The Requiem of Tomás Luis de Victoria (1603)

Victoria's Requiem is among the best-loved and most-performed musical works of the Renaissance, and is often held to be 'a Requiem for an age', representing the summation of golden-age Spanish polyphony. Yet it has been the focus of surprisingly little research. Owen Rees's multifaceted study brings together the historical and ritual contexts for the work's genesis, the first detailed musical analysis of the Requiem itself, and the long story of its circulation and reception. Victoria composed this music in 1603 for the exequies of María of Austria, and oversaw its publication two years later. A rich variety of contemporary documentation allows these events – and the nature of music in Habsburg exequies – to be reconstructed vividly. Rees then locates Victoria's music within the context of a vast international repertory of Requiems, much of it previously unstudied, and identifies the techniques which render this work so powerfully distinctive and coherent.

Owen Rees is Professor of Music at the University of Oxford, and Fellow in Music at The Queen's College, Oxford. He specialises in Spanish and Portuguese sacred music of the 'golden age' and has published on the principal composers of the period – Morales, Guerrero, and Victoria – and on numerous other repertories, genres, and sources from the Iberian Peninsula.

MUSIC IN CONTEXT

Series editors

J. P. E. Harper-Scott
Royal Holloway, University of London

Julian Rushton
University of Leeds

The aim of Music in Context is to illuminate specific musical works, repertoires, or practices in historical, critical, socio-economic, or other contexts; or to illuminate particular cultural and critical contexts in which music operates through the study of specific musical works, repertoires, or practices. A specific musical focus is essential, while avoiding the decontextualisation of traditional aesthetics and music analysis. The series title invites engagement with both its main terms; the aim is to challenge notions of what contexts are appropriate or necessary in studies of music, and to extend the conceptual framework of musicology into other disciplines or into new theoretical directions.

Books in the series

The Requiem of Tomás Luis de Victoria (1603)

OWEN REES

University of Oxford

CAMBRIDGE
UNIVERSITY PRESS

CAMBRIDGE
UNIVERSITY PRESS

University Printing House, Cambridge CB2 8BS, United Kingdom

One Liberty Plaza, 20th Floor, New York, NY 10006, USA

477 Williamstown Road, Port Melbourne, VIC 3207, Australia

314–321, 3rd Floor, Plot 3, Splendor Forum, Jasola District Centre,
New Delhi – 110025, India

79 Anson Road, #06–04/06, Singapore 079906

Cambridge University Press is part of the University of Cambridge.

It furthers the University's mission by disseminating knowledge in the pursuit of
education, learning, and research at the highest international levels of excellence.

www.cambridge.org
Information on this title: www.cambridge.org/9781107054424
DOI: 10.1017/9781107294301

First published 2019

Printed in the United Kingdom by TJ International Ltd, Padstow Cornwall

A catalogue record for this publication is available from the British Library.

Library of Congress Cataloging-in-Publication Data
Names: Rees, Owen, author.
Title: The Requiem of Tomás Luis de Victoria (1603) / Owen Rees.
Description: Cambridge, United Kingdom; New York, NY: Cambridge University Press,
[2019] | Series: Music in context | Includes bibliographical references and index.
Identifiers: LCCN 2018041953 | ISBN 9781107054424 (alk. paper)
Subjects: LCSH: Victoria, Tomás Luis de, approximately 1548–1611. *Officium defunctorum.* |
María, Empress, consort of Maximilian II, Holy Roman Emperor, 1528–1603 – Death and
burial.
Classification: LCC ML410.V63 R4 2019 | DDC 782.32/38–dc23
LC record available at https://lccn.loc.gov/2018041953

ISBN 978-1-107-05442-4 Hardback

Additional resources for this publication at www.cambridge.org/reesappendix

Cambridge University Press has no responsibility for the persistence or accuracy of
URLs for external or third-party internet websites referred to in this publication
and does not guarantee that any content on such websites is, or will remain,
accurate or appropriate.

For Roya

Contents

The Online Appendix, '*Officium defunctorum*: Edition of the Music',
can be accessed at www.cambridge.org/reesappendix

Illustrations

Tables

Music Examples

Acknowledgements

I am most grateful to the numerous scholars who have generously provided assistance and advice. Bruno Turner was characteristically unstinting in sharing reproductions of polyphony and chant sources, and his own transcriptions, as well as in his stimulating replies to questions; it is good to have this opportunity to acknowledge the encouragement and help he has offered over many years. Other reproductions of musical sources were kindly supplied by Emilio Ros-Fábregas, José Abreu, Paulo Estudante, and Clive Walkley. Martin Ham contributed to my efforts to build up as comprehensive as possible a list of Requiems of the period, while Javier Marín generously furnished information about sources both within the Iberian Peninsula and beyond. I would like to thank Bernadette Nelson and João Pedro d'Alvarenga in particular for their friendship, collegiality, and sharing of ideas and material relating to Iberian *pro defunctis* repertory. Xavier Bray advised on Habsburg royal portraiture. John Milsom provided stimulating comments on typographical aspects of the *Officium defunctorum*, and I am grateful to him, Jane Bernstein, Magnus Williamson, Louisa Hunter-Bradley, and Stephen Rose for sharing other material helpful to the international contextualisation of Victoria's 1605 publication and to analysis of it as a publication project. I would like to thank Leofranc Holford-Strevens for undertaking the translation of the paratextual material and answering my questions concerning that material. For information about the funeral of Manuel de Falla and the singing of Victoria's Requiem there, discussed in Chapter 5, I am most grateful to Nancy Lee Harper, Elena García de Paredes (great niece of Manuel de Falla), and Dácil Gonzalez Mesa of the Archivo Manuel de Falla. Further assistance with the research for Chapter 5 and the Epilogue was provided by Timothy Day, Katharine Ellis, Jimmy Reynolds, Jeremy Summerly, and Peter Phillips.

My work in Roman archives and on the Roman copies of the *Officium defunctorum* benefited greatly from the generous assistance and advice of Noel O'Regan, who was also kind enough to share unpublished work. Antonio Chemotti provided great stimulation to my consideration of the *pro defunctis* repertory and exequies in Italy, through numerous discussions while he was based in Oxford during 2016, and through his ready sharing of material acquired during his doctoral research. I am deeply indebted to him, Christian Leitmeir, and John Edwards for their thoughtful comments on draft versions of the book, and in particular to Sean Curran who was unstinting in his provision of feedback. Elements of the material in this book were presented in papers delivered as part of various seminar series and conferences in Oxford, London, Birmingham, Lisbon, and León, and of the contributors to ensuing discussions I would like to thank in particular Margaret Bent, Barbara Eichner, Gervase Rosser, and Anthony Wright.

I offer my thanks to the staff of the following libraries and archives: Biblioteca Nacional de España; Archivo Manuel de Falla, Granada; Biblioteca Apostolica Vaticana; Archivio of San Giovanni in Laterano, Rome; Biblioteca Musicale Governativa del Conservatorio di Santa Cecilia, Rome; Haus-, Hof- und Staatsarchiv (within the Österreichisches Staatsarchiv), Vienna; Archives Générales du Royaume / Algemeen Rijksarchief, Brussels; Raymond Dittrich of the Proskesche Musikabteilung in the Bischöfliche Zentralbibliothek Regensburg; the Library of Christ Church, Oxford; and the British Library.

I am most grateful to the editors of this series, Paul Harper-Scott and Julian Rushton, for their support and patience, and – at Cambridge University Press – to Vicki Cooper (Senior Commissioning Editor when the book proposal was accepted), Kate Brett, Sophie Taylor and Lisa Sinclair. Finally, heartfelt thanks are due to my wife Roya – to whom this book is dedicated – for her patience and support as the project developed: the length of its gestation must have seemed ironic, given that Victoria managed to produce the music of the *Officium defunctorum* in just a few weeks. My fascination with the *siglo de oro* I owe in significant part to my mother, Margaret Ann Rees, who passed away in the year that this project was initiated.

Author's Note

Victoria's first name was 'Thome': he gave it thus when signing correspondence, and it appears in this form (or with the spelling 'Tome') in other documents concerning the composer in Castilian. In modern accounts, of course, his first name is given as 'Tomás', as it is (for ease of recognition) in the title of this book. Most of the letters bearing his signature which have so far been discovered are reproduced in Alfonso de Vicente, *Tomás Luis de Victoria: Cartas (1582–1606)* (Madrid: Fundación Caja Madrid, 2008).

Note on the Abbreviations

Notated pitches are designated using the Helmholtz system, whereby c' denotes middle C, c the note an octave below middle C, and c'' the note an octave above middle C. Pitch classes are given in upper-case Roman letters. Clefs are designated using a subscript numeral to indicate the staff-line on which the clef is located, such that g_2, for example, denotes a G clef on the second staff-line from the bottom.

For printed musical sources of the sixteenth and seventeenth centuries, the sigla employed are those of the *Répertoire International des Sources Musicales*, where such a siglum exists for a given book.

Introduction: 'Requiem for an Age'?

In the early hours of Wednesday 26 February, 1603, the Empress María of Austria lay dying in the great chamber of her apartments annexed to the Convent of the Descalzas Reales in Madrid. Among those attending her death bed would have been Thome Luis de Victoria, who had served María as one of her four personal chaplains for fifteen years. Although his official duties in María's service were concerned with spiritual rather than musical matters, to him fell the task of providing music for the Empress's exequies held in the chapel of the Descalzas Reales Convent – adjoining her apartments – three weeks after her death. This remarkable music, nowadays commonly referred to simply as 'the Victoria Requiem', survives thanks to its appearance in print two years later in a slim commemorative volume entitled *Officium defunctorum*. The dissemination of the book may well have been limited in comparison to that of other collections of Victoria's works, and the music that it contains seems to have been much less widely known and performed in its day than was the *pro defunctis* polyphony of his Spanish predecessor Morales, but in modern times Victoria's Requiem has become the most famous Requiem polyphony of its era, and has acquired extraordinary status both within his oeuvre and within the music of that period. As well as being widely viewed as Victoria's crowning achievement (an accolade which it first received in 1853),[1] it has been assigned much wider iconic significance. It is seen as typifying the characteristics of polyphonic Requiems, and – moreover – the supposedly distinctive traits of Spanish sacred music of the 'golden age', or even of Renaissance music *tout court*. A notice for a recent concert performance claimed that 'for many, it represents what Renaissance polyphony is, what it sounds and feels like, and how expressive it can be'.[2] The work's status both draws upon and contributes to the widespread modern perception

---

[1] Carl Proske wrote: 'Es ist diess die Krone aller Werke unsers Meisters und gehört zu dem Erhabensten, was jemals für die Kirche geschaffen wurde.' ('This is the crown of all the works of our master, and is one of the most sublime ever created for the church.') *Musica divina*, Annus Primus, I, liii (Regensburg: Pustet, 1853).

[2] Brochure for the *2017 International Choral Festival*, SJE Arts, Oxford, advertising a concert performance by the group Tenebrae, directed by Nigel Short.

that Spain had a leading and singular role in the cultivation of the Requiem at that time, a perception which is itself reinforced by notions of a Spanish obsession with death and its rituals. Bruno Turner memorably encapsulated the work's reputation and perceived historical position thus:

It has become revered as well as admired, for it seems to be somehow a Requiem for an Age – the end of Spain's golden century, the end of Renaissance music, the last work, indeed, of Victoria himself.[3]

This appealingly romanticised view of the piece as valedictory in both individual and epochal terms, the latter encapsulated in the phrase 'a Requiem for an Age', is long-established and enduring.[4] In viewing the Requiem as marking the end of an era, it is convenient that the dates of the work's creation and publication coincide neatly with the most conventional placing of the Renaissance–Baroque period boundary by music historians. Beyond this, Turner's phrase evokes and accords with the common but much debated notion of 'the decline of Spain' from the end of the sixteenth century onwards, particularly in political, military, economic, and demographic terms,[5] but also in terms of supposed musical decadence,[6] and the concept of the *siglo de oro* in our construction of Iberian music history is of course a potent one. The mythology attached to the *Officium defunctorum* – and specifically the view of it as consummative – was strengthened in the early twentieth century by the French hispanophile Henri Collet (1885–1951), who highlighted the fact that Victoria described the work as a 'swan song' in the dedicatory epistle that

---

[3] Bruno Turner, *Tomás Luis de Victoria (1548–1611): Officium defunctorum, Requiem, 1605*, Mapa Mundi Renaissance Performing Scores, Series A, No. 75 (London: Vanderbeek & Imrie, 1988), 3.

[4] For example, in the BBC documentary *God's Composer*, the work is described by Simon Russell Beale as 'a requiem not just for his patron but for an age, representative perhaps of the dying embers of Spain's golden era'. This documentary, created to mark the fourth centenary of Victoria's death in 1611, was first broadcast on 2 December that year, and released as a DVD with the same title (Coro CORDVD6).

[5] See, for example, John Huxtable Elliott, *Spain and Its World 1500–1700* (New Haven and London: Yale University Press, 1989), Part IV, 'The Question of Decline', which incorporates various of his essays on the subject dating from 1961 onwards. See also: Henry Kamen, 'The Decline of Spain, A Historical Myth?', *Past and Present* 81 (1978), 24–50, Jonathan Israel's critique of Kamen's view in *Past and Present* 91 (1981), 170–80, Henry Kamen's rejoinder in the same issue, 181–5, and John Lynch, *The Hispanic World in Crisis and Change, 1598–1700* (Oxford and Cambridge, MA: Blackwell, 1992).

[6] See Maria Pilar Ramos López, 'The Construction of the Myth of Spanish Renaissance Music as a Golden Age', in Karol Berger, Lubomir Chalupka, and Albert Dunning (eds), *Early Music – Context and Ideas (International Conference in Musicology, Kraków 18–21 September 2003)* (Krakow: Jagiellonian University, 2003), 77–82, at 80.

opens the liminary matter of the printed book of 1605.[7] In fact, and as discussed in Chapter 3, it seems clear that Victoria simply meant 'swan song' in the sense of 'lament', i.e. that his music was a lament for María, and not that he viewed it as his final work. However, Collet (who – wrongly – thought it likely that Victoria died just three years after the publication of the volume) bound into the concept of swan song both a lament for the age and the last musical testament of the composer, describing the work as follows:

The swan song, the grave Requiem, the serene lament for the whole Spanish faith, gathered in this particular work as in many a page of the dying but immortal musician, who enters into glory at the same hour as his obscure death.[8]

Collet elaborated the swan-song theme by engaging in a lengthy and colourful comparison with Mozart's Requiem, highlighting their similar status as marking the end of their composer's artistic life.[9] The circumstance that the *Officium defunctorum* was indeed Victoria's last published work has reinforced this view and the sense of pathos associated with swan song, although to presume that Victoria stopped composing with the Requiem would be rash.[10] For example, David Wulstan has written that 'the composer's description of this work as his "swan song" was unhappily apt; it is a Requiem for both an Empress and a composer, and indeed for a style; the New Music of the seventeenth century was to render the polyphony of Victoria and his contemporaries old-fashioned.'[11] Perceptions of the work may thus have been coloured by

---

[7] The relevant passage in the dedicatory epistle is: 'Nothing seemed to me more suitable than to revise the music that I wrote for the exequies of your Most Serene mother, and publish it as a swan song under the protection of your name.' ('Nihil magis idoneum visum est, quam ut Harmoniam illam, quam in exequias Serenissimæ tuæ Matris composui, recognoscerem, & tanquam Cygneam cantionem, sub tui nominis patrocinio in lucem æderem.') See Appendix 1 for a translation of the entire epistle.

[8] 'Le chant du cygne, le grave Requiem, la sereine déploration de la foi espagnole tout entière, ramassée dans cette œuvre particulière comme dans mainte page du musicien mourant, mais immortel, et qui entre dans la gloire à l'heure même d'un obscur trépas'; Collet, *Victoria* (Paris: Félix Alcan, 1914), 197.

[9] *Ibid.*, 163.

[10] In his liner notes to the famous recording of the *Officium defunctorum* by Westminster Cathedral Choir (Hyperion Records, 1987), Turner remarks that Victoria composed 'less and less after 1600 and nothing, so far as we know, after the publication in 1605 of the great Office of the Dead'. Turner's cautionary phrase 'so far as we know' is crucial, since absence of evidence is not evidence of absence.

[11] David Wulstan, *Tomás Luis de Victoria: Requiem à 6 (1605)*, revised edition (Oxford: Oxenford Imprint, 1984), i. In a crowd-funded novela, *Victoria, un réquiem para María*, inspired by the *Officium defunctorum* and the circumstances of its genesis, Juan Diego Ortiz Izquierdo

the notions of 'late style' that are common in writing on the arts (and particularly music) from the later nineteenth century onwards, and which have been applied most famously to the case of Beethoven. Gordon McMullan notes that in accounts of the late style of writers, artists, and composers, one frequently finds that the artist's 'final phase of production, a phase which is associated with the proximity of death, is characterised in one of two modes: either as serene, synthetic, and consummatory, or as irascible, discordant, and recalcitrant'.[12] It is of course the first of these two *topoi* that has attached itself to Victoria's Requiem, while the idea that the work represents the 'last gasp' of a style that was becoming outmoded in the face of the 'new music' resonates with other cases, such as that of Bach.

However, in contrast to such emphasis on the Requiem as an end-point (Wulstan goes on to describe it as 'a fitting monument to the "Golden Age"', a phrase anticipating Turner's 'a Requiem for an Age'), others have proposed a different special status for Victoria's Requiem, pointing in the other direction historically, by claiming that it constituted a model for later works in the genre within the Iberian Peninsula, and thus emphasising the continuation of the polyphonic Requiem tradition well beyond Victoria's.[13] As mentioned above, a third strand in descriptions of the music of the *Officium defunctorum* – beyond the emphases on its con- summative position or its influence – is to see the piece as exemplary of some of the principal traits of 'Spanishness' in music of the era. Many accounts repeat (often in reverential terms, as Turner notes) the ubiquitous

develops the myth by imagining Victoria's thoughts as he conceives (some years before María's death) the setting of the Matins lesson *Tædet animam meam* which forms part of the *Officium defunctorum*: 'Surge en mi cabeza la música para esta lectura, dará comienzo a mi última obra ... Aquí, retirado en el convento, escribiré estas tranquilas notas dando forma a un nuevo Réquiem. Un oficio de difuntos para mí, para mi música. Para una música y un tiempo que muere y que tendrá ya escrito su fin.' ('The music for this lesson arises in my mind, which will open my final work ... Here, secluded in the convent, I shall write these tranquil notes giving form to a new Requiem. An Office of the Dead for me, for my music. For a music and an age that is dying and which will already have written its ending.') (p. 18).

[12] Gordon McMullan, 'Introduction', in Gordon McMullan and Sam Smiles (eds), *Late Style and its Discontents: Essays in Art, Literature, and Music* (Oxford University Press, 2016), 3.

[13] See Noel O'Regan, 'Historia de dos ciudades: Victoria como mediador musical entre Roma y Madrid', in Alfonso de Vicente and Pilar Tomás (eds), *Tomás Luis de Victoria y la cultura musical en la España de Felipe III* (Madrid: Centro de Estudios Europa Hispánica and Machado Libros, 2012), 279–300, at 299: 'su *Officium defunctorum* de 1605 ... proporcionó un modelo para las futuras misas de réquiem en la Península' ('his *Officium defunctorum* of 1605 ... provided a model for future Requiem Masses in the Peninsula'). Peter Phillips has argued in particular for its influence in Portugal: 'It seems that this great work became a model for all the later Portuguese versions, so powerful that every significant composer in the country felt drawn into reinterpreting its possibilities for himself.' Booklet notes to the CD recording *Duarte Lôbo: Requiem*, The Tallis Scholars, directed by Peter Phillips (Gimell, 1992), 2.

view that its defining quality is the commingling of passionate intensity and dignified serenity, the latter also being one common marker of 'late style'. Such a combination of expressivity and austerity, the avoidance of musical artifice or elaboration for its own sake, and a powerful religiosity free from all secular influence, became established in modern writing as defining characteristics of Spanish music.[14] Furthermore, as explored in Chapter 4, Iberian *Requiem* polyphony has come to be associated particularly strongly with stylistic sobriety and simplicity. A major role in promoting such a vision of distinct traits in Spanish Golden-Age music was played by Collet, who promulgated the concept of 'Spanish musical mysticism' which constitutes another enduring and prominent element of writing about Iberian polyphony in general and Victoria's music in particular.[15] Higini Anglès expressed the view thus, epitomising the way in which such concepts and qualities were valorised within Spanish musicology:

Like the mystical writers and painters of Spanish humanism, [Victoria] was able to harmonise artistic severity with loving emotion. The secret of this aesthetic achievement lies in the dramatic mysticism with which he infused his works.[16]

---

[14] This historiographical phenomenon has been subjected to considerable analysis and critique in recent musicological writings. See Emilio Ros-Fábregas, 'Cristóbal de Morales: A Problem of Musical Mysticism and National Identity in the Historiography of the Renaissance', in Owen Rees and Bernadette Nelson (eds), *Cristóbal de Morales: Sources, Influences, Reception* (Woodbridge: Boydell, 2007), 215–34; see also Pilar Ramos López, 'The Construction of the Myth of Spanish Renaissance Music'.

[15] Henri Collet, *Le mysticisme musical espagnol au XVIe siècle* (Paris: Félix Alcan, 1913), and *Victoria*. Recent historiographical and critical studies of the concept of 'Spanish musical mysticism' include Maria Pilar Ramos López, 'Mysticism as a Key Concept of Spanish Early Music Historiography', in *Early Music: Context and Ideas II (International Conference in Musicology, Kraków* (Krakow: Jagiellonian University, 2008), 69–82, and Tess Knighton, '"Through a Glass Darkly": Music and Mysticism in Golden Age Spain', in Hilaire Kallendorf (ed.), *A New Companion to Hispanic Mysticism* (Leiden and Boston: Brill, 2010), 411–36, at 431–6. The application of the concept of 'mysticism' to the six-voice Requiem is exemplified by Peter Phillips's description of the work, which also typifies the enduring emphasis on the 'Spanish' approach observable there: 'Its mystical intensity of expression, achieved by the simplest musical means, obviously sets it apart from contemporary English and Italian music, and has led to comparisons of it with the equally intense religious paintings of Velazquez and El Greco. There is no doubt that this masterpiece conveys much of the highly individual Spanish view of religion and death.' Booklet notes accompanying the CD recording *Victoria Requiem*, The Tallis Scholars, directed by Peter Phillips (Gimell, 1987), 2.

[16] Higini Anglès, 'Latin Church Music on the Continent – 3: Spain and Portugal', in Gerald Abraham (ed.), *The New Oxford History of Music*, 10 vols (Oxford University Press, 1954–1990), IV, 372–418, at 400.

Reflecting such an ideology, emphasis on the significance of Victoria being a priest is ubiquitous in accounts of his musical approach,[17] as are the fact that he apparently composed no secular music and the association between his native Ávila and the most famous of the Spanish mystics, St Teresa.

And yet – despite its status as a 'masterwork', the power and pathos of the stories that surround it, the unusual richness of the information concerning its genesis, the special historical and aesthetic stature which it has been given (including as a paragon of the Spanish qualities just described), and the frequency with which it is performed and recorded[18] – Victoria's *Officium defunctorum* has formed the subject of surprisingly little detailed critical writing or contextual study. Furthermore, an attempt to fill this gap and to comprehend the work better through contextual comparison faces a much larger challenge: the paucity of wide-ranging studies of the polyphonic Requiem Mass and other genres of polyphony *pro defunctis* in the relevant period. In particular, the enormous repertory of Requiem Masses by Italian composers from the later sixteenth and early seventeenth centuries has largely escaped attention, with a consequent distorting effect on our generic understanding, encouraging the modern perception that the Iberian *pro defunctis* repertoire was especially prominent and significant in this period.[19] This perception also chimes with – and has perhaps been bolstered by – widely held and frequently voiced beliefs that the fascination with death was unusually strong in early-modern

---

[17] Another comment by Anglès typifies this strand in writings about Victoria: 'Combining the vocations of priest and musician, Victoria created an art of incomparable spirituality . . . He had no other aim than to sing of the Cross and the mysteries of the Redemption, using means uncontaminated by profane art.' Anglès, 'Latin Church Music on the Continent', 399.

[18] There have been at least thirty-two commercial recordings since the 1950s, nearly half of them released after the turn of the millennium.

[19] The current foci of scholarly interest on Requiems are apparent, for example, in the first volume of Pieter Bergé and David Burn (eds), *The Book of Requiems* (Leuven University Press, forthcoming), which represents much the most ambitious study of this genre to date. Of the twenty-eight works that the volume covers, only one – Palestrina's five-voice Requiem – is by an Italian, and it should be noted that this setting is atypical of both Italian and international practice in this genre. Of the twenty-five other Masses considered in detail in the volume, thirteen are by Northerners, eleven by Spanish or Portuguese composers, and the remaining one by a Northerner who made his career in Spain. The volume is ordered chronologically, and it is particularly striking that in its second half Iberian works are dominant: from the chapter on Guerrero's Requiem onwards, no fewer than nine of the fourteen works covered are Iberian. The perception that the Iberian Requiem repertory was particularly prominent is exemplified by Fabrice Fitch's comments that 'the polyphonic requiem flourished with a particular intensity on the Iberian peninsula' and that 'It was in Spain and Portugal that the tradition of *stile antico* requiem settings had the greatest longevity, its ramifications extending well into the [seventeenth] century (as with Victoria's setting).' *Grove Music Online*, 'Requiem Mass', 2: 'Polyphonic Settings to 1600', last accessed 30 July 2015.

Spain.[20] In fact, the surviving repertory of polyphonic Requiem Masses attributed to Iberian composers and dating before about 1650 is very much smaller than that from the same period attributed to Italians. The prominence of Italian composers in the repertory of Requiems written between 1570 and the end of the century was signalled by Harold Luce in his doctoral dissertation of 1958.[21] However, this repertory and the early-seventeenth-century examples of Italian Requiems have in general attracted little scholarly attention since then, in part (one suspects) because such Masses have been of less interest than motets and music for Vespers in more 'modern' styles.[22] The degree to which the Italian Requiems of the early seventeenth century have tended to constitute a hidden repertory is exemplified by the following comment in Jerome Roche's *North Italian Church Music in the Age of Monteverdi*:

To judge from the many masterly settings of the Requiem Mass written during the Renaissance that are well known to us, we might be surprised to find that very few were published in northern Italy in the early seventeenth century. Arcangelo Borsaro issued a set of Requiem music for double choir in 1608, and Olindio Bartolini's 1633 Masses included a Requiem which may have been written for special circumstances. It is likely that simple plainsong or older polyphonic settings

---

[20] That Spanish society displayed a distinctively powerful preoccupation with death is emphasised in, for example, Bartolomé Bennassar, *L'Homme Espagnol: Attitudes et mentalités du XVIe au XIXe siècle* (Paris: Hachette, 1975), Chapter 9, trans. Benjamin Keen as *The Spanish Character: Attitudes and Mentalities from the Sixteenth to the Nineteenth Century* (Berkeley and Los Angeles: University of California Press, 1979), and such a view is accepted in Carlos M. N. Eire's influential *From Madrid to Purgatory: The Art and Craft of Dying in Sixteenth-Century Spain* (Cambridge University Press, 1995). Eire sets out his belief in this particularity of Spanish culture in both his Prologue and Epilogue; for example, in explaining his choice of scope for his study of the history of death, he states that 'I settled on Spain, the staunchest defender of the Catholic faith in the sixteenth century, because I had read enough Spanish devotional literature to know that heaven, hell, and purgatory were as much a part of that nation's topography as Madrid, Gibraltar, and the Pyrenees . . . I also suspected that this apparent fascination with death and the hereafter drew upon the collective psychology of the nation.' (6–7). There may be a danger of an exaggerated exceptionalism when dealing with this aspect of Spanish early-modern culture (perhaps reminiscent of the long history of the stereotyping of Spain by other European cultures), and there is a need to test the consensus through further comparison with other Catholic areas of Europe (as Eire acknowledges on p. 529). Some useful contextualisation in this regard (for example, through juxtaposition with the situation in France) is attempted by Fernando Martínez Gil in *Muerte y sociedad en la España de los Austrias* (Cuenca: Ediciones de la Universidad de Castilla-La Mancha, 2000).

[21] Harold Luce, 'The Requiem Mass from its Plainsong Beginnings to 1600', unpublished PhD thesis, The Florida State University (1958).

[22] Antonio Chemotti has recently cast fresh light on the extent and nature of the Italian repertory of polyphony *pro mortuis* in 'Polyphonic Music pro mortuis in Italy (1550–1650): Context and Intertext', unpublished PhD thesis, Ludwig-Maximilians-Universität, Munich (2017).

were considered more fitting for obsequies, so that there was no demand for settings in the new style.[23]

One could easily conclude from Roche's statement that just two Requiem Masses appeared from north-Italian presses in the early seventeenth century. In truth, more than forty Requiems by Italian composers were included in the output of such presses between 1600 and 1630 alone. If we take the period of a century from 1550 to 1650, at least eighty Requiems by Italians were published in Northern Italy, whereas the total number of such Masses (in print and manuscript) attributed to Iberian composers active before about 1650 is only about half this. The relatively greater scholarly attention given to the Iberian repertory than to the Italian is reflected in – and is in part a reflection of – the fact that almost all of those Iberian Requiem Masses that reached print at the time are available in modern editions (and many in separate performing editions), whereas a tiny proportion of the much larger Italian printed repertory of Requiems is thus visible. It is a commonplace, and frequently true, that Iberian early-modern repertories languish in obscurity in terms of scholarship, editing, and performance, in comparison to repertories from Italy and northern Europe, but in this case the situation is reversed.

Awareness of the huge Italian Requiem repertory has the potential significantly to influence our understanding of practices and regional conventions within the genre of the polyphonic Requiem, and in particular to assess the current scholarly emphasis on the distinctiveness of the Iberian tradition. While thorough and comprehensive study of the Italian works is an enormous undertaking which is beyond the scope of this book, a large number of these settings – as well as of the Northern and Iberian repertories of Requiems – is here considered as part of the attempt to apprehend more fully the approach taken by Victoria in the *Officium defunctorum* and how that approach relates to particular regional practices. In the process, I consider afresh in Chapter 4 to what extent and in what ways Iberian traditions in the composition of Requiems were distinctive, addressing such matters as chant-use and the tendency to employ different mensurations for particular movements, and challenging the idea that stylistic austerity should be viewed as a general distinguishing mark of Iberian Requiems.[24]

---

[23] Jerome Roche, *North Italian Church Music in the Age of Monteverdi* (Oxford University Press, 1984), 39–40.

[24] The most detailed modern study to date of Iberian polyphony *pro mortuis* is Grayson Wagstaff, 'Music for the Dead: Polyphonic Settings of the *Officium* and *Missa Pro Defunctis* by Spanish and Latin American Composers before 1630', unpublished PhD thesis, The University of Texas at Austin (1995). Wagstaff there presents his view of well defined, firmly established, and

Chapter 4 also contextualises the music of the *Officium defunctorum* within Victoria's output, a process that allows the identification of 'signature' elements and approaches that characterise the work and render it distinctive within that output.[25] Most prominent amongst the small-scale signature devices is a particular contrapuntal module which – it transpires – Victoria introduced only in his later career and which he used in a far more concentrated fashion in the *Officium defunctorum* than anywhere else. Victoria's employment of this and other compositional devices and strategies examined in Chapter 4 (including tonal manipulation and juxtaposition, and particular structural ploys) encourages a reading of the *Officium defunctorum* as a coherent and internally integrated compositional project, and their identification helps to explain why the *Officium defunctorum* seems to occupy a powerfully individual sound-world. Polyphonic Requiems generally lack some of the main generators of unification found in cyclic Mass Ordinaries (including use of the same pre-existing material in each 'movement', and consistency of modal representation and tonal type between movements). Nevertheless, it will be argued that Victoria deploys multiple means of drawing together the music that he wrote for María's exequies. Furthermore, these centripetal tendencies apply in various ways to the items in the *Officium defunctorum* beyond the polyphonic Mass itself: the motet *Versa est in luctum*, the responsory *Libera me Domine*, and the Matins lesson *Tædet animam meam*. As will be shown, the degree to which Victoria integrates (for example) his *pro defunctis* motet and responsory setting with the accompanying music for Mass was unusual.

Another type of contextualisation is pursued in Chapter 3, which examines the *Officium defunctorum* of 1605 as a material artefact in the context of music publishing in the period, and in so doing calls attention to its exceptional – perhaps, indeed, unique – nature in both Iberian and international terms: a slender printed book containing one polyphonic Requiem and which memorialises a particular person (here, the composer's employer) and their exequies, highlighting the occasion of the music's genesis. Victoria's publication project – which provides us with a remarkably uncommon opportunity to place surviving *pro defunctis* polyphony within its original context – thus belongs in some sense within the same sphere as the festival books commemorating major dynastic

---

distinctive Spanish traditions of how to compose a Requiem, and argues that the music of Victoria's *Officium defunctorum* stands somewhat apart from these.

[25] In this connection, one should observe that the commonplace view that the *Officium defunctorum* is based in significant part on his earlier four-voice Requiem is erroneous.

ceremonies, and specifically the *libros de exequias* and published sermons that recorded the deaths and exequies of the senior Spanish Habsburgs.

These *libros de exequias* are considered in Chapter 2, within an account and study of the local context within which Victoria's Requiem originated and was first performed: the death, burial, and exequies of María of Austria. In placing these specific events and ceremonies – and Victoria's provision of music for them – within the relevant contexts of Spanish Habsburg exequial traditions and practices, attention is paid to what *libros de exequias* can tell us about the role, nature, and manner of performance of the music embedded within such complexes of ceremony, rhetoric, written texts, and iconographical art. The chapter draws on hitherto overlooked sources and reinterprets those already known in order to construct as vivid as possible a narrative of María's death and burial, and of the ceremonies at the Descalzas for which Victoria prepared the music of the *Officium defunctorum*. The oft-repeated modern view that this music was written not for María's household exequies at the Descalzas but for the later ceremonies organised by the Jesuit College in Madrid is shown to be untenable, but the references to music in the contemporary published description of these Jesuit exequies are also scrutinised. Among the materials upon which the account of events at the Descalzas is constructed is the wealth of correspondence between María's lord high steward Juan de Borja and the Duke of Lerma at the royal court, revealing the frenzied process of determining whether María would be buried at the Descalzas or in the royal mausoleum at El Escorial, and the subsequent hurried organisation by her household (including Victoria) of the exequies which were held some seventeen days later within the convent chapel.

María's household at the Descalzas is scrutinised in broader terms in Chapter 1 as a context for Victoria's service as chaplain and musician. Although his appointment as one of Mariá's chaplains in 1587 was a religious rather than a musical one, and although the Empress's house-hold apparently included no *capilla de música*, it seems that Victoria also acted unofficially as *maestro de capilla* of the royal chapel maintained at the convent. His music performed there in the presence of María and other members of the family could acquire strongly dynastic significance, the most clear-cut example of which is represented by the Requiem itself. Victoria's move to Madrid naturally facilitated his cultivation of Habsburg patronage, including that of the royal court, and this was man-ifest not least in the series of publications leading up to the *Officium defunctorum*.

As explored in Chapter 3, Victoria himself disseminated copies of the *Officium defunctorum* in Spain and beyond. Although the Requiem seems to have achieved very limited purchase within institutional repertories in the seventeenth century, it was thanks to one or more of the copies that Victoria sent to Rome that in the 1700s the work came to the attention of Roman church musicians and collectors with interests in older polyphonic repertories, and thence within the purview of the internationally famous Padre Martini in Bologna. Chapter 5 traces this renewed knowledge of the work in Italy, before considering various stages in the growth of its extra-ordinary modern reputation from the late eighteenth century onwards: its treatment in the general music histories of John Hawkins and Charles Burney; the publishing and liturgical performance of the work within the context of the German Cecilian movement in the 1860s and 70s, and the elevated veneration of the work in these circles, reflecting its encapsulation of the principal values of the movement; widening knowledge of the Requiem – including in England – through the medium of the editions by Franz Xaver Haberl and Charles Bordes; the problematic 'authoritative' edition by Felip Pedrell published as part of the *opera omnia*, and its enduring influence upon modern performing editions and hence on performances and recordings; and finally the choice of the work for use at the funeral of Manuel de Falla in 1947, and the political/nationalist overtones of that choice.

The remarkable popularity of the Requiem in the current century – with new recordings appearing at the rate of about one a year, and a multitude of concert performances – carries an element of the ironic: its appeal as primarily a concert or recorded work divorced from its religious and liturgical context draws substantially on the degree to which it is perceived to carry an aura of profound sacredness and solemn liturgy, and to evoke the mysticism of Victoria and of Spain's 'golden century'. In the epilogue to this book I consider briefly such aspects of the work's reception since the 1980s. More perhaps than any other Requiem Mass in the five hundred years of the genre, Victoria's Requiem has come to be viewed and prized as both epitome and acme.

1 | Chaplain of the Empress

> Most Serene María, the empress, . . . whose illustrious nobility, second to none, for all the ornament of her being born of imperial blood in a long and ancient line and also being the daughter, niece, daughter-in-law, wife, sister, and mother of emperors, and the sister and mother-in-law of the mightiest kings, surpassed and enhanced the glory of her line in her supreme zeal for piety and religion (which was always your family's honour); she is renowned everywhere not only on account of her lineage, but of her offspring, in that she bore four sons now living, the lights of the world, of whom one is emperor, the others are equal in authority to kings, and saw her daughters married to the most powerful kings, and her grandson by one of those daughters the greatest king.[1]

Thus Victoria – or whoever he commissioned to write the text on his behalf – extolled María of Austria in the dedicatory epistle of the *Officium defunctorum*. The composer served María in Madrid from 1587 until her death in 1603. The dual emphasis in the passage above upon (on the one hand) María's exceptionally elevated status as daughter, wife, and mother of emperors and (on the other) her exemplary 'zeal for piety and religion' are among the most common *topoi* in contemporary or near-contemporary accounts of her life and death, including the literature and sermons associated with her death and exequies, for which Victoria composed the music of the *Officium defunctorum*.[2] Despite such conventionality, the juxtaposition of these two eulogistic themes here nevertheless serves to introduce the particular context for Victoria's life and work

---

[1] Thome Luis de Victoria, *Thomæ Ludovici de Victoria abulensis, sacræ cæsaræcæ maiestatis capellani, officium defunctorum, sex vocibus, in obitu et obsequiis sacræ imperatricis* (Madrid: Juan Flamenco, 1605), f. [ii]ᵛ. The translation is by Leofranc Holford-Strevens. See Appendix 1 for the complete Latin text of this dedicatory epistle.

[2] The same dual emphasis is found in the description of María in the *carmen* by Martin Pesserio which follows the dedicatory epistle in the *Officium defunctorum*: 'the elevated, Caesar-blooded, and diadem-lustrous Empress María, to whom alone fell the glory that a Caesar should be her son, her father, and her husband, a Caesar himself her father-in-law, and that she herself should be the sister and mother-in-law of kings, a marked nobility! But a higher honour had befallen her, that she nurtured Christ with her whole bosom, and gave herself entirely to his love.' For the original text, see Appendix 1.

during this period: the household of a senior member of Europe's most powerful family, but a household which occupied part of the same complex as a royal convent.[3] María's status and piety – and the conflation of the courtly and monastic represented by her life in Madrid – are likewise simultaneously emphasised in the well known portrait of her in old age which one can see at the Descalzas Reales convent, and which has been attributed (probably erroneously) to Juan Pantoja de la Cruz (Figure 1.1).[4] The portrait echoes equivalent conventional portraits of the male ruler in armour, the left hand grasping the sword hilt, and the crown or helmet on a table at the side, as in Titian's influential portrait of María's brother Philip (Figure 1.2). María's left hand holds not a sword hilt but a rosary, reflecting the common reference to the rosary as a spiritual weapon (indeed, a sword) in the fight against sin and heresy. Beside her rests the imperial crown, and she wears widow's weeds, reinforcing her imperial status through her marriage to Maximilian II, but the impression of her costume is nevertheless quasi-monastic: she was a Franciscan tertiary, i.e. a member of the Third Order of St Francis, and a nun's habit was regarded as armour against sin and vice. The message is that she is as staunch a defender of the catholic church – a *miles Christi*, soldier of Christ – as her male Habsburg relatives, and carries equivalent authority, but that this defence is achieved through her piety.[5] As we shall see, one of the preachers at María's exequies emphasised that she had fought for the faith through her prayers and exemplary piety just as her sons Rudolf and Matthias had defended it through military prowess.

María, born in Madrid in 1528, was daughter of the Holy Roman Emperor Charles V, and therefore sister of Philip II.[6] Her marriage to her cousin Archduke Maximilian of Austria (the future Emperor Maximilian II) resulted in her enduring involvement with the Austrian

---

[3] The most famous example of this Spanish Habsburg model of combining monastery and palace is seen at El Escorial, where the royal apartments surround the East end of the basilica, and where the King's and Queen's (or Infanta's) chambers have prayer grilles looking into the chancel of the basilica.

[4] Concerning the attribution, see Maria Kusche, *Juan Pantoja de la Cruz* (Madrid: Editorial Castalia, 1964), 196.

[5] The portrait of María is analysed in Fernando Checa Cremades, 'Monasterio de las Descalzas Reales: origenes de su colección artística', *Reales Sitios* 102/4 (1989), 21–30, at 27, and the garb shown in the portrait is considered by Cordula van Wyhe in 'The Making and Meaning of the Monastic Habit at Spanish Habsburg Courts', in Anne J. Cruz and Galli Stampino (eds), *Early Modern Habsburg Women: Transnational Contexts, Cultural Conflicts, Dynastic Continuities* (London & New York: Routledge, 2016), 243–74.

[6] The dedicatory epistle of the *Officium defunctorum* is thus inaccurate in describing her as sister of an emperor: Philip did not hold the Imperial title.

Figure 1.1 María of Austria, attrib. Juan Pantoja de la Cruz; Monasterio de las Descalzas Reales, Madrid, © Patrimonio Nacional

Figure 1.2 Prince Philip (later King Philip II) of Spain, 1550, Titian (Tiziano Vecellio);
© Photographic Archive Museo Nacional del Prado

branch of the Habsburgs, whose interests she continued to represent at the Spanish court during the period in which Victoria served her. Of María's and Maximilian's offspring, two (Rudolf and Matthias) became Holy Roman Emperor, while their daughter Anna of Austria was the fourth and last wife of Philip II of Spain; Anna's and Philip's son inherited the Spanish throne in 1598 as Philip III, and this is the grandson of María who is described as the 'greatest king' at the end of the passage from the dedicatory epistle above.[7] Following Maximilian's death in 1576, María returned to Spain (the journey from Prague to Madrid via Italy taking from August 1581 until March 1582), and after a period in Lisbon she took up permanent residence in 1583 in the extensive royal apartments attached to the convent of the Descalzas Reales in Madrid, a convent of Clarist (Franciscan) nuns founded by her sister Juana, and a highly prestigious institution for the Spanish Habsburgs.[8] María's daughter Margarita, the dedicatee of the *Officium defunctorum*, became a nun within the convent. The Empress's life and concerns during her period of residence at the Descalzas combined (often inseparably) the political, the familial, and the pious. Aspects of this combination are, however, largely obscured in the contemporary hagiographical accounts of María, for example that by Juan Carrillo, who dubs her 'la santa' and focuses on her deep involvement in the convent's life and withdrawal from worldly matters, and the degree to which her routine approximated that of the nuns, but who is, conversely, nearly silent on her participation in Habsburg politics and maintenance of her own household in that part of the Descalzas complex which constituted her palace.[9] The multifaceted nature of the court/convent at the Descalzas is important for considering Victoria's work as chaplain and musician while in María's service and the opportunities that it offered him.

A prime example of the combination of the courtly, the political, the dynastic, and the pious is the manner in which the Descalzas Reales and its royal apartments formed in some senses an extension of the royal court

---

[7] Philip III was both María's nephew and her grandson.

[8] The official title is the Monasterio de la Madre de Dios de Consolación. The building originated as a private palace (in which, indeed, Juana had been born), and was rebuilt to accommodate its new dual purpose as royal residence and convent.

[9] Juan Carrillo, *Relación histórica de la real fundación del monasterio de las descalzas de santa Clara de la villa de Madrid* (Madrid: Luis Sánchez, 1616). The description of María as 'la santa' is at f. 215v. Such idealised representations of María which emphasise her life of piety and prayer rather than the political and courtly aspects of her existence are considered by Magdalena S. Sánchez in *The Empress, the Queen, and the Nun: Women and Power at the Court of Philip III of Spain* (Baltimore and London: The Johns Hopkins University Press, 1998), 62–71.

while that was resident in Madrid.[10] While Philip II visited the Empress relatively rarely at the Descalzas during his final years,[11] Philip III and his Queen, Margaret of Austria, typically attended the convent daily when the royal court was in Madrid. The King and Queen habitually heard their second Mass of the day at the convent, the Queen would often take her midday meal there, and the King regularly visited the Empress: for example, such visits occurred daily during October 1598, and within the last three months of 1599 the King called on her eleven times.[12] The *capilla* of the Descalzas was under royal jurisdiction, and both Philip II and Philip III issued new sets of regulations for this musical establishment,[13] maintaining thus a degree of musical ornament which reflected the convent's regal profile, and which contrasted with the austerity of its monastic life in accordance with its reformed Rule, and the associated restrictions (in theory, at least) on nuns' music-making.[14] Victoria's cultivation of Philip III's patronage must have been assisted by the royal status of the convent and by the King's frequent attendance at the Descalzas, until the court moved to Valladolid in 1601, a move passionately opposed by María, since it reduced her opportunities to influence royal policy. Even thereafter, there were occasions for Victoria to renew his direct contacts with senior members of the royal court. Thus, when the King and Queen (and the Duke of Lerma) visited Madrid in April 1602, they spent the whole of

[10] Further on the close relationship between the convent and the court, see María Luisa López-Vidriero, 'Por la imprenta hacia Dios', in Pedro M. Cátedra and María Luisa López-Vidriero (eds), *De libros, librerías, imprentas y lectores* (Salamanca: Ediciones Universidad de Salamanca, Seminario de Estudios, 2002), 193–218, at 207.

[11] Magdalena S. Sánchez, 'Empress María and the Making of Political Policy in the Early Years of Philip III's Reign', in Alain Saint-Saëns (ed.), *Religion, Body and Gender in Early Modern Spain* (San Francisco: Mellen Research University Press, 1991), 139–47, at 140.

[12] See Sánchez, *The Empress, the Queen, and the Nun*, 11–13, 27, 92.

[13] See Rafael Mota Murillo, *Sebastián López de Velasco (1584–1659), Libro de missas, motetes, salmos, magníficas y otras cosas tocantes al culto divino*, 4 vols (Madrid: Sociedad Española de Musicología, 1980–1993), I, 40–8. The relevant *declaraciones* of Philip II and Philip III are transcribed at 126–35. For a summary of matters relevant to the conduct of the liturgy and the provision of music as set out in Princess Juana's foundation document and in the additions made by Philip III in 1602, see Paulino Capdepón Verdú, 'Música y liturgia en el monasterio de las Descalzas Reales de Madrid', in Francisco Javier Campos and Fernández de Sevilla (eds), *La clausura femenina en el mundo hispánico: una fidelidad secular, Simposium (XIX edición) San Lorenzo del Escorial, 2 al 5 de septiembre*, I (El Escorial: Instituto Escurialense de Investigaciones Históricas y Artísticas, 2001), 563–86.

[14] On such issues, see Janet Hathaway, 'Spirituality and Devotional Music in the Royal Convent of the Descalzas, Madrid', *Journal of Musicological Research* 30 (2011), 202–26, and – more generally on the implications of monastic reform for the use of music in the Divine Office within Spanish convents – Colleen Ruth Baade, 'Music and Music-Making in Female Monasteries in Seventeenth-Century Castile', unpublished PhD thesis, Duke University (2001), 38–44.

the day following their entry with the Empress and her daughter at the Descalzas, and since this was the feast day of St Mark it is likely that Mass in the convent chapel – doubtless attended by the royals – was decorated with polyphony.[15]

María's court was also the main focal point for connections between Madrid and the Austrian branch of the Habsburgs, including the Imperial court of her son Rudolf; the Imperial Ambassador to the Spanish court, Hans Khevenhüller, was a close confidant of the Empress and attended her daily at the Descalzas. There were likewise close links with the Brussels court of Archduke Albert (another of María's sons) and his wife Isabella Clara Eugenia (María's niece, and daughter of Philip II), who ruled the Habsburg Netherlands. Juan Carrillo, secretary to María, was Albert's representative at the Spanish court. Victoria would have had regular contact with both Khevenhüller and Carrillo, and it was via Carrillo that in 1604 (after María's death) Victoria sent books of music to Albert, for which the composer received the very substantial sum of 100 ducats.[16]

The importance of the Habsburg familial network to Victoria during his years in María's service is reflected in his choices of dedicatees for the three new printed collections which he issued within that period.[17] The last of these was of course the *Officium defunctorum*, dedicated to María's daughter Margarita. The 1592 collection of Masses is dedicated to Albert, at that point Viceroy of Portugal, and in the prefatory epistle Victoria states that the first consideration that had led him to offer the volume to the Archduke was the fact that the composer was a chaplain to

---

[15] The visit to Madrid is recorded by the royal chronicler, Luis Cabrera de Córdoba, in his 'Relaciones de las cosas sucedidas, principalmente el la Corte, desde el año de 1599 hasta el de 1614'. The earliest known copy (Madrid, Biblioteca Nacional de España, Ms 9129) dates from 1626, and is declared on the title page to have been copied from the original in the author's hand. This manuscript version is available online in the *Biblioteca Digital Hispanica*. It formed the basis for a nineteenth-century edition with the title *Relaciones de las cosas sucedidas en la córte de España, desde 1599 hasta 1614* (Madrid: J. Martín Alegría, 1857), of which a facsimile is available (Valladolid: Junta de Castilla y León, Consejería de Educación y Cultura, 1997). The relevant passage concerning events in April 1602 is at p. 142 of the edition of 1857.

[16] See Cristóbal Pérez Pastor, *Bibliografía Madrileña: ó, descripción de las obras impresas en Madrid*, 3 vols (Madrid: Tipografía de los huérfanos, Tipografía de la Revista de Archivos, Bibliotecas y Museos, 1891–1907), III, 520; a more recent transcription is in Alfonso de Vicente (ed.), *El mayordomo de Tomás Luis y otros documentos de Victoria* (Ávila: Miján, 2015), 143–4. As I note in Chapter 4, the court chapel of Albert and Isabella in Brussels possessed a copy of Victoria's *Missæ* of 1600 and also 'una . . . missa de Requiem' by the composer, which was probably the *Officium defunctorum*.

[17] I ignore here fresh editions, published during the same period, of Victoria's collections first issued during his Roman career.

Albert's mother.[18] María made particular efforts to influence Albert – and engineered strikingly close links between her household and that of her son – following his return to Madrid from Portugal in September 1593, which was shortly after the copies of Victoria's new printed collection became available for distribution.[19] One can imagine not only that this collection proved useful to María as a cultural gift from artistically the most famous member of her household, but also that Albert's presence in Madrid and the interchanges between the two households assisted Victoria in further cultivating Albert's patronage, which (as observed above) he continued to enjoy after Albert became governor – and later sovereign – of the Netherlands.

The other printed collection issued by Victoria during his period in María's service was dedicated to Philip III: the *Missæ, magnificat, motecta, psalmi* published by the Royal Press in 1600 (V1435). In the liminary matter Victoria highlighted the fact that he was chaplain to Philip's grandmother by declaring it prominently on the title-page and again at the head of the dedicatory epistle, as well as mentioning it a third time within that epistle.[20] A further illustration of the professional relevance to Victoria of the Austrian Habsburg networks to which he had access is a letter from the composer, dated 16 April 1602, addressed to Archduke Ferdinand of Austria in Graz.[21] The letter was sent with a member of the Queen's household, and Victoria enclosed a copy of his *Missæ* of 1600, requesting that Ferdinand provide financial recompense to assist with the cost of publication, recompense which (upon the written recommendation of

---

[18] 'Multa me, Serenissime Princeps, impulerunt, ut hoc opusculum, quod nunc denuo conscripsi, tibi dicarem: Primum, quia Augustæ, ac Cæsareæ Imperatricis matris tuæ singulari beneficio in eorum sacerdotum, qui illi res sacras procurant, numerum adscitus sum.' *Thomæ Ludovici de Victoria Abulensis Missæ, quattuor, quinque, sex, et octo vocibus concinendæ* (Rome: Francisco Coattino, 1592; V1434), f. 1.

[19] The dedicatory epistle is dated 13 November 1592. On 20 July 1593 Victoria sent a copy to Jaén Cathedral (see Vicente, *Tomás Luis de Victoria: Cartas*, 72). María saw to it that Albert was accommodated in the house of Juan de Borja, her lord high steward, near the Descalzas, and she arranged for Hans Khevenhüller to be appointed lord high steward of Albert's household. See José Eloy Hortal Muñoz, 'The Household of Archduke Albert of Austria from His Arrival in Madrid until His Election as Governor of the Low Countries: 1570–1595', in René Vermeir, Dries Raeymaekers, and José Eloy Hortal Muñoz (eds), *A Constellation of Courts: The Courts and Households of Habsburg Europe, 1555–1665* (Leuven University Press, 2014), 101–22, at 120.

[20] The same relevant wording – 'sacræ cæsarææ maiestatis capellani' – appears on the title pages of the 1600 collection and the *Officium defunctorum*. These are the only printed collections of Victoria's works in which his status or employment is thus declared on the title page apart from the *Liber primus qui missas, psalmos, Magnificat ... complectitur* of 1576 (V1427).

[21] Ferdinand was a nephew of Mariá's husband Maximilian, and a brother of Margaret of Austria, Philip III's wife. He was later to become Holy Roman Emperor.

Pietro Antonio Bianco, Hofkapellmeister to Ferdinand) the Archduke duly furnished.[22] Bianco had visited Madrid in 1598 in the company of the Archduchess Maria of Bavaria, mother of Queen Margaret, and may well have met Victoria then. Victoria makes a point of mentioning in his letter that one of the Masses in the collection, the *Missa pro victoria*, was much liked by King Philip: 'una misa de la batalla de que el Rey n(uest)ro s(eño)r gusto mucho'.

Victoria entered María's service as one of her chaplains in September 1587.[23] This post was not itself a musical one, but it seems likely that Victoria was appointed in part because of his considerable reputation as a musician and in the expectation that he could contribute in this capacity to the life of the household and convent, in addition to his religious duties to the Empress. It is worth noting in this regard that among Victoria's fellow chaplains was the poet Bartolomé Leonardo de Argensola, indicating once again María's desire to maintain the cultural life of her household through such appointments of chaplains.[24] In the dedicatory epistle of the *Officium defunctorum* Victoria avers that the favour and support that he had received from the members of the House of Austria had provided him with the 'leisure' to compose.[25] Since his service within María's household represented the only part of his career

---

[22] The texts of Victoria's letter, Bianco's recommendation, and Ferdinand's decision are transcribed in Hellmut Federhofer, 'Graz Court Musicians and their Contributions to the *Parnassus musicus Ferinandaeus* (1615)', *Musica disciplina* 9 (1955), 167–244, at 243. See also Vicente, *Tomás Luis de Victoria: Cartas*, 96–101, which includes a reproduction of Victoria's letter and a transcription.

[23] The date of the commencement of his service is recorded in a document of 9 September 1603 drawn up by María's executors: Madrid, Archivo Histórico de Protocolos, prot. 2016. A transcription of the relevant passage, at f. 1647v, may be found in Mota Murillo, *Sebastián López de Velasco*, I, 49: 'A Tome de Victoria capellan de su Majestad que sirve desde septiembre del año de [1]587'. A charter issued by King Philip III on 2 July 1611 records that Victoria had reported to the King that he had by then served for twenty-four years as María's chaplain and (after her death) as holder of one of the three chaplaincies at the Descalzas that she endowed. This document thus confirms 1587 as the year in which Victoria's service of María began. The text of the charter (Madrid, Archivo Histórico Nacional, Consejos, book 253, f. 116) is transcribed in Mota Murillo, *Sebastián López de Velasco*, I, 153–4.

[24] Sadly, the inventories of María's belongings and from the sale of her estate (in Archivo General de Simancas, Patronato Real, 31–38) do not include lists of books or music books, although two chests for books are mentioned; nor are musical instruments listed. I am grateful to Annemarie Jordan Gschwend for her assistance in this regard.

[25] He writes thus to Margarita in the epistle: 'Now, as I pondered how I may strive in some measure to recompense your favours to me, no more suitable way reveals itself to me than that I should offer you such gifts as have befallen me through your and your Austrian family's kindness, musical [gifts], naturally, and harmonic. And since it is by your [plural, including the House of Austria] propitious support for me that I obtained this leisure, I give you its fruits.' For the original text, see Appendix 1.

that he spent in Habsburg employ, his comment in the epistle may to a large degree reflect the opportunities for composition that this appointment had allowed.[26] It is indeed possible that through Victoria's appointment María wished to ensure that she once again had an eminent composer in her household, to replace Matheo Flecha the Younger who had recently left her service as chaplain.[27] Flecha, who was also a poet,[28] had served María and her sister Juana during their youth, and he became a chaplain to María from 1568. The composer returned with María to Spain in 1581, accompanying her when she took up residence at the Descalzas.[29] In January 1583 he was paid for his services (presumably as a musician) at the celebration of the feasts of the Annunciation and Christmas at the Descalzas the previous year.[30] On 23 October 1585 Hans Khevenhüller (who, as mentioned above, was Imperial Ambassador to Spain, and a key figure at María's court) sent Flecha to the Emperor in Prague with three boy castrati.[31] While we do not know whether Flecha then remained at the Imperial court or returned briefly to Madrid, the former is perhaps more likely, since by 1 July 1586 Flecha was serving as a member of the Imperial chapel.[32]

Although Victoria did not join María's household until September 1587 (that is, nearly two years after Flecha was sent to Prague), we know that he was in Madrid in October 1586, since on the 17th of that month he wrote thence to his friend Giovanni Giovenale Ancina in Rome.[33] The last record

---

[26] One should however note that his output of collections of newly published works after the return to Madrid was much less than it had been between 1572 and 1585.

[27] The possibility that Victoria was brought into María's employ specifically to fill the place vacated by Flecha has been raised by Alfonso de Vicente, 'El entorno femenino de la dinastía: el complejo conventual de las Descalzas Reales (1574–1633)', in Alfonso de Vicente and Pilar Tomás (eds), *Tomás Luis de Victoria y la cultura musical en la España de Felipe III* (Madrid: Centro de Estudios Europa Hispánica & Machado Libros, 2012), 197–246, at 207.

[28] See Maria Carmen Gómez, 'Un libro de poemas de Fray Matheo Flecha (ca. 1530–1604)', *Revista de Musicología* 8 (1985), 343–70.

[29] Maria Carmen Gómez, 'Precisiones en torno a la vida y obra de Matheo Felcha el joven', *Revista de Musicología* 9 (1986), 41–56.

[30] The relevant payments to Flecha are recorded in Biblioteca del Monasterio de las Descalzas Reales, F/8, ff. 41v, and 42. See Alfonso de Vicente, 'El entorno femenino', 203.

[31] Hans Khevenhüller, *Geheimes Tagebuch, 1548–1605*, ed. Georg Khevenhüller-Metsch (Graz: Akademische Druck- und Verlagsanstalt, 1971), 147. This reference to Flecha, and therefore to the likely date of his move from Madrid to Prague, has apparently escaped previous notice.

[32] Gómez, 'Precisiones', 47. One should note, however, Higini Anglès's claim that Flecha was sent from the Imperial court to Spain in 1586 to recruit boy singers for the Imperial chapel. Anglès, 'Mateo Flecha el Joven', *Studia Musicologica Academiæ Scientiarum Hungaricæ* 3 (1962), 45–51, at 49. Anglès provides no reference to the source of his information, other than indicating that it came from 'los archivos de la cancillería austríaca'.

[33] See Daniele V. Filippi, *Tomás Luis de Victoria* (Palermo: L'Epos, 2008), 37–8.

we currently possess of his being in Rome (where he had lived since the mid 1560s) is from 30 April 1585,[34] and his move to Madrid might have occurred at any point during the year and a half between then and October 1586. In his letter to Ancina, Victoria expresses satisfaction with the favourable reception of his printed collections at the Spanish royal court, and mentions in particular the pleasure which Philip II had taken in the 1583 book of Masses (dedicated to the King) and the *Motecta festorum totius anni* of 1585.

In addition to its international links and connections to the royal court, María's household constituted an artistically rich environment for Victoria's life and work in Madrid.[35] For example, the Empress's apartments at the Descalzas were the location for the performance of *La fábula de Dafne*, a dramatic entertainment with vocal and instrumental music, sponsored by the Empress and attended by Prince Philip and the Infanta Isabella Clara Eugenia, which took place on a Sunday afternoon during Carnival, possibly between 1585 and 1595.[36] The performers included members of María's household together with musicians of 'la Capilla de Su Magestad', which we can presume to mean the King's chapel rather than Maria's.[37] If the event occurred after September 1587, Victoria was surely involved.

Among the named participants in *La fábula de Dafne* were two sons of the senior member of María's household, her lord high steward Juan de Borja. Borja was an important musical patron, a collector of printed and manuscript music, and a practising musician.[38] He was the dedicatee of *Las ensaladas* (Prague: Jorge Negrino, 1591), a collection by María's

JUAN DE BORJA

---

[34] Noel O'Regan, 'Tomás Luis de Victoria's Roman Churches Revisited', *Early Music* 28 (2000), 403–18, at 413.

[35] The cultural richness of María's court is vividly described by José Simón Días, 'Libros dedicados a la Infanta Sor Margarita de la Cruz', in *Homenaje a Luis Morales Oliver* (Madrid: Fundacion Universitaria Española, 1986), 429–44, at 429.

[36] See: López-Vidriero, 'Por la imprenta hacia Dios', 207–8; Pilar Ramos López, '*Dafne*, una fábula en la corte de Felipe II', *Anuario Musical* 50 (1995), 23–46; Louise K. Stein, 'The Musicians of the Spanish Royal Chapel and Court Entertainments, 1590–1648', in Juan José Carreras, Bernardo García García, and Tess Knighton (eds), *The Royal Chapel in the Time of the Habsburgs: Music and Court Ceremony in Early Modern Europe*, Studies in Medieval and Renaissance Music 3 (Woodbridge: Boydell & Brewer, 2005), 173–94, at 178–9; Luis Robledo Estaire, 'La música en la casa de la reina, príncipe e infantas', in Luis Robledo Estaire, Tess Knighton, Cristina Bordas Ibáñez, and Juan José Carreras (eds), *Aspectos de la cultura musical en la corte de Felipe II* (Madrid: Fundación Caja Madrid / Editorial Alpuerto, 2000), 195–212, at 212.

[37] See Stein, 'The Musicians of the Spanish Royal Chapel', 178. Although 'Su Magestad' could refer to either Philip or María, the *capilla* which formed part of María's household, discussed later in the present chapter, did not incorporate a *capilla de música* as did that of the King.

[38] On Borja and his musical interests and connections, see Ferran Escrivà Llorca, 'Eruditio, pietas et honor: Joan de Borja i la música del seu temps (1533–1606)', unpublished PhD thesis, Universitat Politècnica de València (2015). On his activity as musical collector,

ex-chaplain Matheo Flecha containing predominantly works by his similarly named uncle and by himself. More strikingly, Pietro Cerone singled Borja out in *El melopeo y maestro* (1613, dedicated to Philip III) as the only Spanish nobleman known to him among those resident in Madrid who maintained a private musical academy akin to those found in Italy.[39] Since Cerone served the Spanish royal court in the 1590s, it seems likely that he was involved in this academy, and Victoria, as the only eminent musician in María's household, would surely have attended also. In a letter from the renowned composer Francisco Guerrero (chapelmaster at Seville Cathedral) to Juan de Borja, Guerrero notes that Borja had permitted him to attend Borja's 'conversación de música', which is presumably the academy to which Cerone refers.[40] Guerrero's letter is of particular interest to us here, since he says that he is sending with it a motet which he had composed for the exequies of Philip II (which must mean the exequies at Seville Cathedral), and invites Borja to perform it 'on your viols'.[41]

see also: Carmelo Peter Comberiati, *Late Renaissance Music at the Habsburg Court* (Montreux: Gordon and Breach, 1987), 192–5; Trevor Dadson, 'Libros e instrumentos de música en inventarios *post-mortem* del siglo de oro español: el caso de don Juan de Borja (1607)', *Pliegos de Bibliofilia* 14 (2001), 3–18; Trevor Dadson, 'Music Books and Instruments in Spanish Golden-Age Inventories: The Case of Don Juan de Borja (1607)', in Iain Fenlon and Tess Knighton (eds), *Early Music Printing and Publishing in the Iberian World* (Kassell: Edition Reichenberger, 2007), 95–116; Douglas Kirk, 'A Tale of Two Queens, Their Music Books, and the Village of Lerma', in Tess Knighton and Bernadette Nelson (eds), *Pure Gold: Golden Age Sacred Music in the Iberian World. A Homage to Bruno Turner*, DeMusica 15 (Kassel: Edition Reichenberger, 2011), 79–92, at 89–92; Ferran Escrivà Llorca, 'La vida en las Descalzas Reales a través de los epistolarios de Juan de Borja (1584–1604)', in Javier Suáres-Pajares and Manuel del Sol (eds), *Estudios. Tomás Luis de Victoria. Studies*, Colección Música hispana, textos, estudios 18 (Madrid: Instituto Complutense de Ciencias Musicales, 2013), 437–52. See also Luis Robledo Estaire, 'Música y virtud en los pentagramas de Juan de Borja y Alejandro Luzón de Millares', in Rafael Zafra Molina and José Javier Azanza (eds), *Emblemática trascendente: hermenéutica de la imagen, iconología del texto* (Pamplona: Sociedad Española de Emblemática/ Universidad de Navarra, 2011), 709–17.

[39] See Escrivà Llorca, 'Eruditio, pietas et honor', 122–3, and María Sanhuesa Fonseca, '*Armería del ingenio y recreación de los sentidos*: la música en las academias literarias españolas del siglo XVII', *Revista de Musicología* 21.1 (1998), 297–530, at 503–4. Cerone writes: 'Y si tengo à dezir verdad, digo que no hallo mas que uno, que guste tener en su casa semejante exercicio: y este Señor es, Don Iuan de Borja, Mayordomo mayor de la S. C. M. de la Emperatriz Doña María de Austria, (que está en cielo) hermana del Rey D. PHILIPPE II.' *El melopeo y maestro* (Naples: J. B. Gargano y Lucrecio Nucci, 1613), 151.

[40] 'V(uestra) S(eñoria) . . . me a hecho muchos favores, admitiéndome en su conversación de música'; the letter is in British Library Add. Ms 28426, document 36, at f. 72, and is transcribed in Escrivà Llorca, 'Eruditio, pietas et honor', 149–50 and 260.

[41] 'Ay enbio a V(uestra) S(eñoría) un mottete q(ue) e hecho para las homrras del Rey n(uest)ro s(eñor) q(ue) sea en gloria. Suplico a V(uestra) S(eñoría) lo vea y cante con sus viguelas de arco.' The post-mortem inventory of Juan de Borja's goods includes a chest of viols; see the transcription in Vicente, *El mayordomo*, 179, 180, and 183.

The letter is dated 9 November 1598, and so the motet was of very recent composition (the King had died on 13 September); indeed, it had not yet received the public performance in Seville for which it was written, since the exequies there were delayed until 30 and 31 December. It may be that this was the *Versa est in luctum* attributed to Guerrero and of which the Altus part (the only part known to survive) was added by hand to a copy of the relevant part-book from Guerrero's *Motecta* of 1597, preserved in Barcelona.[42] We can readily imagine that Victoria, who had a well established association with Guerrero, was among the musicians who tried out Guerrero's motet. Upon María's death in February 1603, Borja and Victoria would of necessity have worked closely together regarding the arrangements for the exequies of her household, for which the music of the *Officium defunctorum* (including Victoria's own setting of *Versa est in luctum*) was composed (see Chapter 2), and when Borja himself died in 1606 Victoria was responsible for the valuation of his music books listed in the post-mortem inventory, which include three printed collections of Victoria's music, as well as a 'libro de missas de difuntos del di(ch)o maestro bitoria', which is discussed further in Chapter 3.[43]

The membership of the Dowager Empress's household over which Borja presided is recorded in a number of surviving registers from the period of Victoria's service, the most extensive of them listing 128 people.[44] Among Victoria's fellow chaplains, within the *capilla* department of the household, were his brother Agustín, and (as mentioned) the poet Bartolomé Leonardo de Argensola, whose own brother – the poet, dramatist, and historian Lupercio Leonardo de Argensola – served as a secretary to María and composed a Latin epitaph to be displayed at her exequies

---

[42] Barcelona, Institución Milá y Fontanals, CSIC, Fondo Reservado, 67. I am most grateful to Emilio Ros-Fábregas for providing photographs of this book.

[43] Transcriptions and studies of the list of music books in this post-mortem inventory may be found in Escrivà Llorca, 'Eruditio, pietas et honor', 288–96 and 333–89, Dadson, 'Libros e instrumentos de música', and Dadson, 'Music Books and Instruments'; another transcription is in Vicente, *El mayordomo*, 172–83.

[44] I am aware of four such lists, three of which are preserved in the British Library: Add. Ms 28428, ff. 405–9; Add. Ms 28428, ff. 451–3; Add. Ms 28707, f. 68. The fourth list is Madrid, Real Academia de Historia, Papeles de Jesuitas, 9/3661, doc. 121, with another copy in 9/3669. Transcriptions of the first two of these lists may be found in Escrivà Llorca, 'La vida en las Descalzas Reales', 444–6, and Escrivà Llorca, 'Eruditio, pietas et honor', 273–8; the third is transcribed in Elías Tormo y Monzó, *En las Descalzas Reales: estudios históricos, iconográficos y artísticos* (Madrid: Blass y cía, 1917), 226–8; a transcription of the fourth list is in José Millán Martínez, 'La emperatriz María y las pugnas cortesanas en tiempos de Felipe II', in Ernest Belenguer Cebrià (ed.), *Felipe II y el Mediterráneo*, 4 vols (Madrid: Sociedad Estatal para la Conmemoración de los Centenarios de Felipe II y Carlos V, 1999), III, 143–60, at 156–60.

(see Chapter 2). Another of the chaplains, Martin Pesserio,[45] contributed a eulogistic Latin *carmen* to the liminary matter of Victoria's *Officium defunctorum* (see Chapter 3). In addition to his service within María's household, Pesserio held chaplaincies at the royal court.[46] Only one specifically musical post (and within the *cámara* rather than the *capilla*) is mentioned in one of the lists of María's household personnel: Juan Vizcaíno appears as a *chantre de cámara*, receiving the same annual stipend as did Victoria and the other chaplains according to this particular list.[47] On another of the personnel registers Victoria's stipend is given as 67,500 *maravedís* annually, which is a modest amount in comparison to his very substantial annual income from benefices.[48] Following María's death Victoria was appointed to one of three chaplaincies (for singers) at the Descalzas which the Empress endowed, bringing a stipend of 45,000 *maravedís*, and in addition he was allotted the post of organist within the *capilla* of the Descalzas, which carried a stipend of 40,000 *maravedís*, increased to 75,000 *maravedís* from 1606. The opening section of the dedicatory epistle in the *Officium defunctorum* (see Appendix 1) suggests that he also served Margarita as chaplain following her mother's death.

Modern writings about Victoria have not always maintained clearly the distinction between the chaplains of María's household and the chaplains belonging to the *capilla* of the Descalzas, that is, the *capilla* created as part of Doña Juana's foundation of the convent. The *capilla* of the Descalzas had its own *maestro*, elected – during the period of Victoria's service in María's household – from amongst the chaplains of that establishment. Although

---

[45] His name is spelled variously Pesserio, Pessenio, Perserio, Persenio, and Porselio, and sometimes with the addition of the further name Hasdale.

[46] See the entry on Pesserio within the biographical database of members of the Spanish royal courts from the time of Charles V to that of Philip V, administered by the Instituto Universitario 'La Corte en Europa', www.iulce.es, a project of the Universidad Autónoma de Madrid. In one of the lists of María's household personnel (British Library Add. Ms 28428, f. 405), Pesserio appears among the chaplains belonging to María's *capilla*, but is there described as 'capellán de la corte', reflecting his parallel service in the royal court. Pesserio is the only one of María's chaplains mentioned by name in her wills, codicils, and memorials: Victoria's name does not appear. In the final testamentary document which María dictated and signed on 4 February 1603 (three weeks before her death), she mentioned Pesserio and two others, among the German members of her household, as particularly worthy of financial assistance: *Recopilacion de los testamentos, codicilo y memoriales de la Magestad Cesarea de la Emperatriz y de otros papeles concernientes a ellos* (np, nd), printed by the Jesuits, of which a copy is preserved as Madrid, Biblioteca Nacional de España, R/39135; the relevant text is at f. 12ᵛ.

[47] Real Academia de la Historia, Papeles de Jesuitas, 9/3661, doc. 121.

[48] See the summaries of these in Robert Murrell Stevenson, *Spanish Cathedral Music in the Golden Age* (Berkeley and Los Angeles: University of California Press, 1961), 365, and Mota Murillo, *Sebastián López de Velasco*, I, 54.

Victoria never held this official post (which, indeed, was not open to him, since he did not occupy one of the relevant chaplaincies within the *capilla* of the Descalzas), there are strong indications that he did act in the capacity of *maestro*, albeit informally. The principal evidence in this regard is found in a royal charter issued in July 1611.[49] This document was drawn up in response to a request from Victoria that upon his death (which in fact occurred on 27 August of that same year) he be succeeded as organist of the Descalzas by Bernardo Pérez de Medrano. As part of this petition, Victoria drew to the King's attention the fact that he had served as *maestro de capilla* of the Descalzas for seventeen years, but without any stipend ('sin interes ninguno'). The wording of the charter implies that these seventeen years' service had begun in the very year (1587) in which Victoria entered María's service. Victoria's claim to have acted as *maestro* over this extended period must have had at least some validity, since it seems highly unlikely that King Philip (who attended the convent regularly when in Madrid, as noted above, and under whose jurisdiction as patron the *capilla* of the Descalzas lay) would have been ignorant of this aspect of Victoria's work at the Descalzas, and Victoria would therefore hardly have dissembled in this respect. However, a complication arises from the fact that we have records of other men – from among the chaplains in the *capilla* of the Descalzas – who officially held this post of *maestro* during parts of the relevant period.[50] The tenor Antonio Bechio (/Bochio/Vecchio) was elected to the position in December 1587 (that is, three months after Victoria's appointment as chaplain to María), but in September 1590 he took up a post as singer-chaplain in the *capilla real* in Granada.[51] We then have no notice of a *maestro de capilla* at the Descalzas until Francisco Montero quitted that office in March 1604.[52] It is not known when Montero was

---

[49] Madrid, Archivo Histórico Nacional, Consejos, libro 253, f. 116. The text is transcribed in Mota Murillo, *Sebastián López de Velasco*, I, 153.

[50] The information currently available concerning the *maestros de capilla* at the Descalzas is presented in Ángel Manuel Olmos Sáez, 'Aportaciones a la temprana historia musical de la Capilla de las Descalzas Reales de Madrid (1576–1618)', *Revista de Musicología* 26/2 (2003), 339–489, and Kelly Huff, 'Demystifying the Life and Madrid Works of Tomás Luis de Victoria', unpublished PhD thesis, University of Kansas (2015), 140. See also Vicente, 'El entorno femenino', 202–3.

[51] See Juan Ruiz Jiménez, 'Patronazgo musical en la capilla real de Granada durante el siglo XVI. 1.– Los musicos prebendados', in David Crawford (ed.), *Encomium musicæ: Essays in Honor of Robert J. Snow* (Hillsdale: Pendragon, 2002), 341–63, at 358.

[52] Thereafter, we can establish the identities of the *maestros de capilla* for the entire period until after Victoria's death in 1611: Antonio Fernández de Alameda succeeded Francisco Montero in March 1604, and Francisco Dávila y Páez succeeded Fernández de Alameda in March 1608. See Olmos Sáez, 'Aportaciones'.

elected,[53] and there may have been a gap between Bechio's tenure and Montero's during which Victoria alone acted as *maestro*, although that would still fail to account satisfactorily for Victoria's statement to the King about the duration of his service as *maestro*. In considering this issue, it is also worth noting that capitular documents from various Spanish ecclesiastical institutions (the cathedrals of Guadix, León, Palencia, Plasencia, and Zaragoza, and the Royal Chapel in Granada) and dating from between August 1593 and May 1608 describe Victoria as *maestro de capilla* of the Descalzas, as does a letter written in Madrid in 1601 by a canon of Jáen Cathedral.[54] To be sure, not all of these references to Victoria's employment are accurate in other respects: one of the documents concerned also claims that he had previously been *maestro de capilla* to the pope.[55] Nevertheless, the body of evidence is sufficient to suggest once again that Victoria did indeed undertake at least some of the duties of *maestro* at the Descalzas, and over the course of many years. Since Victoria was immeasurably more eminent as a musician than those Descalzas chaplains elected to the position of *maestro* during this period, it would have made great sense for him to assume effective musical direction of the *capilla*, while the fact that he held no official appointment might have suited Victoria well, allowing flexibility of commitment and perhaps permitting him to leave to the official *maestro* such regular duties as the teaching of the choirboys.[56] Such an arrangement might also have reflected the fact that the official post of *maestro* was not, until several years after María's death, equivalent in level to those of the Spanish cathedrals: appointments made by seeking – and sometimes examining – external

[53] Mariano Soriano Fuertes gave the date of his appointment as 1598, but provided no reference to the source of this information: *Historia de la música española desde la venida de los fenicios hasta el año de 1850*, II (Madrid: Martin y Salazar; Barcelona: Narciso Ramirez, 1856), 134. Huff, 'Demystifying the Life and Madrid Works', 140, notes that he was a chaplain by 17 January 1600.

[54] The fullest discussion and listing of these documentary references to Victoria is that in Vicente, *Tomás Luis de Victoria: Cartas*, 12, 41–9. The relevant capitular document of 16 May 1608 from Plasencia Cathedral (*ibid.*, 49) refers to Victoria as 'capellán de la emperatriz y maestro de la capilla real': this is presumably a reference to the *capilla real* of the Descalzas, rather than that of the monarch.

[55] Vicente, *Tomás Luis de Victoria: Cartas*, 12.

[56] On the regulations governing the chaplains of the *capilla*, see Mota Murillo, *Sebastián López de Velasco*, I, 45–8, and Maria Leticia Sánchez Hernández, *Patronato regio y órdenes religiosas femeninas en el Madrid delos Austrias: Descalzas Reales, Encarnación, y Santa Isabel* (Madrid: Fundación Universitaria Española, 1997), 155. The chaplains were required to live in a common house, and to seek permission from the *capillán major* for periods of absence. The salary of the singer-chaplains was considerably more – 150,000 *maravedís* – than what Victoria received as chaplain to the Empress, and the *maestro de capilla* received an additional 10,000 *maravedís*.

candidates, and which carried by this period expectations of compositional skill. At the time of María's death and Victoria's composition of the music for her exequies, it is possible that Francisco Montero held the official position of *maestro* at the Descalzas. Nevertheless, given what has been said above, it seems quite likely that Victoria was in musical charge of these services at which the music of his *Officium defunctorum* was first performed.

In another contemporary source Victoria is described as chapelmaster not of the Descalzas but of María herself, in other words, of María's household chapel. This occurs in the recommendation concerning remuneration of the composer written by Pietro Antonio Bianco to Archduke Ferdinand, already mentioned,[57] but may represent a simple misunderstanding on Bianco's part: in the relevant letter to Ferdinand Victoria gives his position simply as 'capellan de la enperatriz'. María's household chapel was, of course, administratively distinct from the *capilla real* of the Descalzas, which was under the king's jurisdiction, but in none of the four lists of María's household mentioned above, including the two which have a distinct section headed 'Capilla', is Victoria (or anyone else) designated *maestro de capilla*.[58] Judging from these lists, María's chapel establishment was small, perhaps because she was resident at the Descalzas, where the performance of the liturgy was undertaken by the nuns and by the monastery's *capilla*. As members of María's household chapel are listed the grand almoner (*limosnero mayor*), the chaplains (usually four), two – or, on one list, four – *mozos de capilla*, and the Empress's confessor (on one list). We can presume that the *mozos*, whose stipend was similar to that of the chaplains, were grooms of the chapel, rather than boy singers.[59] There is no evidence that any of the other chaplains besides Victoria – and Flecha before him – were musicians, and the lists do not include any musicians within the *capilla* establishment: it seems therefore that the Empress's court did not incorporate a *capilla de música*. María's chapel personnel (besides Flecha and Victoria, as already mentioned) did however

---

[57] See Federhofer, 'Graz Court Musicians', 243. In his order of payment, Ferdinand correspondingly refers to Victoria as 'der verwittibten Römischen Kaiserin Capelmaister in Hispanien'.

[58] The household lists which name the members of the household *capilla* under this heading are those in British Library Add. Ms 28428, at ff. 405–9 and ff. 451–3. See Escrivà Llorca, 'La vida en las Descalzas Reales', 442 and 446.

[59] In the household list at ff. 405–9 of British Library Add. Ms 28428, the stipend of the *mozos* is given as 10 florins (= 37,500 *maravedís*), the same as that of the chaplain Martin Pesserio. In the list in Madrid, Real Academia de Historia, Papeles de Jesuitas, 9/3661, the one *mozo* included on the list receives the same stipend as the four chaplains.

contribute on occasion to the performance of the liturgy in the Descalzas chapel, alongside the members of the *capilla real* of the convent,[60] and one of her chaplains, Mateo Moreno, is described as also being *sacristan mayor* of the Descalzas chapel in a document of 1583.[61] However, when the Empress's *capilla* operated as a separate entity in the conduct of the liturgy the usual location for this would presumably have been the oratory which constituted part of María's apartments at the Descalzas, and members of the household chapel, including Victoria, doubtless accompanied the Empress when she travelled, as for example when she was at El Escorial in September 1593 to welcome her son Albert back to Spain after his period as Viceroy of Portugal.

But this small household *capilla* is surely of limited relevance to our consideration of Victoria's activities as a musician while in María's service, the principal context for which was clearly the *capilla* of the Descalzas. At the conclusion of the dedicatory epistle to Philip III of the *Missæ* of 1600, Victoria focuses on performance of the music in that collection at Mass in the convent chapel (and not, for example, on performance by the king's chapel):

> If you accept this gift, it will come about, not only that it is safe from all wantonness of tongues, but also that those who perform Masses with hymns and canticles in this most renowned temple of your most august aunt Juana are made daily more eager for the cult of the true God.[62]

Some or all of the multi-choir works first published in this collection may well have received their initial performances, very likely under Victoria's direction, in the Descalzas chapel and in the presence of the Empress. It is therefore appropriate – given that María was Victoria's patron and that the Blessed Virgin Mary was the patron of the Descalzas convent as well as of the Empress – that there is a notably strong Marian emphasis in the collection: the first three of the five Masses are Marian works, based on Victoria's double-choir settings of the antiphons *Alma redemptoris mater*, *Ave regina cælorum*, and *Salve regina*. The collection includes also these antiphon settings, together with Victoria's eight-voice settings of the other principal Marian antiphon, *Regina cæli*, and of the Marian litany and *Ave*

---

[60] For example, in 1582 'the Empress's chaplains' were among those paid for assisting in the celebration of the Octave of Corpus Christi. See Vicente, 'El entorno femenino', 203.

[61] See Huff, 'Demystifying the Life and Madrid Works', 126.

[62] 'Te munus hoc accipiente fiet, non modo ut tutum sit ab omni linguarum procacitate, sed etiam ut qui Missarum solemnia Hymnis, et Canticis peragunt in clarissimo hoc Templo Augustissimæ Amitæ tuæ Ioanne alacriores quotidie ad veri numinis cultum reddantur.'

Maria. The fifth Mass in the collection, and Victoria's grandest in terms of scoring, is the twelve-voice *Missa Lætatus sum*, based on the third of the five psalms in the female cursus used at Marian Vespers, and Victoria's setting of this psalm on which his Mass is based is also printed here, as is a setting of the last Vespers psalm of the female cursus, *Nisi Dominus*. The *Missa Lætatus sum* is followed by a setting of the Marian canticle Magnificat, likewise for twelve voices. The collection also includes a motet in honour of St Ildephonso, the seventh-century Archbishop of Toledo to whom the Virgin miraculously appeared in Toledo Cathedral to bestow on him a chasuble in recognition of his veneration of her. Among the non-Marian works in the 1600 collection, another features the name 'Maria' more prominently even than any of the works mentioned so far, but this Mary is Mary Magdalene: *Dic nobis Maria* is a setting of part of the sequence *Victimæ paschali laudes*, in which the opening double-choir setting of the verse 'Dic nobis Maria, quid vidistis in via' is repeated after each single-choir verse.

The reverence in which María held her saint's name, her use of it in preference to her titles, and the connection between the Empress and the Blessed Virgin Mary are all emphasised in one of the emblematic 'hieroglyphs' created for the exequies of the Empress organised by the Jesuit College in Madrid (Figure 1.3). As usual with such hieroglyphs, the significance of the image is revealed in stages, firstly by the Latin motto 'et nomen illius Maria' – 'and her name was Mary', an adaptation of 'et nomen virginis Maria' ('and the virgin's name was Mary') from St Luke's Gospel – and then by a verse in Spanish:

She regarded so highly this title and name,
That she fled from grandiose titles,
And signed herself with the name of Mary.[63]

The published *relación* of these exequies provides a further level of explanation:

In her dispatches and letters she would sign herself simply 'Maria', omitting the names signifying Majesty; she did not write 'I, the Empress', although she could have done so, in the same way that kings normally write 'I, the king'. And not only in her dispatches and letters, but also in her wills, codicils, and many other writings ... This gave rise to the hieroglyph, where the name 'Maria' is so

---

[63] *Libro de las honras que hizo el colegio de la compañia de Iesus de Madrid, à la m(agestad) c(æsarea) de la emperatriz doña Maria de Austria, fundadora del dicho colegio, que se celebraron a 21. de abril de 1603* (Madrid: Luis Sánchez, 1603), f. 48.

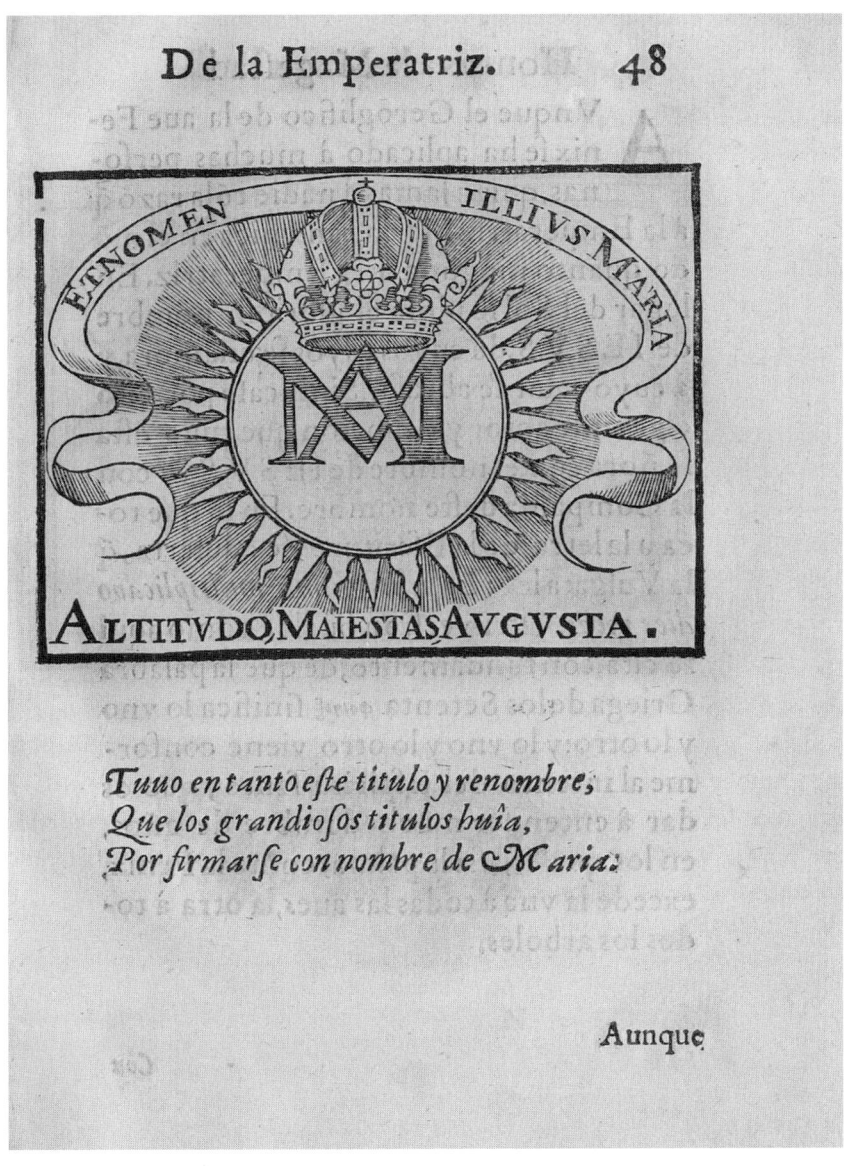

Figure 1.3 *Libro de las honras que hizo el colegio de la compañia de Iesus de Madrid, à la m(agestad) c(æsarea) de la emperatriz doña Maria de Austria, fundadora del dicho colegio, que se celebraron a 21. de abril de 1603* (Madrid: Luis Sánchez, 1603), f. 48; Getty Research Institute

respected, and so surrounded with rays and sunbursts, signifying the esteem in which this lady held this name.[64]

---

[64] 'En sus despachos y cartas se firmava solamente, Maria, dexando los nombres de Magestad: no dezia: Yo la Emperatriz, y pudiera, al modo que los Reyes usan dezir: Yo el Rey. Y no solo en sus

The hieroglyph concerned employs a traditional monogram of the Blessed Virgin Mary, formed of the intertwined letters 'M' and 'A'.[65]

The other Mass in the 1600 collection, the nine-voice *Missa pro victoria*, may have been conceived particularly in honour of Victoria's Habsburg patrons. Although the title conceals the fact, this work belongs to the genre of parody Masses based on Janequin's chanson *La bataille*, but the 'battle' and 'victory' which it expressed presumably included Christ's victory over death, celebrated at Mass, and the victories in defence of the faith achieved and yet to be achieved by the House of Austria.[66] In the dedicatory epistle of the *Officium defunctorum* Victoria lauds María's father and brother in these terms:

> That invincible terror of the world, Charles V, who like a new sun began to blaze in the West against the sun of the East, who with a boldness greater than Alexander's durst pass the Pillars of Hercules, and changed the inscription from *Non ultra* [No further] to *Plus ultra* [Beyond]; then the great-hearted Philip II, who governed and expanded his ancestral dominion 'neither by hope nor by fear' but by arms and counsel.[67]

Victoria himself recorded that Philip III displayed particular fondness for the *Missa pro victoria*.[68] However, according to the view of María propounded by biographers and preachers after her death, such victories for the Catholic cause were achieved not only through the military prowess of her male relatives, but also through the saintly piety of the Empress and the tireless round of devotion and prayer which she maintained at the Descalzas. Daniele Filippi has drawn attention, when discussing the

despachos y cartas, sino en sus testamentos, codicilos, y otras muchas escrituras ... Esto dio ocasion al Geroglifico, donde el nombre de Maria està tan autorizado, y tan lleno de rayos y resplandores, sinificando la estima que ésta señora tenia deste nombre.' *Libro de las honras*, f. 47v. The Empress was the dedicatee of a treatise in support of the dogma of the Immaculate Conception of Mary, by the Franciscan Cristóbal Moreno: *Libro intitulado Limpieza de la Virgen y Madre de Dios* (Valencia: Juan Navarro, 1582).

[65] María's particular devotion to Our Lady was emphasised also in the sermon preached by Fray Juan de los Angeles at her household exequies at the Descalzas: *Sermon que en las honras de la catolica ceserea magestad de la emperatriz nuestra señora predicó el padre fray Iuan de los Angeles* (Madrid: Juan de la Cuesta, 1604), f. 13.

[66] Daniele Filippi discusses the *Missa pro victoria* in the context of contemporary concepts of (for example) Christ as warrior and spiritual battle in *Tomás Luis de Victoria*, 131–4. For a summary of modern views of this Mass and of the possible circumstances of its genesis, see Alfonso de Vicente, 'Introducción: *Pro victoria*. El poder del sonido', in Vicente and Tomás (eds), *Tomás Luis de Victoria*, 9–32, at 22–7.

[67] See Appendix 1 for the original text.

[68] Victoria comments thus in the letter to Archduke Ferdinand in Graz, mentioned above, and in another to Francesco Maria II della Rovere, Duke of Urbino, to whom Victoria had likewise sent a copy of the *Missæ* of 1600. See Vicente, *Tomás Luis de Victoria: Cartas*, 96 and 102.

Missa pro victoria, to a particularly vivid passage in the sermon delivered by Jerónimo de Florencia during the exequies for María organised by the Jesuit College in Madrid:

The sons of our royal eagle [i.e. María], as sons of a mother who was so zealous a defender of our holy faith, have defended it with lance in hand, and they defend it on the battlefield, desiring to drink the blood of its enemies, and their holy mother helped their fight, not on the battlefield with lance in hand, but from the quire with prayers, and from a holy monastery through an exemplary life: for from there with that so harmonious army of so many devotional exercises, and with such magnificent squadrons of such heroic virtues, prayers, and sighs to heaven, she fought for our holy faith against its enemies better than do great armies of soldiers on the battlefield . . . In quires where the servants of God pray, the magnificent squadrons against the enemies of the faith and of virtue are formed.[69]

Thus, according to this metaphor those singing Mass in the quire of the Descalzas acted as soldiers for the faith. This kind of imagery would have acquired a particular power when the *Missa pro victoria* was performed, especially in the presence of María, her grandson Philip, and indeed her daughter Margarita, dedicatee of the *Officium defunctorum*, whom Victoria addressed in the title of his dedicatory epistle as 'a soldier for Christ' ('Christo . . . militanti'). The likelihood of particular connections between the *Missa pro victoria* and Victoria's Habsburg patrons is increased by the fact that the Archangel St Michael, captain of the heavenly host in its battle with the forces of Satan, was not only patron saint of the Holy Roman Empire and hence of the House of Austria but was also held in special reverence by the rulers of Spain, and was declared protector of the Spanish monarchy at the instigation of Philip IV.[70] In an allegorical

[69] 'Los hijos de nuestra Real aguila, como hijos de madre tan zeladora y defensora de nuestra santa Fé con la lança en la mano la han defendido, y defienden en el campo, desseando beverles la sangre à los enemigos della, à los quales su santa madre ayudava à pelear, sino desde el campo con la lança en la mano, a lo menos desde el coro con oraciones, y desde un santo monasterio con vida exemplar: porque desde alli con aquel tan concertado exercito de tantos exercicios de devocion, y con los esquadrones tan lucidos de tan heroycas virtudes, oraciones y suspiros al Cielo, peleava por nuestra santa Fè contra los enemigos della, mejor que lo hazen los grandes exercitos de soldados en el campo . . . en los coros donde oran los siervos de Dios, se forman los lucidos esquadrones contra los enemigos de la Fè y de la virtud.' *Libro de las honras*, f. 40. See Filippi, *Tomás Luis de Victoria*, 134. Alfonso de Vicente – likewise when discussing the *Missa pro victoria* – has highlighted a similar passage, based on that just quoted, in Juan Carrillo's biography of María: 'Introducción: *Pro victoria*', 26–7.
[70] The Jesuit Juan Eusebio Nieremberg, who taught at the Order's Colegio Imperial in Madrid founded by María, wrote of the devotion of the House of Austria and of Spanish monarchs to the saint in a work dedicated to Philip IV, *De la devocion, y patrocinio de San Miguel principe de los angeles, antiguo tutelar de los godos, y protector de España* (Madrid: María de Quiñones, 1643).

painting at the Descalzas, St Michael stands on a pedestal at the entrance of the 'harbour of salvation' ('portus salutis'), acting as a beacon for the ship of the church (the centrepiece of the painting), and following in the wake of that ship are two smaller boats containing male and female members of the House of Austria, including María. In the sky appears the Blessed Virgin Mary, 'star of the sea' ('stella maris'). Since María is dressed as a widow, the painting was probably made during the period of her residence at the Descalzas.[71]

The Offertory text of the Requiem Mass introduces St Michael in this role of welcoming the souls of the righteous to heaven: 'but may the standard-bearer St Michael lead them into the holy light' ('sed signifer Sanctus Michael repræsentet eas in lucem sanctam'). In setting this text for María's exequies in 1603, Victoria treated the opening words, 'sed signifer', in a way that would have been striking to contemporary singers and listeners, using the most famous musical motive of the period, the four-note 'Salve' figure with which the *Salve regina* chant begins. This motive enters immediately at the beginning of the 'sed signifer' section, in the topmost voice, and is sung three times in all.[72] The 'Salve' figure functioned in vocal and instrumental music as the musical sign *par excellence* for the Blessed Virgin Mary.[73] Within the Offertory of his six-voice Requiem, Victoria was perhaps playing with the fact that 'signifer' means not only 'standard bearer' but also 'sign-bearing', and by introducing the sign of Mary at this point in the Offertory text he recalls the role of the Queen of Heaven as mediatrix and 'gate of heaven' ('cæli porta'). 'Signifer' also means 'starry', and Mary was 'star of the sea' ('stella maris'), as represented on the painting at the Descalzas just described. Among the poems composed for María's exequies at the Jesuit College in Madrid we find the Empress similarly likened to a star lighting the way to harbour, and those poems include more explicit parallels between the Empress and her namesake the Queen of Heaven.[74] Such explicit parallels – which we have

---

[71] Regarding this painting, see: Ana García Sanz and María Victoria Triviño, *Iconografía de Santa Clara en el Monasterio de las Descalzas Reales* (Madrid: Patrimonio Nacional / Caja de Madrid, 1993), 121–2; Orlando Amado Hernández Ying, 'Angels in the Americas: Paintings of Apocryphal Angels in Spain and its American Viceroyalties', unpublished PhD thesis, The City University of New York (2009), 84.

[72] It is placed in counterpoint with a rising tetrachord motive belonging to the Offertory chant.

[73] In his six-voice *Salve regina* Victoria had echoed Josquin's famous five-voice setting of that text by employing the 'Salve' motive as a *soggetto ostinato*.

[74] See *Libro de las exequias*, f. 82 (on the Empress María as guiding star) and f. 83v and f. 85v (on the Empress María 'transformed into the mother of Jesus', in that she suckles the Jesuit College with her milk (her will provided substantial funds for its refoundation) as Mary had suckled Jesus.

already encountered in one of the hieroglyphs for those exequies – occur also in the sermon preached on the second day of the exequies by Jerónimo de Florencia, who associates the 'holy Empress, named María' with 'the Empress of heaven, Maria mother of God'.[75] At the end of his oration at the same exequies, Juan Luis de la Cerda addresses the Empress María as mediatrix in a manner which again evokes the parallels with the Blessed Virgin, and which in this case brings to mind specifically the *Salve regina*, a prayer calling thus on Mary as our advocate: 'to thee we sigh, lamenting and weeping in this valley of tears. Therefore, our advocate, turn those your merciful eyes towards us.'[76] De la Cerda's words are:

You, now a most divine Empress (when those in heaven pay heed to our affairs, and are moved by the tears of the wretched) look on us troubled with weeping, oppressed by unusual sadness, full of filth, deformed with tears ... From your heavenly dwellings ... send aid, so that crossing this vast ocean of miseries with you, and (following your example) attaining the heavenly ports ... we may enjoy everlasting bliss.[77]

The quotation of the *Salve* motive within the Offertory of Victoria's Requiem may have served a similar evocative purpose, reflecting both the association of María and Mary and the Empress's new heavenly status and authority. As we shall see in Chapter 4, the *Salve* motive also forms part of a 'signature' contrapuntal module which is used frequently and prominently in the *Officium defunctorum*, rendering it thereby a work which is 'proper' to Victoria's patroness, and repeatedly honouring her by reinforcing the association between the Empress and the Blessed Virgin.

[75] *Libro de las honras*, f. 21v: 'Y pues las honras que hazemos son de una santa Emperatriz, por nombre Maria, valganos oy la Emperatriz del cielo Maria madre de Dios, y de nos su favor para que acertemos, y para obligarla mas, digamos, Ave Maria.' 'And since the exequies which we are conducting are those of a holy Empress named Mary, may the Empress of heaven, Mary the mother of God, vindicate [the Empress] for us today, and grant us her favour so that we may be assured, and to oblige her more, let us say Ave Maria.'

[76] 'Ad te suspiramus, gementes et flentes in hac lacrimarum valle. Eia ergo, advocata nostra, illos tuos misericordes oculos ad nos converte.'

[77] 'Tu iam divinissima Augusta (quando cœlestibus nostrarum rerum sensus inest, et miserorum lachrymis tanguntur) aspice nos turpatos fletu, insolita mœstitia conspersos, illuvie plenos, lachrymis deformatos ... è cœlestibus domiciliis ... opem mitte, ut vasto hoc transmisso miseriarum pelago, una tecum, atque ad exemplum tuum cœlestibus portubus ocupatis ... sempiterna lætitia perfruamur.' *Libro de las honras*, f. 19v.

2 | María's Exequies in Context

The death of the Empress María on 26 February 1603 plunged the senior members of her household into weeks of frenetic activity, leading up to the exequies held at the Descalzas Reales convent on 18 and 19 March. All four of her chaplains would have had formidable commitments during this period, not least in contributing to the burial ceremonies and to the great number of post-mortem services held at the Descalzas before the exequies themselves. But it seems likely that the heaviest responsibility among the chaplains was Victoria's: the preparation of music for the household exequies or *honras fúnebres*, and perhaps – at extremely short notice – for the burial also. The abundance of surviving documentary material relating to María's death and the consequent post-mortem arrangements opens a window onto the context in which Victoria's Requiem was composed and first performed, and this documentation is usefully varied in type, including information from several of those who were eyewitnesses of events at the Descalzas. In attempting to piece together these events we shall also need to consider aspects of the broader context, such as the nature of Spanish Habsburg exequies and of the festival books that memorialise them, and what these sources indicate about music and manners of performance. This chapter takes the form of a narrative beginning with María's final illness and ending with the exequies organised by the Jesuits in Madrid in April, a narrative that is complemented by contextual explanations – some of them necessarily protracted – at the relevant points. Before proceeding further with that narrative, however, one needs to deal with the misguided view, which arose in twentieth-century writings concerning the *Officium defunctorum* and continues periodically to be repeated, that Victoria's Requiem was not in fact composed for María's exequies at the Descalzas.

In the dedicatory epistle of the *Officium defunctorum,* addressed to María's daughter Margarita, Victoria describes its contents as 'the music that I composed for the exequies of your Most Serene mother',[1] and he entitled the volume 'Office of the Dead for six voices upon the death and for

---

[1] 'Harmoniam illam, quam in exequias Serenissimæ tuæ Matris composui'.

the exequies of the Holy Empress'.[2] The most obvious and straightforward reading of these statements is that Victoria was here referring to the exequies organised by and for María's household in which he served, held in the chapel of the Descalzas in Margarita's presence. The idea in modern writings that he was *not* referring to these exequies emerged for four reasons: firstly, the most extensive contemporary account of the household exequies happens not to mention Victoria;[3] secondly, some have doubted that Victoria could have written the music of the *Officium defunctorum* in time for the exequies at the Descalzas; thirdly, it has been claimed that the chapel of the Descalzas was too small to accommodate the exequies; and fourthly, the exequies for María organised by the Jesuit College in Madrid and held in April 1603 were recorded in an extensive and lavishly illustrated published festival book, whereas no such published account of the household exequies survives, and some have consequently presumed that the Jesuit exequies were the more important ceremonies of the two and therefore the more likely and fitting occasion for Victoria's provision of the music published in the *Officium defunctorum*. None of these arguments against Victoria having written this music for María's household exequies holds water, but it is worth setting out the history of their development. In dismissing them, I am not suggesting that Victoria's music might not have been sung at the Jesuit exequies also: in fact, as set out below, I think it very likely that it was, and it is indeed possible that other music composed for that occasion and mentioned in the published festival book was by Victoria. But if his Requiem was indeed used at this event, then this was probably its third performance, not the first, and the piece's genesis certainly occurred as part of Victoria's service within María's household and not through his association with the Jesuits.

Doubts about Victoria's musical contribution to the household exequies at the Descalzas were expressed already in 1914 by Henri Collet. Collet seized upon the observation made previously by Felip Pedrell that the account (by Diego de Urbina) of these exequies does not mention Victoria's participation.[4] This led Collet to conclude that Victoria's

---

[2] 'Officium Defunctorum, sex vocibus. In obitu et obsequiis, Sacræ Imperatricis.'

[3] This manuscript account, by Diego de Urbina, constitutes a document of six folios, now bound into Biblioteca Nacional de España Ms 11773, at ff. 573–8 in the modern pencil foliation, and ff. 560–5 in the older ink foliation.

[4] Pedrell, unlike Collet, drew no particular conclusions from this, although he thought the absence of Victoria's name odd. See Felip Pedrell, 'Estudio biográfico-bibliográfico sobre el Maestro abulense Tomás Luis de Victoria y la presente edición completa de sus obras', in Pedrell (ed.), *Thomae Ludovici Victoria abulensis opera omnia* VIII (Leipzig: Breitkopf and Härtel, 1913), lxx, reprinted as *Tomás Luis de Victoria Abulense* (Valencia: Manuel Villar, 1918), 142.

contribution to the Descalzas exequies was, at best, a modest one, perhaps reflecting the fact that Victoria's status as chaplain did not confer a significant musical role. He speculated that the music sung on the occasion might have been restricted to plainchant, and that Victoria might not even have been there.[5] A related view, which has proved influential over the last half century, was set out by Robert Stevenson in the study of Victoria in his *Spanish Cathedral Music of the Golden Age* (1961). Discussing the same description of the Descalzas exequies to which Pedrell and Collet referred, Stevenson observes:

Although his account bears every mark of being painstakingly complete, he says nothing of Victoria's *Officium Defunctorum*: nor indeed does he so much as mention Victoria. Perhaps then we need not believe that Victoria composed so lengthy a work for performance only three weeks after [María's] death. A much more imposing occasion for the first performance would have been the *solenísimas y grandiosas honras* conducted on April 21–22 at SS. Peter and Paul, the Jesuit church completed in 1567 on the present site of the Madrid Cathedral . . . Victoria, whose intimate associations with the society dated from 1565 if not earlier, cannot have been overlooked when the Jesuit superiors combed Madrid for the finest talent in the capital. Moreover, the supremely beautiful *Officium Defunctorum*, published at Madrid in 1605, and hitherto always considered the pearl of his works, would still have been hastily composed, even if it waited until so late as April 21–22 for its first performance.[6]

Bruno Turner went even further than Stevenson in giving priority to the Jesuit exequies, describing these as 'the great obsequies', stating categorically that Victoria wrote the Requiem for them, and affirming that the Descalzas chapel was 'much too small for such a memorial

---

[5] *Victoria*, 94–5.

[6] Stevenson, *Spanish Cathedral Music*, 370. A view similar to Stevenson's has recently been expressed by Daniele Filippi: 'Probably the *Officium* was composed and performed not for the funeral of the deceased sovereign, nor for the succeeding commemoration held in March, but rather for the solemn ceremonies held on 21 and 22 April at the Jesuit church of Saints Peter and Paul.' ('Probabilmente l'*Officium* fu composto ed eseguito non per il funerale della sovrana defunta, né per la successiva commemorazione tenuta in marzo, bensí per le solenni cerimonie svoltesi il 21 e 22 aprile presso la chiesa gesuita dei Santi Petro e Paolo.') *Tomás Luis de Victoria*, 50. Another recent iteration of this view is in Huff, 'Demystifying the Life and Madrid Works', 158, who also repeats the doubts about the practicality of Victoria composing the relevant music 'at short notice' in time for the Descalzas exequies. The same argument is made by Josep Cercós and Josep Cabré (*Victoria* (Madrid: Espasa-Calpe, 1981), 66–7 and 106), and they once again attribute significance to the absence of Victoria's name from Diego de Urbina's account. They also regard the fact that the *Officium defunctorum* was published only much later as relevant to consideration of its likely date of composition.

service'.[7] This is clearly not the case: the chapel of the Descalzas had, in fact, been used already for Habsburg exequies, namely the royal court exequies of Queen Isabel de Valois (third wife of Philip II) in 1568 and those of the founder of the monastery, Princess Juana (María's sister), in 1573; furthermore, exequies for Queen Margaret of Austria (wife of Philip III) were held at the Descalzas in 1611. Turner bolsters the view that the exequies at the Jesuit College were the principal ones by claiming that Philip III and 'all the dignitaries of church and state' attended those ceremonies: in fact, the King and the members of the royal household were not there.[8] Indeed, as judged by these criteria 'the great obsequies' were neither those of the Jesuits nor those of María's household at the Descalzas, but rather the exequies held for the royal court in Valladolid, which were attended by the King and Queen, the members of the royal councils, the papal nuncio, and the French and Venetian ambassadors, together with many grandees. (The imperial ambassador, Khevenhüller, was duly summoned to attend by the King, but elected to attend the exequies at the Descalzas instead.)[9]

In countering such arguments, it needs to be emphasised firstly that no significance whatever can be attributed to the absence of Victoria's name from the account (or *relación*) of the exequies for María at the Descalzas. It was very uncommon to include musicians' names in such *relaciones*, and indeed the lengthy and detailed *relación* of the Jesuit ceremonies in 1603 likewise 'fails' to mention Victoria, weakening the arguments of Collet, Stevenson, and others further. Second, the hyperbolic language with which the printed *relación* of the Jesuit exequies describes them, and to which Stevenson refers, should not itself lead us to believe that they were extraordinary, or significantly more lavish than her household exequies at the Descalzas: such language is ubiquitous in accounts of this type, and we need give no more special weight to the way the Jesuits portrayed their exequies than to Diego de Urbina's claim in his *relación* of the Descalzas exequies that those exequies were 'among the most solemn and sumptuous which had ever been held in Spain'.[10] While – as we shall see below – the

---

[7] Bruno Turner, sleeve notes to *Victoria Requiem, Officium defunctorum, 1605*, Westminster Cathedral Choir, directed by David Hill (London: Hyperion Records, 1987). These points are repeated in the Introduction to Turner's edition of the work, 3.

[8] The printed account of the Jesuit exequies mentions simply that gentlemen who were in Madrid attended, together with Juan de Borja and the other members of María's household. Hans Khevenhüller was, it seems, the only ambassador present, and his presence is explained by his prominent role in María's household, discussed in Chapter 1. *Libro de las honras*, f. 10v.

[9] Hans Khevenhüller, *Geheimes Tagebuch*, 279.

[10] 'de las mas solenes y sumptuosas q(ue) se han hecho en España'. The writer notes that their stature was diminished only by the absence of the King.

preparations for the Descalzas exequies were certainly conducted in haste, that does not mean that they lacked the solemnity and grandeur appropriate for such commemoration of the Empress.

The printed account of the Jesuit *honras fúnebres* for María is an example of the *libro de exequias*, a genre which became commonplace in the Spanish Habsburg kingdoms by the seventeenth century, as it did in Italy also. *Libros de exequias* – representing a sub-genre of the *relación de sucesos* or festival book – served several purposes: they memorialised the deceased, constituted a record of these ephemeral events for the institutions and participants concerned, and were also used as models of protocol for those responsible for planning subsequent exequies. *Relaciones* of the royal court's own *honras* for senior members of the royal family were distributed to provide information throughout the Spanish kingdoms about the death, burial, and exequies, thus disseminating an idealised and propagandistic image of such *honras* as symbolic representations and affirmations of dynastic power.[11] Conversely, copies of festival books recording civic or institutional exequies held in other cities were sent to the royal court as a demonstration that the ceremonies had been enacted promptly according to royal command, and they served also to highlight the magnificence, ingenuity, and propriety of the decorative and emblematic schemes and the solemnity and grandeur with which the exequies were conducted. Given their functions as panegyrics, *relaciones* naturally tend towards hyperbole (as do all types of festival books of the period, whether recounting weddings, entries, coronations, or other events), and regularly present the exequies concerned as unsurpassed in splendour. But they also – while thus frequently claiming the exceptionally fine nature of the exequies described – assume highly conventional and generic forms and employ standardised vocabulary, reflecting the emphasis on tradition and decorum in the exequies themselves. Given these and other characteristics, one should avoid a naïve reading of such *relaciones* as straightforwardly factual, and it is invaluable to consider them alongside other types of documentation relevant to the process of planning and organising funerals and exequies, including wills, correspondence, and records of payments.

---

[11] The print run of an account of Philip IV's court exequies by Pedro Rodríguez de Monforte – *Descripcion de la honras que se hicieron a la catholica mag(esta)d de don Phelippe quarto rey delas Españas y del nuevo mundo* (Madrid: Francisco Nieto, 1666) – was no less than 1,750 copies. See Steven N. Orso, *Art and Death at the Spanish Habsburg Court: The Royal Exequies for Philip IV* (Columbia, Missouri: University of Missouri Press, 1989), 115.

Returning now to the argument that Victoria could hardly have composed the relevant music (some 575 breves' worth of polyphony) in the period between María's death and the Descalzas *honras*, such a claim seems very rash, even given that he had other heavy duties as chaplain, and even if he received the commission to undertake this task only when the work of arranging the exequies began.[12] Of course, it is conceivable that Victoria started to prepare some of the relevant music before María's death, which might have appeared prudent given the Empress's advanced age (seventy-four).[13] On the other hand, he might not have presumed that there would

---

[12] For comparison, this is similar in length to Victoria's six-voice *Missa Dum complerentur,* and significantly less than his six-voice *Missa Gaudeamus* (about 650 breves). It may also be worth noting, when considering the possible impact of the time available between María's death and exequies, that in most cases Victoria set the equivalent texts much more concisely here than in his earlier four-voice Requiem. The contrast is particularly marked in the cases of the Gradual (occupying 78 breves in the four-voice work but just 44 breves in the six-voice setting) and the Offertory (109 breves and 77 breves respectively). Such increased concision is apparent also in the newly-composed sections of the responsory *Libera me Domine*, which – as mentioned below – might have been written especially quickly, for performance at María's burial: the 'Dies illa' verse is 25 breves long in the setting published in 1583, but just 16 breves long in the later one, while in the final verse ('Requiem æternam') the equivalent figures are 21 breves and 16 breves. Within this picture of increased brevity, the Communion of the *Officium defunctorum* is however exceptional, being 55 breves in length whereas Victoria's earlier setting occupies just 40 breves.

[13] As discussed below, for the first verse – 'Tremens factus sum' – of *Libera me Domine* Victoria re-used the setting associated with his older four-voice Requiem. However, the frequently repeated observation that the *Officium defunctorum* draws much more substantially than this on the four-voice Requiem, or is essentially a reworking of that work, is inaccurate. See, for example, Eugene Casjen Cramer, *Studies in the Music of Tomás Luis de Victoria* (Aldershot: Ashgate, 2001), 277: 'Most of the *Missa* had appeared earlier in a four-voice version ... the *Introit*, which along with the *Kyrie/Christe/Kyrie*, forms the first movement, is the only part of the mass itself that does not draw on the earlier work.' It is nevertheless the case that at various points Victoria adopts the same harmonic or cadential solution and/or melodic gesture at equivalent points (in relation to chant and text) in the two works. Samuel Rubio regarded as 'ridiculous' ('ridículo') the suggestions by previous writers (he cites, for example, Josep Cercós's and Josep Cabré's *Victoria*, mentioned above) that Victoria could not have composed the music of the *Officium defunctorum* in the approximately three weeks available between María's death and the Descalzas exequies (Rubio mentions the burial here rather than the exequies, clearly in error), but he considered it significant with regard to this task that the four-voice Requiem formed the 'foundation' ('fundamento') of the new work. He also raised the possibility that Victoria commenced the planning of the music before the death of the Empress; Samuel Rubio, 'El *Officium defunctorum* de Tomás Luis de Victoria', originally published within the booklet accompanying the recording *Tomás Luis de Victoria: Officium Hebdomadæ Sanctae, Roma 1585. Officium Defunctorum, Madrid 1605*, Cuarteto vocal 'Tomás Luis de Victoria' (Columbia, 1981), 42–6, and reprinted as part of the introductory material to Rubio's edition, *Tomás Luis de Victoria: Officium Defunctorum a seis voces* (Ávila: Caja d'Ahorros d'Ávila, 2000), 13–23, at 14. If Victoria had indeed prepared some or all of the *Officium defunctorum* before María's death, he certainly could not have performed this music liturgically at the Descalzas (in the hearing of, for example Margarita), since this would have rendered obviously fallacious (to

be a requirement to provide new music – including a Requiem Mass – for the occasion. It is difficult to estimate how frequently music performed at Spanish Habsburg exequies was freshly composed, since *libros de exequias* are typically silent on such matters. Among the rare exceptions are *relaciones* of the exequies for Philip III held in Murcia, those marking the death of Philip IV in Mexico City, and those for Margaret of Austria in Coimbra and Lima. In all of these cases the new music was (as one would expect) provided by the cathedral *maestro de capilla*: Manuel de Tavares in Murcia, Francisco López Capillas in Mexico City (whose 'sleeplessness and dedication' in creating music for the occasion is lauded by the chronicler), Cosme de Baena Ferreira in Coimbra, and Estacio de la Serna in Lima.[14] In addition, an entry in the printed catalogue of the great music library of King John IV of Portugal indicates that a later set of *honras* for Margaret of Austria, held at the new royal convent of the Encarnación in Madrid in 1617, included music by Gabriel Díaz Bessón, who had been vice-chapelmaster of the *capilla real* from 1606 until 1614.[15] It seems, however, that the triple-choir Requiem concerned was an expansion of an existing work (the library catalogue states that the Mass was 'based upon another for six voices'), and – as argued in Chapter 3 – the most likely candidate for that work was in fact Victoria's. The catalogue of John IV's library also allows identification of another Requiem Mass (likewise apparently lost) written specially for a set of Habsburg exequies: those of Albert of Austria, sovereign of the Spanish Netherlands, who died in July 1621. The Requiem Mass listed in the library catalogue is by Géry de Ghersem, master of the household chapel of Albert and Isabella in Brussels, and the catalogue entry specifies

---

Margarita not least) his statement in the 1605 print that the music was composed for the exequies of María.

[14] See: Alonso Enriquez, *Las honras que celebró en la muerte del muy alto, y religioso monarca rey don Felipe tercero la muy noble ciudad de Murcia* (n.p., 1622), 60–4; Isidro Sariñana, *Llanto del occidente en el ocaso del mas claro sol de las Españas, funebres demonstraciones, que hizo, pyra real, que erigio en las exequias del rey n(uestro) señor d(on) Felipe IIII* (Mexico City: widow of Bernardo Calderon, 1666), f. 32 and f. 112v; *Relacion de las exequias q(ue) el ex(celentisi)mo s(eño)r d(on) Iuan de mendoça y luna marques de Montesclaros, virrey del Piru hizo en la muerte de la reina nuestra s(eñora) doña Margarita* (Lima: Pedro de Marchán y Calderón, 1612), f. 26. The relevant passages from the account of the Coimbra University exequies for Margaret of Austria are quoted by Ernesto Vieira in his *Diccionario biographico de musicos portugueses*, 2 vols (Lisbon: Mattos Moreira de Pinheiro, 1900), I, 415, but Vieira gives no bibliographical information about his source.

[15] *Primeira parte do index da livraria de musica do muyto alto e poderoso rey dom João o IV nosso senhor* (Lisbon: Paulo Craesbeeck, 1649), 340 (note that this is the second page so numbered), forming part of item 745.

further that it was for nine voices and included a setting of the Sequence
Dies iræ.[16]

In contrast to such cases, however, it seems that even the grandest of
Spanish royal exequies were not always adorned with specially composed
music. This is indicated by a draft order of service for the court exequies of
Philip II in October 1598, which provides an unusual level of detail
regarding music. While we cannot be certain that the musical items listed
there were those actually performed (since the document concerned is
a plan for the ceremonies, not a record of them), it at least shows what was
considered appropriate by one of those at court involved in the arrangements. The writer of the document states that the polyphonic Requiem
Mass would be either the six-voice Mass based on 'Circumdederunt' or
Certon's five-voice Mass.[17] The former is clearly a reference to the six-voice
Requiem by Jean Richafort, which is based on the chant 'Circumdederunt
me gemitus mortis'.[18] The allusion to a five-voice Mass by Certon is
intriguing, and may simply be an error, since only a four-voice Requiem
by Certon is known. Both Richafort's and Certon's Requiems include not
the Gradual from the Roman formulary (beginning 'Requiem æternam')
which would have been the text sung at Philip's exequies, but 'Si ambulem',
the Gradual used within the French tradition and the Dominican rite.
The order of service accordingly indicates that the Gradual (and also the
Tract) should be sung to the settings which form part of the four-voice
Requiem of Francisco Guerrero.[19] The other polyphonic item for which
the composer's name is given is the Matins invitatory *Regem cui omnia
vivunt*, of which Morales's widely disseminated setting was to be used. It is
thus noteworthy that the music proposed for one of the most important
sets of exequies organised by the royal court during the period of Habsburg
rule did not represent a fresh and unified compositional project, akin to

[16] *Primeira parte do index*, 360. The exequies took place in Brussels in March 1622.
[17] 'La misa de difunctos será la de *Çircundederunt*, a seis, o la de Çerton, a çinco.' See
Luis Robledo, 'Questions of Performance Practice in Philip III's Chapel', *Early Music* 22 (1994),
198–218, at 209, and Robledo Estaire, 'La música en la casa del rey', in Robledo Estaire et al.,
Aspectos de la cultura musical, 99–193, at 172.
[18] On this, and for further discussion of the repertory indicated by the order of service, see
Bruno Turner, 'Glimpses of P-Rex: Aspects of the Gentle Art of Music in the Reign of Philip II',
Leading Notes 8/1 (Spring 1998), 2–8.
[19] The order of service also stipulates that the setting of the Sequence be by the *teniente* (that is, the
deputy chapelmaster of the Royal Chapel). This could refer to a lost setting by Adrien Capy,
acting *maestro* of the Royal Chapel following the death of Philippe Rogier in 1596, which was
copied for the use of that chapel between May and August of 1598; see Robledo, 'La música en la
casa del rey', 164. Alternatively, the setting may have been by Géry de Ghersem, who was the
deputy chapelmaster at the time of the exequies.

Victoria's creation of music for María's exequies in 1603. Rather, it was a strikingly varied mélange of the very old (Richafort's Requiem was published in 1532, and Certon's in 1558; Morales died in 1553) and the more recent (Guerrero published the revised version of his Requiem – incorporating the Tract text specified in the reformed Roman Missal – in 1582). Perhaps most surprising is that, according to this proposed order of service, no single polyphonic Requiem Mass setting was to be either composed (by a member of the *capilla real*) or used, and the five-voice setting by the recently deceased *maestro* of the *capilla real*, Philippe Rogier, does not feature in the plan, even though it presumably included a setting of the Roman Gradual text rather than the Parisian-rite text used in Richafort's Requiem.[20]

It is also worth noting that the surviving proposed order of service – including the selection of music – was drawn up only after Philip's death. Philip was famous for his eye for detail and precise planning, but he clearly did not design his own exequies. One might similarly mention that although María included in her testamentary documents detailed specifications regarding Masses to be sung and said upon her death, and concerning her burial, nothing is mentioned there about the exequies: these were for her household to organise, in consultation with the royal court, as we shall see. It thus seems most likely that Victoria set to work on the music of the *Officium defunctorum* only once it became clear what the post-mortem arrangements were to be. Even then, the question of *how much* music he should compose for the exequies would have needed to be considered, since there was clearly no presumption that even the Requiem Mass itself would necessarily be new in such circumstances. At Seville Cathedral in the later seventeenth century there was a requirement for the *maestro de capilla* to compose a motet (and, by implication, only a motet, rather than a Requiem also) for solemn exequies such as those of an archbishop of Seville, as is stipulated in a *ceremonial* compiled in 1687.[21] As noted in Chapter 1, Guerrero wrote a motet for the Seville exequies of Philip II (a copy of which he sent to Juan de Borja in

---

[20] No copy of this Mass has been located, but the work is listed in the catalogue of John IV's music library, *Primeira parte do index*, 373. The compiler of the proposed order of service for Philip's exequies likewise ignored another Requiem Mass (again for five voices) by a previous *maestro de capilla* of the Royal Chapel, Pierre de Manchicourt, although Manchicourt's setting – like those of Richafort and Certon – sets the Gradual 'Si ambulem', inappropriate for use at the 1598 exequies.

[21] The relevant passage is transcribed in Juan Ruiz Jiménez, *La librería de canto de órgano: creación y pervivencia del repertorio del Renacimiento en la actividad musical de la catedral de Sevilla* (Granada: Junta de Andalucía, 2007), 286: 'compondrá por motete una cláusula de la sagrada escritura que diga en particular con el difunto'.

Madrid), as did Alonso Lobo for the equivalent exequies in Toledo
Cathedral, but Lobo included no Requiem Mass in the *Liber primus missarum* of 1602 in which this motet was published (with a heading noting
the circumstances of its creation),[22] and no Requiem by Guerrero composed for the Seville exequies survives in Seville Cathedral sources, which
one might have expected had such a work connected with this important
occasion existed. It is also worth observing that the exceptionally detailed
listing and description of the music performed at the Murcia Cathedral
exequies for Philip III, mentioned above, specifies each item that was newly
composed by Manuel de Tavares for each day of the event, and thus implies
that the other items were not; the Requiem Masses are not among these
new items, with the exception of the Sequence at one of the Masses. Tavares
provided a new motet for one Mass, while on another day of the exequies
the Elevation motet at Mass was an existing work by Philippe Rogier,
which – the writer claims – Rogier had composed for performance at his
own exequies.[23] We should thus bear in mind that the music for María's
exequies may have included existing music and music by composers other
than Victoria, in other words that the contents of the *Officium defunctorum*
might not include all of the polyphony sung at those exequies, although it
does seem safe to presume that Victoria included in the publication everything that he had written for the occasion.

If Victoria did indeed start work on the music for María's exequies only
after her death, then he had some twenty days to complete the task.
The period between the Empress's death on 26 February and the exequies
on 18 and 19 March was briefer than was typical, in order to accommodate
the exequies (and the subsequent exequies of the city of Madrid, likewise
held at the Descalzas) before Holy Week, which that year began on
23 March, since the ritual demands of Holy Week were not readily compatible with the holding of extended *honras* and the decorative transformation of the chapels which they entailed. Royal court exequies in Spain most
often occurred about five or six weeks after the death,[24] but the gap was

---

[22] As observed in Chapter 3, it was common practice among Iberian composers to place
a Requiem as the last Mass in a printed collection of Masses, as had Morales, Guerrero (in two
collections), and Victoria (likewise in two collections).

[23] Enriquez, *Las honras*, 60–4. A copy of Rogier's motet, *Tædet animam meam*, is listed in the
catalogue of John IV's music library, *Primeira parte do index*, 371, where it is described as the
composer's last work.

[24] Orso (*Art and Death*, 28) tabulates the intervals between death and court exequies for Margaret
of Austria, Philip III, Isabella of Bourbon, Prince Baltasar Carlos, and Philip IV. The shortest
period in these cases was 33 days, and the longest 45. In the case of Philip II the interval was 35
days.

sometimes significantly shorter: to take two examples of *honras* at the Descalzas, only a fortnight separated the death of Isabel de Valois and her exequies, and the *honras* for Juana (María's sister) were held just over three weeks after her death. Clearly, such a brief span rendered more challenging the completion of the decorative scheme and other preparations for the ceremonies. The royal court exequies of Don Carlos, son of Philip II, commenced just seventeen days after his death, and Juan López de Hoyos remarks in his *relación* that this caused 'no small difficulty'.[25]

María's Death, Burial, and Exequies

The written materials relating to María's death, burial, and exequies – used in constructing the narrative which follows – may be divided into four categories, ranging in terms of nature and function from relatively private to public: firstly, a daybook kept by a senior member of María's household; secondly, correspondence; thirdly, printed and manuscript *relaciones* of the exequies; and fourthly, encomiastic chronicles and biographical writings, some of which long post-date the events concerned. The most personal account is in the diary of the Imperial Ambassador, Hans Khevenhüller,[26] who was (as noted in Chapter 1) among the most

[25] 'no poca dificultad'; Juan López de Hoyos, *Relacion de la muerte y honras funebres del s(ereni)s(simo) principe d(on) Carlos, hijo de la mag(estad) del catholico rey d(on) Philippe el segundo nuestro señor* (Madrid: Pierres Cosin, 1568), transcribed in José Simón Díaz (ed.), *Fuentes para la historia de Madrid y su provincia* (Madrid: Patronato José Ma. Quadrado del Consejo Superior de Investigaciones Científicas, 1964), I, 8–20, at 14. Another example of exequies which were organised within a particularly short time span occurred in 1610. News reached the Spanish royal court in Lerma on 24 May that King Henry IV of France had died. Philip III summoned the singers of the royal chapel from Madrid, and the exequies took place on 8 and 9 June. See Luis Cervera Vera, 'Túmulos reales diseñados por Francisco de Mora', *Academia: Boletín de la Real Academia de Bellas Artes de San Fernando* 42 (1976), 27–46, at 30 and 45.

[26] Khevenhüller, *Geheimes Tagebuch*. The section of the journal covering the period from January to April 1603 is at 276–81. An abbreviated version of this account in Spanish may be found within the biography of Khevenhüller (constituting volume 14 of a history of his family) compiled after his death, which survives in two copies, in Biblioteca Nacional de España Ms 2751 (with the title 'Historia de Joan Kevenhuller de Aichelberg') and in the Lobkowicz Library at Nelahozeves Castle in the Czech Republic. A modern edition of the Madrid copy has been published as *Diario de Hans Khevenhüller, embajador imperial en la corte de Felipe II*, ed. Félix Labrador Arroyo, with introduction by Sara Veronelli (Madrid: Sociedad estatal para la conmemoración de los centenarios de Felipe II y Carlos V, 2001). The section of the account relevant to María's death and exequies is at pp. 999–1000 of the Madrid manuscript, and 550–53 of the modern edition. See also Sara Veronelli, 'La Historia de Hans Khevenhüller, embajador cesáreo en la corte de España', in José Martínez Millán (ed.), *Felipe II (1527–1598). Europa y la Monarquía Católica* (Madrid: Editorial Parteluz, 1998), 517–37.

important members of María's inner circle, serving her faithfully for many years, and remaining at her side in Madrid even after the court moved to Valladolid, despite his status as the most senior ambassador at court apart from the papal nuncio. Fortunately for our purposes, Khevenhüller's typically concise approach within his journal is here abandoned in favour of an extensive narration, reflecting the depth with which he felt María's death. The richest and most important array of letters concerning María's death and exequies forms part of the correspondence between her Lord High Steward Juan de Borja, writing from Madrid, and the Duke of Lerma (Francisco Gómez de Sandoval y Rojas) at the royal court in Valladolid, but we also have Khevenhüller's letters to his master Emperor Rudolf in Prague, and correspondence between Juan Carrillo and the Archduke Albert in Brussels. In the third category of documentation, besides the *Libro de las honras* concerned with the Jesuit College exequies there survive manuscript *relaciones* of the exequies at the Descalzas and of the royal court's exequies in Valladolid.[27] As mentioned above, the former is by Diego de Urbina, an eyewitness to the ceremonies, who was a *regidor* of Madrid (that is, one of the senior civic officials) and a king of arms of the royal court. There is also a manuscript report of the ceremonies in Vienna – particularly those in the cathedral – written for the Archduke Matthias (another of María's sons, and governor of Austria).[28] Within the category of chronicles and biographical writings, eulogistic portraits of María's life and death at the Descalzas include (in chronological order of publication) Juan Carrillo's *Relación historica* of the Descalzas (1616), Juan de Palma's *Vida* of María's daughter Margarita (1636),[29] and Rodrigo Méndez Silva's *Vida* of María herself (1655),[30] together with a manuscript account of uncertain authorship preserved in the British

---

[27] The text of the *relación* of the Valladolid exequies, preserved in Vienna, Haus- Hof-, und Staatsarchiv, Familienakten, Karton 75, is transcribed as Appendix A of Annemarie Jordan, 'Las dos águilas del Emperador Carlos V. Las colleciones y el mecenazgo de Juana y María de Austria en la corte de Felipe II', in Luis A. Ribot García (ed.), *La monarquía de Felipe II a debate* (Madrid: Sociedad estatal para la conmemoración de los centenarios de Felipe II y Carlos V, 2000), 429–72, at 467–9.

[28] Vienna, Haus- Hof-, und Staatsarchiv, Hofakten des Ministeriums des Inneren, 5–7.

[29] *Vida de la serenissima infanta sor Margarita de la cruz, religiosa descalça de santa Clara* (Madrid: Imprenta Real, 1636). This biography was later (1664) published as the work of Juan de Palafox y Mendoza, by his brother José de Palafox.

[30] *Admirable vida, y heroycas virtudes de aquel glorioso blasón de España ... la esclarecida emperatriz María* (Madrid: Diego Díaz de la Carrera, 1655). The account of the exequies for María at the Descalzas is clearly derived from that of Diego de Urbina, but is shorter.

Library.[31] Luis Cabrera de Córdoba's 'Relaciones de las cosas sucedidas, principalmente el la Corte, desde el año de 1599 hasta el de 1614' provides a summary of the events surrounding María's death from the perspective of the court in Valladolid (Cabrera de Córdoba was royal chronicler),[32] and thus complements the Madrid-centred laudatory accounts just mentioned.

María fell ill on Friday 21 February 1603, and retired the next day to the great chamber in her apartments (now known as the *salón de reyes*) which adjoined the convent on one side and – on another – the oratory to which she had habitually resorted to pray and which housed the monastery's renowned collection of relics. Juan Carrillo's account emphasises the presence of the nuns at her deathbed and their role in the prayers and other rites, but he paints a deliberately incomplete picture, characteristic of his emphasis on her withdrawal from the world and engagement with the life of the monastery, mentioned in Chapter 1. So while he tells us of the nuns singing psalms antiphonally and reciting prayers in María's chamber, and (as her death approached) performing the liturgical rites used for a dying nun, we have to populate the scene in the *salón de reyes* further with Victoria and the other three chaplains.[33] In the city's churches prayers

[31] In Add. Ms 10236. The account is entitled 'Naçimiento, Vida y muerte de la emperatriz Doña María Infanta de Castilla Hija Del Emperador Carlos y hermana del Rey don Felipe 2°'. The book as a whole is entitled, in a later hand, 'Tratados varios de las coronas de españa … recogidas por el P. F. Diego Gascon de Torquemada Religioso del orden de N. P. S. Augustin'. The compiler of the accounts, Diego Gascón de Torquemada, who professed as an Augustinian in Madrid in 1630, was probably the nephew of the chronicler Jerónimo Gascón de Torquemada (d. 1637), gentleman of the chamber to the Princes of Savoy at the Spanish court from 1603, and *aposentador del rey* from 1620. It may be, indeed, that the *vida* of María in the 'Tratados varios' is by Jerónimo, as is suggested by the nearly identical wording of a passage concerned with María's burial in the account in Ms 10236 and in a briefer account of María's death by Jerónimo which survives in two manuscripts. A modern edition of this latter account is in Alfonso de Ceballos-Escalera y Gila (ed.), *Don Jerónimo Gascón de Torquemada: Gaçeta y nuevas de la corte de españa desde el año 1600 en adelante* (Madrid: Real Academia Matritense de Heráldica y Genealogía, 1991), 22.

[32] Cabrera de Córdoba constructs his narrative as a series of dated reports written approximately four weeks apart; the relevant section for María's death, funeral, and exequies is dated 22 March 1603, and is found at ff. 181v-183v of the manuscript copy, and at 169–71 of the edition of 1857.

[33] We should perhaps also treat with some scepticism Juan de Palma's claim (*Vida*, f. 111v) that during María's final illness the conventual boundary (the *clausura*) was specially extended to included the *salón de reyes* where María lay, so that Margarita could visit her mother, and that the door between this room and the rest of María's apartments was blocked up in order to exclude most members of her household except for a few, including the doctors, the ambassador (Khevenhüller), and her confessor. This contradicts the picture of María's pattern of life at the Descalzas painted by Jerónimo de Florencia in his sermon preached at the Jesuit College exequies, in which he states that María had been attended by the nuns every day in her apartments, and that Margarita likewise spent parts of each day with the Empress. Since he was preaching to a congregation which included Margarita herself as well as members of María's household, he would hardly have misrepresented the situation in such respects. See *Libro de las honras*, f. 33v; for a translation of the sermon, see

were said for María, and the famous statue of Our Lady of Atocha was brought in procession to the Descalzas. On Tuesday the 25th María made her confession, and at 8 pm she received extreme unction,[34] Khevenhüller noting that it was conducted 'truly solemnly and with the greatest devotion' ('gar solemniter und devotissimamente'), in the presence of all the nuns of the convent. At 10 pm Juan de Borja sent a letter (his second of the day) to the Duke of Lerma, reporting that the Empress was not expected to live long, and asking for urgent instructions about where she should be buried, and the executors also wrote directly to the King that evening asking the same thing.[35] María died between 4 and 5 o'clock in the morning of Wednesday the 26th.[36] The nuns dressed her in the Clarist habit in accordance with her wishes,[37] and continued their prayers around

Antonio Bernat Vistarini, John T. Cull, and Tamás Sajó (eds), *Book of Honors for Empress Maria of Austria Composed by the College of the Society of Jesus of Madrid on the Occasion of her Death, 1603*, Early Modern Catholicism and the Visual Arts Series 5 (Philadelphia, Saint Joseph's University Press, 2011), where the relevant passage is at 86. Juan de Palma's account here may reflect the need – at the time of writing – to emphasise the strictness with which *clausura* was enforced, particularly since there was greater emphasis on such observance within orders of discalced nuns. This rigidity in observing *clausura* and other regulations at the Descalzas is thus praised in Pedro de Salazar's *Coronica* [sic] *y historia de la fundacion y progreso de la provincia de Castilla de la orden del bienaventurado padre San Francisco* (Madrid: Imprenta Real, 1612), 352. However, Roberta Schwartz has noted a more general tendency towards freedom in applying such restrictions in sixteenth-century Spain, even with regard to the Tridentine regulations: see her 'The Greatest Miracle of San Blas: A Convent as Noble Chapel in Early Modern Spain', in Michael O'Connor and Walter Aaron Clark (eds), *Treasures of the Golden Age: Essays on Music of the Iberian and Latin American Renaissance in Honour of Robert M. Stevenson*, Festschrift Series 27 (Hillsdale, NY: Pendragon Press, 2012), 213–27, at 217.

[34] This is the time given by Khevenhüller (*Geheimes Tagebuch*, 278), who was with the Empress. Jerónimo de Florencia gave the time as 9 pm in his sermon at the Jesuit exequies, reproduced in *Libro de las honras*, f. 41, and the same time is stated in the *vida* of María in British Library Add. Ms 10236.

[35] Borja's letter is at ff. 37–8 of British Library Add. Ms 28425. The executors refer to their letter of the evening of the 25th (which seems not to have survived) in a subsequent letter to the King written on 28 February, preserved in British Library Add. Ms 28707 at f. 50.

[36] This timing of her death is reported in Juan de Borja's next letter to the Duke of Lerma, written on the 26th (British Library Add. Ms 28425, f. 32), and in a letter written to the King by María's executors (British Library Add. Ms 28707, f. 50), and the same timing appears in the account by Khevenhüller, who was present at her death: *Geheimes Tagebuch*, 279.

[37] From the time of the Catholic Monarchs until that of Philip IV, it was normal for members of the Spanish royal house to be buried in the habit of the religious order to which they were most devoted: see María Adelaida Allo Manero, 'Exequias de la Casa de Austria en España, Italia e Hispanoamérica', unpublished PhD thesis, University of Zaragoza (1993), 26. More generally, it became common practice in Spain for people to be buried in the habit of one of the religious orders: see Martínez Gil, *Muerte y sociedad*, 559–61. María expressed her desire to be buried in the Clarist habit in a codicil of 1593: see Joseph Antonio de Abreu y Bertodano, *Coleccion de tratados de paz, alianza, neutralidad, garantia, proteccion* (Madrid: Diego Peralta, Antonio Marin, Juan de Zuñiga, 1740–1752), 140.

the body, which was removed to the *coro* of the monastery chapel (located above the chapel's West end) and lay there until her burial three days later.

In the immediate aftermath of María's death three practical questions were of most relevance to her chaplains and to the musicians of the Descalzas. Firstly, where and when would she be buried? Secondly, what post-mortem services at the Descalzas were stipulated in María's wills and codicils? And thirdly, what would the arrangements be for the household exequies, and when would they be held? Regarding the first and third of these matters the King's decisions and the instructions of the Duke of Lerma were crucial, but the process was rendered vastly more cumbersome by the fact that the royal court was in Valladolid, more than one hundred miles away. Lerma, the King's *valido* or favourite, effectively controlled the court, and thus the stream of correspondence between Lerma and Borja (his uncle) represented a central element in the decision-making and the communication of decisions: Lerma wrote three letters to Borja on 27 February alone.[38] Normally, upon the occurrence of such a death within the Spanish Habsburg family, the court apparatus promptly swung into action to make the necessary arrangements, including for the burial, but in this case those royal court personnel who were experienced in such events and who had important roles in their organisation and ceremonial were not available to assist. If the court had still been resident in Madrid Lerma himself would doubtless have played a more active part, since (as Schwartz observes), he 'assumed the unofficial role of royal master of ceremonies, organizing most major celebrations'.[39] The King – when he heard of his grandmother's deteriorating health – could not come to Madrid because of the serious illness of the baby infanta María, who was to die on 1 March, the day of María's burial.

Besides the practical difficulties in conducting such business at a distance, the decisions about the post-mortem arrangements were not – in the main – straightforward, partly because of María's status (although an Empress, and in many respects the most eminent woman within the royal family, her rank was below that of the Queen), but principally due to conflicting instructions about her place of burial. The court needed to issue prompt directives, paying due regard to

---

[38] The correspondence between Borja and the royal court for the period between 22 February and 1 March (the date of María's burial) preserved in British Library Add. Ms 28425 consists of nine letters and replies.

[39] Roberta Schwartz, '*En busca de liberalidad*: Music and Musicians in the Courts of the Spanish Nobility, 1470–1640', unpublished PhD thesis, University of Illinois at Urbana-Champaign (2001), 156.

established etiquette, on how widely mourning dress and decoration was to be adopted at court and elsewhere, and on how widely within the King's realms exequies were to be observed and at what level of solemnity, instructions that were usually issued by royal letter shortly after the death. Regarding mourning dress, Juan Carrillo reported to Archduke Albert on Saturday 1 March (the third day after María's death) that the King had ordered that such dress be worn (only) by the royal household, guards, and members of the councils of state,[40] while Cabrera de Córdoba adds that the King originally intended to extend this obligation more widely – to the chancelleries, *audiencias*, and cities – but was dissuaded because of the cost, and thus restricted the order for civic mourning to Madrid, since the Empress had died there.[41] However, Khevenhüller in Madrid was apparently unaware of this restriction when he informed the Emperor Rudolf in a letter of 10 March that the King had ordered general mourning at the same level as had been adopted upon the death of his father Philip II.[42] Regarding exequies, the deaths of the most senior figures in the royal family occasioned *honras* throughout the vast areas under the authority of the Spanish Habsburgs, in Europe (including, for example, Naples and Milan) and in the overseas colonies of Spain and Portugal (the latter between 1580 and 1640, when the kings of Spain ruled Portugal also). They were organised by cities, towns, cathedrals, convents, royal chapels, and universities. Exequies for Spanish monarchs were also held in Rome (both at the papal court and for the Spanish nation in Rome), and by the Duchy of Florence and the Imperial court. However, given María's status in the royal hierarchy, her death did not automatically require this level of exequial ceremonies throughout the Spanish realms according to the royal etiquette then in force.[43] Méndez Silva claims that Philip III nevertheless ordered exequies for María 'as for the kings of Spain',[44] but there seems to be no evidence for such widespread exequies for her, although Jerónimo de

---

[40] The relevant letter is in Brussels, Archives Générales du Royaume / Algemeen Rijksarchief, Secretarie van Staat en Oorlog / Sécretairerie d'État et de Guerre, no. 492, at f. 172.

[41] Cabrera de Córdoba, *Relaciones*, 169 (in the edition of 1857).

[42] Vienna, Haus- Hof-, und Staatsarchiv, Spanien, Diplomatische Korrespondenz, Karton 13, f. 169v.

[43] On the relevant etiquette at the court of the Spanish Habsburgs, see Allo Manero, 'Exequias de la Casa de Austria', 25–33. According to that etiquette, the deaths of foreign emperors, kings, and princes who were the parents of queens of Spain were to be marked by royal court exequies. Allo Manero notes that, besides this, in exceptional circumstances exequies for foreign monarchs were also held in certain cities or towns.

[44] Méndez Silva, *Admirable vida*, f. 50.

Sepúlveda reports that *honras* were held in his own monastery of El Escorial,[45] and Juan Carrillo states in his history of the Descalzas that the General of the Observant Franciscans, Fray Francisco de Sosa, wrote to all monasteries and convents of the Order (including, presumably, outside Spain) instructing them to organise *honras* for the Empress, to which local dignitaries should be invited.[46] Beyond this, it is striking that we lack manuscript or printed *relaciones* of exequies for María even from centres such as Zaragoza and Seville from which we otherwise have abundant evidence of royal exequies. Finally, the fact that (as we shall see) the city of Madrid wrote to the King – rather than vice versa – asking for permission to conduct civic exequies for María, and that the King gave special authorisation for this, renders it very unlikely that royal letters commissioning exequies throughout the kingdoms had indeed been issued in María's case, as Méndez Silva states. We should remember that Méndez Silva's account was published more than half a century after María's death, and his eulogistic purposes were well served by claiming that the King had required her death to be marked so widely and so solemnly. (He reports likewise that the King ordered the adoption of mourning dress throughout his realm, which – as noted above – did not occur.)

Within the territories governed by the Austrian Habsburgs, María's death was marked in the Imperial capital, Prague, in the presence of her son the Emperor Rudolf, and exequies were also held in the Cathedral of St Stephen, Vienna, and thereafter in other churches and monasteries in the city and in parishes elsewhere in the Archduchy of Austria. We do not currently know the date of the Prague exequies, but it is worth noting in this regard that only on 10 March did Khevenhüller write to the Emperor with news of his mother's death, and so – given the distance of some 1,400 miles between Madrid and Prague – the exequies cannot realistically have taken place until well after Easter (as did those in Vienna).[47] The exequies in Vienna and elsewhere in the Archduchy of Austria are reported in an account sent to the Archduke Matthias by his councillors in that city, which mentions the participation of both the Cathedral's *Kantorei* and (placed apart from the singers in the cathedral)

---

[45] 'Historia de varios sucesos y de las cosas notables que han sucedido de veinte años a esta parte en toda España y en toda la Iglesia Católica y otras naciones desde el año de 1584 hasta el de 1603', Biblioteca Nacional de España Ms 2577, f. 183r.

[46] Carrillo, *Relación histórica*, f. 219v. As noted in Chapter 1, María was a Franciscan Tertiary, i.e. a member of the Third Order of St Francis.

[47] Vienna, Haus- Hof-, und Staatsarchiv, Spanien, Diplomatische Korrespondenz, Karton 13, ff. 168v-169v. Although it is dated 10 March, the letter may have been sent two days later, as Khevenhüller states in his diary: *Diario de Hans Khevenhüller*, 552.

a substantial and varied group of instrumentalists, and records that sacred *carmina* were sung after the Latin oration.[48]

As intimated, the most troublesome issue that confronted Borja, Khevenhüller, and the Empress's other executors when they opened her wills and codicils on the day of her death concerned the place of burial, and the distance between the court and Madrid caused especial difficulties in resolving this. They were already aware of an agreement between María and Philip II that she would be buried at the great monastery-palace of El Escorial north of Madrid, by then established as the mausoleum for the Spanish Habsburgs. The intention that María be interred there is indeed reflected in the inclusion of her statue in the group of monumental gilded bronze effigies (by Pompeo Leoni) of Charles V's family on the north side of the sanctuary in the monastery's basilica. These were completed in 1597, just six years before María's death, and the wall inscription above the group includes the words 'iacent simul Elisabetha uxor et Maria filia imperatrices' ('here lie also his wife Isabella and his daughter María, empresses'), making explicit the intended presence of María's body in the mausoleum: see the jacket illustration of this book, which shows Juan Pantoja de la Cruz's painting (1599) of Leoni's group of figures and the inscription. However, if this was indeed María's original wish, then the codicils of 1593 and 1600 revealed a change of mind: the first signalled that she was to be buried at the Descalzas until Margarita's death, and then reburied at El Escorial, but the later codicil simply states that she was to be buried at the Madrid convent, without reference to El Escorial. María further specified that the site of her burial in the Descalzas be that used for the nuns: the lower cloister. However, Khevenhüller reports that the executors considered such a burial place as unsuitable for a person of María's status, and they were also uneasy because of the agreement between María and Philip II that she be buried at El Escorial.[49] Although anxious not to act contrary to the wishes of their sovereign, they were caught between a rock and a hard place, since Margarita was determined that her mother be buried at the Descalzas. Cabrera de Córdoba (who, as royal chronicler, presumably reflects the view of these events from the Valladolid court) highlights the fact that Margarita and the nuns promptly removed María's body within the enclosed part of the convent, in order (he implies) to control her place

---

[48] Vienna, Haus- Hof-, und Staatsarchiv, Hofakten des Ministeriums des Inneren, 5–7. The letter is dated 29 May 1603. I am grateful to Christian Leitmeier for assistance in the transcription of this document.

[49] Khevenhüller, *Geheimes Tagebuch*, 279.

of burial.[50] In the first of three letters to Borja which Lerma wrote on 27 February (before he knew the contents of María's codicils), he set out the King's orders that, were María to die before the King could reach Madrid, her body was to be buried temporarily in the chapel of the Descalzas until after Easter (30 March), and that subsequently it was to be taken to El Escorial, and buried there in the presence of the King.[51] Apparently, however, these instructions had not reached Borja by the end of 28 February, and that day the executors wrote to the King to say that the burial could not be delayed further,[52] and that it seemed best to them – given both the fervent requests of Margarita and the fact that removal of the body to El Escorial would cause further delay – to bury María at the Descalzas.[53] The burial duly occurred the next day, Saturday 1 March, in the lower cloister, but this final scene of the drama included an element of the bizarre: while the burial was in progress the Marquis of San Germán, the King's emissary, arrived bearing the letters from Lerma (presumably all three of those written on the 27th) and informing Borja of the King's instructions about the burial. Borja immediately passed the message on to Margarita, but it was clearly too late to alter the burial arrangements.[54]

The surviving material concerning María's burial reveals a contrast between an ideal of pious simplicity on the one hand and a requirement for due ceremoniousness reflecting the status of the deceased on the other,

---

[50] *Relaciones*, 169.

[51] A letter from Juan Carrillo to Archduke Albert likewise reports the King's order that María's translation to El Escorial take place after Easter. Brussels, Archives Générales du Royaume / Algemeen Rijksarchief, Secretarie van Staat en Oorlog / Sécretairerie d'État et de Guerre, no. 492, at f. 172.

[52] Barbara Haggh-Huglo discusses the tradition, relevant to Burgundian/Habsburg circles, of waiting three days before burial; see 'Singing for the Most Noble Souls: Funerals and Memorials for the Burgundian and Habsburg Dynasties in Dijon and Brussels as Models for the Funeral of Philip the Fair in 1507', in Stefan Gasch and Birgit Lodes (eds), *Tod in Musik und Kultur. Zum 500. Todestag Philipps des Schönen*, Wiener Forum fur ältere Musikgeschichte 2 (Tutzing: Hans Schneider Verlag, 2007), 57–85, at 63. However, this seems not to have been normal practice among the Spanish Habsburgs at the time of María's death. For example, the burial of Philip II in 1598 occurred on the day following his death, and the same happened in the case of Margaret of Austria in 1611, while Don Carlos, son of Philip II, was buried on the evening of the same day on which he had died. Juan Carrillo reports in the *Relación histórica* (f. 60r) that the burial of María's sister Juana at the Descalzas took place more than three days after her death, but that was because her body had to be transported from El Escorial, where she died. One notes, however, that Charles V was buried on the fifth day after his death.

[53] British Library Add Ms 28707, f. 50. Enclosed with their letter was one from Margarita to the King.

[54] British Library Add Ms 28425, f. 43. Khevenhüller, conversely, states in his diary that the Marquis of San Germán had arrived in Madrid on 27 February: *Geheimes Tagebuch*, 279.

thus mirroring the debates about her place of burial.[55] The former ideal is represented in María's codicils, and is emphasised in the hagiographical accounts of her life and death. In contrast, the reports and letters of the courtiers involved – Borja, Khevenhüller, and Lerma – reveal their concern that there be an appropriate level of ritual solemnity. In the codicil of 1600 María had stipulated that her burial be 'without any ceremony, but done entirely plainly',[56] and in both this codicil and the earlier one of 1593 she asked to be buried in the manner of the nuns of the Descalzas – specifying the altar of Christ at the Mount of Olives, in the North-East corner of the lower cloister – and with only a plain gravestone.[57] Jerónimo de Florencia, preaching at the Jesuit exequies, reported these details of her simple burial, presenting it as a demonstration of her piety and 'profound humility',[58] and these same details were endlessly repeated in the chronicles of her death, and were highlighted by the chronicler Carrillo as a sign that she had eschewed 'superfluous things' and 'vain honours'.[59] He develops this theme by arguing that it was the tears of the poor whom she had assisted through alms and pious bequests that constituted the most solemn *honras* at her burial, and that 'the most honourable music, and the most agreeable to the ears of God, was the voices and laments of the poor people [whom she had assisted through charity] that accompanied her to her tomb'.[60] He thereby implies that such 'music' was of more worth than music provided by the elite musicians of the Descalzas for the occasion, just as the mourning of the poor had been worth more than ritual solemnity. María's request for a simple burial might reflect the emphasis on austerity in the first Rule of St Clare, followed at the Descalzas. However, it might also be a manifestation of Spanish royal traditions of piety and the projection of piety: similar

---

[55] Contemporary debates concerning the proper level of pomp at burials are discussed in Martínez Gil, *Muerte y sociedad*, 420–26.

[56] 'sin ninguna ceremonia, sino todo llanamente'; the relevant codicil is transcribed in Abreu y Bertodano, *Coleccion de tratados*, 152–5, and the relevant passage is at 153.

[57] See Abreu y Bertodano, *Coleccion de tratados*, 140 and 153, for the relevant passages in the two codicils.

[58] 'su profunda humildad'; *Libro de las honras*, f. 37v.

[59] 'cosas superfluas', 'honras vanas'; Carrillo, *Relación histórica*, f. 219. See also: Gil González Dávila, *Teatro de las grandezas de la Villa de Madrid Corte de los Reyes Catolicos de España* (Madrid: Tomás Junti, 1623), 149; Jerónimo Gascón de Torquemada, *Gaçeta y nuevas*, p. 22 of the modern edition; Méndez Silva, *Admirable vida*, f. 50; Diego Gascon de Torquemada in British Library 10236, f. 100; Antonio de León Pinelo, *Anales de Madrid desde el año 447 al de 1658*, ed. Pedro Fernández Martín (Madrid: Instituto de Estudios Madrileños, 1971), 180–1; the manuscript copy on which this modern edition is based is Biblioteca Nacional de España Ms 12.55.

[60] Carrillo, *Relación histórica*, f. 221: 'la musica mas honrosa y agradable a los oidos de Dios, fueron las Vozes, y lagrimas de los pobres que la acompañaron hasta la sepultura'.

requests for simple burial are found in the wills of Isabella of Castile and María's father Charles V, and Philip III ordered that he be buried 'with the least possible pomp'.[61] With regard to music, in an anonymous account of Philip II's funeral and exequies printed in Rome it is reported that the funeral ceremonies at El Escorial preceding the burial were conducted without music (i.e. presumably, part-music) or the use of instruments, in accordance with Philip's instructions.[62]

However, in contrast to this ideal of simplicity, the first of Lerma's three letters to Borja dated 27 February transmitted the King's instruction that the burial at the Descalzas be conducted with the solemnity appropriate to Maria's rank,[63] and Borja reassured Lerma in a letter of 1 March that the office had indeed been conducted 'with all possible solemnity',[64] while Khevenhüller in his diary noted that she was buried 'truly solemnly'.[65] Although such remarks are conventional and even platitudinous, that should not cause us to underestimate the demand for – and manifestation of – solemnity, and we may presume that such solemnity encompassed the musical aspects. Furthermore, while it might appear that 'solemnity' and 'simplicity' could co-exist in the conduct of such rituals (such as those at El Escorial just mentioned), the more usual way of understanding 'solemnity' in this context is surely in relation to the spectrum of ritual ceremoniousness and elaboration operating in ecclesiastical institutions at the time, whereby the more important the liturgical occasion the more elaborate was the performance of the ritual and the music.

Unfortunately, while Borja and Khevenhüller provide details regarding María's burial ceremonies, they do not mention the musical element. Borja tells us that 'the chaplains' were present, by which he presumably means the chaplains of the *capilla* of the Descalzas, but María's four household chaplains (including Victoria) would also have participated, and it seems entirely likely that Victoria was in charge of the music for the occasion, given that he acted as *maestro de capilla* of the Descalzas (see Chapter 1). It is indeed possible that the setting of the responsory *Libera me Domine* which he published in the *Officium defunctorum* received its first

---

[61] 'con la menor pompa que fuere posible'. See Martínez Gil, *Muerte y sociedad*, 610 and 613.

[62] 'Lunedi alli 14. del medesimo l'interrorno, senza Musica, ne altri Instrumenti, havendo così essa Maestà commandato.' *Relatione del solenne mortorio fatto nell morte del cattolico Filippo II re di Spagna* (Rome: Bartholomeo Bonfadino, 1598). I am grateful to Antonio Chemotti for drawing this account to my attention.

[63] 'con el authoridad y solenidad q(ue) se deva a su grandeza'. British Library Add. Ms 28425, f. 37v.

[64] 'El offiçio de la yglesia se hizo con toda la solenidad que fue posible.' British Library Add. Ms 28425, f. 44r.

[65] 'gar solemniter'; Khevenhüller, *Geheimes Tagebuch*, 279.

performance then. (In the burial ritual the responsory *Libera me Domine* would have been sung before the body was carried from the *coro* to the lower cloister.)[66] If so, Victoria may have had to compose this setting very rapidly indeed,[67] particularly if he delayed starting work because of the uncertainties about where María would be buried: if the burial had taken place at El Escorial rather than the Descalzas, then it might well have transpired that Victoria would have played no role in the provision of any polyphony for the occasion. These circumstances of haste could explain why here alone – in all the music of the 1605 collection – he reused part of his existing four-voice Requiem, as mentioned above, and may also be reflected in the brevity of the newly set sections: for example, the new 'Dies illa' verse is only two-thirds as long as the re-cycled 'Tremens' verse, even though the 'Dies illa' text is longer, and overall Victoria composed just 63 breves worth of new music for this setting. On the other hand, the requirement for due solemnity reflecting the Empress's status, just mentioned, may be reflected in the adoption of six-voice scoring for all sections of the responsory apart from the section borrowed from the older piece – the first verse, 'Tremens factus sum ego' – and the second verse, 'Dies illa'. A further sign that Victoria may have been working to an extremely tight deadline is the fact that the 'Tremens' verse fits rather poorly into its new context in terms of vocal scoring. The four-voice setting of *Libera me Domine* published in 1583 and 1592 is scored for an ensemble of narrow overall range, using c_2 c_3 c_4 and f_4 clefs. The Altus part has a wide ambitus of a twelfth, descending periodically to d (below the Tenor) and once to c, the same lowest note as is used in the Tenor; indeed, in the respond (i.e. the opening lengthy section of polyphony) Altus and Tenor have similar functions, frequently singing their imitative entries at the same pitch. The chant is assigned to the Cantus part throughout the setting, including in the 'Tremens' verse, which is scored for a trio of voices: Cantus, Altus, and Bassus. In contrast, Victoria's setting of the *Libera me* published in the *Officium defunctorum* has no part notated in c_2 clef (and so the top part of the 'Tremens' trio is here given to one of the Cantus parts, using c_1 clef),

---

[66] For an account of the ceremonies for the burial of nuns at the Descalzas, including the singing of responsories by the *capilla* and the nuns, see María Leticia Sánchez Hernández, 'La vida cotidiana de la primera comunidad de las Descalzas Reales de Madrid', in Ana García Sanz (ed.), *Las Descalzas Reales: orígines de una comunidad religiosa en el siglo XVI* (Madrid: Patrimonio Nacional / Fundación Caja Madrid, 2010), 107–47, at 146–7.

[67] An example of the speedy composition of music for burials comes from Seville Cathedral: according to a late-seventeenth-century account, the chapelmaster Juan Sanz composed 'in one night' ('en una noche') settings of the Invitatory and one lesson for the burial of the Duke of Medina Sidonia in February 1667; see Ruiz Jiménez, *La librería*, 287.

and its Altus part does not descend below *g*, but in this imported 'Tremens' verse it has to descend a fourth lower than this (see b. 32 of the edition in the Online Appendix). The issues created by the importation of this differently-scored music into the new *Libera me* are reflected in the handling of it by some modern editors and performers: in the most widely used modern edition (that by Bruno Turner), and hence in many recordings, the topmost voice is assigned to altos (even though it is presented as a Cantus part in the 1605 publication), and the sometimes uncomfortably low Altus part to tenors.

Victoria may also have had to oversee and/or provide music on the day on which María died and for the rituals that constituted the novena (the nine days after death), as well as contributing as chaplain to the saying and singing of post-mortem Masses. As was the norm among senior members of the Spanish Habsburgs, María had left instructions in her wills and codicils for enormous numbers of Masses to be said or sung on the day of her death, during the novena, and thereafter. The purpose of these and other types of suffrages was to shorten the time which María's soul would spend enduring the purifying sufferings of purgatory. Borja estimated the total of Masses included in her *obras pias* or pious bequests to be about 30,000,[68] whereas a manuscript list of the number of Masses to be recited at particular religious institutions in Madrid (including the Descalzas) and elsewhere, apparently compiled a few months later, gives the total as 37,000.[69] María had specified that – if she were to die in the morning, and sufficiently early to allow it – all the monasteries, convents, and parish churches of Madrid should hold a solemn sung Mass with Vigil (i.e. Office of the Dead) and responsory on the day of death, and since she died in the early hours of the 26th, this requirement came into effect.[70] There would certainly have been such a Vigil and Mass at the Descalzas, and it is reasonable to assume that the *capilla* of the monastery and Victoria would have contributed to it musically. With regard to the novena, she instructed that as many Masses as possible be said in the monasteries of Madrid, and particularly *misas de alma* (said at an *altar privilegiado*,

---

[68] In his letter to Lerma of 26 February, British Library Add. Ms 28425, at f. 33r.

[69] British Library Add. Ms 28707, at f. 49. This total of Masses ordered in María's wills and codicils is given at the head of the document. The listing of Masses at specific institutions which follows produces a rather lower total of 33,253. Of these, the list specifies that 453 Masses had been recited at the Descalzas by the end of July, and then mentions a further 1,500 Masses to be recited there by specified priests.

[70] British Library Add. Ms 28707, f. 3. María also required that as many said Masses as possible be recited that day in Madrid.

causing one soul to be released from purgatory). In addition, during each day of the novena the members of one or two of Madrid's religious houses or churches were to come to the Descalzas to sing a Requiem Mass for her.[71]

Following María's burial, the main task for Borja, the executors, and other senior members of María's household was the organisation of the exequies at the Descalzas. In this undertaking Borja had the role of superintendent, although Margarita may also have been influential in the planning, and it might have been either of them that engaged Victoria to provide the music. Such *honras fúnebres* for senior members of the House of Austria were designed to honour, commemorate, and mourn them, to contribute to the ritual acts designed to ensure the eternal repose of their souls, and to project idealised images of the dynastic stability, magnificence, power, and piety of the Spanish Habsburgs. The liturgical element of each set of exequies typically consisted of an afternoon Vigil (to which was frequently added a Latin oration) and – the next morning – a succession of three Masses: votive Masses of the Holy Spirit and of the Blessed Virgin Mary, and then the solemn Requiem Mass. This was followed by a sermon in Spanish, and finally by the ceremony of Absolution at the catafalque, featuring a series of sung responsories. In addition to their ritual solemnity and splendour, these exequies were characterised by opulent and spectacular ephemeral decoration, rich in symbolic content, forming an imposing and awe-inspiring stage and backdrop for the liturgical ceremonies. The walls of the church or chapel were draped in black from floor to ceiling and bedecked with appropriate emblems. The dominant element and focal point of such decorative and iconographic programmes was the enormous catafalque or *túmulo*, constructed of wood but painted, gilded, and silvered, and adorned with sculptures, paintings, banners, epitaphs and other inscriptions, and the coats of arms of the deceased and their family. Such catafalques – which supported enormous numbers of candles – were also known as *capillas ardentes*, 'burning chapels'.[72] The catafalque might reach almost to the

---

[71] The will of 1589 specifies that it should be the monasteries that performed this requirement, while the codicil of 1593 allowed for parish churches also to undertake it.

[72] There is a brief summary of the long-established international tradition of the *chapelle ardente* or *castrum doloris* and of the emergence of the term 'catafalque' in the sixteenth century in Minon Schraven, *Festive Funerals in Early Modern Italy: The Art and Culture of Conspicuous Commemoration* (Farnham: Ashgate, 2014), 10–15. On catafalques in Spain, see Andrew Arbury, 'Spanish Catafalques of the Sixteenth and Seventeenth Centuries', unpublished PhD thesis, Rutgers University (1992). On Spanish royal exequies, including the role of the decorative arts within them, see also Orso, *Art and Death*, Allo Manero, 'Exequias de la Casa de Austria', and Javier Varela, *La muerte del rey: el ceremonial funerario de la monarquía española, 1500–1885* (Madrid: Turner, 1990).

vaulting: that constructed in Seville Cathedral for the exequies of Philip II was some 130 feet tall. The bottom tier of the catafalque incorporated the *tumba* (bier, or representation of the tomb), around which took place the ceremony of Absolution that concluded the exequies. On the catafalque and the walls of the church, and sometimes outside it, was displayed a profusion of 'hieroglyphs', further poems in Latin, Spanish, and often other languages, coats of arms, and other images, particularly personifications of death. The hieroglyphs (*Jeroglíficos*) were emblematic pictures, some of great size, accompanied by Latin mottos within banderoles, and including brief verses (usually in Spanish) beneath the image; the motto (or *inscriptio*) and verses (or *subscriptio*) enabled the viewer to interpret the picture.[73]

The usual location for the *honras fúnebres* organised by the Spanish royal court for kings, queens, and crown princes[74] between 1581 and 1665 was the church of the Hieronymite monastery of San Jerónimo in Madrid. However, the royal court exequies for María in 1603 were of course in Valladolid, not Madrid. Within three days of María's death, the King had decided to hold these exequies in the chapel of the monastery of San Benito el Real,[75] and they took place on 20 and 21 March.[76] It seems likely that Lerma played a dominant role in their organisation, and he may also have been responsible for the additional set of exequies which were held at the Dominican convent of San Pablo in Valladolid: a document in the hand of Francisco de Mora, who designed the catafalques for other exequies of the Spanish Habsburg court, includes mention of a catafalque constructed by

---

[73] The hieroglyphs created for María's exequies at the Jesuit College in Madrid, and the other poems written for the occasion, were reproduced in the published commemorative account of these exequies, *Libro de las honras*. This seems to be the earliest such printed account of exequies in Habsburg Spain to include illustrations showing the hieroglyphs. Following the reproduction of each hieroglyph and its appended text is an explanation of its significance in relation to María's qualities and achievements, with notable emphasis on her support for the Jesuits. The hieroglyphs are reproduced in Vistarini, Cull, and Sajó, *Book of Honors*.

[74] That is, *príncipes jurados*, heirs apparent to the throne of Castile.

[75] Cabrera de Córdoba, *Relaciones*, 169 of the 1857 edition; Juan Carrillo mentions the decision to hold the court exequies at San Benito in a letter to Archduke Albert dated 2 March: Brussels, Archives Générales du Royaume / Algemeen Rijksarchief, Sécretairerie d'État et de Guerre / Secretarie van Staat en Oorlog, 492, f. 174.

[76] The dates are reported in a letter from Juan Carrillo to Archduke Albert dated 8 April: Brussels, Archives Générales du Royaume / Algemeen Rijksarchief, Sécretairerie d'État et de Guerre / Secretarie van Staat en Oorlog, 492, f. 177. Likewise, Doña Catalina de Zúñiga y Sandoval reported from the royal court to Juan de Borja in a letter of 21 March that the *honras* had concluded that afternoon; her letter is in British Library Add. Ms 28427, at f. 196. However, the manuscript *relación* of the exequies gives the dates as 21–22 March; see the transcription in Jordan, 'Dos aguilas', 467.

Jerónimo Hernández for the Empress in San Pablo.[77] This convent, a royal
foundation, faces the royal palace (across the Plaza de San Pablo) which
was occupied by the court when in Valladolid. Lerma became patron of the
convent in 1601, oversaw the renovation of the West façade and the
construction of two side towers, and was buried there. In 1608 he organised
at San Pablo exequies for the Archduchess María, mother of Margaret of
Austria (Philip III's queen).[78]

Although the essential outline of exequies was uniform throughout the
Iberian world, the royal court had its own specific protocols for such
events. Two manuscript sets of regulations for the *capilla real* include
protocols for various categories of *pro defunctis* services, including
exequies.[79] Of these, Clause 32 in the 'Leges et constitutiones capellæ
Catholicæ Maiestatis' provides information about music for exequies of
the king, the queen, or a prince of the royal house. During the Vigil, the first
lesson at Matins was to be sung by a boy, the second in *fabordón*, and the
third by a priest. This clause also indicates that at the Absolution after Mass
one (i.e. only one) responsory should be sung 'in music', which may well
mean 'in polyphony'.[80] There are parallels between the treatment of Matins
of the Dead prescribed here and the instructions for the conduct of Matins
in the proposed order of service for the royal court exequies of Philip II
(discussed above).[81] Here again the first lesson of Matins was to be sung by

---

[77] See Cervera Vera, 'Túmulos reales', 33.

[78] Cabrera de Córdoba, *Relaciones*, 346 of the 1857 edition; Diego de Guzmán, *Reina Catolica:
      Vida y muerte de D. Margarita de Austria* (Madrid: Luis Sánchez, 1617), f. 182.

[79] One of these sets of regulations was drawn up in about 1550, but both of them were current in
      the early part of Philip II's reign, and to some extent still in force thereafter. The set of
      regulations entitled 'La Orden que se tiene en los Officios en la Capilla de su Magestad' –
      updated early in Philip's reign, and preserved in a seventeenth-century copy – is considered in
      detail in Bernadette Nelson, 'Ritual and Ceremony in the Spanish Royal Chapel, *c.* 1559–*c.*
      1561', *Early Music History* 19 (2000), 105–200; see in particular her discussion of the protocols
      for *pro defunctis* services at 151–67, and the transcription of the relevant text at 176–9 and 182.
      Nelson compares the regulations set out there with those in the other – and better known – set
      of regulations for the *capilla real*, 'Leges et constitutiones capellæ Catholicæ Maiestatis'.
      Transcriptions of the part of this document relevant to *pro defunctis* services may be found in
      Edmond Vander Straeten, *La musique aux Pays-Bas avant le XIXe siècle*, 8 vols (Brussels:
      G.-A. van Trigt, 1867–88), VII, 185, and in Robledo Estaire et al., *Aspectos de la cultura
      musical*, 332.

[80] The relevant clause (as transcribed in Robledo Estaire et al., *Aspectos de la cultura musical*, 332)
      is: 'In exeq[u]iis imperatoris, imperatricis, regis, regine, principis d[omi]norum nostroru[m]
      defunctorum, Vesperas, cum uno nocturno et Laudes, primam lectionem puer unus, secundum
      in fabordon, tertiam sacerdos, missam solemniter et deinde responsorium musicae canunto.'
      The poor Latin here is typical of the document as a whole. The phrase 'cum uno nocturno'
      applies to Matins.

[81] The relevant document is transcribed and translated in Robledo, 'Questions of Performance
      Practice', 209, and is also transcribed and discussed in the same author's 'La música en la casa

a boy, and the second lesson (alone) was to be sung in parts. However, this lesson would be performed not in *fabordón* as directed in the 'Leges et constitutiones' (one should note that *fabordón* is indeed specified elsewhere in this order of service) but in four-voice polyphony (*canto de órgano*).[82] Although Clause 32 in the 'Leges et constitutiones' further stipulates that Matins at such royal exequies is to have one nocturn only (i.e. with three psalms with antiphons, and three lessons with the associated responsories), contemporary sources suggest that it was common – perhaps indeed standard practice – for Matins to include three nocturns on these royal occasions.[83] Although the Murcia exequies for Philip III, considered above, involved Matins of one nocturn, the order of service for the court exequies of Philip II indicates three, as do printed accounts of the exequies for Don Carlos and Queen Isabel de Valois (both in 1568).[84] The traditions governing the performance of lessons at Matins of royal exequies apparent from the order of service for Philip II's exequies were still in evidence in the later seventeenth century: the printed account of the court exequies for Philip IV in 1665 specifies that the second lesson was sung by all the members of the *capilla* 'à papel' (i.e. from a music book or books), whereas the other lessons were chanted, each by a different singer, the first by a boy from the choir school, and lessons 3 to 9 by chaplains. The account adds that this manner of performing the nine Matins lessons was 'according to the manner of the Royal Chapel'.[85] These royal-chapel conventions of the treatment of Matins find a parallel in Victoria's inclusion in his *Officium*

---

del rey', 169 and 172. Robledo notes (at 164) that separate written plans for these *honras* had been submitted by various members of the royal household, the first by Manuel de Sousa, and the second by Gerónimo de Talamantes and Gaspar de Arratia. We do not know whether the surviving document corresponds to either of these plans.

[82] 'La primera lecçión del primer nocturno dirá un cantorçico, la 2ª. cuatro cantores en canto de órgano, la 3ª. un capellán de banco. El segundo nocturno se dirá como el primero y las liçiones dirán los capellanes de banco. El 3°. nocturno de dirá de la mesma manera.' See Robledo Estaire, 'La música en la casa del rey', 169.

[83] It is also worth noting that Clause 35 in the 'Leges et constitutiones' stipulates that Matins of the dead for a king, queen, or any member of the Habsburg family is to be sung with three nocturns. Wagstaff ('Music for the Dead', 360) concludes, surely correctly, that this refers to the ceremonies on the day of death, rather than the later exequies.

[84] López de Hoyos, *Relacion de la muerte,* and *Hystoria y relación verdadera de la enfermedad felicíssimo tránsito, y sumptuosas exequias funebres de la serenissima reyna de España doña Isabel de Valoys nuestra señora* (Madrid: Pierres Cosin, 1569). These *relaciones* are transcribed in Díaz (ed.), *Fuentes para la historia,* I, at 8–20 and 20–55 respectively.

[85] Rodríguez de Monforte, *Descripcion de la honras,* f. 87v.

defunctorum of a polyphonic setting of the second Matins lesson, *Tædet animam meam*, but of no other lessons.[86]

In the days following María's burial it was decided to press ahead with the organisation of the exequies as quickly as possible, in order (as noted) to hold them before Holy Week: on 8 March, one week after the burial, Borja reported to Lerma that work on the catafalque was proceeding with great haste ('muy gran prisa'), and that it would hopefully be possible to hold the exequies before Palm Sunday,[87] and four days later he informed Lerma that the dates of the *honras* had been settled as 17 and 18 March,[88] just five days thence, although they were subsequently postponed by one day, to 18 and 19 March.[89] Since the civic exequies took place in the Descalzas chapel immediately afterwards, on 19 and 20 March, this left two days before Palm Sunday for the public to admire the decorative apparatus and for it then to be dismantled. If the planning of María's household exequies was subject to considerable time constraints, the civic authorities of Madrid were confronted with a still more frenetic timetable in organising their own exequies. As mentioned, it seems that no royal letters were issued to cities requiring the holding of exequies after María's death. Rather, it was the King who received a petition from the city officials of Madrid, asking that they be allowed to hold *honras* at the Descalzas. He granted permission in a letter of 12 March,[90] but this left extremely little time to arrange the ceremonies if they were to take place before Easter, which would be of great advantage (organisationally and financially), since the city officials could thus use the catafalque and decorations being installed for the household exequies, rather than having to reassemble these or commission new ones to be put in place after the chapel had been restored to its normal appearance for Holy Week. It was in any case frequent practice in Spanish cities that the civic exequies began on the second day of the preceding (court or cathedral) exequies. At a meeting on the 16th, called upon receipt of the

---

[86] It is also worth observing that Victoria's setting is for four voices, corresponding in this respect with the scoring stipulated for this item at Philip II's exequies, whereas the rest of the music in the *Officium defunctorum* is for six voices. Regarding the number of nocturns of Matins at exequies and other *pro defunctis* services at the Spanish court and more widely, see Nelson, 'Ritual and Ceremony', 154–8, and Wagstaff, 'Music for the Dead', 357–61.

[87] British Library Add. Ms 28425, f. 49r.   [88] British Library Add. Ms 28425, f. 54r.

[89] The title-page of the printed sermon from the exequies – *Sermon que ... predicó el padre fray Iuan de los Angeles ... en 17 de março de 1603* – gives the date on which it was preached as 17 March, i.e. two days before the date on which it was actually delivered.

[90] The king's letter is in Madrid, Archivo de la Villa, A. S. A. 2–311-60. The letter's text is reproduced in Diego de Urbina's *relación* of the Madrid exequies, in Biblioteca Nacional de España Ms 11773 (f. 576), and also in Méndez Silva's later account in *Admirable vida* (f. 53), which is here clearly derived from that of Diego de Urbina.

King's letter, the city officials duly agreed to hold their exequies on the 19th and 20th, and appointed commissioners who set about making the arrangements 'with incredible alacrity'.[91] These arrangements included inviting the singers, who were to be those of the *capilla* of the Descalzas. It seems very likely that – just as the civic exequies were to re-use the catafalque from the court exequies – the singers of the Descalzas chapel were to re-use Victoria's music, which they would just have performed at the household *honras*. It also appears likely that Victoria directed his own music for these civic exequies.

As Victoria worked on the Requiem, others were creating the literary elements of the chapel decorations. María's secretary Lupercio Leonardo de Argensola provided a Latin epitaph, which may well have been the one displayed on the *túmulo*, and most probably in front of the *tumba* itself.[92] Since Lupercio was a noted poet, as well as dramatist and historian, it seems safe to presume that he contributed further items for the *honras*, and among María's chaplains Lupercio's brother Bartolomé (likewise a poet) and Martin Pesserio (who wrote the Latin *carmen* for the prefatory matter of the *Officium defunctorum*) may well likewise have been involved in this element of the exequies. The liturgical aspects were planned and overseen by Diego de Guzmán,[93] *capellán mayor* of the *capilla* of the Descalzas, with whom Victoria – as the provider of the polyphony for the ceremonies – would have liaised closely. Regarding the musical forces to be employed, it may have been Victoria who pointed out to Borja the need to recruit additional singers – besides those of the *capilla* of the Descalzas – for the occasion, perhaps reflecting the decision to use six-voice textures in his music for the Mass, and more generally the requirements (already discussed) for a level of solemnity and grandeur appropriate to María's status. In a letter to Lerma of 12 March, six days before the exequies, Borja

---

[91] 'con increyble presteza'; Biblioteca Nacional de España Ms 11773, f. 577.

[92] The epitaph is transcribed in Cipriano Muñoz y Manzano, Conde de la Viñaza, *Los cronistas de Aragón: Discurso leido ante S. M. el Rey Don Alfonso XIII, presidiendo la Real Academia de la Historia, en la recepción pública del Excmo. Sr. Conde de la Viñaza* (Madrid: Fortanet, 1904), 79, Appendix 118, carta 11. The source is a letter by Lupercio, dated 20 March 1603 (that is, the day after María's household exequies), to Dr Bartolomé Llorente, canon and *capellán mayor* of the Basilica of El Pilar in Zaragoza, and preserved in Zaragoza, Archivo de la Basílica del Pilar, Orden 2, Lig. 70. Sup. Alm. 5, vol. 2, no. 11. The placement of the catafalque epitaph on the front of the *tumba*, facing the nave, became the norm at royal exequies from those for Philip III onwards: see Orso, *Art and Death*, 19 and 31. While it is possible that the epitaph transcribed in Lupercio's letter was not the principal one on display, but simply one of several or many epitaphs penned for María's exequies, the former interpretation is suggested by Lupercio's use of the definite article ('el epitaphio de la emperatriz') in his letter.

[93] As stated by Diego de Urbina in his *relación* of the exequies, Biblioteca Nacional de España Ms 11773, at f. 575v.

reported that he had written to Bernardo Sandoval y Rojas, Cardinal Archbishop of Toledo (and Lerma's uncle), to request 'some singers which we lack' for the *honras*.[94] Four singers from Toledo Cathedral duly came to perform at the exequies: the *tiples* Juan García and Juan Fernández, the alto Hernando de Lerma, and the bass Tomás de Miranda.[95] Of possible relevance to the securing of such musical help from Toledo is the fact that at the time of María's death Victoria was assisting the chapelmaster of Toledo Cathedral, Alonso Lobo, acting as his proxy in dealings with the royal press in Madrid regarding the publication of Lobo's *Liber primus missarum*.[96] We cannot be sure of the precise numbers singing at María's exequies. As reformed in 1601 by Philip III, the *capilla* of the Descalzas had nine singer-chaplains, two of each voice-type plus the *capellán* elected *maestro*;[97] there were also to be two salaried chaplains with good voices whose duties included acting as deacon and subdeacon at Mass. If the establishment was at full strength for María's exequies, then thirteen singers (including the four from Toledo and the *maestro*) performed the polyphony of the *Officium defunctorum*; the two salaried chaplains might have swelled the number further if they were skilled in polyphony, and it is possible of course that Victoria sang, so it may be that the forces were as great as sixteen.

As mentioned above, the only *relación* of the two sets of exequies for María at the Descalzas is that by Diego de Urbina, who (as a *regidor* of

---

[94] 'algunos cantores que nos faltan'; British Library Add. Ms 28425, f. 54r.

[95] For references to the entries in the *actas capitulares* of Toledo Cathedral in which the singers sent to Madrid are named, see François Reynaud, *La polyphonie tolédane et son milieu, des premiers témoignages aux environs de 1600* (Turnhout: Brepols, 1996), 44, n. 326 and n. 327. There are, however, errors in Reynaud's account: earlier in the same paragraph he claims that three (different) singers were sent to sing at María's exequies in June 1581 (i.e. twenty-two years before her death). The same error of date occurs in Reynaud's otherwise valuable summary of the regular practice of Toledo Cathedral singers performing in other institutions, within his 'Música y músicos toledanos: grupos e individuos fuera de la catedral', in John Griffiths and Javier Suárez-Pajares (eds), *Políticas y prácticas musicales en el mundo de Felipe II* (Madrid: Ediciones del ICCMU, 2004), 241–52, at 243. Natalia Medina Hernández states that the *actas capitulares* for 14 March 1603 name just two singers in connection with María's exequies: Tomás de Miranda and Hernando de Segura: see 'La vida musical en la catedral de Toledo durante el siglo XIII: capilla de música y obras', unpublished PhD thesis., Universidad Autonoma de Madrid (2015), 34.

[96] Lobo appointed Victoria his proxy for this publication project in July 1602. A document of 4 March 1603 records Victoria's receipt of the 130 copies, and transfer of payment for them on Lobo's behalf. The relevant documents are transcribed in Vicente (ed.), *El mayordomo*, documents 34, 35, and 41. See also Stevenson, *Spanish Cathedral Music*, 263.

[97] The relevant passage in Philip III's *declaración* of 1601 regarding the *capilla* is transcribed in Mota Murillo, *Sebastián López de Velasco*, I, 131. A document of 9 January 1603, shortly before María's death, lists the eight singers and *maestro* who were in post at that point. See Huff, 'Demystifying the Life and Madrid Works', 142.

Madrid) was certainly present for the civic exequies, while two eyewitnesses (Borja and Khevenhüller) offer brief comment on the household
exequies. All three underline their due solemnity in conventional terms:
Borja reported to Lerma on 19 March that the household exequies had
been conducted 'with the greatest solemnity possible',[98] while
Khevenhüller noted in his diary that both the Vigil and the Masses were
carried out 'truly solemnly',[99] and informed the Emperor Rudolf that they
were 'truly stately'.[100] Diego de Urbina – as was commonplace in *libros de
exequias* – attributes the duration of the Vigil (two and a half hours) to its
'great solemnity'.[101] While he says nothing about the music, other than that
the musicians were the chaplains and singers of the *capilla* of the Descalzas
and the four singers from Toledo,[102] his account does assist us in picturing
the scene while Victoria's new music was performed. The space was
brilliantly lit (there were more than two thousand candles on the catafalque
alone), un-resonant (as was conventional, the walls and pillars of the entire
chapel were draped in black, as were the altar and the pulpit), and very
crowded: the members of the Empress's household stood ranged along the
walls of the *capilla mayor* (the Eastern part of the chapel, in which the
catafalque had been erected), presumably because there was no room for
seating to accommodate them. Indeed, Urbina highlights the fact that of all
those in the *capilla mayor* the only people seated were the three presiding
bishops, the royal chaplains, the Abbot of the Benedictine Monastery of
San Martín (adjacent to the Descalzas), and – in the seats of honour either
side of the catafalque – Khevenhüller and Borja. The three other stewards
of the household stood behind the catafalque, and mace-bearers were
stationed at each of its corners; the rest of the chapel between the *capilla
mayor* and the West doors was fitted with benches, occupied by *señores* and
caballeros of Madrid.[103]

---

[98] 'con la mayor solenidad que havemos podido'; British Library Add. Ms 28525, f. 62v.

[99] 'gar solemniter'; Khevenhüller, *Geheimes Tagebuch*, 280.

[100] 'gar statlich'; letter of 22 March from Khevenhüller to Rudolf. The relevant passage is at p. 177 of a typed transcription of the relevant correspondence, entitled *Die geheime Korrespondenz des kaiserlichen Botshafters am Königlich spanischen Hof in Madrid, Hans Khevenhüller, Graf von Frankenburg*, in Vienna, Haus- Hof-, und Staatsarchiv, Spanien, Diplomatische Korrespondenz, Karton 13.

[101] 'gran solemnidad'; Biblioteca Nacional de España Ms 11773, f. 575v. One might note by way of comparison that the Vigil of the royal court exequies for Philip II at San Jerónimo in Madrid lasted between three and four hours, according to a manuscript *relación* entitled 'Honrras que se Hiçieron en S(an)t(o) Geronimo de Madrid Por el Rey Don Felipe segundo', copied at ff. 44v–45v (in the modern pencil foliation) of British Library Add. Ms 10236.

[102] Biblioteca Nacional de España Ms 11773, f. 575v.

[103] Biblioteca Nacional de España Ms 11773, ff. 573v-574.

'Con gravedad y pausa': Musical and Performance Ideals

It is clear from the accounts in *libros de exequias* and other documents that both the composed music and the chant at such Habsburg exequies was performed at a slow pace, and that such unhurried performance was viewed as an appropriate contribution to the solemnity of the occasion (noted in the remarks of Urbina, Borja, and Khevenhüller) and to the maintenance of a duly contemplative and reverential atmosphere. This reflected the general practice of relating the speed of liturgical chanting to the degree of solemnity of the service concerned.[104] It invites contextualisation through consideration of the ideals of singing the Divine Office with *pausa, gravedad,* and *solemnidad* apparent for example within the Jeronymite order,[105] and of singing the psalmody of the Office with sufficient *pausa* between the half verses to which numerous monastic constitutions refer.

Thus the draft order of service for the royal court exequies for Philip II, discussed above, specifies that the chanting of the psalms and antiphons at Vespers and the singing of Lauds (including the canticle *Benedictus* performed in *fabordón*) should be 'very slow' ('muy despaçio'),[106] while at the ceremonies marking the translation of royal corpses to El Escorial in 1574

---

[104] This is stipulated in, for example, a mid seventeenth-century Benedictine Ceremonial from Portugal: Frei Manuel da Ascenção, *Ceremonial da Congregação dos Monges Negros da Ordem do Patriarcha S. Bento do Reyno de Portugal* (Coimbra: Diogo Gomes de Loureiro and Lourenço Crasbeeck, 1647), p. x. The celebrated moralist Martín de Azpilcueta, in his manual on prayer and conduct of the Divine Office and abuses in such conduct, specifically warned against excessively fast recitation of Requiem Masses, the Office of the Dead, and responsories *pro defunctis: Enchiridion sive manuale de oratione et horis canonicis* (Rome: Joseph de Angelis, 1578), 247. (The original Spanish version was published in 1545 as *Commento en romance ... sobre el capitulo Quando de consecratione.*) It may be that Azpilcueta was thus reinforcing the need for such *pro mortuis* services to be recited particularly slowly, or alternatively that his comment reflects a tendency for these services to be rushed given the enormous numbers which had to be conducted. Comments by the chapelmaster of the Sistine Chapel in 1652 show that in that institution also there was a tradition of performing the chant of Requiem Masses (and music for Holy Week) slowly. The relevant document is transcribed in Giancarlo Rostirolla, 'Alcune note storico-istituzionali sulla cappella pontificia in relazione alla formazione e all'impiego dei repertori polifonici nel periodo post-palestriniano, fino a tutto il Settecento', in Bernhard Janz (ed.), *Collectanea II: Studien zur Geschichte der päpstlichen Kapelle: Tagungsbericht, Heidelberg, 1989* (Vatican City: Biblioteca apostolica Vaticana, 1994), 631–788, at 754. I am grateful to Antonio Chemotti for drawing this passage to my attention.

[105] See José López-Calo, 'La música en la Orden y en el Rito Jeronimianos', *Studia Hieronymiana* 1 (1973), 123–38, and Alfonso de Vicente Delgado, 'Los cargos musicales y las capillas de música en los monasterios de la Orden de San Jerónimo (siglos XVI–XIX)', unpublished PhD thesis, Universidad Complutense de Madrid (2010).

[106] See the transcription in Robledo Estaire, 'La música en la casa del rey', 169.

the chant 'Subvenite' was sung 'so slowly that it appeared ... that this responsory was never going to end'.[107] Similarly, in a *relación* of the civic exequies for Margaret of Austria in Córdoba Cathedral we read that the Requiem Mass was performed 'with such solemnity that the *capilla*'s singing of the Sequence alone took half an hour'.[108] Some of the relevant passages in *relaciones* indicate slow performance through reference to the *compás* (i.e. beat, a term applied to both polyphonic and chant performance). For example, at the exequies for Philip II organised by the Inquisition of New Spain in Mexico City in 1599 the first psalm of Matins was sung in polyphony with a *compás* that was 'slow and sedate' ('grave y sosegado'),[109] while the Vigil of the exequies for Queen Isabel at S. Jerónimo in Madrid in 1644 is described thus:

> When all were in their places, the signal was given, and the Royal Chapel began Vespers of the Dead. Immediately thereafter they sang Matins with three nocturns and nine lessons, and Lauds, all with the solemnity, sweetness, and *compás*, and numbers of instruments and voices that are customary in such important ceremonies; and consequently [the services] lasted until the seventh hour in the evening.[110]

[107] 'tan despacio, que nos pareció que nunca se había de acabar aquel responso'. See Michael Noone, 'Processions to the "City of the Dead": The Spanish Royal Chapel and an Anonymous Requiem from El Escorial', in Juan José Carreras and Bernardo García García (eds), *The Royal Chapel in the Time of the Habsburgs: Music and Court Ceremony in Early Modern Europe*, Studies in Medieval and Renaissance Music 3 (Woodbridge: Boydell, 2005), 144–61, at 147 and n. 17.

[108] 'con tanta solemnidad, que la sequentia sola cantada por la capilla, duró media ora.' *Relacion de las honras que se hizieron en la ciudad de Cordova, à la muerte de la serenissima reyna señora, doña Margarita de Austria* (Córdoba: widow of Andres Barrera, 1612), f. 31v.

[109] Dionisio de Ribera Florez, *Relacion historiada de las exequias funerales de la magestad del rey d(on) Philippo II nuestro senor* (Mexico City: Pedro Balli, 1600), f. 163v.

[110] 'Estando ya todos en sus lugares, hecha la seña, empeço la Capilla Real las Visperas de Difuntos. Luego cantò el Oficio de tres Nocturnos, i nueve Lecciones, i sus Laudes: todo con la solenidad, dulçura, i compàs, i el numero de instrumentos, i vozes, que en actos tan graves se acostumbra: i assi tardò hasta las siete de la noche.' *Pompa funeral honras y exequias en la muerte de la muy alta y católica señora doña Isabel de Borbon* (Madrid: Diego Díaz de la Carrera, 1645), ff. 49v–50. As discussed in Chapter 4, a significant number of Spanish and Portuguese Requiem Masses employ *proportio dupla* mensuration (using a breve rather than semibreve tactus, and known as *compás mayor* in Spain) in some sections and *integer valor* (with a semibreve tactus, and known as *compasillo* in Spain) in others. The sections under *proportio dupla* move predominantly in the longer note values. However, it is difficult to perceive a connection between this particular practice and the remarks about the use of a slow *compás* in *relaciones* of exequies, since (as pointed out in that chapter) it is exceptional for a Spanish or Portuguese Requiem to adopt the *compás mayor* manner of writing throughout. Rather, it seems likely that at exequies a slow *compás* was adopted for the polyphony in general (whether in the *compasillo* or *compás mayor* manner of writing), with whatever relationship

Some Spanish accounts further emphasise the use of appropriately generous *pausas* – rests, or breaks between phrases or sections – as an element of the solemnity and gravity of performance (whether of entirely chanted items or of those involving polyphony) at exequies. Thus in Juan Gómez de Mora's description of the royal court exequies for Margaret of Austria in 1611 we read that the responsories at the Absolution were sung 'in three choirs with a grand sonorousness and ensemble of voices, and with such tranquil *pausas* that they stirred devotion and sorrow',[111] and the first responsory at the exequies for Margaret in Lima Cathedral was performed 'with great *pausa* and solemnity for four choirs',[112] while Pedro Rodríguez de Monforte observed that all of the music sung at the court exequies for Philip IV was marked by 'gravity in the *pausas*' ('grave-dad en las pausas').[113] As he noted, the *pausas* were adjusted to mark points of particular solemnity: the last of the five responsories at the Absolution (*Libera me Domine*) was performed with 'greater *pausa* and solemnity in the singing' ('mayor pausa y solemnidad de canto') than were the preceding responsories.[114] As early as 1425 there exists a reference from Ferrara to the singing of *pro defunctis* chants on anniversaries with a restrained voice and 'faciendo punctum cum pausa'.[115] At the period of Victoria's *Officium defunctorum*, to sing any chant of the Office or Mass 'con pausa' or 'con pausas' seems most straightforwardly to have meant leaving a gap between the end of one textual phrase (for example, a verse of a psalm or canticle) and the start of the next, or at the least to avoid overlap between phrases. The proper lengths of such *pausas*, measured in terms of the *compás* of the chant, is mentioned for example in Martín de la Vera's *Ordinario y Ceremonial* setting out Jeronymite practice and specifically that at El

---

was conventional at that time and in a particular institution between the speeds of tactus for these two mensurations and styles of composition.

[111] 'a tres coros con gran sonoridad y concierto de vozes, y pauses tan suaves, que movian a devocion y ternura'. Juan Gómez de Mora, *Relación de las honras funerales que se hizieron por la reyna doña Margarita de Austria nuestra señora, en esta villa de Madrid por su magestad del rey don Felipe nuestro señor* (Madrid, n.d.). A transcription of this *relación* is in *Relaciones breves de actos públicos celebrados en Madrid de 1541 a 1650*, ed. José Simón Díaz, El Madrid de los Austrias, Serie Documentación 1 (Madrid: Instituto de Estudios Madrileños, 1982), 72–8. The relevant passage is at 78.

[112] 'con gran pausa y solemnidad a quatro choros'. Fray Martín de León, *Relación de las exequias q(ue) el ex(celentisi)mo s(eño)r D. Iuan de Mendoça y Luna Marques de Montesclaros, Virrey del Piru hizo en la muerte de la reina nuestra s(eñora) doña Margarita* (Lima: Pedro de Marchán y Calderón, 1612), f. 27.

[113] *Descripcion de la honras*, f. 88.   [114] *Ibid.*, f. 112.

[115] Quoted in Enrico Peverada, *Vita musicale nella chiesa ferrarese del Quattrocento* (Ferrara: Capitolo Cattedrale, 1991), 106, and discussed by Rob Wegman in *The Crisis of Music in Early Modern Europe, 1470–1530* (New York and London: Routledge, 2008), 32.

Escorial.[116] In 1788 Joaquin Lorenzo Villanueva, a chaplain at the royal Encarnación convent in Madrid, devoted a whole book to the need for priests to say or sing Mass 'con gravedad y pausa', rather than conducting it with unseemly haste and with abbreviations, as was commonplace.[117] Among the abuses which he mentions is the practice in some churches of omitting four to six verses at a time during the singing of the (lengthy) Sequence *Dies iræ* in Requiem Masses.[118] It is worth noting that in highly sectionalised forms such as polyphonic settings of responsories *pro mortuis* – with their alternation of polyphony and chant and their responsorial structure – there was abundant opportunity to increase the *pausas*, and it may be that singing such items 'con gravedad y pausa' also involved sustaining the final sonorities of polyphonic sections. For example, in performance – i.e. with all the necessary repetitions of the respond and sections of the respond – Victoria's setting of the responsory *Libera me Domine* published in the *Officium defunctorum* falls into no fewer than sixteen sections, nine of them sung in polyphony and the remainder in chant. With regard to the singing of *Libera me Domine* with 'mayor pausa y solemnidad' than the other responsories at Philip IV's exequies, one notes that at El Escorial there existed a convention that the three verses of this responsory should be chanted more slowly than the other responsories.[119]

Beyond their comments on such matters of pacing in performance, and the associated qualities of *gravedad* and *solemnidad, relaciones* contain traces of the desired and/or experienced affective attributes of the music of Habsburg exequies, although such evidence requires circumspect interpretation, given the function and nature of *relaciones*. The descriptions in many *relaciones* point to the ideal – particularly in the seventeenth century, when polychoral settings became more common – that the music should

---

[116] *Ordinario y ceremonial según las costumbres y rito de la orden de nuestro padre san Geronymo* (Madrid: Imprenta Real, 1636). The relevant passage is translated in Michael Noone, *Music and Musicians in the Escorial Liturgy under the Habsburgs, 1563–1700* (Rochester, NY, and Woodbridge: University of Rochester Press, 1998), 135.

[117] Joaquin Lorenzo Villanueva, *De la obligacion de decir la Misa con circunspeccion y pausa* (Madrid: Imprenta Real, 1788).

[118] *Ibid.*, unnumbered seventh page of the Prologue.

[119] The relevant passage from the *Quadernos de las costumbres* is transcribed in Noone, *Music and Musicians*, 299. Other references to the singing of the fifth responsory at the Absolution 'with greater solemnity' ('con mayor solemnidad') than the others are in the account of the exequies for Margaret of Austria held in Lima (Martín de León, *Relacion de las exequias*, f. 27v) and that of the exequies for Philip III conducted by the Spanish nation in Rome: Geronimo Fernandez de Cordova, *Relacion de las funerales exequias que la nacion española hizo en Roma a la majestad del rey n(uestro) s(eñor) d(on) Philippo III de Austria, el piadoso* (Rome: Giacomo Mascardo, 1622), 39.

combine the qualities of requisite gravity and solemnity on the one hand with sonorous splendour on the other, in a manner which echoed both the mixing of sobriety and sumptuous flamboyance in the decorative schemes of such exequies, and the manner in which royal exequies combined themes of mourning and of triumph over death, of mortal frailty and immortal glory. The official *relación* of the court exequies for Isabel of Bourbon describes the visual impression within the church thus: 'majesty was equalled by sadness; the sumptuous by the funereal; and the noble by the sorrowful'.[120] We might compare this with the manner in which Isidro Sariñana, in his *relación* of the Mexico City exequies for Philip IV in 1666, describes the music composed for the occasion by Francisco López Capillas, chapelmaster of the cathedral. He praises the music as conjoining the artistic and the devotional, 'without annulling harmoniousness through the funereal, nor negating sweetness through religiousness'.[121] One can reasonably argue that the music which Victoria wrote for María's exequies in 1603 represents a remarkable manifestation of such a balancing of the sumptuous and the sombre, and in Chapter 4 I explore the pervasive intermingling of sweet and doleful affects which characterise it. Thus exequial music had the power to intensify the particular character of *honras* as communicated also by the visual and ritual elements, and the published *Libro de las honras* of the exequies for María held at the Jesuit College in Madrid on 21 and 22 April explicitly praises this combination of sadness and sweetness in one of the specially written musical items, as well as demonstrating an especially vivid way in which music could dramatise both the personal (familial) and dynastic aspects of *honras fúnebres*.

The Jesuit Exequies for María

The item concerned was a Latin *monodia* sung at the end of Matins, the text of which – beginning 'Quis dabit capiti meo aquam' – is reproduced in the *Libro de las honras*. This text is based on the *monodia* (signifying, in this context, a funeral song) written by Angelo Poliziano upon the death of Lorenzo de' Medici in 1492, which was set to music by Heinrich Isaac, and later (for example) by Nicholas Payen, chapelmaster of Charles V's

---

[120] 'La magestad igualava à la tristeza; lo sumptuoso, à lo funesto; i lo grave, à lo doloroso.' *Pompa funeral honras*, f. 37.

[121] 'sin derogar à lo funebre lo armonico, ni desdecir de lo religioso lo suave'; Sariñana, *Llanto del occidente*, f. 32.

chapel.[122] These settings lie within a wider tradition of mourning pieces with texts beginning 'Quis dabit', the most important of the other texts being 'Quis dabit oculis', the opening of which – like that of Poliziano's *monodia* – is derived from the beginning of Chapter 9 of the Book of Jeremiah.[123] The *monodia* sung at the Jesuit exequies in Madrid retains the first two stanzas of Poliziano's almost unchanged, and adds five more stanzas (presumably the work of a member of the College), so as to make the poem specific to María and her family. Indeed, the conceit is that it is Margarita who speaks: as noted in the *Libro de las honras*, the *monodia* was intended to represent Margarita's feelings upon her mother's death,[124] and in the final verse she calls upon her sisters Ana and Isabel (who had died in 1580 and 1592 respectively) to raise their mother into heaven. The music of the *monodia* is described as 'so well fitted to the text, and so sad on the one hand, and so sweet on the other, that it captivated the listeners'.[125] This was not the only occasion on which Poliziano's *monodia* was appropriated for royal exequies in Habsburg Spain: for the *honras fúnebres* upon the death of Philip III in 1621, the University of Salamanca held its traditional poetry competition, the assigned task on that occasion being to compose a '*monodia* in imitation of Poliziano'.[126]

The performance of the *monodia* in the Jesuit exequies of 1603 preceded the Latin *oratio*, after which the *capilla* sang a six-stanza Sapphic poem 'with very fine music' to end that day's ceremonies,[127] a poem which again

[122] See Wolfgang Fuhrmann, 'Pierre de la Rues Trauermotetten und die *Quis dabit*-Tradition', in Gasch and Lodes (eds), *Tod in Musik*, 189–244, especially 212 onwards.

[123] On settings of *Quis dabit oculis* associated with the deaths of the Habsburg emperors Maximilian I and Ferdinand I, see Erika Honisch, 'Sacred Music in Prague, 1580–1612', unpublished PhD thesis, University of Chicago (2011), 200–1. Antonio Chemotti notes that among the inscriptions displayed at the Florentine exequies of Emperor Matthias (María's son) was 'Quis dabit capiti meo aquam et oculis meis fontem lacrymarum?'; see Alessandro Stufa de Conti del Calcione, *Esequie della maestà cesarea dell'imperador Mattia* (Florence: nella stamperia del Cecconcelli, 1619), 46, and Antonio Chemotti, 'Motets and Liturgy for the Dead in Italy: Text Typologies and Contexts of Performance', in Esperanza Rodríguez-García and Daniele V. Filippi (eds), *Mapping the Motet in the post-Tridentine Era* (London: Routledge, 2018), 57–84, at 80.

[124] 'representando el justo sentimiento de la Alteza de la señora Infanta doña Margarita, por la muerte de la serenissima Emperatriz su madre'; *Libro de las honras*, f. 10v.

[125] 'la musica . . . era tan conforme a la letra, y tan triste por una parte, y por otra tan suave, que suspendia el auditorio.' *Ibid.*

[126] Ángel Manrique, *Exequias, túmulo y pompa funeral que la universidad de Salamanca hizo en las honras del rey . . . Felipe III* (Salamanca: Antonio Vásquez, 1621). See Antonio Ramajo Caño, 'Notas sobre la recepción del Poliziano latino en España: una "monodia" del catedrático salmantino Blas López', *Criticón* 55 (1992), 1–52, esp. 46–8, where the poem in imitation of Poliziano's *monodia* by Blas López is discussed.

[127] 'con muy buena musica'; *Libro de las honras*, ff. 19v–20.

draws upon Poliziano.[128] The account in the *Libro de las honras* says nothing about the music at the Requiem Mass the next morning, but notes that 'the responsory' ('el responso') after Mass was performed 'with very fine polyphony' ('con muy buena musica de canto de organo'), after which came the sermon.[129] Nowhere is it stated who the musicians (referred to simply as 'la capilla') were, nor is/are the composer(s) named. It seems that the College was without a polyphonic *capilla* of its own, and therefore the musicians must have been brought in for the occasion. Indeed, we know that the music for certain major events at the College during the seventeenth century was provided by the members of the king's *capilla real*, and on the feast of the Conception of the Blessed Virgin Mary in 1631 this ensemble was joined by the *capilla real* of the Descalzas.[130] But the King's *capilla real* was not available for the exequies of 1603 given the court's absence from Madrid,[131] and it therefore seems most likely that the *capilla real* of the Descalzas supplied the music. Since the members of the Empress's household, led by Juan de Borja, attended the exequies,[132] Victoria was presumably present in any case, and he may well have played a role in the musical provision; indeed, very possibly his music for the exequies at the Descalzas was heard again on this occasion. The 'responso' sung before the sermon might thus have been Victoria's setting of *Libera me Domine*, or (if the account is imprecisely worded) his motet *Versa est in luctum*, the text of which is the respond section of a *pro mortuis* responsory. It is also not unlikely that the *monodia* and the setting of the Sapphic poem were his work. One should note in this connection the strength of Victoria's links with the Jesuits: educated at the Colegium Germanicum in Rome, he then served that College as musical director. It thus seems logical that the superiors of the Madrid College would have welcomed, and perhaps sought, the provision and direction of music for their exequies in 1603 by such an eminent Jesuit alumnus. This was a major

---

[128] The quotation is identified in Escrivà Llorca, 'Eruditio, pietas et honor', 116. In this case, just one line ('Vindicat nostros sibi jure cantus') is quoted, from the thirteen-stanza Latin Sapphic ode in honour of Cardinal Francesco Gonzaga inserted within Poliziano's *Fabola di Orfeo*.

[129] *Libro de las honras*, f. 20v.

[130] See José Simón Díaz, *Historia del Colegio Imperial de Madrid*, 2 vols (Madrid: Consejo Superior de Investigaciones Científicas, 1952), I, 138, n. 10. Occasions in 1607, 1622, 1651, and 1672 for which the king's *capilla real* provided music for the College are noted by Díaz at I, 47, 234–5, 272, 452, and 482. On the lavish musical provision by the *capilla real* for the feast of St Ignatius Loyola in 1607, see Simón Díaz, *Relaciones breves*, 70, and the discussion in Huff, 'Demystifying the Life and Madrid Works', 79.

[131] The King was then at the royal palace of Aranjuez, thirty miles South of Madrid, as is recorded in Biblioteca Nacional de España Ms 2347, at f. 351.

[132] *Libro de las honras*, f. 10v. Margarita was also present.

event for the Society: the Jesuits elected to hold the *honras* on 21 and 22 April so that they coincided with a Provincial Congregation of the Society, and could thus be attended by the senior members of the Society within the Province of Toledo,[133] and the decision to organise these exequies – and to publish a lavish souvenir of the occasion – reflects the extremely bountiful testamentary provision which the Empress had made for the College.[134]

Commemorating the Empress

The exequies performed and Requiem Masses sung and said during the months after María's death[135] represented only the beginning of what was intended (according to the stipulations in her wills and codicils) to be a perpetual round of prayer for her soul, at the Descalzas and the Jesuit College in Madrid as well as in other institutions in Spain and elsewhere. Victoria himself was obliged to say a weekly Mass for her, having been appointed to one of the chaplaincies at the Descalzas endowed in her testamentary documents and for which he was to receive 45,000 *maravedís* a year until his own death.[136] It is for this reason that he could still be described on the title page of the 1605 *Officium defunctorum* as a chaplain of the Empress. Among the services at the Descalzas for which María made testamentary provision were a biannual office and Mass of the dead, to be sung on the anniversary of her death and upon the feast of All Saints (or

---

[133] The date on which the exequies commenced is given erroneously as 25 April on f. 10 of the *Libro de las honras*, but correctly on the title page. The former is clearly an error since the day of the week stated there does not match the date.

[134] She bequeathed a large proportion of her fortune to the College, and this munificent patronage was reflected in the College's refoundation with the title 'Colegio Imperial'. See José Simón Días, 'Libros dedicados a la infanta sor Margarita de la Cruz', in Hipólito Escolar Sobrino (ed.), *Homenaje a Luis Morales Oliver* (Madrid: Fundacion Universitaria Española, 1986), 429–44, at 433.

[135] To give a further idea of the number of Masses involved: in the dedicatory epistle of the *Libro de las honras* it is claimed that the Society of Jesus had already said 35,000 or more Masses for the Empress. These were in addition to the more than 37,000 Masses mentioned on the list in British Library Add. Ms 28707, noted above.

[136] 'Cuentas de los testamentarios de la Emperatriz', Madrid, Archivo Histórico de Protocolos, prot. 2016, f. 1647v. The relevant passage is transcribed and discussed in Mota Murillo, *Sebastián López de Velasco*, I, 49; another transcription is in Vicente, *El mayordomo*, document 82, the passage concerning Victoria being at 229. In a document of 1605 Victoria assigns this annual income (here given as 120 *ducados*) to a certain Isabel Díaz y Poe, in return for 720 *ducados*. As noted in Chapter 3, there has been speculation that this transaction was related to Victoria's expenses in publishing the *Officium defunctorum*, but this seems unlikely. For this document, see Pérez Pastor, *Bibliografía madrileña*, III, 520.

the day within its Octave which was most free from other liturgical demands),[137] and these were occasions on which Victoria's *Officium defunctorum* is likely to have been sung.[138] Another ceremony at which it may well have been used was the translation of the Empress's remains in 1615. Although Philip III acceded to María's wishes and the requests of Margarita and others of her children that her body not be moved to El Escorial during Margarita's lifetime, he was not in the end content with her humble burial place in the lower cloister of the Descalzas, and on 11 March 1615 her body was removed to the monastic *coro*, in a ceremony attended by the King, the royal children, and members of the court. When the body had been brought from the lower cloister to the *coro* in solemn procession, the office of the dead was celebrated in the chapel below 'with much music'.[139] The ceremonies recalled the original exequies for María, in that a catafalque was installed and the chapel was decorated with imperial crowns. The next day a Requiem Mass was conducted 'with great solemnity and music'.[140] Méndez Silva states that the music was provided by the *capilla real*, without specifying whether he means the *capilla real* of the Descalzas or the King's *capilla*.[141] According to Juan de Palma, Margarita used this occasion to entreat the King to permit the Empress's body to remain at the Descalzas in perpetuity, and he acceded.[142] He commissioned the jasper sarcophagus – set prominently on the West wall of the *coro* – in which María's remains still lie. Apart from the possible continued use of Victoria's six-voice Requiem Mass at anniversary services in the Descalzas chapel, it may be that his setting of *Libera me Domine*, perhaps written for the Empress's original burial (see above), continued to be sung regularly in the *coro* beside her tomb after her reburial and after the burial there of her daughter Margarita, who died in 1633: it seems that a responsory for the Empress and the Infanta was sung in the *coro* during

---

[137] 'Iten mando, que el dia, que Yo muriere, y el de Todos Santos, ù el mas desocupado de su Octava, se me diga cada año, un Ofizio de Muertos, con su Missa, todo cantado, aquì, en este Monasterio.' See Abreu y Bertodano, *Coleccion de tratados*, 142. Documents in the archive of the Descalzas refer to the continued performance of these services by the *capilla* more than a century later, in the 1720s: see Consuelo García López, *Archivo del Monasterio de las Descalzas Reales de Madrid*, 2 vols (Madrid: Patrimonio Nacional, 2003), documents 1334, 1336, 1588, 1592, 1595, 1596, and 1598. On these and other services for the soul of the Empress at the Descalzas, see also the extract from a document of 1614 transcribed as Appendix 4 of Vicente, 'El entorno femenino', 238.

[138] It might also have been used for the exequies held at the Descalzas for Margaret of Austria, who died in 1611; these exequies are mentioned by Diego de Guzmán in his *Reina Catolica*, f. 259v.

[139] Carrillo, *Relación histórica*, f. 224.   [140] 'con muy grande solemnidad y musica'; *ibid.*

[141] Méndez Silva, *Admirable vida*, f. 54v. Mota Murillo (*Sebastián López de Velasco*, I, 53) notes that the participation of the King's chapel is not unlikely, given the King's presence.

[142] Palma, *Vida*, f. 143v.

the burial ceremonies for each nun of the Descalzas, and no responsory setting was more firmly associated with María and Margarita than was Victoria's of 1603.[143] We cannot, sadly, track directly the durability of his exequial music at the Descalzas beyond an inventory of music books of 1608, which includes a copy of the *Officium defunctorum*.[144] We thus do not know whether Victoria's Requiem attained anything like the long repertorial life and status that Guerrero's Requiem did at Seville Cathedral, where it was still the usual choice in the eighteenth century.[145] Beyond the walls of the Descalzas, the longevity of the Victoria Requiem relied on its publication in 1605, the subject of Chapter 3.

[143]   See Sánchez Hernández, 'La vida cotidiana', 146–7. Sánchez Hernández fails to provide a reference to the source of her information about this aspect of the burials of nuns.

[144]   'Libro ynpreso en papel con la misa de requien de Vitoria con cubierta de papelón y quero negro'. See Vicente, 'El entorno femenino', 237, and Vicente, *El mayordomo*, 125.

[145]   See Ruiz Jiménez, *La librería*, 283–93.

3 | Publishing the *Officium defunctorum*

The *Officium defunctorum* is – in the context of its time – an extraordinary book and represents a highly original publication project, although its modern fame has perhaps obscured that singular nature. It is a printed folio choirbook, but contains essentially just one 'work' and is only thirty folios in length; indeed, Victoria referred to it as a 'librito' ('booklet').[1] It combines two purposes and identities, being both the musical equivalent of a commemorative festival book and a means of disseminating widely a small quantity of *pro mortuis* polyphony. It thus stands apart not only from all other editions of the composer's music published during his lifetime,[2] but also from the output of the Venetian and Roman publishers who had issued most of his works, and is furthermore exceptional within the context of both music books and occasional books printed elsewhere in Europe. Not only was the project unusual, but its execution reveals curious and contradictory features: the book is presented as, in Alfonso de Vicente's words, 'a veritable monument to the [Habsburg] dynasty',[3] but was printed in a strikingly less sumptuous manner than other choirbooks from the Royal Press, and with a clear desire to keep costs to a minimum; its imposing title page is dominated by a Habsburg coat of arms, but these are the arms of Charles V (that is, María's paternal arms), rather than the marital arms which she apparently still employed at the time of her death, and which appear in the *Libro de las honras* marking the Jesuits' exequies for her; since the *Officium defunctorum* was printed in Madrid, Victoria could oversee the process, and he elsewhere demonstrated exacting standards regarding the presentation of his music in print, but the presswork of the 1605 book is incompetent in significant respects, including those particularly relevant to a Requiem that makes heavy use of chant, and the

---

[1] He did so in a letter dated 25 August 1605 accompanying the copy of the *Officium defunctorum* sent to the Chapter of Zaragoza Cathedral. The text of the letter, which was discovered by Alfonso de Vicente, is transcribed in Vicente, *Libros y obras de Tomás Luis de Victoria (y otros) en Aragón*, Cuadernos Tomás Luis de Victoria 4 (Ávila: Miján, 2016), 37.

[2] Although the *Officium Hebdomadæ Sanctæ* (V1432) likewise has a specific liturgical focus, it is a very much larger collection, and does not commemorate a particular event.

[3] 'Un verdadero "monumento a la dinastía"': 'El entorno femenino', 224.

project was completed with an untoward haste that impaired its appearance and legibility; and Victoria professed to have disseminated the book very widely, but there are few signs that his efforts bore much fruit in terms of institutional purchase (in comparison to his other printed collections) or repertorial embedding of his Requiem, despite the status of María and of Victoria, and the substantial need for *pro mortuis* polyphony: in striking contrast with its modern stature within Victoria's output and the music of the period, the *Officium defunctorum* may have been one of the least widely known of his published collections. In this chapter, expanding on the points introduced above, I scrutinise the nature and multiple functions of the *Officium defunctorum*, viewing it against the background of contemporary music printing and publishing, analysing the implementation of the project, and considering the evidence of its dissemination.

The dedicatory epistle of the *Officium defunctorum* sets out its particular purpose – a lament for the Empress, and a gift to Margarita:

Nothing seemed to me more suitable than to revise the music that I wrote for the exequies of your Most Serene mother, and publish it as a swan song under the protection of your name.[4]

It might seem that the most straightforward reading of Victoria's famous reference to 'swan song' here is that he wished to present the *Officium defunctorum* as his own valedictory,[5] and – as discussed in the Introduction – much has indeed been made of this in constructing the mythology surrounding the work. However, several writers from Collet onwards pointed out that this interpretation is gainsaid by the fact that at the end of the same epistle Victoria expresses to Margarita his ambition to produce further works:

But may you – regarding not the gift but the spirit of the giver, and his most humble devotion to your late Most Serene mother, to you, and to all yours – show favour to

---

[4] 'Nihil magis idoneum visum est, quam ut Harmoniam illam, quam in exequias Serenissimæ tuæ Matris composui, recognoscerem, & tanquam Cygneam cantionem, sub tui nominis patrocinio in lucem æderem.'

[5] William Byrd signalled such valedictory intent for his *Gradualia* (of which the first volume was published in the same year as the *Officium defunctorum*) by including on the title page the well known distich by Martial concerning swan song: 'Dulcia defecta modulatur carmina lingua / Cantator cygnus funeris ipse sui.' Byrd was in his mid 60s in 1605 (and thus significantly older than Victoria), and may well have believed that this was likely to be his last project, but as it happened he – unlike Victoria – went on to publish further works after the two volumes of *Gradualia*.

this enterprise, expecting that one day, if God grant me longer life, they [i.e. such gifts] will be greater.[6]

Collet argued that this second passage has the effect of narrowing the sense of the first, such that 'swan song' should be taken to refer to the exequies of the Empress,[7] although that did not discourage him from making a great deal of the work's status as Victoria's own swan song. That Collet was correct in interpreting Victoria's wording is supported by the fact that, in the eulogistic *carmen* which follows the epistle, Martin Pesserio both likens Victoria's exequial music for María to the 'sad plaints' of the dying swan and then immediately wishes the composer long life and exhorts him to 'join [more] musical trophies to [your existing] trophies'.[8] These two passages in the *carmen* present no potential contradiction in the way that the two portions of the dedicatory epistle cited above might (albeit mistakenly) be seen as doing. It is clear that Pesserio here refers to swan-song not because he regarded this as the composer's last work but simply because such song was a lament or funeral song:

With such exequies, with such a song, Victoria, do you bewail the pious funeral of our common mistress as Thracian Orpheus (lamented) at the death of Eurydice, or such sad plaints as the dying swan, or the Daulian bird redoubles with mournful voices.[9]

The Daulian bird was the nightingale, whose song was traditionally regarded as a lament.[10] Allusion to the lamenting songs of the swan and the nightingale is likewise found in the *monodia* sung at the Jesuit exequies

---

[6] 'Tu vero non munus, sed animum dantis, & humillimum in Serenissimam Matrem tuam defuncta, in te, tuisque, omnes obsequium respiciens, his incœptis fave, maiora, si Deus mihi dies longiores dederit, olim expectans.'

[7] Collet, *Victoria*, 96. Bruno Turner similarly states that 'in his dedication to Princess Margaret it is clear that *Cygneam Cantionem* refers to the Empress. Victoria could hardly have known in 1603 or 1605 that he was to die in 1611 aged sixty-three.' *Tomás Luis de Victoria (1548–1611): Officium defunctorum*, 3.

[8] 'Coniunge trophæa trophæis, Musica'; see the complete translation of this poem in Appendix 1. It was partly on this basis that Robert Stevenson argued, as had Collet, that 'doubtless [Victoria] means "swan song" in an illative sense. The *Officium Defunctorum* would be a swan song for the empress . . . The references to *cygnus* in lines 28 and 32 of [Pesserio's] poem should forever silence those critics who, because of Victoria's own reference to *Cygneam cantionem*, would see him spelling out his intention to retire henceforth from artistic labors.' (*Spanish Cathedral Music*, 370–1)

[9] 'Talibus exequiis, cantu (Victoria) tali
Comunis nostræ Dominæ pia funera defles,
Quales Euridices in funere Thracius Orpheus,
Aut quales cygnus moriens, vel Daulias ales,
Ingeminat tristes lugubri voce querelas.'

[10] See, for example, Virgil's *Georgics*, Book IV, lines 515–20, where the poet likens Orpheus's laments for Eurydice to the night-long mourning song of the nightingale who has lost her

for María, within one of the stanzas taken from Poliziano's poem.[11] Thus, it seems clear that in describing his musical gift to Margarita as 'like swan song' Victoria was merely reflecting the fact that it was a lament for her mother.[12] In this capacity, and within the Habsburg context, the 1605 volume may be understood more fully if situated alongside Margarita's desire to keep her mother close (as evinced by her desire that the body remain at the Descalzas, discussed in Chapter 2), and – beyond this – her marked fascination with the dead members of her family; for example, she commissioned the decoration of a breviary with representations of these family members from Charles V onwards in the form of crowned skulls and cross bones, annotated with their date of death.[13] Such fascination was itself part of the wider focus of the Spanish Habsburgs on veneration of their dead, exemplified by the role of El Escorial as the principal family mausoleum.

This dynastic trait and Margarita's particular desire to commemorate her mother may have encouraged Victoria, as a servant of the Habsburgs, to embark on the innovative project of creating a printed musical memorial, in the expectation that the nature of the book would imbue it – and the music it contains – with prestige within Habsburg circles. The project was probably unsolicited, since Victoria states in the dedicatory epistle that 'nothing seemed to me more suitable than to revise the music that I wrote for the exequies of your Most Serene mother, and publish it as a swan song under the protection of your name': this would hardly have been appropriate wording if he was fulfilling a commission from Margarita, and the *Officium defunctorum* was certainly not commissioned by the royal court either, since this would have been reflected in the liminary matter. (It is possible that Margarita nevertheless underwrote all or part of the production costs, and/or rewarded Victoria once the book was printed.) Nothing

---

young. Given that Pesserio likewise links these two laments, it is possible that he was thinking of, and intended to evoke, this very passage.

[11] The relevant stanza (see *Libro de las honras*, f. 11) is:

   'Sic turtur viduus solet,
   Sic cycnus moriens solet,
   Sic luscinia conqueri:
   Heu me miseram,
   O dolor, ò dolor.'

[12] In encouraging Victoria to achieve further compositional success, Pesserio once again refers to the swan, but this time not in relation to the myths of swan song, but as the bird of Apollo, the god of music: he calls upon Victoria to be like 'a swan seeking the lofty stars on Apolline wings' ('summa petens alis Phæbeis Sydera cygnus').

[13] See Palma, *Vida*, ff. 255v–256v, which includes a reproduction of these drawings. Margarita is also reported as having treasured a book of engraved miniatures of members of the House of Austria, *Santos de la Casa de Austria*, in which each portrait was accompanied by details of where that person was buried; see López-Vidriero, 'Por la imprenta', 202.

equivalent to the *Officium defunctorum* had (as far as we know) appeared previously in the Iberian world, and the book apparently spawned no successors there. Of the five Spanish composers who published *pro defunctis* polyphony before 1605 – Cristóbal de Morales, Juan Vázquez, Francisco Guerrero, Pedro Rimonte, and Victoria himself – four included their Requiem Masses as the final items in extensive collections of their Masses.[14] This way of publishing a Requiem remained the norm among Iberian composers – including Manuel Cardoso, Juan Esquivel, Francisco Garro, Duarte Lobo, and Filipe de Magalhães – for decades after the appearance of Victoria's 1605 publication: see Table 3.1. Several of these collections also include *pro defunctis* motets or items for the Absolution or Matins of the Dead, as did Victoria in 1605. Victoria had himself published Requiem polyphony at the end of his collections of Masses issued in 1583 and 1592:[15] the 1583 collection ends with his four-voice Requiem, while in the 1592 volume the same Requiem – again standing as the last Mass in the book – is followed by settings of two responsories *pro defunctis*. However, the fifth Iberian composer to have published *pro defunctis* music before the appearance of Victoria's 1605 publication, Juan Vázquez, took a different approach. His *Agenda defunctorum* is devoted entirely to music for the liturgies of the dead, and in this respect it resembles Victoria's *Officium defunctorum*.[16] Nevertheless, it differs markedly from the latter in that it is not a commemorative volume, and also in the scope of its contents: besides the Requiem Mass, Vázquez provided for Matins of the Dead polyphonic settings of the invitatory, all nine antiphons, the three lessons of the first nocturn, the first lessons of the second and third nocturns, and the ninth responsory, while for Lauds he set the Benedictus and *Requiescat in pace*.[17] The resulting book is more than twice the length (62 folios) of the *Officium defunctorum*.

Looking beyond the Iberian context to the outputs of music publishers elsewhere, there once again seem to be no precise equivalents to Victoria's

---

[14] Morales's five-voice Requiem appears at the end of his *Missarum liber secundus* first published by Dorico in Rome in 1544 (M3582); Guerrero included his Requiem as the last item in his *Liber primus missarum* (Paris: du Chemin, 1566; G4870), and the revised version of the work at the end of his *Missarum liber secundus* (Rome: Francesco Zanetto, 1582; G4872); Pedro Rimonte's six-voice Requiem likewise stands as the last Mass in his *Missæ sex* published by Pierre Phalèse the younger in Antwerp in 1604 (R1712).

[15] *Missarum libri duo* (Rome: Alessandro Gardano, 1583; V1431); *Missæ . . . liber secundus* (Rome: Francisco Coattino, 1592; V1434).

[16] Seville: Martín de Montesdoca, 1556; V996.

[17] The publication also includes the chant for the Matins psalms, the other Matins responsories, and the psalms and antiphons for Lauds, and the texts of the other lessons at Matins.

Table 3.1 Printed Requiems by Iberian composers to 1650, arranged by date of publication

Composer	Voices	Printed collection (and RISM siglum where one exists)	Date	Position of Requiem in the collection
Cristóbal de Morales	5	*Missarum liber secundus* (M3582)	1544	Final Mass (of 8)
Juan Vázquez	4	*Agenda defunctorum* (V996)	1556	At end of this collection of *pro defunctis* music
Francisco Guerrero	4	*Liber primus missarum* (G4870)	1566	Final Mass (of 9)
Francisco Guerrero	4	*Missarum liber secundus* (G4872)	1582	Final Mass (of 8) (a revised version of the Requiem published in 1566)
Thome Luis de Victoria	4	*Missarum libri duo* (V1431)	1583	Final Mass (of 9)
Pedro Rimonte	6	*Missæ sex* (R1712)	1604	Final Mass (of 6)
Thome Luis de Victoria	**6**	***Officium defunctorum*** (V1436)	**1605**	**Only Mass, with 1 *pro defunctis* lesson & 1 responsory**
Juan Esquivel	5	*Missarum ... liber primus* (E825)	1608	Final Mass (of 6)
Francisco Garro	8	*Opera aliquot ... Missæ quatuor ... defunctorum lectiones tres*	1609	Final Mass (of 4), with 3 *pro defunctis* lessons
Juan Esquivel	4	*Psalmorum, hymnorum ... tomus secundus*	1613	Final Mass (of 7) in the Mass section of the collection
Duarte Lobo	8	*Liber missarum* (L2591)	1621	Final Mass (of 8), followed by *pro defunctis* motet
Manuel Cardoso	6	*Missæ quaternis, quinis, et sex vocibus* (C1039)	1625	Final Mass (of 7), followed by 2 *pro defunctis* motets & 1 responsory
Francisco Dávila y Páez	8	Sebastián López de Velasco, *Libro de missas* (L2822)	1628	Final Mass (of 5) in the Mass section of the collection
Filipe de Magalhães	6	*Missarum liber* (M122)	1636	Final Mass (of 8), followed by *pro defunctis* motet
Duarte Lobo	6	[Second book of Masses] (L2592)	1639	Final Mass (of 7), followed by *pro defunctis* reponsory
Manuel Cardoso	4	*Livro de varios motetes* (C1042)	1648	Within *pro defunctis* section at end of the collection

Officium defunctorum, if one takes into account (in combination) the format of the volume (a choirbook only thirty folios in length), its contents (a single Mass, together with some music for other parts of the *pro defunctis* liturgy), and its purpose (of presenting the music composed for the exequies of a particular person). On the one hand, Italian presses did issue a significant number of single-composer collections with the title *Officium defunctorum* or variants thereupon from the 1580s onwards. However, these differ from Victoria's collection in three respects: none commemorates a particular occasion or figure; all make significantly more extensive provision for the Office of the Dead than did Victoria;[18] and all were issued in part-books rather than as choirbooks. Furthermore, one should note that the great majority of Requiem Masses by Italian composers which were published between 1560 and 1650 appeared not as part of such *Officia defunctorum* but – as in Spain and Portugal – within collections of Masses by a single composer (and were likewise typically placed as the final Mass within these collections).[19] Only a few Italian Requiems were issued in separate publications (and hence akin to Victoria's in this respect at least): two of the Requiems by Giovanni Matteo Asola,[20] and works by Giovanni Francesco Anerio,[21] Arcangelo Borsaro,[22] Mario Capuana,[23] and Lodovico Viadana.[24] In addition, one finds a few Italian publications containing

---

[18] However, not every such collection includes a Requiem Mass.

[19] Almost all of the relevant publications of Italian composers' Masses are in part-book format, rather than in choirbook format as was usual in the publications of Iberian repertoire. An exception is the *Missarum liber primus* of Costanzo Porta (Venice: Angelo Gardano, 1578; P5180). On the favouring of part-book over choirbook format by Venetian music publishers, even for collections of liturgical music, see Jane Bernstein, 'Made to Order: Choirbooks Publications in Cinquecento Rome', in M. Jennifer Bloxam, Gioia Filocamo, and Leofranc Holford-Strevens (eds), *Uno gentile et subtile ingenio: Studies in Renaissance Music in Honour of Bonnie J. Blackburn* (Turnhout: Brepols, 2009), 669–76, at 671.

[20] One of Asola's three four-voice Requiems was first issued as *Missa pro defunctis a quatro voci pari* (Venice: Angelo Gardano, 1576; A2529), and subsequently in A2530 (1585), A2531 (1590), and AA2530a (1598). Asola's three-voice Requiem appeared as *Missa defunctorum tribus vocibus* (n.d.; A2609).

[21] This Requiem was originally published in a collection of Anerio's Masses, *Missarum quatuor, quinque, et sex vocibus, missa quoque pro defunctis una cum sequentia, et resp. Libera me Domine . . . liber primus* (Rome: Giovanni Battista Robletti, 1614; A1110), but was later issued separately in publications of 1630 (A1111), 1649 (A1112), and 1677 (A1113).

[22] His eight-voice Requiem appeared as *Sacri sacrificii per gli defonti . . . a otto voci . . . opera decima* (Venice: Ricciardo Amadino, 1608; B3780).

[23] His eight-voice Requiem was published as *Missa octo vocibus duobus alternantibus choris ad organum modulanda* (Venice: Alessando Vincenti, 1645; C950). His four-voice Requiem appeared, together with music for Compline, in *Messa di defonti, e compieta a quattro voci . . . opera quarta* (Venice: Alessandro Vincenti, 1650; C953).

[24] *Missa defunctorum tribus vocibus* (Venice: Ricciardo Amadino, 1592), with later editions of 1598 (V1355) and 1667 (V1356).

more than one Requiem Mass as the sole contents, such as Antonio Brunelli's *Missæ tres pro defunctis,*[25] and Giovanni Cavaccio's *Missæ quatuor pro defunctis . . . pars secunda* and *Messe per i defunti.*[26]

In contrast with the situation in Italy, certain music publishers in Paris and the Low Countries did produce significant numbers of folio editions containing just a single Mass and using choirbook layout, and the majority of Requiems by French composers which reached print in the sixteenth and seventeenth centuries were indeed published in such a form: those by Pierre Clereau,[27] Simon de Bonnefond,[28] Pierre Certon,[29] Pierre Lauverjat,[30] Eustache du Caurroy,[31] Étienne Moulinié,[32] and Charles d'Helfer.[33] Of the sixteenth-century singleton Mass folio publications from northern presses, most appeared within a short period in the mid to late 1550s. They featured prominently in the output of Nicolas du Chemin in Paris between 1554 and 1557, with further examples between 1564 and 1568; Du Chemin issued two such publications in 1554 (one of which is Clereau's Requiem) and no fewer than twelve in 1556 (including Bonnefond's Requiem), with four more appearing in 1557. Seven single-Mass publications were issued by the Parisian press of Adrian le Roy and Robert Ballard between 1557 and 1559, and several more containing Masses by Lassus appeared from the same press in the 1580s; Phalèse of Leuven published a ten-volume series of Masses by Jacobus Clement (Clemens non Papa) between 1556 and 1560, and issued the same composer's Requiem in 1570;[34] and Plantin of Antwerp printed a Mass by Philippe de Monte as a separate item in 1579.[35] In the seventeenth century such single-Mass publications appeared in large numbers from the Ballard firm, which produced no fewer than 125 such editions in the period up to 1673.[36]

While in various respects these singleton Mass prints from Paris, Leuven, and Antwerp resemble Victoria's *Officium defunctorum*, there also exist significant distinctions in nature and function between many of

---

[25] Venice: Giacomo Vincenti, 1619; B4650.

[26] The former was published in Venice by Ricciardo Amadino in 1593 (C1551). This collection contains two Masses, and clearly the *pars prima* (of which I am unaware of a surviving copy) contained another two. All four Masses are in the *Messe per i defunti* (Milan: Simone Tini & Filippo Lomazzo, 1611; C1554).

[27] Paris: Du Chemin, 1554; C3186.   [28] Paris: Du Chemin, 1556; B3455.

[29] Paris: Le Roy & Ballard, 1558; C1713.   [30] Paris: Pierre Ballard, 1623; L1128.

[31] Paris: Pierre Ballard, 1636; D3618.   [32] Paris: Pierre Ballard, 1636; M3940.

[33] Paris: Robert Ballard, 1656; H4985.   [34] No copy of this 1570 edition has been located.

[35] *Missa ad modulum Benedicta es* (Antwerp: Christophe Plantin, 1579; M3315).

[36] These publications are discussed and listed in Laurent Guillo, *Pierre I Ballard et Robert III Ballard: Imprimeurs du roy pour la musique (1599–1673)*, 2 vols (Sprimont: Mardaga, 2003), I, 107–11.

them and the 1605 volume. Crucially, none of the singleton Requiem Mass prints are overtly commemorative as is Victoria's: no association with an individual or set of exequies is mentioned therein, and Jean-Paul Montagnier has observed, for example, that for none of the Requiems published thus by the Ballard firm in the seventeenth century can one establish with any certainty for whose exequies the piece concerned was written.[37] The similarities between some of the French prints and Victoria's lie in certain physical aspects of the books, and in their contents. The seventeenth-century editions of single Requiem Masses (those by Lauverjat, Du Caurroy, Moulinié, and Helfer) issued by the Ballard firm are of the same folio size as the *Officium defunctorum* (between 400 and 420 mm high, and between 270 and 290 mm wide): as discussed below, the typical size of printed choirbooks of polyphony by Iberian composers was larger than this by the period concerned. In addition, the *Missa pro defunctis quatuor vocum* of Lauverjat and the *Missa pro defunctis quinque vocum* of Moulinié, issued by Pierre Ballard in 1623 and 1636 respectively, bear comparison with the *Officium defunctorum* not only in size but also in length (at twenty and twenty-two folios respectively, they are lengthier than most of the single-Mass publications of the sixteenth and seventeenth centuries, although still shorter than Victoria's) and in their inclusion of a modest amount of additional material besides the Requiem itself: Lauverjat provided settings of the third responsory for each nocturn of Matins of the Dead (in addition to a setting of *Libera me Domine de morte*), and Moulinié a motet for the Elevation at Mass and settings of Psalm 129 and of *Libera me Domine de morte*. However, it is important to note that while Victoria's volume was of course intended to stand alone as a separate commemorative book (and clearly circulated thus, as we shall see), the single-Mass prints issued by Du Chemin and other northern publishers were of a kind that allowed or encouraged purchasers to assemble several such Masses to form anthologies, and the single-Mass publications of the Ballard firm in the seventeenth century were frequently sold thus in groups.[38] Earlier publishers sometimes made this option explicit by presenting singleton Mass editions as parts of a series; the resulting book, if one purchased the set, would resemble the *Liber missarum* type of collection, of which the renowned earliest extant example is Andrea Antico's *Liber quindecim missarum* (Rome, 1516[1]), and which was later represented

---

[37] Jean-Paul C. Montagnier, *The Polyphonic Mass in France, 1600–1780: The Evidence of the Printed Choirbooks* (Cambridge University Press, 2017), 251–3.

[38] See Guillo, *Pierre I Ballard*, I, 107.

by Jacques Moderne's *Liber decem missarum* (Lyons, 1532[8]) and by the single-composer collections of Masses which became the dominant kind, such as Moderne's *Liber octo missarum* of music by Pierre Colin (Lyons, 1542; C3307), the Dorico and Moderne publications of Morales's Masses in the 1540s and early 1550s, and the *Missarum liber primus* of Palestrina (Rome: Valerio & Luigi Dorico, 1554; P655). Standing part-way between such *Liber missarum* collections and the singleton Mass publications of Du Chemin and Le Roy & Ballard is Pierre Attaingnant's project to print twenty Masses in seven volumes (and thus in groups of three or, in one case, two, per volume) under the general title *Viginti missarum* in 1532.[39] In 1568 Nicolas du Chemin gathered twenty of his previous singleton Mass editions into a two-volume set, under the title *Missarum musicalium*;[40] the fact that he intended such anthologising when initially publishing singleton Masses is indicated by his use of signatures in those separate editions which allowed for their assembly into groups with sequential signatures.

The commemorative function of the *Officium defunctorum* aligns it to some extent with the *libros de exequias* considered in Chapter 2. It rendered the ephemeral musical element of María's exequies durable and allowed it to be perused, admired, and emulated, just as *libros de exequias* permitted readers (whether or not they had been present at the exequies concerned) to consider at leisure the fine points of the ephemeral decoration and its rich symbolic content, and to use them as exemplars for future exequies. However, while the printing of such festival books in the Iberian world became increasingly common during the seventeenth century, none have been identified that include (for example) a motet performed at the relevant exequies, and although the *Libro de las honras* describing the Jesuit exequies for María in 1603 devotes considerable space to reproductions of the ephemeral art created for the occasion, it incorporates no music. Such a tradition did exist in Lutheran cities in the same period, where printed *Leichenpredigten* reproduced the sermon and

---

[39] The copies of the set at the Boston Athenæum and the Österreichische Nationalbibliothek in Vienna include the whole series bound as a single book. The *sextus liber* includes Jean Richafort's Requiem as one of its two Masses. In 1557 and 1558 Le Roy and Ballard published three books containing three Masses each, and each with the title *Missæ tres*: A1384 (Jacques Arcadelt), 1558[2] (Claudin de Sermisy, Claude Goudimel, and Jean Maillard), and C1715 (Pierre Certon).

[40] Among the ten Masses in the second volume is Bonnefond's Requiem. On this project see Kate van Orden, *Music, Authorship, and the Book in the First Century of Print* (Berkeley, Los Angeles, and London: University of California Press, 2014), 41. Du Chemin had previously, in 1554, incorporated Clereau's Requiem into a larger volume entitled *Missæ duodecim*, which included Clereau's *Missæ quatuor*.

epitaphs from a funeral as well as (often) a funerary Lied, and it was also common to issue a single funeral motet or cantional lied as a separate souvenir pamphlet.[41] The published festival-book account of the Venetian exequies for Cosimo II de' Medici in 1621 announces publication of the music for the occasion, composed by Monteverdi and others, but no copy of such a publication is known.[42] There are, however, the books that present the music (for *intermedi*, and opera) for Medici weddings in the sixteenth century and at the start of the seventeenth, including Peri's *Euridice* published in 1601.[43] John Butt has commented thus in relation to the function of these and similar publications:

One especially common use of print throughout Europe was to commemorate a specific event such as a court celebration or funeral. Here the edition was normally designed as a reflection of something that was effectively unrepeatable, a way of distributing the aura of that event to a wider audience, but certainly not as a record of an enduring 'work' or as a prescription for later performance. Something similar might apply to the more extravagant prints of early seventeenth-century Italian secular music (opera and monody).[44]

Lorenzo Bianconi (to whom Butt here refers) remarks, regarding the publication of the complete scores of Italian courtly operas in the early decades of the new century:

These publications serve less as the basis of future performances (i.e. the musical 'reproduction' of what, in reality, is a unique and unrepeatable theatrical event) than as simple souvenirs: retrospective testimony to the splendour of some politically and/or artistically important 'happening', the self-glorification of a court in the eyes of its peers.[45]

[41] See Stephen Rose, 'Schein's Occasional Music and the Social Order in 1620s Leipzig', *Early Music History* 23 (2004), 253–84, and chapter 3 of the same author's 'Music, Print & Authority in Leipzig during the Thirty Years' War', unpublished PhD thesis, University of Cambridge (2002).

[42] See *Esequie fatte in Venetia dalla natione fiorentina al serenissimo D. Cosimo II* (Venice: appresso il Ciotti, [1621]), and Paolo Fabbri, *Monteverdi* (Torino: E.D.T., 1985), 240.

[43] The sixteenth-century publications of music for Florentine intermedi are *Musiche fatte nelle nozze dello illustrissimo duca di Firenze il Signor Cosimo de Medici* (Venice: Antonio Gardano, 1539), and Cristofano Malvezzi, *Intermedii e concerti, fatti per la commedia rappresentata in Firenze nelle nozze del Serenissimo Don Ferdinando Medici e Madama Christiana di Lorena Gran Duchi di Toscana* (Venice: Giacomo Vincenti, 1591).

[44] John Butt, 'The Seventeenth-Century Musical "Work"', in Tim Carter and John Butt (eds), *The Cambridge History of Seventeenth-Century Music* (Cambridge University Press, 2005), 27–54, at 35.

[45] Lorenzo Bianconi, *Music in the Seventeenth Century*, translated by David Bryant (Cambridge University Press, 1982), 74.

Butt and Bianconi may be correct that the majority of those who owned (for example) the 1609 or 1615 edition of Monteverdi's *Orfeo* were not principally interested in performing the work (although that hardly precludes performance of some of the contents by certain owners). But the balance of the two functions – as souvenir and as means of performance – was surely more equal than this in the case of the *Officium defunctorum*, which is both a souvenir of a 'happening' (like the editions of courtly operas) and a book which could be used to sing the polyphony required at any Requiem Mass; it is simultaneously (to return to Butt's phrases) 'a way of distributing the aura' of María's death and exequies and 'a record of an enduring work'. Indeed, the two functions are not only compatible but are crucially linked here: the performances of María's exequial music in Spain and beyond which were made possible through its printing sustained and increased the commemorative devotions for her. When Victoria sent copies of the book to institutions he cannot have intended that it would be treated simply as a commemorative object, but rather that his music for María would be sung again and repeatedly, not only to his credit, but also in her honour and for the sake of her soul.

Printing the *Officium defunctorum*

Libros de exequias were normally issued promptly after the events concerned, but more than two years elapsed between María's household exequies and the publication of the *Officium defunctorum*.[46] To be sure, there was a similar gap between Victoria's agreement with Julio Junti for the printing of his *Missæ, Magnificat, Motecta, Psalmi, et alia* (on 1 October 1598) and the appearance of the volume in 1600,[47] but this was a much more complex and substantial publishing task than the *Officium defunctorum*: ten partbooks, containing a repertory many times as large as that in the 1605 volume. It is possible that, had the royal court been in Madrid rather than Valladolid when María died and had the Descalzas thus continued to fulfil its previous role as part of the court's devotional ambit, this official record of the music sung at the Empress's

---

[46] The dedicatory epistle is dated 13 June 1605, and printing was complete by 25 August, the date of a letter from Victoria to the Chapter of Zaragoza Cathedral accompanying a copy of the book. The title page makes clear that all four copies we have of the *Officium defunctorum* represent the first edition: 'nunc primum in lucem æditum'.

[47] The agreement is transcribed in Vicente, *El mayordomo*, 59–61. Printing was to begin within six months of the agreement, but no deadline was stated for its completion.

exequies issued by the Royal Press would have reached print much more promptly. As it was, the circumstances were unpropitious: María's household was disbanded after her death, Juan de Borja left for Valladolid, and the King clearly did not fund the publication. As noted, it seems to have been left to Victoria to instigate the project.

Like his 1600 collection, Victoria's new volume was produced by the Royal Press in Madrid. The bookman responsible was Juan Flamenco (Joannes Flandrus in Latinised form), foreman of the Press from 1597 until his death in 1612. He worked on behalf of two members of the Junti/ Giunta family of printers and booksellers, Julio Junti de Modesti and his nephew Tomás Junti.[48] In addition to royal commissions, many individuals arranged for their works to be published by the Royal Press, which had a reputation for fine typography. No contract between Victoria and the printer has been located, but we do possess the contract between Victoria and Junti for the *Missæ, Magnificat, Motecta, Psalmi, et alia* of 1600,[49] and also the agreement between Alonso Lobo and Juan Flamenco (on behalf of Julio Junti) for Lobo's *Liber primus missarum* (L2588) issued in 1602; in this latter case, Victoria acted as an intermediary between Lobo and Flamenco regarding the printing of and payments for the volume, as mentioned in Chapter 2.[50] Victoria dedicated his 1600 collection to Philip III, and the title-page bears the royal coat of arms, but the contract reveals that it was the composer, not the King, who paid for publication, and it seems likely that the *Officium defunctorum* was likewise privately funded, although – by way of contrast – in 1598 Philip II had ordered that the costs of printing the *Missæ sex* (R1937) by the late Philippe Rogier

---

[48] On the Giunta/Junta/Junti family in Spain, and the Royal Press established by Philip II in 1594, see: William Pettas, *A History and Bibliography of the Giunti Printing Family in Spain, 1526–1628* (New Castle, Del.: Oak Knoll Press, 2005), especially 68–73; Verónica Rioja Fernández, 'Aspectos de la impresión musical durante la etapa madrileña de Victoria', in Ana Sabe Andreu (ed.), *Tomás Luis de Victoria 1611–2011: Homenaje en el IV centenario de su muerte* (Ávila: Diputación de Ávila, 2011), 207–67, at 221–6; Maurice Esses, *Dance and Instrumental diferencias in Spain during the 17th and early 18th centuries*, 3 vols (Stuyvesant: Pendragon, 1992–1994), I, 89–90; Jaime Moll, *De la imprenta al lector: estudios sobre el libro español de los siglos XVI al XVIII* (Madrid: Arco/Libros, 1994), 133–41; Pérez Pastor, *Bibliografía madrileña*, I, xxix–xxxv; Vicente, *Tomás Luis de Victoria: Cartas*, 27–30. For a discussion of the Press's output of printed polyphony, see Tess Knighton, 'Preliminary Thoughts on the Dynamics of Music Printing in the Iberian Peninsula during the Sixteenth Century', *Bulletin of Spanish Studies* 89 (2012), 521–56, at 540–3.

[49] Pérez Pastor, *Bibliografía madrileña*, III, 518–19.

[50] For transcriptions of the relevant contemporary documents, see Vicente, *El mayordomo*, documents 34, 35, and 41.

(again undertaken by Juan Flamenco at the Royal Press) be met from the royal purse.[51]

The *Officium defunctorum* was a much more modest project than the choirbooks of Rogier's and Lobo's Masses printed by the Royal Press. Publishers' charges per printed leaf varied in accordance with the size and quality of the paper (which constituted the largest single component of the costs of printing), as well as the elaborateness of the edition. The paper used for the *Officium defunctorum* is significantly smaller than that employed for the Rogier and Lobo choirbooks, and of markedly lower quality than that constituting Lobo's book. Furthermore, the *mise en page* is very crowded in comparison to that in these books: economising on paper was clearly a priority. Finally, the music pages bear much less decoration than in the earlier choirbooks. Similar comparisons with, for example, the choirbooks of Victoria's music printed in Rome in the 1580s again highlight the modesty of the *Officium defunctorum*. This assessment of the book may seem surprising, since modern writers have tended to regard it as a magnificent example of the music printer's art. For example, José Maria Llorens Cisteró describes it as a 'very luxurious edition',[52] and Daniele Filippi as 'very elegant in its spacious *mise en page*'.[53] We might indeed have expected the book to reflect in its lavish production the elevated and monumental status of the work it contains, as if that work – set apart thus by Victoria as no other of his works were – deserved and so must necessarily have received particularly magnificent treatment in print. More generally, as Jane Bernstein has observed, printed folio choirbooks functioned as 'sumptuous presentation objects' directed at existing or potential patrons,[54] and Victoria certainly used the 1605 volume thus. Why, then, is the *Officium defunctorum* not more sumptuous, particularly given its commemorative and dynastic functions? We can only speculate. Perhaps Victoria had limited funds available for the project, or chose to divert only restricted funds towards it. With a substantial published output

---

[51] The text of the royal order is transcribed in Nicolás A. Solar-Quintes, 'Nuevos documentos sobre ministriles, trompetas, cantorcicos, organistas y capilla real de Felipe II', in *Miscelánea en homenaje a monseñor Higinio Anglés*, 2 vols (Barcelona: Consejo Superior de Investigaciones Científicas, 1958, 1961), II, 866. In the dedicatory epistle of the volume, addressed to Philip III, Géry de Ghersem (who had edited the collection) reminds the new king that his father had decided to cover the costs of its production.

[52] 'edición muy lujosa'; José Maria Llorens Cisteró, 'Victoria, Tomás Luis de', in Emilio Casares Rodicio, José López-Calo, and Ismael Fernández de la Cuesta (eds), *Diccionario de la Música Española y Hispanoamericana*, 10 vols (Madrid: Sociedad General de Autores y Editores, 1999–2002), X, 854.

[53] 'elegantissima nella sua *mise en page* ariosa'; *Tomás Luis de Victoria*, 167.

[54] Bernstein, 'Made to Order', 670–1.

to his name, perhaps he did not see the need to contract with the Royal Press for this work to appear in so impressive and hence expensive a form as (for example) did his younger acquaintance Alonso Lobo, whose *Liber primus missarum* was his first foray into print. Perhaps, finally, the *Officium defunctorum* was intended decorously to reflect in its relative unostentatiousness the famed tempering of majesty with sobriety and modesty which was so heavily emphasised in the hagiographical accounts of María's life, death, and burial, and which likewise was central to depictions of the Clarist nun Margarita, the volume's dedicatee.

As just mentioned, the relatively modest nature of Victoria's publication is manifest partly in the paper size. It was printed on a size of paper which had been commonly used for printed choirbooks of Masses from the 1530s until the 1570s, and which belongs to the general category of paper-size known as 'royal'.[55] The paper-type represented by the *Officium defunctorum* had sheet dimensions in the region of 600×420 mm.[56] In a folio book such as this, each sheet was folded once along the longer edge, producing in the case of this paper-size a leaf (or folio) size of about 420×300 mm before trimming. Such trimming resulted in varying folio sizes among the surviving copies of a publication: the four known copies of the *Officium defunctorum* have leaves varying in height between 400 mm and 418 mm, and in width between 270 mm and 280 mm.[57]

This size of folio volume – typical (as mentioned) of printed choirbooks of Masses for a significant part of the sixteenth century – is represented by Victoria's first publication of Masses, issued by Angelo Gardano in Venice in 1576 (V1427), and the book of his Masses published by Francesco Coattino in Rome in 1592 (V1434), but his second such collection (Rome: Domenico Basa and Alessandro Gardano, 1583; V1431) has a much larger page-size (540×390 mm), produced by using broadsheet format, whereby each folio of the royal-size paper forms a leaf of the book,

[55] Regarding this paper size, see for example Philip Gaskell, *A New Introduction to Bibliography* (Oxford: Clarendon Press, 1974), 73.

[56] The three sixteenth-century examples of 'royal' paper given in Gaskell, *A New Introduction*, 73, measure 570×435, 600×440, and 580×420 respectively. Mary Lewis gives a size of about 580×420 for paper of this category in the mid-sixteenth century: *Antonio Gardano, Venetian Music Printer, 1538–1569: A Descriptive Bibliography and Historical Study*, 2 vols (New York and London: Garland, 1988, 1997), I, 39.

[57] The page measurements are as follows: Biblioteca Musicale Governativa del Conservatorio di Santa Cecilia, Rome: 410×280 mm; Basilica di San Giovanni in Laterano, Archivio Musicale, Rari, st. mus. 43: 418×278; Biblioteca Apostolica Vaticana, Cappella Giulia XV.2: 410×278; Segorbe, Archivo de la Catedral: 400×270. Thus the Segorbe copy has been more severely trimmed than the three Roman copies.

rather than having been folded to form a bifolio.[58] This format was used for four other choirbook publications of music by Victoria, and three by his compatriot Francisco Guerrero, all issued in Rome between 1581 and 1585 under the auspices of the publisher Domenico Basa. Christophe Plantin of Antwerp adopted a similarly prodigious book size for five publications of Masses issued between 1578 and 1587,[59] and his successors Jan and Balthasar Moretus retained this format for their publications of the Masses (including two Requiem Masses) and Magnificat settings of the Portuguese composer Duarte Lobo between 1605 and 1636,[60] while a cheaper alternative for printing such monumental choirbooks in Portugal was the royal press of Craesbeeck in Lisbon, which issued collections by Manuel Cardoso, for example. It was this very large format that Juan Flamenco in Madrid employed for the collections of Masses by Philippe Rogier and Alonso Lobo mentioned above. These volumes have dimensions of approximately 550×400 mm,[61] and thus resemble (for example) Victoria's Roman editions in choirbook format of the 1580s rather than the *Officium defunctorum*, which was the only publication of polyphony by Flamenco and the Royal Press to use the smaller size.

The contract for the *Liber primus missarum* of Alonso Lobo gives us the price per leaf which the Royal Press charged the composer: one third of a *real*.[62] Given that the *Officium defunctorum* was printed on smaller and lower-quality paper, has shorter and less elaborate prefatory matter, and uses more modest decoration on the music pages, we can presume that Victoria paid significantly less per sheet than did Lobo. Each copy of the

---

[58] I am grateful to Jane Bernstein for furnishing me with this information.

[59] Unlike the Roman editions just described, Plantin's volumes use exceptionally large paper, with the sheets folded into bifolios, rather than broadsheet layout. The 1578 publication is described in the Plantin *Index librorum* of 1584 as 'in maximo folio regali': see Voet, *The Golden Compasses: A History and Evaluation of the Printing and Publishing Activities of the Officiana Plantiniana at Antwerp*, 2 vols (Amsterdam: Vangendt / New York: Abner Schram, 1969–1972), II, 162, n. 4. Voet gives the size of the volume as 550×407 mm: see his *The Plantin Press (1555–1589): A Bibliography of the Works Printed and Published by Christopher Plantin at Antwerp and Leiden*, 6 vols (Amsterdam: Van Hoeve, 1980–1983), III, 1097.

[60] For example, Armindo Borges gives measurements of 570×424 for the *Cantica Beatæ Mariæ Virginis* (1605; L2590) and 560×420 for the *Liber missarum* (1621; L2591). See Borges, *Duarte Lobo (156?–1646): Studien zum Leben und Schaffen des portugiesischen Komponisten* (Regensburg: Gustav Bosse Verlag, 1986), 116 and 128. The copy of the Moretus edition of Palestrina's *Hymni sacri* (1644; P741) in Rome, Basilica di San Giovanni in Laterano, Archivio Musicale, measures 593×470.

[61] Once again, the sizes of the surviving copies vary significantly depending on trimming. For example, the copy of Lobo's *Liber primus missarum* in Rome, Basilica di San Giovanni in Laterano, Archivio Musicale (Rari, st. mus. 21), measures 537×393.

[62] The contract is transcribed in Pérez Pastor, *Bibliografía madrileña*, II, 39. See also Stevenson, *Spanish Cathedral Music*, 262–3.

Officium defunctorum has only thirty folios, and it is therefore safe to assume that the cost per copy charged by the printer was well under ten *reales*.[63] On 1 February 1605, Victoria entered into a financial deal to obtain 720 *ducados*,[64] and both Robert Stevenson and Alfonso de Vicente speculated that this was to fund the printing of the *Officium defunctorum*.[65] However, while Victoria may well have used part of this sum to pay the printer, it is unrealistic to suppose that this was the sole purpose of the financial transaction concerned: if each copy of the *Officium defunctorum* cost less than ten *reales*, the sum of 720 *ducados* (7,951 *reales*) would have paid for 800 or more copies, and it seems most unlikely that the print run was so large. The initial print run of Victoria's previous publication with the Royal Press, the *Missæ, Magnificat, Motecta, Psalmi, et alia* of 1600, was 200,[66] while the print runs of the Rogier and Lobo choirbooks were smaller still: 100 and 130 respectively. Several scholars have estimated a figure of 500 as an average print run for music books in the mid to late sixteenth century, although numbers varied widely, reflecting (for example) differences in format.[67] Dorico contracted with Cristóbal de Morales to print 525 copies of his *Missarum liber primus*,[68] and Plantin produced approximately 375 copies of the *Octo missæ* of George de La Hèle,[69] while the folio publications of single Masses by the Ballard firm in the seventeenth century had print runs of between 300 and 400.[70] The Plantin-Moretus folio

[63] However, as noted below, when Victoria sent a copy of the book to the chapter of Zaragoza Cathedral he requested a reward of 4 *ducados* (that is, just over 44 *reales*), claiming that this was the sum the book had cost. See Vicente, *El mayordomo*, 13. Presumably Victoria was overstating the cost per book, in order to allow for the fact that only a proportion of those to whom he sent the book would furnish payment and that not all copies would be thus 'sold'.

[64] The contract between Victoria and Isabel Díaz y Poe is transcribed in Pérez Pastor, *Bibliografía madrileña*, III, 520.

[65] Stevenson, *Spanish Cathedral Music*, 366; Vicente, *Tomás Luis de Victoria: Cartas*, 29–30.

[66] The contract allowed the publisher to print an additional 100 copies, on condition that they not be sold until the year following the initial publication. The contract is transcribed in Pérez Pastor, *Bibliografía madrileña*, III, 518–19.

[67] See: Jane Bernstein, *Music Printing in Renaissance Venice: The Scotto Press (1539–1572)* (Oxford University Press, 1998), 117, where she proposes 500 as the average print run for commissioned music books; Samuel Pogue, *Jacques Moderne, Lyons Music Printer of the Sixteenth Century* (Geneva: Librairie Droz, 1969), 45, who considers 500 as an approximate norm, and 'probably a maximum' for Moderne; and Richard Agee, *The Gardano Music Printing Firms, 1569–1611* (University of Rochester Press, 1998), 423 n. 27.

[68] Suzanne Cusick, *Valerio Dorico: Music Printer in Sixteenth-Century Rome* (Ann Arbor, Mich.: UMI Research Press, 1981), 297–301.

[69] Lavern J. Wagner, 'Some Considerations on Plantin's Printing of De La Hèle's *Octo Missae*', *De Gulden passer* 64 (1986), 49–59, at 57.

[70] Guillo, *Pierre I Ballard*, I, 232–3. Guillo estimates that the print runs for quarto publications of *airs* or motets by the Ballard firm were around 500.

volumes of Duarte Lobo's Masses and Magnificat settings were printed in numbers varying between 130 and 350.[71] Towards the upper end of the spectrum for publications of polyphonic music was Francisco Guerrero's *Sacræ cantiones* of 1555, published in part-book format by Martín de Montesdoca in Seville, which had a print run of 750 copies.[72] Significantly larger print runs between 1,000 and 1,500 are found among some instrumental collections published in Spain, but these were unusual within the context of Spanish publishing (including music publishing).[73] At the other end of the spectrum, the lowest print run of which I am aware for a Spanish publication of sacred polyphony in this period is forty copies, as contracted between the composer Diego de Bruçeña and the printer Susana Muñoz in 1620 for a book of Masses, Magnificat settings, and motets.[74]

As mentioned, the elegance and clarity of the *mise en page* characteristic of the Rogier and Lobo choirbooks published by the Royal Press is notably lacking in parts of the *Officium defunctorum*, which frequently has a cluttered appearance. Beyond the aesthetic aspect, this had consequences for singers reading from the book. The problem was caused not by the smaller page size *per se*, but by two factors: use of music type which was unsuitably large for the space available, and the attempt to accommodate the music on as few pages as possible. Flamenco employed the same music type as he had for those previous choirbooks (with a printed staff height of 21.5 mm),[75] but the printed area of the page in Lobo's *Liber primus missarum* is 502×306 mm, whereas that in the *Officium defunctorum* is just 355×227 mm.[76] The issue is highlighted by comparison with printed

---

[71] Borges, *Duarte Lobo*, 116, 128, and 151.

[72] The contract is transcribed in Klaus Wagner, *Martín de Montesdoca y su prensa: contribución al estudio de la imprenta y de la bibliografía sevillanas del siglo XVI* (Seville: University of Seville, 1982), 114–15. The contracted print run of 1008 copies of Andrea Antico's *Liber quindecim missarum* (Rome, 1516) was apparently exceptional; see Catherine Weeks Chapman, 'Andrea Antico', unpublished PhD thesis, Harvard University (1964), 55.

[73] See John Griffiths, 'Printing the Art of Orpheus: Vihuela Tablatures in Sixteenth-Century Spain', in Iain Fenlon and Tess Knighton (eds), *Early Music Printing and Publishing in the Iberian World*, DeMusica 11 (Kassel: Edition Reichenberger, 2006), 181–214, at 191. See also Knighton, 'Preliminary Thoughts on the Dynamics of Music Printing', 530.

[74] See Alejandro Luis Iglesias, 'El maestro de capilla Diego de Bruçeña', in Crawford and Wagstaff (eds), *Encomium musicæ*, 455–62, at 464.

[75] This is only slightly smaller than the staff height of the *grosse musique* type made by Hendrik van den Keere for Plantin in the 1570s; see Guillo, *Pierre I Ballard*, I, 112, and (for a full-sized reproduction of the typeface) Hendrick Vervliet, *Sixteenth-Century Printing Types of the Low Countries* (Amsterdam: Menno Hertzberger, 1968), 335.

[76] When the type owned by Julio Junti de Modesti – that is, the type used by the Royal Press – was valued upon his death in 1619, just two sets of type for polyphonic music were listed, one for

folio choirbooks similar in page-size to the *Officium defunctorum*: Antonio
Gardano had acquired music type with a staff height of 15.8 mm (that is,
only about three-quarters of the height of the type used for the *Officium
defunctorum*) for his folio volumes of Magnificat settings by Morales and
others and of Masses by Jacobus de Kerle, published in 1562, and his heirs
working in Venice continued to use this type, for example for Victoria's
Liber primus qui Missas of 1576.[77] The type employed for the 1572 edition
of Palestrina's *Missarum liber primus* issued by the heirs of Dorico produced a staff height of 16.5 mm,[78] while type with a staff height of 15 mm
created for Le Roy and Ballard in 1555 and used for folio choirbooks was
still employed by the Ballard firm for its seventeenth-century folio publications of Masses.[79] In such books, considerably more music could thus
be accommodated comfortably and elegantly on a page than was the case in
the *Officium defunctorum*, and their type sizes allowed for a layout with
usually twelve staves per page,[80] whereas for the 1605 publication
Flamenco fitted only nine on each page. (In his Rogier and Lobo volumes,
with their larger folios, he had adopted the twelve-staves-per-page layout.)

The use of this over-large type worked against the printer's clear anxiety
to use as few sheets as possible, an anxiety apparent in decisions made
when casting off the music. Whereas in the Rogier and Lobo choirbooks
Flamenco had consistently begun new Mass sections on new openings
(even where that meant leaving numerous blank staves), in the *Officium
defunctorum* a new 'movement' sometimes begins immediately after the
previous one on the same page or even part-way along the same staff line.
In addition, the concluding passage of the final item (*Tædet animam
meam*) was printed with all voice-parts on a single page, rather than spread
across the facing pages of an opening as in normal choirbook layout.

'canto de órgano grande' and one for 'canto de órgano chico'; see Moll, *De la imprenta al lector*,
136. (In addition, there were two sets of type for chant; Juan Flamenco had issued a number of
liturgical books with chant, including editions of the *Graduale Romanum* and *Missale
Romanum* in 1597.) We can presume that the former, larger set was that used for all three of the
polyphonic choirbook volumes, including the *Officium defunctorum*, and that the smaller set
was used for Victoria's part-book collection of 1600.

[77] See Agee, *Gardano*, 121.   [78] Measurements taken from the copies in the British Library.
[79] See Guillo, *Pierre I Ballard*, I, 112 and 210.
[80] This is the number of staves per page in – citing just a few examples of books with similar page-
size to the *Officium defunctorum* – Antico's *Liber quindecim missarum* (1516), Du Chemin's
1556 edition of Bonnefond's Requiem, Gardano's 1562 collection of Magnificat settings by
Morales and others, Gardano's collection of Masses by Kerle of the same year, Palestrina's
Missarum liber primus (both the original 1554 edition and that of 1572), and Victoria's *Liber
primus* (Angelo Gardano, 1576) and his 1592 collection of Masses published by Coattino.
The singleton Mass publications by the Ballard firm in the seventeenth century typically have
ten staves per page.

The restricted number of staves per page and the limited amount of music that could be fitted onto each staff (because of the large type-size) certainly brought disadvantages when casting off. For example, if twelve staves per page had been available, the whole of the Gradual respond would have fitted on one opening. As it was, not only did this respond need more than a single opening, but the entire Gradual (including the verse) could not quite be accommodated on two openings, and hence it was decided to locate the beginning (just five breves' worth) of the Gradual on the same opening as the end of the preceding item (the Kyrie), with undesirable results: the singer(s) on the Bassus part have just three notes of the Gradual before they need to turn the page (Figure 3.1).[81] In addition, there was insufficient space for a large initial (of the size of the 'K' for the final Kyrie, for example) to mark the beginning of the Gradual, and the small initial 'R' which was employed suggests to the eye that the Gradual is merely a sub-section rather than a new liturgical item.[82]

[81] There is another oddity in the typesetting of the Gradual: the opening chanted phrase of the verse – 'In memoria æterna' – was laid out across the two pages of an opening, because this chant phrase was too long to be accommodated within the space available on one staff, and the cramped layout of the book left only one staff free on each page once the polyphony for the rest of the Gradual verse was fitted in. This layout led one modern editor, Rudolf Walter, to believe (astonishingly) that this chant line was to be distributed between the two Cantus parts, with Cantus II taking over in the middle of a melisma where the chant moves to the right-hand page: see the critical commentary to his edition, *Tomás Luis de Victoria: Missa pro defunctis cum responsorio Libera me domine, 1605, 6 gemischte Stimmen a cappella*, Musica divina 15 (Regensburg: Friedrich Pustet, 1962), p. ii. It seems that a user of the Segorbe Cathedral copy was likewise confused by this layout, since they wrote out the opening words of the chant incipit ('In memoria eter') underneath the part of the melisma for 'æterna' on the *recto*. The layout of the opening is unhelpful to singers since the chant incipit was positioned below the Cantus parts for the polyphonic section of the verse, even though the chant precedes the polyphony in performance. On the initial opening of the *Libera me Domine* (ff. 21v-22) the lack of space resulted in the first chanted section ('de morte æterna . . . tremenda') being placed beneath Cantus I, but the second ('Dum veneris . . . ignem') beneath Cantus II. Neither is, in fact, the most logical position for these chanted sections, since the Altus carries the chant during most of the polyphonic sections here.

[82] The uncomfortably crowded typesetting in parts of the *Officium defunctorum* is exemplified by the final Agnus Dei in the Altus: the first system of this Agnus, on f. 15, is set with no spacers between notes, and the initial 'A' signalling where this Agnus begins could not be accommodated on the staff itself before the clef (as it is in the other five voice parts), but is placed before the beginning of the underlaid text, with the odd result that the text appears to begin 'A qui tollis'. The tight spacing of notes here also meant that accidentals could not be positioned on the staff, but appear underneath it, in the horizontal space occupied by the text. Another example of poor *mise en page* in the *Officium defunctorum* resulting from the paucity of staves may be found on f. 9r, the first recto of the Offertory. The Altus sings the lengthy plainchant incipit ('Domine Iesu Christe Rex gloriæ') of this section, and ideally this incipit would of course have begun at the start of a new staff, but instead it commences part-way along a staff, the first part of which is occupied by the final notes of the Cantus II music on this opening.

Figure 3.1 *Thomæ Ludovici de Victoria abulensis, sacræ cæsareæ maiestatis capellani, officium defunctorum, sex vocibus, in obitu et obsequiis sacræ imperatricis* (Madrid: Juan Flamenco, 1605), f. 6; Biblioteca Apostolica Vaticana, Cappella Giulia XV.2. © 2018 Biblioteca Apostolica Vaticana

The constricted layout and typesetting of the 1605 edition might have proved unhelpful to singers in several respects, including the placement of chant incipits, and text underlay. The space between staves was in many cases insufficient to allow a syllable to be aligned with the relevant note where that note lies below the staff,[83] and the syllable had instead to be printed beside the note (to left or right): several occurrences may be seen in the Bassus part in the final verse and Kyrie of *Libera me Domine* (Figure 3.2). This practice might in some instances have caused performers to sing the syllable one note earlier or later than Victoria intended.[84] One such case occurs in the Tenor I part at 'in nomine Domini' in the Benedictus (see b. 39 of the edition in the Online Appendix): it seems likely that Victoria wished 'Do-' to be sung after the descending octave leap here, but since the low note concerned fell below the staff in the 1605 edition, the syllable was put underneath the preceding note, and the next syllable of this word ('mi', in b. 40) was likewise misplaced for the same reason. That such deficiencies in underlay would have troubled Victoria is indicated by a manuscript containing psalm settings by the composer, copied in Rome by his acquaintance Francisco Soto, which was clearly made with publication in mind: among the detailed annotations in Victoria's hand are numerous corrections of underlay, and on an associated sheet now bound as part of the manuscript Victoria sets out instructions to the editor or publisher of the psalms, and asks Soto specifically to take great care with the correction of the book and to ensure that the underlay is accurate.[85]

More serious than the attempts to squeeze a quart into a pint pot in printing the *Officium defunctorum* was the inadequacy of the fount for printing this particular work, a problem exacerbated by incompetence in typsetting. In several sections of the Requiem ligation is commonplace, especially in the voice part carrying the chant (most often Cantus II).

---

[83] The problem is particularly apparent in the Bassus part, since low *F* is quite frequent in the music of the *Officium defunctorum*, and there are several occurrences of *E* and *D*.

[84] Such misleading underlay was avoided in the Rogier *Missæ sex* of 1598, and is very rare in Lobo's *Liber primus missarum*, even though the latter uses a larger text fount for underlay than either the *Missæ sex* or the *Officium defunctorum*. This larger text fount makes an appearance in the *Officium defunctorum* for a 'Christe tacet' indication on f. 5r and an 'Altus' designation on f. 9r.

[85] 'Señor Francisco de Soto: suplico a v(uestra) m(erce)d se tenga gran cuenta con la coreption deste libro, y que la letra se ponga en su lugar.' The manuscript concerned is Rome, Biblioteca Nazionale Vittorio Emanuele II, Ms 130. Victoria's instructions are reproduced and transcribed in Vicente, *Tomás Luis de Victoria: Cartas*, 78–9. On this manuscript, see also Klaus Fischer, 'Unbekannte Kompositionen Victorias in der Biblioteca Nazionale in Rom', *Archiv für Musikwissenschaft* 32/2 (1975), 124–38, and Esteban Hernández Castelló, 'Il manoscritto musicale 130 della Biblioteca Nazionale Vittorio Emanuele II di Roma', *Revista de Musicología* 29/1 (2006), 326–31.

Figure 3.2 *Officium defunctorum*, f. 25; Biblioteca Apostolica Vaticana, Cappella Giulia XV.2. © 2018 Biblioteca Apostolica Vaticana

Unfortunately, Flamenco was inexperienced in printing ligatures,[86] and the type he used for the project was ill suited to doing so: the pieces of type for breves and longs, when juxtaposed, left gaps between note-heads (and therefore do not clearly indicate a ligature), whereas, for example, the sets of type used by Angelo Gardano for Victoria's 1576 collection of Masses, by Alessandro Gardano for the 1583 collection (containing his four-voice Requiem), and by Francesco Coattino for his 1592 collection (again including his four-voice Requiem) produced no significant gaps of this kind. The gaps are more apparent still in the passages sung in plainsong, where black full notation is used,[87] whereas the equivalent chant passages in the four-voice Requiem as printed in 1583 and 1592 are markedly more satisfactory in their juxtaposition of note-heads to form ligatures, and indeed the printing of the Requiem Mass chants in the Madrid Royal Press's *Missale cantorale proprium missarum de tempore* (1597) was executed better than that in the 1605 publication. In the surviving copies of the *Officium defunctorum* these gaps have mostly been filled in by hand in the polyphonic sections (but not in the plainchant sections), a laborious job clearly undertaken in the printer's shop.[88] Besides these technical imperfections, the typesetting of ligatures in the *Officium defunctorum* was carelessly or ignorantly done, without a proper understanding of the rules for rhythmic interpretation of ligatures: there are no fewer than nine instances (almost all in the voice carrying the chant) where the second, third, or fourth note of a ligature was given an extraneous downward tail on the left.[89] To be sure, in all cases but one these stems would probably have been ignored by singers who understood the relevant

[86] Ligature are very rare in the printed Masses of Rogier and Lobo. None of the works in these two books is a chant-based cantus-firmus Mass, which might have involved significant use of ligation. Furthermore, only one type of ligature – *cum opposita proprietate* – occurs in Lobo's *Liber primus missarum*, and in the *Missæ sex* all but five of the ligatures are of this type.

[87] The only symbol used in the plainsong sections throughout the *Officium defunctorum* is the punctum (or black brevis).

[88] These numerous amendments to ligatures and other changes to stems were implemented rather carelessly, such that although most of them correspond in all four copies, no copy carries all of the same amendments as any other. The copy from the Cappella Giulia has significantly fewer of the amendments than do the other three copies.

[89] There are also errors in the typesetting of the text which suggest that those responsible were unfamiliar with the liturgical texts involved. The second syllable of 'cadant' in the Offertory falls at the beginning of a new opening, and was set with a capital 'D' as if it were a separate word, 'Dant'; in addition, in the Index at the end of the volume the initial word of the Matins lesson 'Tedet' is given as two words, 'Te det'. An error in the texting of the Altus part in the Benedictus – where 'in nomini Domini' was printed instead of 'in nomine Domini' – was (mis)corrected in the Segorbe Cathedral copy to 'in nomine Domine'. The error remained uncorrected in the other three surviving copies.

rules, since what was printed was clearly meaningless given where these tails appear,[90] but one instance (in the Cantus II part at the end of the Introit antiphon) might have caused the singers to err, singing the previous note – to which this downward tail could plausibly have been seen as applying – as a long rather than a breve. (This is the breve in b. 30 of the edition in the Online Appendix.)

Clearly, then, Victoria was not present at the print shop when galley-proofs were pulled from the press, since if he had been he would surely have asked for stop-press corrections at the relevant points.[91] That he was not involved at this stage is very surprising, given that the book was being printed in Madrid, although one notes that the contract between Victoria and Junti regarding publication of the 1600 collection does not mention proofreading by the composer, and indeed the printing of the 1600 collection was likewise rather careless.[92] The fair copy with which Victoria provided Flamenco cannot of course have employed the erroneous ligature-stems, but there may be a simple explanation for the occurrence of these errors. It seems likely that Victoria wrote oblique ligatures at these

---

[90] Two of the extraneous stems were crossed out by hand in the Segorbe Cathedral copy.

[91] Comparison of the surviving copies reveals five stop-press corrections. Four of these are present in all copies except that in Segorbe Cathedral: folio numbers were added to folios 5 and 6, the second digit was added to the folio number 12, and an extraneous letter 'e' after the second syllable of 'leonis' in the second Tenor part of the Offertory was removed. In addition, a folio number was added on folio 2; this correction is present in the Cappella Giulia and San Giovanni in Laterano copies, but not those in the Conservatorio di Santa Cecilia or Segorbe Cathedral. One paste-down correction was made after the press-run was complete: this correction is to the second note of the *cum opposita proprietate* ligature in the Bassus four notes from the end of the Introit antiphon. Inked amendments in all copies, besides those already mentioned, include diagonal lines drawn between text and notes in two places where the printer had failed to align the syllables and music properly. In addition, in *Tædet animam meam* a sharp sign was added to the g' in the Cantus at the second syllable of 'dimittam' (b. 6 in the edition in the Online Appendix), an important annotation, since the Cantus continues to recite on this pitch for the subsequent four syllables. This sharp is present in all surviving copies except that from the Cappella Giulia. The amendments to underlay and addition of an accidental just described were apparently mistaken by Daniele Filippi as 'small signs of use' ('piccoli segni d'uso') of the copy from the Chiesa Nuova (*Tomás Luis de Victoria*, 38, n. 40). There are no such 'signs of use' in this copy, nor in that from the Cappella Giulia. The other two surviving copies do however bear a few markings relevant to performance: there are more such indications in the Segorbe Cathedral copy than in that belonging to San Giovanni in Laterano, and the Segorbe copy also underwent numerous repairs, including the replacement of missing sections of staff, notes, *custodes*, and text. It therefore seems likely that the Segorbe copy was much more heavily used in performance than was any of the three Roman copies.

[92] For a discussion of the errors in the printing of the 1600 collection, see Huff, 'Demystifying the Life and Madrid Works', 214–16. Some consideration of how frequent it was for composers to be present during the printing of their works, in order to check proofs, may be found in Stephen Rose, 'Publication and the Anxiety of Judgement in German Musical Life of the Seventeenth Century', *Music and Letters* 85 (2004), 22–40, at 27.

points; the compositor, lacking such a ligature-shape in the set of type, was obliged to use separate notes, and for some reason thought that employing a note with a descending stem to show the second note of the oblique ligature was correct.[93] In the copy of Victoria's Requiem dating from 1613 in a choirbook for the Abbey of Saints Ulrich and Afra in Augsburg, oblique ligatures are employed at all but one of the relevant points; likewise, the 'Tremens' verse of the responsory *Libera me Domine*, which had earlier been published as part of Victoria's four-voice Requiem, has an oblique ligature at the place concerned (at the end of the verse, in the Bassus) in the edition of 1592.

Flamenco produced a much more plain and undecorated book for Victoria in 1605 than he did for Alonso Lobo in 1602 or when publishing Rogier's works in 1598: the initials used after the first opening of music are simply black Roman majuscules, and almost all of them lack the decorative frames which the initials in the earlier publications include, as do the 'residuum' markings.[94] These frames are absent even on the first opening of music, although here more elaborate initials appear: the two Cantus parts have initials from a set of calligraphic Gothic letters, the Altus and Tenor I from a set of Roman majuscules with background decoration of foliage and birds, and the Tenor II and Bassus an historiated initial with a scene from the Song of Songs showing the King and the female beloved. The 'R' here is therefore echoed in the figure of the 'rex', and the reference is presumably to Song of Songs 1.3: 'introduxit me rex in cellaria sua'. Daniele Filippi believes that this historiated initial was chosen specifically as part of the purpose of the book to honour and commemorate María,[95] but this seems unlikely, since this set of decorative initials – like the others employed in the 1605 volume – had already been used by Flamenco in the Rogier and Lobo collections, and the 'R' from this set happened to show the scene described. If Flamenco had particularly wished to use an initial appropriate to the purpose of the book here, he might have commissioned

---

[93] In contrast, the printers of Victoria's four-voice Requiem did employ oblique ligatures.

[94] Both the crowded *mise en page* and the limited decoration of the *Officium defunctorum* again become vividly apparent if one compares the book's appearance with the presentation of the five-voice Requiem by Juan Esquivel in that composer's *Missarum ... liber primus*, published three years later by Artus Taberniel in Salamanca. (Iain Fenlon has argued that Flamenco's choirbooks influenced Taberniel's work: 'Artus Taberniel: Music Printing and the Book Trade in Renaissance Salamanca', in Fenlon and Knighton (eds), *Early Music Printing*, 117–46, at 137–8.) The layout of the music (with twelve staves to a page) is notably generous and uncluttered: each item begins on a new opening, and each item and section opens with an initial with fine decorative border and part-name.

[95] *Tomás Luis de Victoria*, 167.

or purchased one incorporating (for example) one of the conventional images of mortality used in the ephemeral decoration at exequies. Valerio and Luigi Dorico, when printing the five-voice Requiem of Morales in the *Missarum liber secundus*, used such an initial 'R', showing the figure of death as a skeleton, and in his edition of the same book published in 1551 (M3583), Moderne similarly employed an initial 'R' which incorporates an image of death striking down a king with his spear, and the inscription 'memento mori'.

Much the most prominent decorative element of the 1605 volume is the woodcut which occupies a significant portion of the title page (Figure 3.3), but even here we find evidence of the desire to minimise costs: the arms shown are not María's marital arms (i.e. those which she employed after her marriage to Maximilian), but rather her paternal arms, the imperial arms of Charles V. In contrast, the *Libro de las honras* recording the Jesuits' exequies for her, published by Luis Sánchez and released early in 1604, did show María's marital coat of arms, in which her father's arms are impaled (i.e. placed side by side) with those of her husband. These arms of María appear both on the title page (Figure 3.4) and on the reproduction of one of the hieroglyphs therein (f. 58), and we can safely presume that this was the version of her arms used for the iconographical scheme at the Jesuit exequies, and furthermore that María utilised these impaled arms as a widow. For the *Officium defunctorum*, however, Flamenco reused an existing woodcut dating back to Charles's reign, rather than commissioning one specially for the project.[96] Such reuse was common practice at the Royal Press, being most apparent among the frequent appearances of the royal coat of arms in their publications between 1594 and 1628,[97] and there exist some other cases of Spanish title pages of the late sixteenth and early seventeenth centuries which use Charles V's imperial arms; but the decision by the Royal Press not to use María's marital arms at the opening of a book whose purpose was to commemorate her and her exequies specifically is striking, given not least the importance of heraldry at such

---

[96] In contrast, the engraving of the royal coat of arms of Philip II, surrounded by musical instruments, used for the title page of Victoria's *Missarum libri duo* of 1583 was apparently made for that publication, since it bears the date 1583.

[97] These all incorporate the arms of Portugal (reflecting Spanish Habsburg rule of Portugal from 1581 onwards), but this element is of course absent from the arms used in the *Officium defunctorum*, which are those of Charles V. The inventory of Julio Junti de Modesti's printing materials, mentioned above, includes twelve engravings of royal arms of various sizes, some of which are there described as old; see Moll, *De la imprenta al lector*, 139 ('ocho planchas de armas reales, grandes y chicas') and 140 ('quatro armas reales viejas'). The imperial arms used for the 1605 publication may have been among them.

Figure 3.3 *Officium defunctorum*, title page; Biblioteca Apostolica Vaticana, Cappella Giulia XV.2. © 2018 Biblioteca Apostolica Vaticana

LIBRO
DE LAS HONRAS QVE
HIZO EL COLEGIO DE
la Cópañia de IESVS de Madrid, à la M.C
de la Emperatriz doña Maria de Auftria,fundadora
del dicho Colegio,que fe celebraron a 21.
de Abril de 1603.
DIRIGIDO ALA SERENISSIMA INFANTA
Soror Margarita de la Cruz,monja de la orden de fanta Clara
en el fagrado monefterio de las Defcalças de Madrid.

CON PRIVILEGIO.
En Madrid,Por Luis Sanchez. Año M.DC.III.

Figure 3.4 *Libro de las honras*, title page; Getty Research Institute

exequies and the fact that Margarita (the dedicatee) would naturally have
taken note of the choice of arms. Presumably – given the apparently limited
finances for this project – it was not thought worth the cost of commissioning a reproduction of her marital arms, since, two years after her death,
there would be no call for their use in any other publication: to employ an
old woodcut showing her paternal arms (which she would have used before

her marriage) was therefore the best solution in such circumstances.[98] I have so far been able to identify one previous use of precisely the same woodcut as was employed by Flamenco for Victoria's volume, on the title page of a book published in Toledo by Juan de Ayala in 1552, *La Pregmatica del obraje de los paños*.[99]

When Victoria received the completed copies of the book, he must have been taken aback by yet another significant deficiency in the pressmen's work. Three of the four surviving copies reveal that some printed sheets were gathered and folded before the ink was dry, so that ink passed from one side of an opening to the other.[100] The problem is most apparent in the copy belonging to San Giovanni in Laterano, where several pages are so badly smudged that elements of the music and text are unclear, in a way that would have been distracting to singers.[101]

No other book bearing Victoria's name on the title page had emerged from the press with such defects as the *Officium defunctorum*, and no such problems had been evident in the previous choirbooks issued by the Royal Press under Flamenco's foremanship.[102] Victoria had himself been responsible on Alonso Lobo's behalf for confirming (before payment was made) that Lobo's book of Masses had been well printed.[103] It is clear that Flamenco took less care over Victoria's 'librito' than he had over his earlier music publications, despite its special commemorative function and its ties to the royal house which he served as printer, suggesting that he regarded it as a private commission rather than an official project for the House of Austria, and it may be that his contract with Victoria left the composer in possession of all of the copies to distribute, rather than Flamenco retaining

---

[98] The arms on the title page of the *Officium defunctorum* feature the imperial bicephalous eagle as 'supporter' (behind the escutcheon), the imperial crown above, the collar of the Order of the Golden Fleece below, and on either side Charles's columnar device: the pillars of Hercules with the motto *plus ultra*.

[99] The title page is reproduced in Francisco Vindel, *Manual gráfico-descriptivo del bibliófilo hispano-americano (1475–1850)*, 10 vols (1930–1931), VII, 236 (item 2261).

[100] In addition, there is significant smudging of some of the staff lines on f. 21r of the copy belonging to the Conservatorio di Santa Cecilia.

[101] The worst affected pages are f. 13v, f. 18r, and f. 19v, but the problem occurs on no fewer than thirteen pages, i.e. almost one quarter of all the pages bearing music.

[102] Navigating the 1605 volume was hindered by the folio numbering, which has a striking level of inaccuracy for so short a book: f. 4 is numbered 11, f. 14 is numbered 13, and f. 27 is numbered 23, in addition to which several folios are unnumbered in the Segorbe Cathedral copy and one folio in the copy in the Conservatorio di Santa Cecilia, Rome (omissions which were corrected during the press-run, as evinced by the other two surviving copies). As in other respects, the other two polyphonic choirbooks printed by the Royal Press in Madrid are much more accurate in their foliation.

[103] See the notarial document of 4 March 1603, transcribed in Vicente, *El mayordomo*, 95.

some to sell. The premature folding of the printed sheets shows the precipitate manner in which the work was completed: as mentioned above, the dedicatory epistle bears the date 13 June 1605, and the copies were in Victoria's hands by 25 August, so the printing took no more than ten weeks.[104] Flamenco may have shoehorned this job into a restricted space because of the need to complete larger (and perhaps more prestigious) projects which required his presses and pressmen. The third volume of Fray José de Sigüenza's *Historia de la Orden de San Jerónimo* – dedicated to Philip III (the Jeronymite order was particularly favoured by Spanish royalty) – was published by Flamenco and the Royal Press in 1605, and the *tasa* (the legally required determination of the maximum sale price) reproduced in the preliminary matter is dated 21 June of that year, a week later than the date of Victoria's dedicatory epistle. Since the title page and other preliminaries of Sigüenza's book would have been printed only after certification of the *tasa*, the completion of this project presumably either overlapped with the printing of Victoria's volume (if Flamenco had sufficient presses and pressmen available to do both simultaneously), or – perhaps more likely – was kept on hold until the *Officium defunctorum* was finished.[105] While just four copies of the *Officium defunctorum* are known, dozens survive of Sigüenza's volume.

Circulation of the *Officium defunctorum*

Overall, evidence for the book's dissemination – in the form of surviving copies and references to copies now apparently lost – is rather limited, and very few manuscript copies of the music have been located. This has been taken by some as an indication that the book was less widely known and used than others of Victoria's publications, a situation which has been attributed to various factors, such as the restricted repertoire which it

---

[104] It was common practice in Spanish early-modern publishing for the main body of the book – without the title page and other preliminary matter – to be printed first, and submitted for approval and licensing. However, the preliminary matter of the *Officium defunctorum*, including the dated dedicatory epistle, forms part of the same gathering as the start of the music, and so printing commenced after the date given in the epistle. On the legalities and practices of publishing in early-modern Spain, see for example Jaime Moll, 'Problemas bibliográficos del libro del Siglo de Oro', *Boletín de la Real Academia Española* 59 (1979), 49–107, and José Simón Díaz, *El libro español antiguo: análisis de su estructura*, 2nd edition (Madrid: Ollero & Ramos, 2000).

[105] Another project may have been waiting in the queue for completion while the *Officium defunctorum* was printed: the *Tercera parte de la vida de Christo* by Cristóbal de Fonseca bears a *tasa* dated 12 August 1605.

contains, its occasional nature, and the fact that by the time of its publication the *pro defunctis* settings by Morales and Guerrero were long established as the staple in Iberian cathedrals.[106] The indications we currently
have of the circulation of the *Officium defunctorum* may all or almost all
reflect the work of distribution undertaken by Victoria himself. He sent out
copies to institutions and to individuals, in accordance with the common
practice whereby composers expected remuneration for at least
a proportion of the copies thus offered. Two of the covering letters accompanying copies of the *Officium defunctorum* have been found: those sent to
the Chapter of Zaragoza Cathedral on 25 August 1605 and to the
Collegium Germanicum in Rome on 1 February 1606.[107] The similarity
in their wording exemplifies the 'mass mailing' nature of his marketing
campaigns.[108] In encouraging a favourable response from the recipients, he
avoided false modesty in these letters, describing the work as 'such an
excellent *Officium*' ('officio … tan excelente').[109] The copies would in
many cases have been inspected by musicians of the institutions and
households concerned, who would make a recommendation regarding
the book's usefulness, and the recompense granted to Victoria might
have depended on assessment of its quality as a printed object (about
which he presumably had anxieties) as well as the perceived merits of the
music.[110] Victoria may have exaggerated when claiming (in the letter to
Zaragoza) that he had sent copies 'to all the princes and prelates of Spain',
or indeed (as he put it in the letter to the Germanicum) 'to all the princes

[106] See Javier Marín López, 'Tomás Luis de Victoria en las Indias: de la circulación a las
reinvención', in Vicente and Tomás (eds), *Tomás Luis de Victoria*, 403–60, at 438; Alfonso de
Vicente, *Tomás Luis de Victoria: Cartas*, 115; Juan Ruiz Jiménez, 'Recepción y pervivencia de la
obra de Victoria en las instituciones eclesiásticas de la Corona de Castilla', in Vicente and
Tomás (eds), *Tomás Luis de Victoria*, 301–51, at 317.

[107] The letter to Zaragoza Cathedral is transcribed and discussed in Vicente, *Libros y obras*, 36–8;
the letter to the Collegium Germanicum is reproduced, transcribed, and discussed in Vicente,
Tomás Luis de Victoria: Cartas, 110–15.

[108] See the overview of Victoria's practice in Daniele Filippi, 'Carlo Borromeo and Tomás Luis de
Victoria: A Gift, Two Letters and a Recruiting Campaign', *Early Music* 43 (2015), 37–51, at 40.
Multiple copies of the covering letters were typically copied by other scribes and signed by
Victoria. The letters accompanying copies of the *Officium defunctorum* sent to Zaragoza
Cathedral and the Collegium Germanicum were copied by different scribes.

[109] The letter to Zaragoza Cathedral begins: 'Este officio hize para la muerte y honras de la
Emp(eratri)z N(uestra) Seño(ra) que este en el cielo el qual por ser a gloria de Dios tan
excelente le he embiado a todos los Principes y Perlados de España.' The letter to the Collegium
Germanicum begins with identical wording except that 'España' is replaced by 'Cristiandad'.

[110] For an example of a printed book being returned to the composer without recompense because
of the number of misprints it contained, see Rose, 'Publication and the Anxiety of Judgement',
29. For instances of the process of musical and physical inspection of printed books on behalf
of the institution receiving them, see *ibid.*, 32–3.

and prelates of Christendom'. The *Officium defunctorum* certainly reached the cathedrals of Albarracín,[111] Badajoz, Burgos, Cádiz, Plasencia, Sigüenza, Teruel, and Zaragoza, and another copy belonged to the Royal Chapel in Granada,[112] but it is striking that many of the wealthiest and musically most important cathedrals – including Seville and Toledo – are absent from this list. Victoria surely included these also in his circulation of copies (we know, for example, that he sent his previous two collections, of 1592 and 1600, to Toledo),[113] but traces of this in chapter acts and inventories have been lost or not yet located. We find a similar situation in the New World: no evidence has emerged of copies received or held by the most important ecclesiastical institutions, such as Mexico City Cathedral, although an inventory from as late as 1902 of Morelia Cathedral (formerly Valladolid de Michoacán) lists a copy of the six-voice Requiem.[114]

[111] A 1619 inventory of the cathedral's music books has an entry for 'quatro quadernos de música de Vitoria, a saber es una misa de diffuntos de seis voces de emprenta'. See Alberto Cebolla Royo, 'Inventarios "musicales" de la catedral de Albarracín (ss. XIV–XX)', *Nassarre. Revista Aragonesa de Musicología* 25 (2009), 137–76, at 156; see also the discussion in Vicente, *Libros y obras*, 39, n. 78. The reference to 'quatro quadernos' (i.e. *cuadernos*) is intriguing: the item concerned comes at the end of the list of choirbooks containing polyphony, described in most cases as 'libro grande', and at the start of the list of sets of part-books, and the latter are all described using the same term as is applied to the copy of Victoria's six-voice Requiem, 'quadernos'. It may be that the compiler of the inventory simply made an error regarding the copy of Victoria's music here, and that there was a single copy of the *Officium defunctorum*, rather than four copies; it is less likely that the reference is to a set of manuscript part-books of Victoria's Requiem, since six part-books would have been required, not four (and the compiler of the inventory elsewhere specifies where a part-book is missing from a set), and since he notes that the copy is printed ('de emprenta'). His placing of the volume within the list is logical, since it was smaller and shorter than the 'libros grandes' preceding it. Furthermore, in inventories of the Cathedral's music books of 1681 and 1743 we find a 'quaderno impresso de Victoria' which is very likely to be the same item, alongside other single volumes described using the term 'quaderno'; see Cebolla Royo, 'Inventarios', 160 and 168. As discussed below, the equivalent term 'quaternio' is used in the inventory of the Brussels court chapel to describe a copy of the *Officium defunctorum* and other books with relatively few pages, and not as a means of referring to part-books. In December 1606 Victoria made arrangements to secure payment of 150 *reales* from the cathedral for 'some books' ('unos libros'), one of which was surely the *Officium defunctorum*; see Vicente, *Libros y obras*, 39, n. 78.

[112] On the copy in Cádiz, see Máximo Pajares, 'Cádiz', in Casares (ed.), *Diccionario de la Música Española*, II, 862. The Badajoz Cathedral inventory of 1631 which includes the *Officium defunctorum* is transcribed in Alonso Gómez Gallego, 'La música de Victoria en la Catedral de Badajoz', *Revista de Musicología* 35/1 (2012), 337–63, at 342. On the copy sent to Teruel see Vicente, *Tomás Luis de Victoria: Cartas*, 48.

[113] See Javier Marín López, 'Music Books for an *iglesia principal y calificada*: The 1657 Inventory of Jaén Cathedral in Context', in Tess Knighton and Emilio Ros-Fábregas (eds), *New Perspectives on Early Music in Spain*, Iberian Early Music Studies 1 (Kassel: Reichenberger, 2015), 108–62, at 126–7.

[114] See Javier Marín López, *Los libros de polifonía de la Catedral de México*, 2 vols (Jaén: Universidad de Jaén, and Madrid, Sociedad Española de Musicología, 2012), II, 1122. His

In his letter to Zaragoza Cathedral, Victoria added a postscript note informing the Chapter that 'the cost of this booklet is four *ducados*',[115] and it is quite likely that he made a similar addition to the letters sent to other cathedrals: certainly, two such institutions (Plasencia and Teruel Cathedrals) paid him precisely this amount (i.e. 1,500 *maravedís*),[116] and Burgos Cathedral granted him 1,700 *maravedís*.[117] However, Sigüenza Cathedral paid 2,250 *maravedís*,[118] while the authorities at Zaragoza Cathedral were more generous still, sending Victoria 100 *reales* (= 3,400 *maravedís*), more than double the sum he had mentioned in his letter to them. There are indications that in the cases of his printed collections of 1592 and 1600 Victoria sent out some copies already bound and others unbound,[119] but the brevity of the *Officium defunctorum* in comparison to his previous folio publications may have encouraged him to circulate it unbound. Certainly, the copy received by Plasencia Cathedral in 1608 was unbound,[120] and that belonging to the Royal Chapel in Granada remained unbound in 1610.[121] Since Teruel Cathedral paid Victoria the same amount as did Plasencia, and Burgos gave a similar sum, those copies were likewise surely unbound, and this may be true also of the three surviving copies in Rome: these retain what are probably their original bindings, and these bindings vary (so that they were therefore clearly not the result of Victoria arranging for multiple copies to be bound).[122] The copy belonging to the *capilla* of the Descalzas – which may have been used regularly – acquired a black-leather binding (as indicated by an inventory of 1608).[123]

source for this information was Francisco Ganegas Galván, 'Ynventario General de las obras de música que tiene el Archivo de esta Santa Iglesia', unpublished, Morelia, Archivo de Música de la Catedral, 1902.

[115] 'su preçio deste librito son quatro ducados'; transcribed in Vicente, *Libros y obras*, 37.

[116] See Vicente, *Tomás Luis de Victoria: Cartas*, 48–9.

[117] José López-Calo, *La música en la catedral de Burgos*, 14 vols (Burgos: Caja de Ahorros y Monte de Piedad del Círculo Católico de Obreros de Burgos, 1995–2004), IV, 108.

[118] See Javier Suárez-Pajares, *La música en la catedral de Sigüenza, 1600–1750*, 2 vols (Madrid: Instituto Complutense de Ciencias Musicales, 1998), II, 4.

[119] See Ruiz Jiménez, 'Recepción y pervivencia', 310–11, who also discusses the sums received by Victoria for these and other publications.

[120] See José López-Calo, *La música en la catedral de Plasencia (Notas históricas)* (Trujillo: Fundación Xavier de Salas, 1995), 38.

[121] See Vander Straeten, *La musique aux Pays-Bas*, VIII, 468.

[122] For example, the copy belonging to the Conservatorio di Santa Cecilia (and previously to the Chiesa Nuova of the Oratorians) has soft leather covers, while the binding (leather over boards) of the copy in the collection of San Giovanni in Laterano resembles closely those of the same institution's copy of Lobo's *Liber primus missarum*, and was surely undertaken by the same local bookbinder.

[123] 'Libro ynpreso en papel con la misa de requien de Victoria con cubierta de papelón y quero negro'. See Vicente, 'El entorno femenino', 237.

Besides the copies which Victoria 'offered' to ecclesiastical institutions, he would have sent copies to Margarita and (we can safely presume) to the King, but neither of these has left any known trace. A list of music books of the royal chapel drawn up by the chapelmaster Matheo Romero in 1612 does not include the *Officium defunctorum*, perhaps indicating that the work was not even within the performing repertory of the royal chapel.[124] One might have expected Juan de Borja to have possessed the volume, and indeed it has been presumed that one item in the post-mortem inventory of his music books, which were valued by none other than Victoria himself, was a copy of the 1605 book. However, the item concerned is described as a 'libro de misas de difuntos del maestro bitoria', that is, a book containing more than one Requiem Mass by the composer. While it is not impossible that this was an error, Victoria's participation in the drawing up of this inventory (which he signed) renders this unlikely, as does the fact that the item is listed at three points in the relevant documentation, always with the plural 'misas'.[125] This item was bought by the Duke of Lerma in the auction of Borja's books, and may logically be identified with the 'cartapacio grande de Vitoria de misas de requien' in an inventory drawn up shortly afterwards of the music books of the new collegiate church of San Pedro which he established on his estate in Lerma.[126] Note that here again, and independently, one finds the plural 'misas' (which recurs in a Lerma inventory of 1708), further reducing the likelihood of error. One suspects therefore that this book was not a copy of the *Officium defunctorum* but a manuscript copy of Victoria's two Requiem Masses, for four and six voices, perhaps commissioned by Borja or presented to him by the composer following María's death (and possibly before the *Officium defunctorum* appeared). Lerma paid for it the amount – 22 *reales* – stated in Victoria's valuation: the book was thus deemed by Victoria to have only a fraction of the value of any of the other choirbooks of Masses (printed and manuscript) in the

---

[124] This list is transcribed in Vicente, *El mayordomo*, as document 81, at 224–7. It does include the two other choirbook publications of polyphony from the royal press (Rogier's and Lobo's Masses), and a manuscript collection of Masses beginning with Clemens non Papa's Requiem.

[125] The post-mortem inventory is transcribed in Escrivà Llorca, 'Eruditio, pietas et honor', 288–96, and Vicente, *El mayordomo*, as document 70 (at 172–83); the relevant book is item 15 in the inventory. Another partial transcription is provided in Dadson, 'Music Books and Instruments', at 111–14. Dadson simply states that this item is the *Officium defunctorum*, and does not address the problem raised by the plural 'misas'. Juan Ruiz Jiménez likewise presumes that this book was the *Officium defunctorum*: see his 'Recepción y pervivencia', 315. The issue is discussed further in Escrivà Llorca, 'Eruditio, pietas et honor', 142, and Vicente, *Libros y obras*, 39.

[126] See Douglas Kirk, 'Churching the Shawms in Renaissance Spain: Lerma, Archivo de San Pedro Ms Mus. 1', unpublished PhD thesis, McGill University (1993), 61.

inventory, all of which were valued at 110 *reales* or more, and which included two of his own published collections. Outside the orbit of the Descalzas and of the royal court, it seems likely that Victoria sent the *Officium defunctorum* to senior members of the Austrian branch of the Habsburgs, but if so no evidence of such copies has been uncovered. In addition, we can presume that he would have sent one to the court of Albert and Isabella Clara Eugenia in Brussels, and what may well be this copy appears in an inventory of the music books of the Brussels chapel drawn up in 1607.[127]

However extensive and vigorous were Victoria's efforts to circulate the book, the fact remains that we know of only four surviving copies of the *Officium defunctorum*, a figure which contrasts notably with the three previous publications of polyphony by the Royal Press in Madrid: twenty-two copies (from the total print-run of 130) of Alonso Lobo's *Liber primus missarum* have been located, and seventeen of Rogier's *Missæ sex*,[128] while at least twelve libraries and archives possess one or more of the part-books of Victoria's *Missæ* of 1600 (of which the initial print run was 200). Furthermore, only one copy of the *Officium defunctorum* has been located in Spain (in Segorbe Cathedral),[129] and none are known in Portugal or the Americas.

It is particularly striking that the published *Index* of the vast music library of King John IV of Portugal, who was tireless in his efforts to

---

[127] The item is described as 'una quaternio missa de Requiem Ludovici de Victoria'. The term 'quaternio' appears to be used here for short items (such as a setting of *Te Deum*), which perhaps were less solidly bound than the items described as 'livres' in the inventory; 'quaternio' clearly does not mean 'part book' (not least because the term is applied here to items of folio size) as claimed by Anne Elizabeth Lyman, who tabulates the contents of the inventory in 'Peter Philips at the Court of Albert and Isabella in Early Seventeenth-Century Brussels: An Examination of the Small-Scale Motets, including an Edition of *Deliciae sacrae*', unpublished DMA thesis, U. of Iowa (2008), 70–71. The inventory is transcribed in François Lesure, 'Inventaire des livres de musique de la chapelle royale de Bruxelles en 1607', *Revue belge de musicologie* 5 (1951), 34–5. The copy of the *Officium defunctorum* is listed once again in an inventory of 1666: 'Item un grand livre Tome Ludovice de Victoria officiom [sic] defunctorum sex vocibus'. This wording was clearly copied directly from the title page of the 1605 publication. The relevant inventory is transcribed in Albert van der Linden, 'Un fragment d'inventaire musical du XVIIe siècle', *Revue belge de musicologie* 3 (1949), 43–4.

[128] These include seven in Spain, three in Portugal, three in the Americas, and two in Italy. The copy in Tournai was destroyed in the Second World War, and that in Zaragoza is apparently lost.

[129] On the history of this copy, and the transcription from it by José Perpiñán (made probably in 1897) which apparently formed the basis for Felip Pedrell's edition, see Magín Arroyas Serrano and Vicente Martínez Molés, 'La primera transcripción moderna del *Oficio de difuntos* de Victoria: el manuscrito del maestro José Perpiñán', *Revista de Musicología* 35/1 (2012), 473–89.

acquire repertoires of sacred music associated with the Spanish court, lists no copy of the work in print or manuscript, although we should remember that this *Index* is described on the title page as only the 'first part',[130] and a subsequent volume (if it was indeed printed) has not been located. While we thus have no evidence that John possessed Victoria's six-voice Requiem, it may be that he did own a copy of a *Missa pro defunctis* based upon Victoria's work. The intriguing entry in his music catalogue which suggests this concerns the triple-choir Requiem by Gabriel Díaz Bessón, whose music featured prominently in John's library. As mentioned in Chapter 2, following the opening in 1616 of the Convent of the Encarnación, a prestigious royal foundation next to the Royal Palace in Madrid, Díaz was engaged to provide music for exequies held there in memory of the convent's founder, Margaret of Austria. Thanks to the catalogue of João's music library, we know that this music was for three choirs, i.e. presumably for twelve voices, and that the Mass was 'based upon another Mass for six voices'.[131] Much the most likely candidate for this other Mass is Victoria's, given the context for which Díaz was composing:[132] connections between Margaret of Austria and the Empress María had been very close; Margaret's foundation of the Encarnación was inspired in part by the example of the Descalzas; and Díaz would almost certainly have known Victoria's six-voice work (and could well have been involved in performances of it), given his employment not only at court but also at the collegiate church of San Pedro in Lerma, which (as noted) may have possessed a copy of Victoria's music for María's exequies.

Beyond the Iberian world, the only surviving copies of the *Officium defunctorum* which have been located are the three in Rome.[133] Of these, the copy in the Biblioteca Musicale Governativa del Conservatorio di Santa

---

[130] *Primeira parte do index.* John did possess a copy of a later printed Requiem by a composer associated with the Descalzas, namely the eight-voice setting by Francisco Dávila y Páez, *maestro de capilla* at the Descalzas from 1607, which was published by the royal press in 1628 within the *Libro de misas* of Sebastián López de Velasco, who was likewise *maestro* at the Descalzas.

[131] *Primeira parte do index*, 340 (this is the second page so numbered), forming part of item 745: 'Esta Missa he feita sobre outra de seis'.

[132] Another, although weaker, candidate is Pedro Rimonte's six-voice Requiem, published in his *Missæ sex* of 1604.

[133] The copy belonging to San Giovanni in Laterano is presumably the 'libro di una Messa di Morti del Vittoria' which is the last item in a list of the music books belonging to the basilica when Cristoforo Guizzardi was chapelmaster, i.e. in 1620–1622. This list appears at the end of Ms 58 in the Archive of San Giovanni, and is transcribed in Raffaele Casimiri, *Il Codice 59 dell'Archivio Musicale Lateranense, autografo di Giov. Pierluigi da Palestrina* (Rome, 1919), 25. On Victoria's proactive marketing of his printed music to Roman institutions, see Noel O'Regan, 'Music Prints by Cristóbal de Morales and Tomás Luis de Victoria in Surviving

Cecilia came from the Chiesa Nova (the church of the Oratorians),[134] and presumably reflects Victoria's close connections with that Congregation, manifest for example in his friendship with the Oratorians and musicians Giovanni Giovenale Ancina and Francisco Soto, with both of whom Victoria corresponded from Madrid.[135] It may well be therefore that Victoria himself sent this copy to the Oratorians, perhaps via Soto (Ancina had died in 1604), who seems to have acted as Victoria's agent in Rome. Victoria used Soto as a recipient for money given as recompense for the copies of his publications which he sent out, including that of the *Officium defunctorum* dispatched to the Collegium Germanicum in Rome on 1 February 1606, as we know from the letter which he enclosed with that copy. Although the body of the letter was written by a scribe, Victoria added a postscript in his own hand in which he asks that the 'reply' (that is, the hoped-for recompense) from the Rectors of the Germanicum should be given to Soto. Victoria also took the opportunity in this postscript to remind the Rectors that he had been the first music director of the College, making it appropriate – he says – that they should reward him now.[136]

Signs that the music of the *Officium defunctorum* was copied for performance in the Iberian world during the seventeenth and eighteenth centuries are extremely few.[137] It may be that a seventeenth-century manuscript copy survives in Segorbe Cathedral (which holds, as noted, the only known Iberian copy of the printed book, and one which was clearly heavily used).[138] A 1657 inventory of music books belonging to Jaén Cathedral lists a copy of a Requiem by Victoria, but it is not clear whether this was the four-voice work or the six-voice, and (if the latter) whether this was a copy

---

Roman Inventories and Archival Records', in Knighton and Nelson (eds), *Pure Gold*, 113–31, at 114.

[134] Its provenance is given in an annotation on the front cover and an ink stamp on the recto of the front flyleaf.

[135] See Filippi, *Tomás Luis de Victoria*, 36–40, and particularly 38 n. 40 regarding the provenance of the relevant copy of the *Officium defunctorum*.

[136] 'y sepa V(uestr)a S(eñori)a que yo fui el primer maestro de ese colegio y que se me deve hazer merçed'; see the transcription and reproduction of the letter in Vicente, *Tomás Luis de Victoria: Cartas*, 110–11. A note in another hand records that the letter was received on 6 September (seven months after it was written), and that reply was made two days later. It also notes that 'un misa funerale in musica' was ordered, which may indicate that Victoria's music was used for a Requiem Mass at the College.

[137] Juan Ruiz Jiménez has observed that the representation of Victoria's works in Iberian manuscripts – including those for church instrumentalists – up to 1800 is low, particularly if compared with that of music by Morales and Guerrero; see 'Recepción y pervivencia', 320–22.

[138] I am grateful to Javier Marín López for this information, which he obtained from the archivist of Segorbe Cathedral.

of the 1605 print or a manuscript copy.[139] Besides this, three copies of *Tædet animam meam* dating from the late eighteenth century are in the Cathedral of Santiago de Cuba.[140]

The only (nearly) complete manuscript copy of the music in the *Officium defunctorum* so far discovered and dating from the seventeenth century is in Germany: this copy is incorporated in a choirbook of Requiem Masses copied in 1613 in Augsburg for the Imperial Benedictine Abbey of Saints Ulrich and Afra.[141] In the copy of Victoria's Requiem the parts are re-arranged so that the Cantus II part in the printed version (i.e. the part that most often bears the chant) is here presented as Cantus I,[142] but it is nevertheless clear that the copyist was working from a copy of the 1605 publication.[143] The presence of Victoria's Requiem in this book might reflect Habsburg connections (given Augsburg's importance within the Empire), or more generally the role of Augsburg in the printed music trade,[144] but it may be that the Fugger family of Augsburg, bankers to the Habsburgs, are of particular relevance.[145] The Fuggers were patrons of the Abbey (for example, paying for a new organ in 1580),[146] and at this period maintained their banking connections with Spain, as a means of

---

[139] See Marín, 'Music Books for an *iglesia principal y calificada*', 118–19 and 146. The inventory entry states that the copy concerned, originating as a separate booklet, was bound in with a manuscript collection of Requiem Masses and *pro defunctis* motets. As Marín notes, this manuscript was probably compiled between 1566 and 1576.

[140] See Javier Marín López, 'Tomás Luis de Victoria en las Indias', 438–9.

[141] Augsburg, Staats- und Stadtbibliothek, Tonkunst Schletterer 21. *Tædet animam meam* was not copied. The motet *Versa est in luctum* is placed after the responsory *Libera me Domine*, rather than before it as in the printed volume.

[142] However, in the opening polyphonic section of *Libera me Domine* the Cantus parts are not reversed in comparison to the printed version.

[143] However, the chant sections of the responsory *Libera me Domine* are significantly different from those in the printed version.

[144] See Stephen Rose, 'The Mechanisms of the Music Trade in Central Germany, 1600–40', *Journal of the Royal Musical Association* 130 (2005), 1–37, at 12–13.

[145] I am grateful to Barbara Eichner for making this suggestion. It may also be worth mentioning previous – indirect – connections between Victoria (or his music) and Augsburg: early in his career the composer enjoyed the patronage of Cardinal Otto Truchsess von Waldburg, Bishop of Augsburg; and Sebald Mayer's 1589 edition of Victoria's motets, published in Dillingen, has dedicatory epistles addressed to von Waldburg and to Johann Otto von Gemmingen, Dean of Augsburg Cathedral. On this edition, see Iain Fenlon, 'From Print to Public: The Milanese and Dillingen Editions of Victoria's Motets', in Javier Suárez-Pajares and Manuel del Sol (eds), *Estudios. Tomás Luis de Victoria. Studies*, Música Hispana, textos, estudios 18 (Madrid: Ediciones del ICCMU, 2013), 27–36.

[146] See Barbara Eichner, 'Sweet Singing in Three Voices: A Musical Source from a South German Convent?', *Early Music* 39 (2011), 335–47, at 345, and Franz Krautwurst, 'Die Fugger und die Musik', in Renate Eikelmann (ed.), *'Lautenschlagen lernen und ieben': Die Fugger und die Musik: Anton Fugger zum 500. Geburtstag* (Augsburg: Hofmann-Verlag, 1993), 41–8, at 43; this latter study considers more widely the musical patronage of the Fugger family.

demonstrating their commitment to the faith. Of the composers represented in the manuscript, Gregor Aichinger (organist of the Abbey) was organist to Jakob Fugger, and Christian Erbach was likewise in the service of the family, both of them dedicating printed collections to family members.

We have seen that the *Officium defunctorum* of 1605 represented an experiment in how to preserve widely in memory and for posterity the exequial music for a patron, as if it were a musical correlate of the *libro de exequias*, but Victoria then treated it in a similar fashion to his earlier and more conventional printed collections in terms of his marketing methods, and he would have made a good return on at least some of the copies which he circulated. As far as we can tell, the experiment remained an isolated and uninfluential one: the book spawned no successor publications in Habsburg circles or – apparently – beyond them. Nor does the book's dissemination seem to have engendered extensive incorporation of Victoria's Requiem into performing repertories within the musically more prominent institutions of the Spanish and Portuguese empires or the Holy Roman Empire. However, thanks to the existence of the copies which Victoria sent to Rome, the *Officium defunctorum* came to the attention of musical antiquaries in the eighteenth and nineteenth centuries, and began its rise to 'crowning' status within his output. This rise, traced in Chapter 5, may well have been aided by the way in which the music was packaged in 1605: as a separate, entire, and reasonably substantial 'work'. But first I turn to the music itself, considering to what extent Victoria's fashioning of his 'excellent *Officium*' was – like that packaging – distinctive.

4 | Fashioning the Requiem

The two most striking gestures in the music of Victoria's Requiem both occur in the motet *Versa est in luctum*. The first, often highlighted in commentaries on the piece, is used to portray the transformation of music into lament: 'My harp is turned into mourning and my organ into the voice of those that weep' ('vocem flentium'). As the word 'flentium' begins, an *f♯* in Tenor I clashes with a *b♭* in Tenor II, producing an acerbic diminished fourth.[1] (See the edition in the Online Appendix, b. 25.) The other most remarkable gesture – or, rather, series of gestures – follows a few breves later, and intensifies the initial statements of the plea which constitutes the remainder of the text, 'spare me, O Lord, for my days are as nothing' ('parce mihi, Domine, nihil enim sunt dies mei'): the upper voices end their phrases (at first on 'Domine', then repeatedly on 'mei') by leaping up a fifth onto the final unstressed syllable (b. 33–4, 38, and 40–1). This is highly abnormal behaviour at a phrase ending for the top voice in polyphony of the period. In so doing, the upper parts reach their peak note *e″*, a note used extremely sparingly throughout the *Officium defunctorum*, and not hitherto in *Versa est*.[2] At these moments the 'mœstum carmen' ('sad song') that Victoria conceived for María's exequies, praised by Pesserio in his prefatory poem, reaches its most intense. But while these two passages stand apart from their surroundings in the motet and the *Officium defunctorum*, *Versa est in luctum* is also, in multiple ways, integrated within and connected to the whole body of music that constitutes the *Officium defunctorum*. Beyond such integration and connection, I shall argue below that *Versa est* provides a concentrated epitome of an employment of harmonic and tonal *chiaroscuro* that marks the music published in that volume as a whole. In other respects also, and despite its variety of (for example) texture and pacing, the music of the *Officium defunctorum* is bound together to form a single entity made up of connected parts. Some of

---

[1] Those who have called particular attention to this moment include Samuel Rubio: 'El *Officium defunctorum* de Tomás Luis de Victoria', 20.

[2] On paper, the Gradual of the *Officium defunctorum* has a higher range in the Cantus parts, but as discussed below this item should be transposed downwards by a fifth in performance, the result being that the Cantus parts here do not reach even to *e″*.

the means employed to characterise this 'sad song' mark the piece as distinctive within Victoria's output (and contribute to its cumulative expressive power), and moreover single out Victoria's approach here to crafting a polyphonic Requiem as an idiosyncratic one. Modern listeners, I think, readily sense both that distinctiveness and aspects of the coherence just mentioned, and it is part of the purpose of this chapter to explore what creates these impressions.

Academic discourse of recent decades has tended to discourage the imposition of what are perceived as anachronistic concepts of coherence and unity in analysis of music of this period, together with emphases on compositional intentionality and – more broadly – on the reified work.[3] Of course, the cyclic Mass displays obvious musical unity, derived especially from the use of a single source of material for all 'movements'. Andrew Kirkman locates the reasons for the development of such musical unification within the music's ritual functions, and specifically in the ways in which Mass was perceived in the thirteenth to fifteenth centuries.[4] He argues that the unifying of the Mass Ordinary movements reflects and accentuates the interpretation of the entire Mass ritual as a reenactment of the Passion of Christ, such musical integration mirroring the thematic coherence of the Mass: 'Through the agency of the cyclic Mass, the unity that was felt to envelop the ritual as a whole in a consistent message

---

[3] In *The Imaginary Museum of Musical Works: An Essay in the Philosophy of Music* (Oxford: Clarendon Press, 1992) Lydia Goehr famously set out the thesis that the work-concept acquired the status of a regulative force in Western music only from about 1800 onwards. Of earlier periods she states, for example, that 'the idea of a work of music existing as a fixed creation independently of its many possible performances had no regulative force in a practice that demanded adaptable and functional music . . . Musicians did not see works as much as they saw individual performances themselves to be the direct outcome of their compositional activity.' (185–6) Reinhard Strohm, in a powerful critique of such scholarly problematising of the work-concept, has argued for the relevance of concepts of 'work-character' to consideration of music of the Renaissance: 'Looking Back at Ourselves: The Problem with the Musical Work-Concept', in Michael Talbot (ed.), *The Musical Work: Reality or Invention?* (Liverpool: Liverpool University Press, 2000). Goehr's and Strohm's positions, and other writings on the subject, are evaluated in John Butt's re-consideration of the issue of the work-concept as applicable to music of the early-modern era: 'What is a "Musical Work"? Reflections on the Origins of the "Work Concept" in Western Art Music', in Andreas Rahmatian (ed.), *Concepts of Music and Copyright: How Music Perceives Itself and How Copyright Perceives Music* (Cheltenham: Edward Elgar Press, 2015), 1–22. Butt covers some of the same issues, but with a narrower focus on the seventeenth century, in 'The Seventeenth-Century Musical "Work"'.

[4] Andrew Kirkman, *The Cultural Life of the Early Polyphonic Mass: Medieval Context to Modern Revival* (Cambridge University Press, 2010). Reinhard Strohm challenges Kirkman's downplaying of the 'internally driven' aesthetic motivations for unification in cyclic Masses, and their treatment as self-contained unified artefacts, in his review of the book in *Early Music History* 30 (2011), 261–70.

received the enhancement of a sonic marker that bound together its various parts.'[5] Beyond this, he notes that the unification of a Mass Ordinary setting and the choice of recurrent cantus firmus on which to base it rendered the resultant polyphonic cycle more apt for marking a particular occasion, and such a multi-section work, extending across the whole ceremony of the Mass, served to stamp that ceremony with its particular theme:

Unity ... is indeed the very lifeblood of the cyclic Mass in its expression of the eschatological needs of those who paid for its production and enactment in sound. In spanning the ritual of Mass, the repeated statement of a cantus firmus offered a means both of embracing [that ritual's] sacramental message as a unified celebration and reenactment of Christ's Passion, and of particularizing its plea to the Redeemer, made flesh, at the point of climax, on the altar. The unity it imposed served, then, a more than merely aesthetic purpose ...: it offered the prospect of a quicker release, after death, from purgatory, and consequently a quicker passage to paradise.[6]

But what, then, of polyphonic Requiem Masses? Such Masses met 'eschatological needs' more directly than did others, and served explicitly to secure quicker release from purgatory. All polyphonic Requiems were in any case 'particularised' by their inclusion of Proper texts, and still more deserving of this description were those Requiems composed for specific exequies, as was Victoria's. Some form of musical unification that reflected that overarching purpose and occasional nature might thus have seemed especially appropriate, if Kirkman is correct in interpreting as he does the efficacy of such 'consistency and unity of utterance across the five component movements' of Mass Ordinaries,[7] and the function of unifying cantus firmi in rendering such compositions 'personalised' in a manner reflecting (for example) a private endowment. Furthermore, a Requiem composed for a certain set of exequies contributed to a ritual and iconographical programme – itself highly 'personalised' – in which unification and consistency of message played a prominent part. Thematic repetitiveness in the iconographical schemes (manifest most obviously, perhaps, in the innumerable reproductions of the deceased's coat of arms) found, indeed, some equivalent in the texts of the items which composers included in their Requiems: of the five Proper texts which Victoria set for the second day of María's exequies (Introit, Gradual, Offertory, Communion, and the responsory *Libera me Domine*), all but one contain the same petition,

---

[5] Kirkman, *The Cultural Life*, 203. [6] Kirkman, *The Cultural Life*, 208–9.
[7] Kirkman, *The Cultural Life*, 204.

'Requiem æternam dona eis Domine, et lux perpetua luceat eis',[8] and the version of the Agnus Dei used in Requiems echoes this with 'dona eis requiem sempiternam', while the Communion begins with 'lux æterna luceat eis'. Such textual repetition is foreign to the cyclic Mass Ordinary. But in musical terms the polyphonic Requiem (like Masses *de beata virgine*) lacks the simple generator of unity present in other cyclic Masses – the sharing of material between movements – and (again like Masses *de beata virgine* and unlike other Ordinary cycles) Requiems do not typically maintain modal consistency between movements, since the modes employed reflect those of the relevant chants. Such modal variety militated against the use of common borrowed material (whether mono-phonic or polyphonic). In other words, while the original function of a work such as Victoria's Requiem was strongly 'particularised', this poly-phonic genre did not adopt the 'particularising' and unifying devices of polyphonic Mass Ordinary cycles. An exception is Richafort's Requiem, possibly sung at Philip II's court exequies. As noted in Chapter 2, the draft order of service for those exequies refers to this Requiem simply as 'the one based on *Circumdederunt*', and the piece was easily identifiable because of its use of canonic voices singing the text and chant 'Circumdederunt me gemitus mortis, dolores inferni circumdederunt me'. This canonic treat-ment of the chant is itself drawn from Josquin's motet-chanson *Nimphes nappés*.[9] But Richafort's appropriation for a Requiem of borrowing and unification techniques associated with cyclic Mass Ordinaries did not spawn successors within the Requiem genre. The only borrowed material identified hitherto in Victoria's Requiem (discussed below) is located in just one item, *Versa est in luctum*, and Victoria's work is therefore not consistently unified – or 'particularised' – by means so explicit or promi-nent as those employed by Richafort. Nevertheless, the multifarious devices he employed to create links between sections and to exert centri-petal pressure on movements which are made distinct by their chants serve to make Victoria's *mœstum carmen* for María distinct, 'particular', and coherent, and – beyond this – his deployment of a particular 'signature'

---

[8] These words constitute the Introit antiphon (sung twice, of course, before and after the verse), the Gradual respond, the Communion verse, and the third verse of the responsory *Libera me Domine*. As discussed below, Victoria reflected this repetition by using the same music for two of the occurrences of 'luceat eis' and the same imitative material for two occurrences of 'et lux perpetua'.

[9] The work also incorporates, in the Gradual and Offertory (and placed in the same two canonic voices), the motive to which the words 'c'est douleur non pareille' are sung in Josquin's *Faulte d'argent*.

module across the movements made the music 'particularised' and proper to María, as we shall see.

In more general terms, and beyond such questions of coherence, the present chapter explores ways of recasting our understanding of the *Officium defunctorum* and of Victoria's compositional choices in two intertwined respects, with the aim of better distinguishing therein the particular or idiosyncratic from the typical, with regard both to generic conventions and the rest of Victoria's output. Firstly, it locates Victoria's music within a much larger frame of reference – in terms of *pro mortuis* repertoire from across Europe – than has been attempted before. In particular, it draws into that frame a substantial body of Italian polyphony which has not attracted significant attention. (Appendix 2 is a list of some eighty Requiems by Italian composers printed between 1560 and 1650; a more restricted selection of Italian works preserved only in manuscript was also considered for the purposes of this study.) Secondly and consequently, it interrogates the current firmly established 'horizons of expectation' surrounding Iberian Requiems in the period, including Victoria's. Some of the musical gestures in the *Officium defunctorum* which may be striking to modern ears turn out to be unexceptional; on the other hand, it emerges that one particular device is rare in his output and constitutes a distinctive 'signature' element of the *Officium defunctorum*. The analysis and contextualisation begins with the two highlighted moments in *Versa est in luctum* mentioned above.

'Vocem flentium', Borrowing from Marenzio, and a Signature Contrapuntal Module for the *Officium defunctorum*

The effect of transformation at 'flentium' in *Versa est in luctum* – mentioned above – is all the more telling because the harmonic gesture is sudden and unexpected. Where Victoria uses an equivalent sonority elsewhere in his output, the result is typically milder – less of a 'stab of pain' – since the diminished fourth (or augmented fifth when inverted) is usually introduced on the *arsis* (up-beat) of the tactus, rather than on the *thesis* (down-beat) as here, and it emerges smoothly from a preceding (usually consonant) harmony which includes both the same lowest pitch and also the note a major third (or tenth) above that pitch that will form the augmented or diminished interval with the moving voice: see, for example, the occurrence in the motet *O vos omnes* shown in Example 4.1. In *Versa est*, on the other hand, all the vocal

Example 4.1 Thome Luis de Victoria, *O vos omnes*: use of augmented fifth

Example 4.2 Thome Luis de Victoria, *Senex puerum portabat*: use of augmented fifth

parts in play move onto new pitches for the start of 'flentium', which they declaim homophonically, and the F *mi* at this moment not only contrasts with the repeated F *fa* pitches of the preceding extended cadence on 'meum' but also causes the Tenor I part to trace a diminished fourth from *bb* to *f♯* melodically. The closest parallels in Victoria's works occur in the motets *Senex puerum portabat* and *Cum beatus Ignatius* (see Examples 4.2 and 4.3): here the diminished fourth does arrive on the *thesis*, but in the case of *Cum beatus Ignatius* the upper note of this interval is prepared, and in both instances only one voice sings the stressed syllable of the word at the relevant moment.[10]

---

[10] The device is deployed in *Cum beatus Ignatius* to reflect the extraordinary text, vividly portraying the physical horrors of martyrdom. As Noel O'Regan has observed, this motet text would have possessed strong relevance for the Collegium Germanicum with which Victoria was closely associated: 'Tomás Luis de Victoria's *Cum Beatus Ignatius* in the Context of Rome's

Example 4.3 Thome Luis de Victoria, *Cum beatus Ignatius*: use of diminished fourth

cor - po - ris   con - tri - - - - - -

-ti - us   cor - po - ris   con - tri - - -

-us   cor - po - ris

cor - po - ris   con - - - - -

-us   cor - po - ris   con-

It is important to note that while the musical gesture at the word 'flentium' is intended to shock, the text here concerns a *transmutation* of 'organum meum' into 'vocem flentium', of music into weeping, rather than simply the appearance of something new, and Victoria evokes this process through the transformed repetition of a single musical device: a syncopated and pre-cadential minim-semibreve-minim figure using a 'consonant fourth', in other words a fourth or compound fourth over the lowest sounding pitch which is not prepared as a consonance as would be the case in other suspension figures, but which then behaves as in a conventional suspension, resolving downwards by step; it subsequently moves upwards by step as the *cantizans* element of the cadence.[11] Victoria places one occurrence of this syncopated figure as the cadential motive ending the 'et organum meum' phrase (with a cadence on F, b. 23–4), and its harmonically caustic alter ego or antithesis occurs two breves later at 'flentium', as the music is wrenched away from F *tritus* modality. Immediately after Tenor I has sung the figure to 'flentium', Cantus II echoes the Tenor's phrase an octave higher (b. 25–6), and indeed the singer(s) on this Cantus line might well have wondered if they should correspondingly sing *f♯'* as the word 'flentium' arrives, to match the Tenor,

Jesuit Colleges', paper delivered at the Medieval and Renaissance International Music Conference, Barcelona, 8 July 2011.

[11] Consonant fourths may be approached from the note above, but in the case of the figures in the *Officium defunctorum* discussed here they are preceded by the note below.

Example 4.4 Luca Marenzio, *Dolorosi martir*, opening

even though this sharp is not indicated in their line: if they did so, then another augmented fifth harmony would result.[12] The local juxtaposition of the suave *mollis* use of the syncopated figure at 'et organum meum' and the outburst at 'flentium' could be seen as the focal point within a broader transformation – matching the theme of the text – involving this figure within the motet. As Noel O'Regan discovered, Victoria based the opening of *Versa est in luctum* on that of Marenzio's famous madrigal *Dolorosi martir*,[13] an exordium which makes repeated use of the syncopated cadential figure (Example 4.4). The figure occurs three times during the madrigal's opening passage, of which the first two occurrences (b. 3 in the

---

[12] Of the modern editors of the piece (see the list of editions in the Select Bibliography), Samuel Rubio and Jon Dixon suggest that this *f*' be sharpened, while Felip Pedrell, Bruno Turner, and David Wulstan do not. Since the majority of recordings use Turner's edition, the less acerbic option has become the more common treatment of this passage, but the sharp is employed in several recordings, including those by the Accademia Corale di Lecco (Vox, 1954), the Gabrieli Consort (Archiv Produktion, 1996), La Stagione Armonica (Symphonia, 2002), Capella de Ministrers and the Cor de la Generalitat Valenciana (Licanus, 2006), and KammerChor Saabrücken (Rondeau, 2012).

[13] The discovery was revealed in O'Regan's papers 'Piracy or Parody? The Exordium of Tomás Luis de Victoria's *Versa est in luctum*', Medieval-Renaissance Music Conference, Utrecht University, 1 July 2009, and 'Tomás L. de Victoria and Luca Marenzio: Cross-Fertilisation and Emulation between two Rome-based Composers in the Shadow of Palestrina', Tomás Luis de Victoria: Werk und Rezeption, Bremen, December 2009, to be published in Michael Zywietz (ed.), *Im Schatten Palestrina? Tomás Luis de Victoria – Werk und Rezeption*. I am most grateful to the author for sending me a copy of the second of these papers prior to publication.

Cantus, b. 4–5 in Tenor I) involve the consonant fourth, and the second coincides with a suspended seventh also. The exordium of *Versa est* extends this ten-breve passage into a more substantial paragraph lasting fourteen breves, and increases the uses of the syncopated figure therein to six. For the very first occurrence (b. 3 of the edition in the Online Appendix), Victoria adopts the second of Marenzio's versions, that involving both consonant fourth and suspended seventh, and a final consonant-fourth figure (b. 13) marks the cadence concluding Victoria's exordium. Of the four other occurrences, two constitute consonant fourths, while the listener's attention is drawn to the remaining two by different means: that in the Bassus in b. 4–5 is doubled in the Altus, and the instance in b. 10 is decorated with an archaic 'under-third' figure. The exordium of *Versa est* thus serves to fix this figure securely in the listener's mind, but in relatively conventional forms, rendering more telling the harmonic metamorphosis of the figure at 'flentium'.

Victoria may indeed have derived the idea for this metamorphosis from Marenzio's piece, for while the syncopated figure is generally absent from the madrigal after the exordium, it reappears twice in the concluding section at two of the three cadences setting the word 'amara' ('bitter'), and in both of these instances we find not only the consonant fourth but – more tellingly – the harmonic effect (here involving an augmented fifth) that Victoria uses at 'flentium'. While Marenzio fittingly deploys this gesture to evoke the meaning of the single word to which it is sung, Victoria (as we have seen) uses the transformation of the relatively tame consonant-fourth figure into this more strikingly dissonant version to dramatise the change from 'music' into 'weeping'. The poem attributed to Luigi Tansillo and set by Marenzio includes no such transformation.

Following the monumental climactic passage with which Victoria ushers in the words 'nihil enim sunt dies mei' (discussed above, and further below), the music gradually subsides, and the syncopated cadential figure again plays a striking role in this process, being deployed twice in direct succession in the Altus (b. 51–2) as one means of achieving the effect of waning. The Altus begins the motive as if intending to cadence on *d'*, but the cadence is evaded by replacing *c♯'* with *c♮'* (not indicated in the print, but necessary), and the line is thus diverted to a second, sequentially lower, iteration of the figure, cadencing instead on *c'*.[14] Four breves later, in the

---

[14]   The affective significance of musical 'descents' was mentioned by Athanasius Kircher in his *Musurgia universalis* (Rome, 1650), who terms them *catabasis* or *descensus*. On this and later

Example 4.5 The 6+5 module

concluding passage of the motet, Victoria again presents the figure twice in direct succession, but this time arranged in two different voices (b. 56 in the Altus; b. 57 in Cantus I) so as to produce a harmonic sequence (a fragment of what would later be termed the circle of fifths) which recalls the opening of the Sanctus of the *Officium defunctorum*, where precisely this arrangement of two statements of the syncopated consonant-fourth figure – beginning on *c♯'* and *f♯'*, in Altus (b. 2) and Cantus I (b. 3) respectively – occurs. (There the process is extended into a longer 'circle-of-fifths' sequence, the harmonic succession being A – D – G – C – F.) But while in the Sanctus both statements involve the conventional (and relatively euphonious) consonant fourth, the first of the two statements in this passage of *Versa est* (b. 56) uses a related polyphonic module that is more harmonically pungent and conspicuous, thereby bringing the motet to a close of particular intensity (although the voices not cadencing here continue with conventional cadence-affirming material). The Altus (with the syncopated figure) takes the *cantizans* role and the Tenor the *tenorizans* role in cadencing onto the final, D.[15] The contrapuntal module used here is shown in its basic form in Example 4.5. This cadence-approach figure uses the same syncopated motive in the *cantizans* part (shown as the Tenor in the example) as does the common form of consonant-fourth figure, but in this case the second note of the motive is not initially dissonant with the lowest voice, but instead behaves as a conventional suspended dissonance (prepared as a consonance). This upper note of the

(related) German writings on the term, see Dietrich Bartel, *Musica poetica: Musical-Rhetorical Figures in German Baroque Music* (Lincoln, Nebraska: University of Nebraska Press, 1997), 214–5.

[15] On such terminology relating to cadence, see for example Bernhard Meier, *The Modes of Classical Vocal Polyphony*, translated by Ellen S. Beebe (New York: Broude Brothers, 1988), 91.

syncopated figure is, however, also dissonant (from its beginning) with another part which is already singing the note a second above or a seventh below (and shown in the Altus in the example). The *bassizans* element of the module, beginning on the note a fifth above (or fourth below) the eventual cadence note, descends and then rises by step before leaping to the cadence note, and at the point where the second of its notes sounds, upper voices are singing both the fifth and sixth notes above the lowest part, notes which they sustain as the *bassizans* part rises again to its initial pitch: it is this particular vertical simultaneity (both fifth and sixth above the lowest part) which lends the figure much of its distinctive character, and it differs from other uses of this vertical simultaneity in music of the period in that the sixth-plus-fifth combination begins on the *arsis* not the *thesis*, in relation to the tactus, and also in that the note forming a sixth with the *bassizans* part is already present before this dissonant moment. Gioseffo Zarlino had ruled out such a combination of fifth and sixth above the lowest part in his influential treatise *Le istitutioni harmoniche* of 1558: 'But if one part has a sixth above the bass, no other part must sound a fifth above the bass, because then these two parts would be separated by a whole tone or semitone, with a resultant dissonance.'[16]

One finds this device (henceforward referred to as the '6+5 module') no fewer than nineteen times in the music of the *Officium defunctorum*: there are occurrences in all items except the Kyrie and Agnus Dei, with three instances in *Tædet animam meam* and no fewer than seven in the Communion.[17] The occurrences in the Communion all treat the chant note sounding at that point as the fifth above the *bassizans* voice at the start of the module, and hence the sixth above the lowest part where the striking 6+5 sonority occurs. Furthermore, Victoria employs an extended and elaborately decorated form of the 6+5 module – lasting two breves – as another unifying device across movements of his Requiem. This extended version is heard first in the Gradual verse, at b. 27–9, and recurs at b. 11–13

---

[16] 'Ma si debbe avertire, che quando si porrà in una della parti la detta Sesta sopra il Basso, di non porre alcun' altra parte, che sia distante per una Quinta sopra di esso: percio che queste due parti verrebbeno ad esser distanti tra loro per un Tuono, overo per un Semituono; di maniera che si udirebbe la dissonanza.' *Le istitutioni harmoniche* (Venice: [Pietro Da Fino?], 1558; reissued with new title page and errata list printed by Francesco Franceschi Senese (Venice) in 1561 and 1562). The quotation from the original text here is taken from the facsimile edition of the 1561 issue, Bibliotheca musica bononiensis, Sezione 2, no. 39 (Bologna: Arnaldo Forni, 1999), 244. The English translation is by Guy Marco, *The Art of Counterpoint*, Music Theory Translation Series 2 (New Haven & London: Yale University Press, 1968), 188.

[17] One of the instances in the Communion, at b. 10, is of a three-voice (and hence incomplete) version of the figure.

of the Sanctus and (in a slightly shorter and simpler form) at b. 46–8 of the Benedictus. Scrutiny of the rest of Victoria's output highlights the degree to which the 6+5 module constitutes a characteristic and distinctive 'signature element' of Victoria's exequial music of 1603, helping to individuate that work even though one could not go so far as to describe it as ubiquitous there. Strikingly, there are no instances of the module in any of his printed collections before the 1585 *Motecta* (which includes just one occurrence of the incomplete three-voice version of the module).[18] It is worth noting, in particular, that Victoria's earlier four-voice Requiem as published in 1583 does not have a single instance of the module. It then begins to feature slightly more often in Victoria's collections published in 1592 and 1600:[19] in the former there are seven occurrences of the full four-voice module, and one of a three-voice version (omitting the part shown as the Cantus in Example 4.5), while in the 1600 collection the module appears seven times in works not published previously. But in the entirety of Victoria's output the 6+5 module is used only eighteen times outside the *Officium defunctorum*, and the full four-voice module only sixteen times, that is, fewer occurrences than in the *Officium defunctorum* alone, which underscores the frequency of its appearance there. It is worth noting, furthermore, that the 6+5 module struck the very first writer to attempt a description of the style and expressive character of Victoria's Requiem: Franz Xaver Haberl, whose edition of the work (the first since that of 1605) was published in 1874. Haberl drew attention to the device as one rarely found among the old masters, citing the instance at b. 20 of the Offertory (at 'pœnis inferni'), and making this remark immediately after commenting that Victoria expresses 'severe pain and bitter grief by the most simple means'.[20]

---

[18] Various similar modules, but which avoid the sounding of the sixth above the Bassus on the second minim of the module (and hence the characteristic dissonance with the *cantizans* part at this point) can however be found in Victoria's output. One version, in which the Bassus behaves as in the module under discussion here, occurs for example in Victoria's Magnificat setting in the first tone (even-numbered verses), published in his 1576 collection; the figure occurs at the cadence on 'sede' in the 'Deposuit' verse; another of the related formulæ, employing the same syncopated figure in the *cantizans* part but placing the Bassus figure in a higher voice, is used for example in the concluding 'alleluia' section of *Gaude Maria virgo*.

[19] For example, while there are no occurrences in the whole of the four-voice Requiem as printed in 1583, both of the *pro defunctis* responsories newly appended to the Requiem in the 1592 edition contain instances of the figure.

[20] *Missa pro defunctis sex vocum auctore Thoma Ludovico a Victoria*, item 5 in vol. I of *Musica divina: sive thesaurus concentuum selectissimorum omni cultui divino totius anni juxta ritum sanctæ ecclesiæ catholicæ inservientium*, Annus II (Regensburg, New York, & Cincinnati: Pustet, 1874), Vorwort, p. [ii]: 'herben Schmerz und bittere Trauer mit den eingachsten Mitteln'.

It would require a much broader survey of contemporary repertory than is possible here in order to assess whether Victoria's adoption of this module in the *Officium defunctorum* in particular, and (less concentratedly) in other late works is best understood in the light of specific influences, local fashions, or wider practices. However, given that Victoria seems to have incorporated the module into his compositional practice only after moving to Madrid,[21] we may note another striking concentration of occurrences of the module, namely within the works of the senior musician of the Spanish court at the time of Victoria's arrival in Madrid and until 1596: Philippe Rogier, *maestro* of the Royal Chapel. Within the motets of Rogier's *Sacrarum modulationum … liber primus* (R1936) of 1595 there are thirteen occurrences of the module, and two of his Masses in the posthumous *Missæ sex* of 1598 make extensive use of it, there being ten instances in the *Missa Dirige gressus meos* (but, notably, none in the motet by Crecquillon on which it is based) and nine in the *Missa Philippus Secundus Rex Hispaniæ*, in honour of María's brother. All of the occurrences in the *Missa Philippus* involve the *soggetto ostinato* which gives the Mass its title, a note of this *soggetto* forming the sixth above the lowest sounding note at the crucial 6+5 point in the module. Similarly, in nearly half of the instances of the module's use in the *Officium defunctorum* (including all those in the Communion) a note of the chant provides the sixth above the lowest note. Is it possible, then, that Rogier or Victoria adopted this device through the influence of the other? They were, after all, working in close proximity in royal service for a decade. Perhaps the recurrence of this musical device in the *Officium* thus reflected a fashion in Philip's and María's households, rather than being deployed as an element 'proper' to the *mæstum carmen* of exequies.

But Victoria's decision to use the 6+5 module so often in the *Officium* for María may also have been a way of personalising the work, rendering it 'proper' to his patroness: as one can see in Example 4.5, the *bassizans* part of the 6+5 module outlines the most famous musical sign for the Blessed Virgin Mary, the four-note 'Salve' motive from the opening of the Marian antiphon *Salve regina*. Those performing the Bassus line of Victoria's exequial music thus found themselves repeatedly singing this familiar theme, one which, as noted in Chapter 1, Victoria had also employed for

---

[21] This view becomes erroneous if Noel O'Regan is correct in viewing the 1600 collection as 'a retrospective publication of his polychoral music, mostly composed for Rome': 'The Counter-Reformation and Music', in Alexandra Bamji, Geert H. Janssen, and Mary Laven (eds), *The Ashgate Research Companion to the Counter Reformation* (Farnham: Ashgate, 2013), 337–54, at 348.

Example 4.6 Francisco Dávila y Páez, Requiem, opening of Introit

his setting of 'sanctus Michael' in the Offertory. Exploiting the associations with the Empress's heavenly patron and namesake, so strongly emphasised during the exequies, Victoria ensured that María was recalled periodically throughout his work, in a manner analogous to the repetitions of her name and her imperial symbols in the textual and iconographic elements of the *honras*.[22]

Victoria's prominent use of the 6+5 module in the *Officium defunctorum* may thus have been engendered by the particular nature and purpose of the work, and does not seem to be representative of a *generic* tradition or fashion. As noted, he did not employ it in his four-voice Requiem; nor does it occur in Guerrero's widely disseminated setting, although the syncopated figure discussed above – used as a consonant fourth, for example – is common there.[23] However, Victoria's employment of it in the exequial music of 1603 may have been locally influential in generic terms, such that the module took on a meaning or association through its frequent appearance in the *Officium* for María: the eight-voice Requiem by Francisco Dávila y Páez, *maestro de capilla* at the Descalzas from 1607, includes no fewer than twelve occurrences of the figure, including two in close succession in the opening phrase of the Introit (Example 4.6), and two (one in the opening phrase sung by each choir) at the beginning of the Sanctus (Example 4.7).[24] Since the 6+5 module shares its syncopated component with the consonant fourth figure which (as noted) is the most striking

[22] More generally, it is worth noting that Marian devotion featured prominently on the second day of exequies, since a votive Mass of the Blessed Virgin Mary preceded the Requiem Mass. Giovanni Cavaccio included a setting of *Salve regina* among the motets in his *Messe per i defunti* (Milan: eredi di Simon Tini e Filippo Lomazzo, 1611, C1554).

[23] There are, however, two occurrences of the module in Lassus's five-voice Requiem, published in 1589, i.e. shortly before the full four-voice figure began to appear in Victoria's publications.

[24] In both cases the second occurrence of the module is of a type where the second note in the *bassizans* part is raised by a semitone. This type – where the second vertical simultaneity of the module is what would later be classified as a 'secondary dominant' chord – occurs only once in

Example 4.7 Francisco Dávila y Páez, Requiem, opening of Sanctus

element of the opening of the Sanctus in the *Officium defunctorum*, the openings of the Sanctus in Victoria's and Dávila y Páez's Requiems are thus made similar (although it is the latter which here quotes the 'Salve' motive prominently, in the Bassus parts), and all the more so since Dávila y Páez constructs this passage using the same 'circle-of-fifths' sequence of harmonies as does Victoria at this point (A – D – G – C). It therefore seems quite likely that the younger composer had Victoria's work in mind here: Dávila y Páez would certainly have known the older piece, and in all probability directed performances of it if – as is very likely – it continued in use at the monastery, not least for the anniversary services for María. Dávila y Páez took up his post at the Descalzas several years before Victoria's death, and would have worked closely with Victoria since the latter held the position of organist there. Given Victoria's own eminence and the eminence that the six-voice Requiem would have acquired because of its association with the Empress, it is unsurprising the Dávila y Páez's setting should display some influences from the work.[25] Indeed, another

---

Victoria's *Officium defunctorum* (in the Benedictus), but no fewer than seven times in the Requiem by Dávila y Páez.

[25] However, in many other respects the Requiem of Dávila y Páez does not resemble Victoria's, including in the texts set (for example, Dávila y Páez set just the verse of the Gradual, but provides polyphony for the whole of this verse, unlike Victoria) and use of chant (the chants used in the Agnus Dei settings are different in the two works). In the 1628 printed source, the

correspondence occurs in the Communion settings: the most concentrated use of the 6+5 module in Victoria's work is found at 'cum sanctis tuis' in this part of the Requiem, where the figure is employed three times within four breves as this unit of text is repeated.[26] Since this whole passage recurs as part of the repetendum of the antiphon after the verse, we reach a total of six occurrences (of the seven instances in the Communion as a whole). Departing from common practice (internationally) in setting this Communion text, Dávila y Páez does not re-use his original music for 'cum sanctis tuis in æternum' at the repetendum; it is when this text is repeated that he employs the 6+5 module, used as in Victoria's setting to set the words 'cum sanctis tuis'.

Victoria's *Versa est in luctum* may also have influenced this later Requiem. In place of the Benedictus there one find the motet *Dies mei transierunt*, the position of which indicates that it was to be sung at the Elevation.[27] The text of the motet is, like that of *Versa est in luctum*, from the Book of Job (17:11–12): 'Dies mei transierunt, cogitationes meæ disipatæ sunt. Torquentes cor meum noctem verterunt in diem, et rursum post tenebras spero lucem.' ('My days have passed away, my hopes have been shattered. The desires of my heart have turned night into day, and after darkness I hope for light.')[28] Indeed, this text constitutes a kind of (eventually) hopeful complement to the consistently despondent character of *Versa est*, beginning with the final two words of that motet, 'dies mei', but moving from darkness to light rather than tracing the transformation of music into lament. There are musical correspondences between the motets. The perturbing harmonic device which Victoria uses at 'flentium' in *Versa est* (described above) appears twice in close succession in *Dies mei transierunt*, the second occurrence being the more striking because (as in Victoria's motet) it is placed on the *thesis* of the tactus. In addition,

---

Requiem of Dávila y Páez is described as having been 'reduzida y vista' ('reduced and examined') by the composer of the rest of the collection, Sebastián López de Velasco, but we do not know what form the relevant revisions took.

[26] The relevant passage, b. 11–16, employs a circle-of-fifths harmonic progression (although with a 'step back' in the opposite direction at one point), with harmonies of E – A – D – G – C – F. The 6+5 module is used at the cadences where the harmony moves from E to A, A to D, and G to C.

[27] It is not clear from the printed source whether this motet is by López de Velasco (described in the print as having edited the Requiem) or Dávila y Páez.

[28] One finds two readings of this text in English translations: the first links 'Torquentes cor meum' (the final words of verse 11) with verse 12, as in the translation provided here; in the second (and much the most common) these three words are linked in sense with verse 11. It is clear that the composer of this motet intended the former reading, given the way in which he highlights musically the point of articulation before 'torquentes' rather than that after it.

the 6+5 module is used no fewer than four times in the opening section of the motet (the section which corresponds most closely in textual affect with *Versa est*). These parallels make it seem more likely that the motivic similarities between the *exordia* of *Dies mei* and *Versa est* (both of which use the, itself quite conventional, device of combining rising and falling motives) are not fortuitous, but reflect Dávila y Páez's contact with Victoria's *Officium*. As with *Versa est* but unlike many other motets printed with Requiems in Spain and Portugal (as noted below), *Dies mei transierunt* is matched to the surrounding Requiem in its scoring.

Beyond this case of apparent influence explicable through a personal and institutional connection, we lack indications that Victoria's use of the 6+5 module in the *Officium defunctorum* influenced other composers of exequial music. One potential exception concerns *Tædet animam meam*, which is (as observed above) the section of the *Officium defunctorum* which has the second highest number of occurrences of the module, after the Communion.[29] It may be that Manuel Cardoso was influenced by this setting when composing the settings of the first lesson of each nocturn for Matins of the Dead, printed immediately before the four-voice Requiem in his *Livro de varios motetes*.[30] The first of these lesson settings, *Parce mihi Domine*, includes no fewer than four instances of the module, while the second and third lessons, *Responde mihi* and *Spiritus meus*, have three each.[31] Besides this, use of the 6+5 module seems to be scarce in the Iberian repertory of music *pro defunctis* composed in the decades after 1605, as it had been before that. For example, one finds no occurrences of it in either Requiem by Juan de Esquivel, or in the settings by Sebastián de Vivanco and Manuel Cardoso, and only one each in Felipe de Magalhães's Requiem and Duarte Lobo's eight-voice work.[32]

---

[29] The module is used twice in quick succession near the opening of the setting, for the cadence at '[animæ] meæ' (b. 13–14) and near the beginning of the succeeding phrase, at '[Dicam] Deo' (b. 15–16); the final occurrence is at 'adjuves' (b. 34–5).

[30] Lisbon: Lourenço de Anveres, 1648, C1042.

[31] In some cases the module appears in a slightly different form to the one discussed so far, for example omitting the suspension formed by the *cantizans* part. The concentration of appearances of the module in Cardoso's settings of lessons for Matins of the Dead is the more striking given that he avoids the figure entirely in the four-voice Requiem Mass and responsory which follow in the 1648 collection, and also in his six-voice Requiem published in 1625.

[32] The six-voice Requiem by Lobo does include no fewer than eight occurrences of this module or related constructions, but the work is unusually rich in various figures involving the simultaneous sounding of the fifth and the sixth above the lowest part. There is also one use of the module in the four-voice setting of the responsory *Memento mei Deus* which follows this Requiem in Lobo's *Liber II missarum* of 1636.

As we have seen, Victoria reserves his use of the 6+5 module for a prominent moment in *Versa est in luctum*: the final cadence. In the context of the motet, the appearance of the module is climactic because it is aurally more striking than the other modules using the same syncopated figure – such as consonant fourths – which precede it in this last section of the motet and which are prominent in the (Marenzio-derived) exordium, with the notable exception of the 'flentium' moment which trumps all others in impact. Specifically, the final cadence of the motet invites comparison with its 'companion' cadence marking the end of the exordium, at b. 13–14. These are the only two such prominent cadences onto the final (D) in the motet, and they are linked by their use of the syncopated figure, but in the first cadence the other parts simply hold their notes for a breve while the Altus sings the syncopated figure (producing a consonant fourth), while in contrast the second cadence has the contrapuntally and harmonically richer 6+5 module. The two passages concerned are also linked because they are among the very few points in the motet where Victoria replaces B *mi* with B *fa* (the other passage which does so is the crucial 'transformation' at 'et organum meum in vocem flentium'), and in this respect once again the second passage is the more intense: in the approach to the cadence at b. 15 a single voice sings a *mi fa mi* (*a'* – *b♭'* – *a'*) figure before the consonant fourth cadential figure, whereas in the final passage of the motet that figure is not only heard as part of the 6+5 module itself, but is also anticipated in the same voice (Cantus II, b. 54–5), after which there are also iterations of *mi fa mi* in Tenor I, Cantus II again, and Cantus I. It might or might not be fortuitous that the item following *Versa est* in the 1605 print, *Libera me Domine*, opens with the *mi fa mi* figure in Cantus I (its use here being logical, since it is an inversion of the initial chant motive D – C♯ – D), and the figure also appears in the Bassus at the end of that initial section of the respond. The *a'* – *b♭'* – *a'* gesture also constitutes a unifying figure in the Offertory through its repeated appearance in the cantus parts: it occurs as the opening gesture in Cantus I (the first word is 'libera', which may be relevant for the musical parallel with the responsory's opening), then in this voice at 'de pœnis' (b. 13–15), 'et de profundo' (b. 22–3), 'tartarus' (b. 39–40), and 'in lucem sanctam' (b. 60–61), and finally in Cantus II at 'quam olim Abrahæ' (b. 62–3).

The listener may well notice that the wider family of modules sharing the syncopated figure prominent in the exordium of *Versa est* (rising by step to the second note, and falling thence by step) are very common in the music of the *Officium defunctorum*, occurring in every 'movement', and sixty-seven times in all, thirty of these being instances of the consonant fourth, and one a 'consonant seventh' (at b. 47 of the Introit verse, discussed below). Consequently, the use of this syncopated figure (including its appearance within the 6+5 module) may to some extent contribute to the impression that the whole work inhabits a particular sound-world, and – like the 6+5 module – its frequent employment in Victoria's six-voice Requiem certainly distinguishes that music from Victoria's four-voice Requiem as published in 1583, where there are just twenty-five occurrences of such motives, only five of which are consonant fourths. We should however be cautious in attributing to this syncopated figure *per se* an equivalent role in making the music of 1603 distinctive as that played by the 6+5 module itself, since Victoria had used the syncopated figure regularly throughout his career,[33] whereas, as we have seen, this was not the case with the 6+5 module. Thus, while the listener to the *Officium defunctorum* might for example be struck by the prominence of the figure in *Tædet animam meam* (it is employed – as a consonant fourth – in the very first cadence, and five more times thereafter), it likewise makes multiple appearances in Victoria's setting of the *Te Deum* published five years earlier in 1600, a setting which employs a similar style to that of *Tædet*, prioritising textual declamation in a freely homophonic texture, with frequent cadential articulation; the resemblance between the pieces in terms of cadential formulæ is highlighted by the fact that their first cadences are identical.

Nevertheless, the prominence of the syncopated figure in the exordium of *Dolorosi martir* might have encouraged Victoria to draw upon that piece for his exequial music for María, given that it thus 'fits',[34] and indeed – as we have seen – these syncopated figures provide a particularly strong link between *Versa est* and the Sanctus. Furthermore, Victoria's deployment of the figure in the opening section of his Mass, the Introit, draws special attention to it; or one might say rather that he exploits the figure as a means of achieving musical highlighting. Thus the most disruptive and therefore striking harmonic device in the first paragraph of the Introit uses a consonant-fourth syncopated figure: hearing the music of b. 8, the

---

[33] To cite just a few examples: the motet *Ardens est cor meum* published in 1576 has six instances of the consonant fourth, among nine occurrences of the syncopated figure, and the *Missa Ave regina cælorum* included in the 1600 collection incorporates many examples of a 'double-speed' version of the figure, with the rhythm semiminim-minim-semiminim; this version of the figure features prominently in *Nigra sum sed formosa* (published in 1576), at the phrase 'ideo dilexit me rex'. The syncopated figure is also common in Victoria's settings of the Magnificat.

[34] Noel O'Regan has indeed gone further, in 'Tomás L. de Victoria and Luca Marenzio', by suggesting that the frequent use of the consonant fourth in the Requiem might have been 'sparked off' by its presence in *Dolorosi martir*.

listener expects a cadence onto F (the final) in b. 9, but the Altus sings *f♯'* rather than the expected *f♮'*, and this voice's consonant-fourth figure redirects the music to a cadence on G (the start of an extended 'circle-of-fifths' progression which reaches all the way to E♭ harmony). There are, indeed, parallels with the 'flentium' gesture in *Versa est*: the consonant-fourth figure is on the same pitch-classes in both cases, the same swerve from F♮ to F♯ occurs, and the start of the figure is preceded by C harmony. Of the three occurrences of the syncopated figure in the Introit verse, the first (b. 47) is striking for the fact that it involves not a consonant fourth but a considerably rarer device, a consonant seventh, the use of which here is unique in the music of the *Officium defunctorum*. Four breves later (at b. 51), Victoria introduces another consonant fourth figure in the topmost voice at the climactic end of the 'orationem meam' phrase. The approach to this cadence in the topmost line is striking in that as it oscillates repeatedly between *d''* and *c''* the first and third occurrences of *c''* are signed with a sharp in the printed edition, but the second is not. The alternation of the two forms of *c''* is itself conspicuous in performance, but singers might well (instead) have treated this note also as *c♯'*, and indeed the note is shown thus in the manuscript copy of the Requiem in Augsburg. Doing so produces an acerbic augmented fourth with the Fs in the Bassus and Altus at this point, and hence a likeness with the 'flentium' gesture in *Versa est*.

Before leaving Victoria's citation of *Dolorosi martir*, it is worth considering how this allusion might have been relevant (beyond the pleasure of recognition) to those hearing or performing the motet who also knew this famous madrigal and the poetry which it sets. How might such allusion and recognition have inflected the meaning and interpretation of the motet?[35]

---

[35] Not only was Marenzio's setting well known, but the poem received numerous other settings, including by Marc'Antonio Ingegneri, Luzzasco Luzzaschi, Giovanni Maria Nanino (two settings), Francesco Soriano, and Alessandro Striggio. Several of the settings are musically connected, including in some cases with Marenzio's. See Anthony Newcomb (ed.), *Luzzasco Luzzaschi, Complete Unaccompanied Madrigals*, 4 vols (Middleton, Wis.: A-R Editions, 2003–2010), II, xxix, and Marco Bizzarini, '"Dolorosi martir, fieri tormenti": il madrigale romano e lo stile grave', in Franco Piperno (ed.), *Luca Marenzio e il madrigale romano* (Rome: Accademia nazionale di Santa Cecilia, 2007), 97–113. Peter Poulos has pointed out in two conference papers certain similarities between the passages setting 'et organum meum' in the *Versa est in luctum* motets of Victoria and Simone Molinaro, the latter published in Molinaro's *Motectorum quinis, et missæ denis vocibus liber primus* (Venice: Vincenti, 1597, M2930), and has suggested that one composer knew the other's setting: 'Victoria a Genova: modelli e influenza', Società Italiana di Musicologia, Genoa, 21–23 October 2011, and 'Victoria and the Motet in Genoa: Models and Influence', Mapping the post-Tridentine Motet (ca. 1560–ca. 1610): Text, Style and Performance, University of Nottingham, 17–19 April 2015. I am most grateful to Prof. Poulos for sharing with me a copy of the first of these papers.

As mentioned, Victoria cited only the exordium of *Dolorosi martir*, a passage which fittingly represented the concept of 'turning' with which his text begins ('versa'), since Marenzio combines a falling and a rising motive to construct this paragraph.[36] (It is also a nice conceit that Victoria chose to employ the parody/imitation technique of *transforming* an existing piece of music into something new, and with new text, when setting a text about transformation.) In Marenzio's piece the falling motive is used to set the second part of the first line of the poem, 'fieri tormenti', and one might have expected Victoria duly to exploit it for the concluding words, 'cithara mea', of the opening independent clause of his text, 'versa est in luctum cithara mea', not least since 'fieri tormenti' and 'cithara mea' have the same number of syllables (as do 'Dolorosi martir' and 'Versa est in luctum'). Indeed, to assign 'cithara mea' – as Victoria does – to a separate section of the piece, after a prominent cadence on the final at 'luctum', seems illogical, and certainly Alonso Lobo had incorporated 'cithara mea' (with its own motive) into the opening paragraph of his *Versa est in luctum*. But Victoria's decision makes sense, since having both the rising and falling motives sung solely to the words 'Versa est in luctum' duly represents the concept of 'reversal' and transformation. The continual alternation of F *mi* and F *fa* produced in large part by the shape of the descending motive contributes to the mixing of antithetical affects in the passage, again appropriate to the concept of sweet music turned into bitter lament. But beyond Marenzio's exordium, adapted by Victoria, the listener/singer might well have recalled also the fifth line of the madrigal's text – 'Triste voci, querele, urli, e lamenti' ('sad voices, complaints, cries, and laments') – which overlaps in topic with the first half of the motet's text (particularly 'triste voci' / 'vocem flentium'). Whether or not in this connection, it is striking that another composer – Giulio Cesare Gabucci – independently used the opening of Marenzio's *Dolorosi martir* when composing a setting of *Versa est in luctum*.[37]

---

[36] Alonso Lobo employed a similar device to represent this text in the (freely composed) opening of *Versa est in luctum*, written for the exequies of Philip II.

[37] Gabucci's motet appeared in *Della nova metamorfosi de diversi autori ... libro secondo* (Milan: A. Tradate, 1605, 1605[6]). Aspects of Victoria's and Gabucci's *exordia* demonstrate that they were *independently* based on Marenzio's exordium. Gabucci's reference to Marenzio's exordium has been pointed out by Poulos in 'Victoria a Genova' and 'Victoria and the Motet in Genoa'. Other works based on Marenzio's *Dolorosi martir* are a Mass by Krystof Harant – who was a chamberlain to the Emperor Rudolf, María's son – and a Magnificat setting by Michael Praetorius. On the latter, see Walter Kreysig, 'The Continuation of the Roman Cinquecento Madrigal as a Sacred Parody in Seventeenth-Century Germany: Luca Marenzio's Five-Voice *Dolorosi martir* (1580) and Michael Praetorius's Six-Voice *Magnificat super Dolorosi martir* (1611)', in Piperno (ed.), *Luca Marenzio*, 213–70.

Returning now to the integration of *Versa est* with the surrounding Requiem polyphony, one observes not only that the motet has the same vocal scoring as the music for Mass and the Absolution, but also that there is a high degree of modal/tonal and harmonic congruence with other items. Such congruence is facilitated by Victoria's transposition downwards by a fifth of the material from Marenzio's madrigal:[38] the exordium of *Dolorosi martir* is constructed with A final (although the whole madrigal ends on E) and Victoria's motet with D final.[39] Although this transposition should theoretically have involved the introduction of a B♭ signature, Victoria's omission of a signature reflects the use of F sharps in Marenzio's initial rising motive (these become B naturals in *Versa est*), and also the very sparing appearance of B *fa* in the whole motet. The cleffing, D final, and lack of flat signature of *Versa est* render its tonal type and modal representation the same as those of the *Libera me* which follows it in the print,[40] and also produce a significant level of harmonic and cadential correspondence with the preceding Mass movements: the Offertory is of the same tonal type (with D final), and the Gradual likewise has a D final once transposed down by a fifth (as it should be: see below), and although the Benedictus, Agnus Dei, and Communion end with cadences on G (and the Sanctus with a cadence on A), they all display a harmonic/cadential orientation similar to that of *Versa est*. Indeed, although the opening two movements of the Requiem – Introit and Kyrie – do have a B♭ signature (as does the Gradual once transposed), the mixture of F *tritus* modality with prominent D *protus* gestures and cadences in the Introit locates this and *Versa est* within similar tonal (in the broad sense) and cadential landscapes. This tonal behaviour in the Introit is logical given that although the Introit chant is in mode 6, psalm tones 6 (with F final) and 1 (with D final) share the same intonation (F – G – A) and reciting note (A), and the mediation formula at 'Hierusalem' in the Introit verse features both in psalm tone 1 and in one version of psalm tone 6. Beyond this, both sections of the Introit (antiphon and verse) begin with Cantus I singing *a′ – b′ – c″*, a transposition of the opening three-note ascent in the chant here (which constitutes, as just mentioned, the psalm-tone

[38] This difference in notated pitch has nothing to do with cleffing: Marenzio's piece does not employ 'high clefs'.

[39] It might not be coincidence that this transposition brings Victoria's motet into a similar modality to the chants associated with the responsory *Versa est in luctum*, which are in mode 2.

[40] An introduction to the terminology and concepts relevant to considering modality and tonality in polyphony, and of contrasting modern approaches to such areas, is provided in Chapter 1 of Franz Wiering, *The Language of the Modes: Studies in the History of Polyphonic Modality* (New York & London: Routledge, 2001).

intonation in the verse), while in *Versa est* both the second and third of the three sections of the motet (at 'cithara mea', b. 14–15, and 'parce mihi', b. 27–8) likewise begin with this $a' - b' - c''$ figure in the highest Cantus part, and its opening of course has the figure $a' - b' - c\sharp''$ (from Marenzio) in Cantus I.

In presenting a motet with a *pro mortuis* text together with a polyphonic Requiem, Victoria's *Officium defunctorum* embodies Iberian practice more strongly than Italian. Motets published with Requiems by Italian composers up to 1650 include a lower proportion of *pro defunctis* texts, and indicate rather that common practice in Italy was to use – at the Elevation of Requiem Masses – motet settings of traditional Elevation and Eucharistic prayers, including *Adoramus te Christe, Ave verum corpus*, and parts of the Prayers (or Verses) of St Gregory, *O Domine Jesu Christe, adoro te*.[41] Conversely, settings of these texts are not found among the motets associated with Iberian Requiems. Rather, in both of the cases before 1605 where Spanish composers had inserted a motet in their published Requiem Masses the motet concerned – the positioning of which shows that it functioned as an Elevation motet – has a text with *pro mortuis* associations. Juan Vázquez's *Agenda defunctorum* includes the motet *Sana me Domine*, the text of which incorporates Psalm 40:5, used as an antiphon at Matins of the Dead. Francisco Guerrero added the six-voice motet *Hei mihi Domine* to his four-voice Requiem when he published a revised edition in 1582, the text in this case being that of a responsory for Matins of the Dead.[42] Likewise, in the decades following the publication of the *Officium defunctorum* the motets associated with printed Requiem Masses in the Iberian Peninsula have 'appropriate' texts as does Victoria's. We have already seen one example of this from the same institutional context as the *Officium defunctorum*: the motet *Dies mei transierunt* within Dávila y Páez's Requiem.

---

[41] The intended use of such motets at the Elevation is indicated in the printed sources by their positioning between Sanctus and Agnus Dei and/or by a specific heading to this effect. Further on the contrast between Iberian and Italian practice with regard to motets associated with Requiems, see the present author's 'Motets *pro defunctis* in the Iberian World: Texts and Performance Contexts', in Esperanza Rodríguez-Garcia and Daniele V. Filippi (eds), *Mapping the Motet in the post-Tridentine Era* (London: Routledge, 2018), 85–101; for a list and discussion of the relevant Italian motets, see Antonio Chemotti, 'Motets and Liturgy'.

[42] A setting of psalm, 129, *De profundis*, follows the Requiem and responsories for the Absolution in Pedro Rimonte's *Missæ sex* (1604). This is in motet style, and indeed Rimonte also published it in his motet collection *Cantiones sacræ* (Antwerp: Pierre Phalèse, 1607, R1711). This psalm is sung at Matins of the Dead. A motet-style setting of the first part of this psalm is, similarly, preserved with the Requiem of Sebastián de Vivanco, and likewise this setting also appeared in a printed motet collection.

Four of the five published Requiems by Portuguese composers include one or more motets placed immediately after the Mass, that is, the same position as in the case of *Versa est* within the *Officium defunctorum*; in some cases these are followed by a responsory setting, as in the 1605 print. Almost all of these motets are textually 'proper' to a Requiem, and several, indeed, have texts from the *pro mortuis* liturgies:[43] Duarte Lobo's *Audivi vocem de cælo* (a versicle sung during the Office of burial),[44] Filipe de Magalhães's *Commissa mea pavesco* (a verse of the responsory *Domine quando veneris* from Matins of the Dead),[45] and Manuel Cardoso's *Sitivit anima mea* (a Matins antiphon). This last motet is preceded in the printed source (Cardoso's *Missæ quaternis, quinis, et sex vocibus* of 1625, which includes his six-voice Requiem) by another, *Non mortui*, which has a striking text adapted from the Apocryphal book of Baruch: 'The dead who are in hell, whose spirit has been taken from their bodies, will not give glory or justice to the Lord, but the soul that is grieved on account of the greatness of its sin and that walks bowed and feeble gives you your glory and righteousness, O Lord.'[46] Cardoso's other Requiem, for four voices, is followed in its printed source (the *Livro de varios motetes*) by a motet *Domine, ne recorderis*, the text of which is almost identical with that of the respond section of the responsory *Ne recorderis* from Matins of the Dead, and a setting of this responsory is the next item in the book.[47] Among the seventeenth-century Iberian Requiems preserved in manuscript, the seven-voice work by Joan Cererols incorporates (in place of the Benedictus) a setting of *Hei mihi Domine*, the same responsory text as used by Guerrero in the revised version of his Requiem.[48]

---

[43] Wagstaff, 'Music for the Dead', 483–4, notes the Iberian tradition of motets with texts taken from the *pro mortuis* liturgies, and copied as part of Requiem Masses. The text of Victoria's *Versa est in luctum* was used as the respond section of a responsory which, although most commonly sung at the feast of St Job, had also been employed at Matins of the Dead in some Uses: see Knud Ottosen, *The Responsories and Versicles of the Latin Office of the Dead* (Aarhus: Aarhus University Press, 1993), 389, 401, 406. Of the motet settings of *Versa est in luctum* by other Spanish composers, those by Alonso Lobo and Sebastián de Vivanco have the same text as Victoria's, while Francisco de Peñalosa's setting includes also the verse 'Cutis mea . . . in statera'.

[44] This follows the eight-voice Requiem in Lobo's *Liber missarum* of 1621, and is preceded by another motet, *Pater peccavi*, with penitential text. The two motets are clearly paired, since they use almost identical opening material.

[45] This follows his Requiem in the *Missarum liber* of 1636.

[46] The text frequently appears in an erroneous translation, beginning 'They are not dead who are in hell', and thus fundamentally altering the sense.

[47] The last phrase of the motet's text, 'quia in inferno nulla est redemptio', comes from another responsory for Matins of the Dead, *Peccantem me quotidie*.

[48] There is an edition by David Pujol in *Joan Cererols*, 5 vols, Mestres de l'Escolania de Montserrat (Monestir de Montserrat, 1931–1981), II, 218–25.

Despite this textually 'proper' nature of motets preserved with Iberian Requiems, the degree to which such motets seem to constitute a *musically* integrated element of their companion Requiems varies considerably. Victoria's *Versa est* stands at one end of this spectrum, while in many other cases the musical association between Mass and motet(s) is less close: Guerrero's *Hei mihi Domine* was, as mentioned, added to the Requiem when it was published for the second time, and is for more voice-parts than the Mass; Lobo's *Audivi vocem de cælo* conversely employs two fewer voices than the Requiem which it follows; Magalhães's *Commissa mea pavesco* is differently scored than its companion Mass; and the two motets printed between the Requiem Mass and the *Libera me* in Cardoso's collection of 1625 have different cleffing to both the Mass and the *Libera me*.

While we have observed the congruities between *Versa est* and Victoria's Mass, what can be said about the most likely location of the motet in performance? The strong musical echoes between the motet and the Sanctus might point towards the employment of the motet at the Elevation. As noted, the placing of motets after the Benedictus in both Vázquez's *Agenda defunctorum* and Guerrero's 1582 collection indicates such a function for those pieces, while an unattributed Requiem Mass in Granada Cathedral, Archivo Capitular 7 similarly includes a motet *Versa est* placed between Sanctus and Agnus, and another *Versa est* motet attributed to a certain Soria was inserted in this position within the Requiem Mass by Pallares copied in Ávila, Monasterio de Santa Ana 6.[49] As we have seen, the motets incorporated in Dávila y Páez's Requiem and Cererols's seven-voice Requiem were certainly also Elevation motets, since they actually replace the Benedictus. The *relaciones* discussed in Chapter 2 reveal other cases where Elevation motets were sung during the Requiem Mass at exequies, and reinforce the distinction – in terms of textual practice at this point in Requiem Masses – with Italian traditions.[50] However, as far as I know, such positioning of Victoria's *Versa est* has not been tried in modern interpretations: rather, recordings – including those which attempt liturgical reconstructions – consistently place it after the Communion (that is, at the end of the items for Mass), reflecting a presumption that its position in the 1605 volume (between the Communion and the *Libera me Domine*) indicates its ritual

---

[49] See Wagstaff, 'Music for the Dead', 603.

[50] One such case of a motet sung at the Elevation is the Mexico City exequies for Charles V. See Francisco Cervantes de Salazar, *Túmulo imperial dela gran ciudad de Mexico* (Mexico City: Antonio de Espinosa, 1560), f. 26.

position.[51] It is certainly possible that *Versa est* was sung at the conclusion of Mass, either before the sermon or after it as those presiding at the Absolution moved to their stations at the four corners of the catafalque:[52] one of the ritual locations for performance of *Libera me Domine* was at the Absolution.[53] But it is also entirely possible that Victoria simply decided to present the three 'additional' items (those not setting texts from the Mass) all together at the end of his 1605 print, after the *Missa pro defunctis*, and that the particular location of *Versa est* in the print therefore tells us nothing regarding its function in performance. After all, one of the other two items placed at the end of the print, *Tædet animam meam*, is in the 'wrong' position liturgically: it belongs to Matins of the Dead, and should therefore precede rather than follow the *Missa pro defunctis*.[54] Some modern editors have duly moved *Tædet* to the start of their editions, but these same editions leave *Versa est* where it stands in the 1605 edition.[55] Certainly, *Versa est* bears no heading indicating its function, and the Index at the end of the book likewise does not stipulate this.

---

[51] Such a view is apparent, for example, in Bruno Turner's liner notes to *Victoria Requiem, Officium defunctorum, 1605*, Westminster Cathedral Choir (Hyperion, 1987), and his Introduction to *Tomás Luis de Victoria (1548–1611): Officium defunctorum, Requiem 1605*, 4. All of the recordings of the *Officium defunctorum* which include *Versa est in luctum* place it after the Mass items and before *Libera me Domine*.

[52] At the Mexico City exequies for Charles V, a psalm was sung after the end of Mass while the clergy positioned themselves for the Absolution; see Cervantes de Salazar, *Túmulo imperial*, f. 26.

[53] We might note the juxtaposition of musical items and preaching on the first day of the Jesuit College's exequies for María, when the Latin oration was preceded by the *monodia* and followed by the Sapphic poem 'with very fine music'.

[54] The 'mis-placement' of this item in the *Officium defunctorum* is unusual, since most other printed collections of the period which provide music for both Office and Mass of the Dead put the Office items first. Among Iberian examples we see this practice in Juan Vázquez's *Agenda defunctorum* of 1556 and Manuel Cardoso's *Livro de varios motetes* of 1648. In the latter case, settings of three lessons for Matins of the Dead are placed before the four-voice *Missa pro defunctis*, whereas a motet and a responsory setting for the Absolution come after it, as in the *Officium defunctorum*. It is true that in Francisco Garro's *Opera aliquot* (Lisbon: Pedro Craesbeck, 1609) three lessons are located after the *Missa pro defunctis*, but since we are dealing here with a collection of several Masses (rather than a publication solely dedicated to music *pro mortuis*), it would have been somewhat odd to interrupt that series of Masses with items belonging to a different liturgical type.

[55] *Tædet* appears as the first item in the editions by Bruno Turner and Jon Dixon (*Tomás Luis de Victoria (1548–1611): Requiem Mass for Six Voices and Settings for the Office of the Dead* (JOED: Carshalton Beeches, 1994)). It might be worth observing that in the manuscript Viseu, Arquivo Distrital, Cod. 3, which preserves the Requiem of Estêvão Lopes Morago, the Mass is followed by a setting of *Versa est in luctum*, another motet, and then an assortment of items for the Office of the Dead, amongst which are pieces for Matins including one lesson (as occurs in Victoria's collection).

The 'parce mihi' Climax

Whether *Versa est* was sung at the Elevation (a climactic point in the Mass) or next to the sermon, it is during the outburst at 'parce mihi Domine' in the motet that Victoria's writing seems most closely equivalent to the impassioned oratory of exequial preaching praised in *relaciones*. The leaps upwards by a fifth for the last (unstressed) syllable of 'Domine' and 'mei' in both Cantus parts (b. 33–41) represent an extraordinary way for an upper voice to conclude a phrase within the musical language of the period.[56] Victoria used such a gesture extremely rarely elsewhere, and never as a thrice-repeated exclamation as here. There are just fourteen cases in his works of such a leap of a fifth in the topmost voice(s) onto the unstressed syllable at the end of a phrase, and only eleven of these where the effect of the leap is not mitigated by the other Cantus part singing an intervening note. Furthermore, the e'' to which the Cantus parts leap here in *Versa est* is the peak note of the whole *Officium defunctorum*, and nowhere else in the music for María's exequies is the climactic part of the Cantus range emphasised thus: the note e'' occurs only five times outside *Versa est*, and each of these occurrences is isolated and uses a stepwise ascent to the e'' rather than a leap.[57] (In only two cases in the rest of his output is the upper note which is reached in such a gesture the peak note of that voice-part.) As with the gesture at 'flentium', the first of these upward leaps of a fifth, in Cantus I (b. 33–4), comes completely out of the blue, but the intensity is then prolonged, with Cantus I reciting on e'' and d'', and Cantus II sustaining for a dotted breve the e'' to which it leaps at 'mei' (b. 38–9); the expressive force is further compounded by the suspensions created by the motive for 'nihil'. On the first occasion that Cantus I sings the words 'nihil enim sunt dies mei' (b. 34–7) its phrase outlines the 'salve' motive (here $e'' - d'' - e'' - a'$), which as we have seen is woven into the Requiem through its appearance in the 6+5 module and at 'sed signifer' in the Offertory. The association between María and her patron saint is thus

---

[56] Exceptions occur when composers match the sung text to the relevant solmization syllables: the expression 'ut sol' ('as the sun') attracts a rising fifth for this reason in Marian motets of the period, where this expression occurs frequently, at the conclusion of the phrase 'pulchra ut luna, electa ut sol' from the Song of Songs, 6:9. But such cases are different from the gestures in *Versa est*, in that the notes A to E forming the leap here do not constitute *ut* and *sol* of one of the three types of *musica recta* hexachord.

[57] Once the Gradual of the *Officium defunctorum* has been subjected to the necessary downwards transposition, its Cantus parts do not reach as high as e''.

evoked at the climax of the motet and – one might argue – of all Victoria's polyphony for the Empress's exequies.[58]

There may be another chant reference at the 'parce mihi' climax also. The text at this point in the motet, 'parce mihi Domine, nihil enim sunt dies mei', is also the opening of the first lesson at Matins of the Dead. The chant tone for this lesson has a falling fifth at ends of sentences, as at 'mihi', and is thus present at this point in, for example, Morales's setting of *Parce mihi*. While falling fifths in the Cantus for the last note and syllable of phrases are by no means uncommon in Victoria's writing, the particular repeated effect in Cantus I here in *Versa est* – recitation of 'dies me-' on an *e″* and then the drop of a fifth to *a′* – would surely have evoked this lesson from Matins.

Libera me Domine

Whatever the order and chronology of composition of the items constituting the *Officium defunctorum*, the outcome was that the setting of *Libera me Domine* which follows *Versa est* in the 1605 volume likewise matches closely the preceding music there. Firstly, it has identical vocal scoring in its six-voice sections to all the six-voice music in the volume.[59] (All the six-voice items in the *Officium defunctorum*, including the motet *Versa est in luctum*, employ cleffing of c_1 c_1 c_3 c_4 c_4 f_4, except the Gradual, where this clef-combination is simply shifted a third higher to g_2 g_2 c_2 c_3 c_3 f_3.) This matching of Mass and *Libera* setting means, besides all else, that Victoria's *Libera me Domine* is unusually grand by the standards of the time regarding this liturgical polyphonic

---

[58] Of course, if *Versa est* was not written for María's exequies, but was an existing piece incorporated into that project, then such an interpretation becomes nonsensical. One cannot dismiss this possibility regarding *Versa est*, but there is no convincing evidence that points to it having been composed before 1603. Adriano Giardina proposed that *Versa est in luctum* may long pre-date the other music in the *Officium defunctorum*, in 'Is *Versa est in luctum* by Victoria an "Early Motet"?', a paper presented at the conference 'Mapping the Post-Tridentine Motet (ca. 1560–ca. 1610): Text, Style and Performance', University of Nottingham, 18 April 2015. Giardina pointed to similarities in, for example, textural devices between *Versa est in luctum* and motets for similar numbers of voices published by Victoria in 1572, but he adduced no evidence that Victoria was likely to have abandoned these particular practices in a late six-voice motet.

[59] The exception to the consistency of cleffing amongst all this music is the four-voice verse 'Tremens factus sum' of *Libera me Domine*, which, as noted in Chapter 2, Victoria took without alteration from his earlier setting published with the four-voice Requiem.

genre.[60] Although a small number of six-voice (and, indeed, eight-voice) Requiem Masses survive which definitely or possibly pre-date Victoria's music of 1603, almost without exception these are not associated with a setting of this responsory.[61] Moving beyond matters of scoring, in modal representation and tonal type Victoria's *Libera me* matches both *Versa est* and (because of a similarity of chant mode) the Offertory of his Mass, a match reflected in the presence of some identical passages: the structurally important cadential passage at 'lucem sanctam' in the Offertory (b. 60–62, before the repetendum section 'quam olim Abrahæ') is the same as that at the end of the second polyphonic section in *Libera me Domine*, at 'et terræ' (b. 17–19).[62] Furthermore, the necessary transposition of the Gradual downwards means that the passage leading to the cadence at 'luceat eis' (b. 20–22) which concludes the respond section of the Gradual is essentially identical to the setting of the same words which ends the third verse of *Libera me Domine* (b. 73–5). (This same cadence-approach also appears at the end of the Gradual verse, at 'non timebit', b. 42–4.) Likewise, the setting of 'et lux perpetua' in the third verse of *Libera me* (b. 69–72) uses the same imitative material as the setting of these words in the Communion (b. 28–32).

Moreover, several sections of *Libera me Domine* exemplify a type of compositional strategy apparent also in other parts of the *Officium defunctorum*: bipartite structures in which the second of the two periods is climactic in relation to the first, and/or in which the second is the more active in terms of (for example) harmonic rhythm, speed of declamation, or animated vocal lines. Thus, for example, in the opening section of the responsory the text 'libera me Domine' is set as a repeated plea in the non-chant voices (the division between these two statements being marked by a cadence on the final D at the third note of the chant in the Altus, b. 5).

---

[60] If Victoria composed the *Libera me Domine* before the movements of the Requiem Mass – a possibility mentioned in Chapter 2 – it is nevertheless entirely possible that he had already decided that the Requiem for María would be for six voices.

[61] The only exception of which I am aware is the case of Pedro Rimonte's *Missæ sex* of 1604, which includes a six-voice *Libera me Domine* as well as a Requiem Mass. The eight-voice Requiem by Giulio Belli, published in his *Missarum sacrarumque cantionum octo vocibus liber primus* (Venice: Amadino, 1595, B1749), is there accompanied by a motet setting of the *Libera me Domine* text.

[62] It is also worth noting that the Offertory and *Libera me Domine* are the two movements of the *Officium defunctorum* where Victoria places the chant not in the Cantus II part but in the Altus. (At 'cum sanctis tuis in æternum' in the Communion, the chant phrase is begun by Cantus II, but is then taken over (transposed downwards by a fifth, to D final) by the Altus in breves and semibreves, for the duration of this one phrase only.) This phenomenon, which reflects the nature of the chant melodies involved, is discussed below.

In the first of these periods, the upper Cantus part is constrained to the *mi fa mi* gesture (*a'* – *b♭'* – *a'*) discussed previously, but in the second it expands upwards to reach the peak note *e''* which, as stated above, is used extremely sparingly in the *Officium defunctorum*, and which had been exploited most prominently in the 'nihil enim sunt dies mei' climax in *Versa est*. This second period is animated by minim declamation in various voices and by semiminim runs in Tenor II as well as by the dotted rhythm in Cantus I after it reaches its *e''* (b. 7). The type of bipartite climactic structure described here occurs in every other section of *Libera me Domine* (apart from the 'Tremens' verse borrowed from his older Requiem, and the brief concluding Kyries), and in these further examples harmonic rhythm is also manipulated as part of the climactic effect. In the next polyphonic section of the respond, 'quando cæli movendi sunt et terra', the speeding-up of the music in the second musical paragraph is prompted directly by the meaning of the text, 'movendi sunt', at which point minim declamation and a matching faster harmonic rhythm appear (b. 15 onwards). For the opening passages of both the second and third verses of the responsory ('Dies illa' and 'Requiem æternam') Victoria began with a breve harmonic rhythm for three bars, accelerating then to a semibreve harmonic rhythm in the fourth bar, and using the syncopated figure (as part of the 6+5 module in the second case) in the fifth bar leading to a cadence in the sixth bar, after which in both cases the next segment of text ('calamitatis' and 'dona eis' respectively) is set at the quicker pace, involving minim or semiminim declamation and a still faster harmonic rhythm.[63] The first part of the Gradual verse in the *Officium defunctorum* provides another example of such methods. As in the opening section of *Libera me Domine*, the text ('erit justus') is declaimed twice in the non-chant voices. The music begins in longs, breves, and semibreves, but after the extended version of the 6+5 module at b. 27–8 the text is repeated (incorporating a brisker 6+5 module) with faster harmonic rhythm and *per arsin et thesin* imitation between Altus and Cantus I. The first Kyrie of the Requiem Mass further exemplifies the creation of a bipartite structure around a single cantus firmus statement. Before the cadence (b. 9) demarcating the two periods the movement is almost entirely in breves and semibreves and the harmonic rhythm in breves (i.e. clear *proportio dupla* behaviour), but thereafter – as in the opening section of *Libera me Domine* – more animation is immediately generated by lower-voice activity. The two Tenor parts act as the engine propelling the new phrase,

---

[63] The 'Dies illa' verse also has a third section ('dies magna et amara valde').

employing syncopated non-imitative entries and semiminim movement. The entry of Tenor I is part of a close concentration of entries in Altus, Tenor I, and Cantus I just a minim apart, highlighting the beginning of the new period. This type of non-imitative animating movement may be one of the elements that Noel O'Regan had in mind when he referred to a 'sort of pseudo-polyphony found in [Victoria's] six-voice *Officium defunctorum*', remarking that it was 'a much-imitated manner'.[64]

The degree to which the *Libera me Domine* thus coheres musically with the preceding movements of the Requiem and the motet may well seem so natural to the modern listener that they would presume that this reflects normal practice when composing and publishing Requiem polyphony at the period. In fact, however, there were few precedents in Italy, Spain, or elsewhere for Victoria's inclusion of a setting of *Libera me Domine* along-side his printed Requiem Mass, and in cases where Iberian publications issued before or after 1605 do include this or other responsories *pro mortuis* as well as a Requiem these responsories do not in several instances match the accompanying Mass in terms of (for example) scoring as is the case in the *Officium defunctorum*. Amongst some forty printed Requiems by Italians pre-dating the *Officium defunctorum* only a couple were printed with a *Libera me Domine*, and one of these is a motet with this text rather than a setting of the liturgical responsory.[65] Regarding printed collections by Iberian composers, Vázquez's *Agenda defunctorum* (1556) and Rimonte's *Missæ sex* (1604) have settings of *Libera me Domine,* but during the half-century following the appearance of Victoria's *Officium defunctorum* the only setting to be published in the same volume as a Requiem Mass by a Peninsular composer is Cardoso's four-voice version included in the volume containing his six-voice Requiem.[66] Given their different

---

[64] Noel O'Regan, 'Victoria in Rome', *Leading Notes* 15 (Spring 1998), 26–30, at 29.

[65] As noted above, this motet is in Belli's *Missarum sacrarumque cantionum octo vocibus* of 1595; although it follows the Requiem Mass in the print, it is listed in the index as the first of the motets in the collection, and is a through-composed setting of parts of the *Libera me Domine* text. In contrast, Floriano Canale's setting in *Missæ, introitus ac motecta* (Brescia: Tomaso Bozzola, 1588, C770) is suitable for liturgical use as a responsory.

[66] *Missæ quaternis, quinis, et sex vocibus* (Lisbon: Pedro Craesbeeck, 1625, C1039). But while most Iberian Requiem Masses that reached publication were thus printed without a setting of *Libera me Domine*, a significant number of Requiems attributed to composers working in Spain and Portugal before about 1670 and preserved in manuscript are associated with a setting of *Libera me Domine* which is certainly or very possibly by the composer of the Requiem concerned. The Masses involved are those by Estêvão de Brito, Joan Brudieu, Juan Cererols (two works, for four and seven voices respectively), Cubells, Manuel Mendes, Estêvão Lopes Morago, and Joan Pau Pujol. There are also many Iberian *Libera me Domine* settings that do not appear together with a Mass, including for example a widely copied setting by Anchieta and a five-voice setting

scoring and cleffing, Cardoso's Mass and *Libera me* were probably conceived independently, and Vázquez's and Rimonte's *Libera me* settings are likewise scored differently from the Masses in the relevant collections. In the early decades of the seventeenth century the inclusion of *Libera me Domine* did become a regular practice in French publications of Requiems, such as those of Jean de Bournonville,[67] Eustache du Caurroy,[68] Pierre Lauverjat,[69] and Étienne Moulinié,[70] but this had previously been rare in France,[71] and among these examples Bournonville's and du Caurroy's are for fewer voices than their accompanying Masses.

Victoria himself had, however, already taken the unusual step of providing (in print) a *Libera me Domine* together with a Requiem twenty years earlier, when he published the *Missarum libri duo* in 1583 containing his four-voice Requiem, and in deciding to do so it seems likely that he was looking to the example of Francisco Guerrero's *Missarum liber secundus* issued the previous year.[72] These two publications form a striking pair of twins. They are both broadsheet choirbooks, published in Rome by Domenico Basa as part of a series of such choirbooks, as described in Chapter 3. But it is in their contents that the twinning of Guerrero's and Victoria's Mass collections is clearly apparent: both end with a four-voice Requiem together with a *Libera me Domine* setting, and both include a *Missa de beata virgine*, but more telling is the fact that in each publication we find a *Missa Simile est regnum cælorum* (Victoria's is, indeed, based on

by Alonso Lobo. Regarding settings of other responsory texts in Iberian publications which include Requiem Masses: Cardoso's four-voice Requiem in the *Livro de varios motetes* is (as mentioned above) preceded and followed by various items for Matins of the Dead, including the responsory *Ne recorderis*; Duarte Lobo's six-voice Requiem which appeared in his second book of Masses of 1639 is followed by a setting of the responsory *Memento mei Deus* for four voices, the cleffing of which again suggests that it was not conceived together with the Mass; the Requiem by Dávila y Páez published in López de Velasco's *Libro de missas* of 1628 is followed by a setting of the responsory *Peccantem me quotidie*, but without specific indication of whether this item is by López de Velasco or Dávila y Páez.

[67] *Missa trecedim IV. V. & VI. vocum quarum ultima pro defunctis* (Douai: Jean Bogard, 1619, B3843).

[68] *Missa pro defunctis, quinque vocum* (Paris: Pierre Ballard, 1636, D3618).

[69] *Missa pro defunctis, quatuor vocum* (Paris: Pierre Ballard, 1623, L1128).

[70] *Missa pro defunctis quinque vocum* (Paris: Pierre Ballard, 1623, M3940).

[71] One example is Pierre Clereau's *Missa pro mortuis, cum duobus motetis* (Paris: Nicolas du Chemin, 1554, C3186).

[72] Victoria may also have known Jacobus de Kerle's four-voice Requiem and *Libera me Domine* setting, which were printed together in his *Sex misse suavissimus modulationibus referte . . . concinende . . . liber primus* (Venice: Antonio Gardano, 1562, K446). Kerle was in the service of Cardinal Otto Truchsess von Waldburg, patron of the Collegium Germanicum where Victoria studied, and the dedicatee of Victoria's first published collection. Kerle subsequently entered imperial service, and was in Prague from 1583 until his death in 1591.

Guerrero's motet) and a *Missa Surge propera*, so that in total almost half of their contents consists of parallel works, and it is a nice conceit also that the parallelism involves works with the word 'simile' in their titles.[73] Besides this twinning between the contents of the books, there are indications that Guerrero's Requiem influenced Victoria's.[74] With regard to the association of a Requiem with a *Libera me Domine* in these two collections, we should note that Guerrero's *Libera me Domine* may well post-date the original composition of his Requiem, since the responsory did not appear in the first published edition of that work, from 1566.

But if Victoria followed Guerrero's example in including a *Libera me Domine* with his published Requiem, he did not adhere to the same procedure as Guerrero in setting the *Libera me Domine* text, regarding which elements were to be sung polyphonically and which chanted. Rather, the respond section of Victoria's work – in which the first two (out of three) sections of the respond are set completely in polyphony, and as a single unit – matches that of numerous works in Roman sources, suggesting that he was here conforming to Roman tradition, as was natural given that he (unlike Guerrero) was working in Rome at that time.[75] The scheme is as follows, with text set in polyphony shown in bold:[76]

[R1a] **Libera me Domine** [R1b] **de morte æterna in die illa tremenda**
[R2a] **quando cœli** [R2b] **movendi sunt et terra**
[R3a] dum veneris [R3b] iudicare sæculum per ignem.

The Roman works exemplifying this approach include a setting which forms part of the Requiem by Charles d'Argentil (a French singer in the *Cappella Pontificia* from the late 1520s until 1556),[77] the setting by Costanzo Festa (who enjoyed a long career in the *Cappella Pontificia*), three settings attributed to Palestrina, one by Francesco Soriano published in 1619, one by Giovanni Andrea Dragoni, and two unattributed settings in the Cappella Giulia book which contains the five-voice *Libera me*

[73] A further symptom of associations between Guerrero and Victoria within the series of Basa choirbook publications of the early 1580s is Victoria's inclusion of two motets by Guerrero in his *Motecta festorum totius anni* of 1585.

[74] For example, their settings of the Introit antiphon are identical for the last two and a half breves'-worth of music.

[75] Guerrero sets only the first section of the respond.

[76] The section labelled R2 is the first repetendum of the responsory, and that labelled R3 is the second repetendum. R2 is repeated after the first verse, R3 after the second verse, and the whole respond after the third. In Victoria's four-voice Requiem, the first repetition of R2 has to be chanted, since its polyphonic setting is joined on to R1 without a break.

[77] The Requiem is preserved in a choirbook copied for the Cappella Giulia in 1543: Biblioteca Apostolica Vaticana, Città del Vaticano, Cappella Giulia, XII.3, at ff. 140–52.

attributed to Palestrina.[78] These settings all resemble Victoria's four-voice work also in their inclusion of polyphony for the whole of all three verses ('Tremens factus sum', 'Dies illa', and 'Requiem'). Beyond this, many of the Roman settings exemplify a broader tradition – which both of Victoria's settings reflect – of using reduced or altered forces for the first two verses,[79] but more specifically we find several examples (particularly in Roman works) of the use of lower voices for verse 1 and higher voices for verse 2, as in Victoria's settings.[80]

However, in his six-voice *Libera me Domine* Victoria abandoned the Roman practice – and therefore his own earlier approach – in terms of how the respond is treated: instead, he set the first part only of the first section of the respond (although he again set the whole of R2), and also the first part of the third section:

[R1a] **Libera me Domine** [R1b] de morte æterna in die illa tremenda
[R2a] **quando cœli** [R2b] **movendi sunt et terra**
[R3a] **dum veneris** [R3b] iudicare sæculum per ignem.

---

[78] The Roman tradition of how to set *Libera me Domine* is explored further in Antonio Chemotti, 'Polyphonic Music pro mortuis in Italy', 177–227. Chemotti argues that this particular practice probably originated in the papal basilicas. The five-voice setting attributed to Palestrina is the last item in Biblioteca Apostolica Vaticana, Città del Vaticano, Cappella Giulia XV.15. It has the same scoring (with cleffing of c_1 c_3 c_4 c_4 f_4) as Palestrina's Requiem, which it follows in the source. One of the four-voice settings attributed to Palestrina is in Basilica di San Giovanni in Laterano, Archivio Musicale, Rari, st. mus. 59, at f. 92v-94; the bulk of the contents of this manuscript are believed to be in Palestrina's own hand. A second four-voice setting is in the eighteenth-century source Biblioteca Apostolica Vaticana, Città del Vaticano, Cappella Sistina Ms 219, at f. 49 onwards. The two four-voice settings are edited by Franz Xaver Haberl in Haberl et al. (eds), *Pierluigi da Palestrina: Werke*, 33 vols (Leipzig, 1862–1907), XXXI, at 19–24 and 140–44, and the five-voice setting in vol. XXXII of the same series, at 155–60. Haberl regarded the five-voice work as an *opus dubium*. The first of the unattributed settings of *Libera me Domine* in Cappella Giulia XV.15 is also preserved as the final item of an unattributed Requiem Mass in Basilica di San Giovanni in Laterano, Archivio Musicale, Rari, Ms 69, at ff. 1v-11. The scribal hand indicates that this copy was made in the seventeenth century, and the attribution of a piece later in the manuscript bears the date 1652.

[79] The practice of allocating the verses to fewer singers may reflect what happened in entirely chanted performance: for example, in the *Directorium chori* (Rome: Francesco Coattino, 1589), 595, we find the rubric that the verses of *Libera me Domine* are to be performed by two singers. The use of reduced scoring for verses is frequent in other polyphonic responsories also, beyond those *pro mortuis*.

[80] In the five-voice setting attributed to Palestrina, the first verse is for the four lower voices, and the second verse uses the four higher voices; Argentil's setting and one of the four-voice settings attributed to Palestrina (preserved in Cappella Sistina 219) use the lower three voices for verse 1 and the upper three for verse 2; in both of the anonymous settings in the Cappella Giulia manuscript verse 1 is likewise a trio, and one of them uses a high-voice quartet for verse 2, while in the other a trio of Cantus, Altus, and Tenor sings this verse; Festa employed two high voices for verse 2.

Not only was this not Roman custom, but I know of no Iberian settings of *Libera me Domine* which match this procedure. Rather, in pieces where, as in Victoria's setting, section R1b is left to be chanted, the same is typically done for R2b, producing the following scheme, consistent in its treatment of the three parts of the respond:[81]

[R1a] **Libera me Domine** [R1b] de morte æterna in die illa tremenda
[R2a] **quando cœli** [R2b] movendi sunt et terra
[R3a] **dum veneris** [R3b] iudicare sæculum per ignem.

Victoria had indeed adopted this scheme in the two responsory settings added to the 1592 edition of his four-voice Requiem, *Peccantem me quotidie* and *Credo quod redemptor*, and it may well be therefore that these were composed after his return to Spain, since they conform to frequent Iberian practice. In Iberian settings it is likewise common for each verse to be treated in this manner, i.e. with polyphony provided for only the first part of the verse, and this is what Victoria does in *Peccantem me quotidie* and *Credo quod redemptor*, whereas in his later setting of *Libera me Domine* he sets the whole of each verse, as he had in his earlier setting, and in common with other Roman settings. Victoria's approach in the six-voice *Libera me Domine* thus appears to be a highly unusual hybrid. Perhaps it reflects performance practice at the Descalzas, and possibly at the royal court also, in terms of how this and other responsories were treated in all-chanted performances and/or in versions with polyphony. Grayson Wagstaff has pointed out the tradition evident in settings of responsories *pro mortuis* of providing polyphony for those segments of the text that were sung by soloists in an all-chanted performance, and to leave in chant those parts which were sung by the entire *coro*.[82] But if Victoria's handling of the *Libera me Domine* in the *Officium defunctorum* does indeed match local practice in such terms, we should note that R2a is treated in two different ways in this setting: in polyphony when the respond is sung initially, and then in chant (which is set out in the 1605 volume) when R2 is repeated after the first verse. Was the first statement sung by soloists and the second by the whole *coro* in chanted performance of *Libera me Domine* at the Descalzas? Or does Victoria's method reflect a tradition applying to polyphonic settings there? Or, finally, might Victoria's treatment of the respond represent his own decision? In this

[81] This scheme is followed in, for example, the settings by Juan de Anchieta, Estêvão de Brito, Manuel Cardoso, Aires Fernandez, Hernando Franco, Alonso Lobo, Manuel Mendes, and Juan Vázquez.
[82] 'Music for the Dead', 147.

last case, the inconsistency between his handling of R1 and R2 in the initial statement of the respond could be explicable in textual (syntactic) terms. Whereas R1a ('Libera me Domine') constitutes a clause, R2a ('quando cœli') is a verbless stump, and so Victoria might have regarded it as less suitable for treatment as a separate musical unit, and preferred to continue in polyphony for the whole clause 'quando cœli movendi sunt et terra'.

Requiem Masses as Composite Forms: Scoring and Tonalities

Victoria's binding together of not only his music for Mass but also the motet and the *Libera me Domine* through the use of consistent scoring extended a practice of unifying the movements of a Requiem Mass in terms of scoring and cleffing,[83] a practice long established beyond the Pyrenees but one that apparently became customary among Iberian composers only during the course of Victoria's composing career, and which was still far from entrenched even by 1603.[84] In Requiems by composers active in the late fifteenth century and the early decades of the sixteenth century, such as La Rue, Brumel, Févin, and Prioris, variety of scoring and cleffing is commonplace. In La Rue's Requiem, for example, almost every movement has a different type of scoring (with a total of eight types employed), and some movements are for four voices and others for five. This variegated approach is likewise apparent in the earliest surviving Iberian Requiem, by Pedro de Escobar. Of the two Iberian Requiems published in the mid-sixteenth century, both by composers born near the start of the century, Morales's five-voice Requiem employs five different scorings and clef-combinations,[85] while Vázquez's Requiem within the *Agenda defunctorum* has six, together with a seventh clef-combination for the motet *Sana me Domine* inserted after the Sanctus. Moving a generation later, in the first published version of Guerrero's Requiem (1566) one finds five

[83] Such consistency is not disturbed by a movement being in high clefs, as is the case with Victoria's setting of the Gradual in the *Officium defunctorum* and as was common practice in Italy in setting the Sequence of the Requiem Mass.

[84] In describing the scoring of the various items for Mass in Victoria's 1605 collection as consistent, I am of course considering the 'basic' scoring of each item, and ignoring for these purposes reductions in the number of voices for the 'Christe' and verses 1 and 2 of *Libera me Domine*.

[85] One should emphasise that the types of variability of scoring discussed here go well beyond the adjustments to the clef of a particular voice which copyists and printers quite routinely undertook.

clef-combinations representing four scoring matrices,[86] while the version published in 1582 (which contains some different items for Mass) has four clef-combinations representing three scoring matrices. A year later Victoria published his four-voice Requiem, and here we see a rather more unified approach, with just two scoring matrices, represented by three clef-combinations. Victoria may have been influenced in this regard by contemporary practice in Italy and/or beyond, since Requiems by Italian composers published up to that point normally use just one or two scoring matrices, and this practice dominates in works by both Italians and Northerners published from the 1550s onwards.[87] But among Victoria's contemporaries working in Spain and Portugal the employment of a variety of scoring continued: we find this, for example, in the Requiems by Sebastián de Vivanco and Manuel Mendes, and the four-voice work by Juan Esquivel (published eight years after the *Officium defunctorum*), all of which have three or four different matrices. Victoria, however, elected for the Italian and Northern-European approach in writing the music for María's exequies, and in so doing may have been at or near the leading edge of the normalising of this practice in the Peninsula, a practice seen also in (for example) the five Requiems by his younger contemporaries in Portugal, Cardoso, Lobo, and Magalhães.

As was mentioned in discussing *Versa est* and *Libera me*, tonal aspects play a significant role in producing the impression of coherence given by Victoria's Requiem. To contextualise his compositional approach in this respect, one needs first to emphasise that polyphonic Requiems drawing upon the relevant chant in each movement (as Victoria's does) had a concomitant tendency towards variety among the movements in terms of modal representation and tonal type; such variety contrasts with polyphonic Mass Ordinary settings (belonging to any of the common types: cantus-firmus, paraphrase, or parody/imitation Masses), where modal representation and tonal type (as well as, to some extent, material) were typically the same across all movements. Victoria's six-voice Requiem exemplifies an approach to the polyphonic Requiem which counteracted that variety to a lesser or greater extent, an approach which brings the best of both worlds: the resulting complex of polyphonic or part-polyphonic

---

[86] Two of the clef-combinations represent the same scoring, but are a third apart in cleffing.

[87] Antonio Chemotti scrutinised the cleffing of a large array of printed Requiems by Italian composers in printed sources, and kindly reported the results to me in a private communication. He found only a handful of cases in which there were changes of scoring matrix (excluding the cases where the Sequence alone is notated in high clefs), and these changes were mainly trivial. My own survey of Italian Requiems produced similar results.

movements gains coherence, but retains the associative and evocative power and authority of using the chants. However, as will be explored below, while thus linking sections of the Requiem in certain respects, Victoria also cultivates *varietas* within sections to a striking degree.

The Introit and Kyrie chants used in Victoria's Requiem are both in mode 6, and the Gradual and Offertory both in mode 2. The Gradual chant, untransposed, ends on A rather than the final D, as does its verse, but this chant appears in many chant source of the period transposed down by a fifth so that it ends on D, like the Offertory, and Victoria's cleffing for the Gradual indicates that he intended this transposition.[88] The chants of the remaining sections – Sanctus, Agnus Dei, and Communion – all have G as final, but they contrast in modal terms, and although all three make reference to – or use of – psalm tones, in each case the psalm tone is a different one. The Sanctus chant employs for almost all its length the sixth psalm tone, with A as recitation note and repeated occurrences of the intonation formula F – G – A; only in its last phrase (the Hosanna of the Benedictus) does it swerve away, beginning this phrase on D and ending (as mentioned) on G rather than the expected F, using one of the terminations of psalm tone 1. Since the sixth psalm tone resembles psalm tone 1 in important respects, the Sanctus chant is thus close to that of the Introit verse, and likewise employs B *fa*. The Agnus Dei chant bears resemblances to the fourth psalm tone, including the G – A – B *mi* formula of that tone's mediation and terminations; this appearance of the *cantus durus* system contrasts with the *cantus mollis* of the formulæ used in the Sanctus chant and that of the Introit verse, although the Agnus chant also traces the F – G – A ascent which is prominent in both Introit and Sanctus chants. The Communion is uncontrovertibly a mode-8 chant, using B *mi*, and its verse is sung to the eighth psalm tone.

With this overview of the chants' modes in mind, we may consider next the tonal types which Victoria employed:[89]

---

[88] This does not, however, render the Gradual modally identical to the Offertory, since the Gradual once transposed represents *cantus mollis*, with flat signature.

[89] On tonal types, see Harold Powers, 'Tonal Types and Modal Categories in Renaissance Polyphony', *Journal of the American Musicological Society* 34 (1981), 428–70. I use here the well established shorthand method of indicating the 'minimal markers' of tonal type, as employed by Powers: ♭ and ♮ indicate respectively *cantus mollis* (with a signature of B♭) and *cantus durus* (with no signature); c_1 and g_2 indicate the cleffing (and therefore ambitus), by showing the clef of the top voice (in the case of Victoria's Mass, the two Cantus parts) and therefore indicating the use of *chiavi naturali* ('normal clefs'), where c_1 is the highest clef, or *chiavette* ('high clefs'), where g_2 is the highest; the capital letter which concludes each designation of tonal type is the pitch class of the lowest note in the final sonority of the relevant movement.

Introit: $\flat$ – c_1 – F
Kyrie: $\flat$ – c_1 – F
Gradual: $\natural$ – g_2 – A
Offertory: $\natural$ – c_1 – D
Sanctus: $\natural$ – c_1 – G
Agnus Dei: $\natural$ – c_1 – G
Communion: $\natural$ – c_1 – G

At this minimally characterised level of tonal categorisation, therefore, we see the modal variety between the chants reflected in his polyphonic treatment, with four different tonal types present among the seven movements: one for Introit and Kyrie, one each for the Gradual and Offertory, and the final one for Sanctus, Agnus Dei, and Communion. If we were to view this music in terms of the 'church keys' which became a prominent part of tonal theory and practice in the seventeenth century, then the initial two movements belong (according to the numerations and categorisation found in Banchieri's *Cartella musicale* (1614) and in other writings) to the sixth *tuono*, the Gradual (once transposed) to the seventh, the Offertory to the first, and the final three movements to the eighth.[90] What if one attempted a twofold division into major and minor modes (one which would acquire growing theoretical currency during the seventeenth century), or *Ut* and *Re* tonalities, to use the terminology developed by Cristle Collins Judd?[91] If such distinction were made on the basis of the final cadences of movements (a method which, as we shall see, is crude and distorting for the music of this Mass), then five out of the seven movements of the Mass (Introit, Kyrie, Sanctus, Agnus Dei, and Communion) would be said to represent the major mode (or *Ut* tonalities) and only two (Gradual and Offertory) the minor (or *Re* tonalities).

And yet Victoria's crafting of these seven movements reveals him both mitigating the tonal variety indicated by considering the chants, tonal types, and church keys,[92] and also manipulating the 'major'-'minor' (or *Ut* versus *Re* tonalities) profile of the piece suggested by the crude measure

[90] See Gregory Barnett, 'Tonal Organization in Seventeenth-Century Music Theory', in Thomas Christensen (ed.), *The Cambridge History of Western Music Theory* (Cambridge University Press, 2008), 407–55, at 419–27, Harold Powers, 'From Psalmody to Tonality', in Cristle Collins Judd (ed.), *Tonal Structures in Early Music* (New York & London: Garland, 1998), 275–340, at 281–306, and Wiering, *The Language of the Modes*, 76–8.

[91] See her 'Modal Types and *Ut, Re, Mi* Tonalities: Tonal Coherence in Sacred Vocal Polyphony from around 1500', *Journal of the American Musicological Society* 45 (1994), 428–67.

[92] In counteracting the Requiem chants' tonal variety Victoria was far from alone among composers of polyphonic Requiems, and such phenomena deserve extensive study in an

just mentioned. The particular pair of tonalities that 'naturally' dominate the Requiem – *Ut* tonality on F and *Re* tonality on D – reflect the chants incorporated, but even where a particular chant did not (or did not most obviously) suggest such tonal treatment we find Victoria often steering the music into this territory of *Ut* F tonality and/or *Re* D tonality. In broad terms, his manipulation of emphasis between *Ut* and *Re* tonalities is in favour of the latter, the 'minor', but – as will be explored below – the characteristic sound-world of the six-voice Requiem is generated in part by nothing so simple as this, but rather by the tendency within movements to mix *Ut* and *Re* tonalities. Such striking *chiaroscuro* effects in which major and minor are regularly juxtaposed constitute a significant part of the affective character of the work.

Chiaroscuro

A good example of such 'major'/'minor' (or *Ut* / *Re* tonality) juxtaposition is the repetentum section of the Offertory ('quam olim Abrahæ promisisti et semini eius'), where alternating F (*Ut*) and D (*Re*) cadences follow in quick succession, the *chiaroscuro* being emphasised by changes in texture: after the F cadence at 'Abrahæ' (b. 65) this word is repeated by upper voices, cadencing on D (b. 66), then 'promisisti' in the chant (here in the Altus) is harmonised with an F cadence (b. 68), and again repeated by upper voices but with the last chant note altered so as to allow a D cadence (b. 69). Thereafter, for 'et semini eius', Victoria uses a circle-of-fifths sequence (b. 70–4), sharpening the initial f of this chant phrase and using major-third harmonies of D, G, C, F, and B♭. This sequence therefore initially contrasts, in its use of the *cantus durus* system, with the *cantus mollis* of the preceding music, but the circle-of-fifths process returns the music to *cantus mollis* in preparation for the final D cadence of the movement.

Victoria introduces a more dramatic clash between *cantus durus* and *cantus mollis* in the Communion. As noted above, the chant here is of the eighth mode, with G final and using the B *mi* of *cantus durus* in both the antiphon and the verse, the latter employing the eighth psalm tone. Victoria's setting is of tonal type ♮ – c_1 – G. However, to mark the start of the second phrase of text in the polyphonic setting of the antiphon, 'cum

attempt to appreciate more fully composers' approaches to the genre given that it was not a naturally unified one (in terms of tonalities) as were most Mass Ordinary settings.

sanctis tuis', Tenor II unexpectedly switches to *b fa* (b. 8), clashing with the preceding occurrences of B *mi* in both the chant-bearing voice (Cantus II, as usual in this Mass) and the Altus, and contradicting the modality of the chant by employing the minor third above the modal final G. This phrase of text, 'cum sanctis tuis', is then repeated several times, each repetition marked (as in the passage from the Offertory just described) by a shift to a new texture, and these repetitions alternate between use of B *fa* and B *mi*. Thus two breves after the Tenor II *b fa* the chant-bearing voice sings a sustained *b′ mi* (b. 10), and this is emphasised by forming part of a 6+5 module. Two breves later again, the same voice then has *b′ fa* (b. 12), the shift back to *mollis* being intensified by the fact that this too occurs as part of a 6+5 module. After these statements of 'cum sanctis tuis' for low, high, and low voices respectively, all the voices contribute to the culminating statement, and here yet again the form of B switches, this *b mi* (in Tenor I, b. 13–14) forming part of the syncopated figure of yet another 6+5 module: this section of the Communion involves more concentrated use of the module than does any other passage in the *Officium defunctorum*. Moreover, since this passage constitutes the first part of the repetendum of the Communion, its impact in performance is enhanced through repetition. Its second occurrence follows without break from the end of the verse ('et lux perpetua luceat eis'), and once again at this point Victoria dramatises the point of articulation by means of a *mi – fa* confrontation: approaching the G-cadence that ends 'luceat eis' Tenor I sings *b mi* (b. 34), but at the moment of cadence Tenor II contradicts this with its *b fa* (b. 35), the effect being (as at b. 8) a strange reversal of the conventional 'tierce de Picardie'.

Victoria's remarkable setting of the remaining repetendum text, 'quia pius es', likewise exploits the *mi – fa* contrast as one means of highlighting textual repetition. The passage is constructed such that we hear a threefold statement of 'quia pius es' (even though not all the voices sing the text three times). I know of no other instances of such threefold declamatory treatment of this text in the international Requiem repertoire of the period.[93]

---

[93] Closest to Victoria's approach among the Requiems known to me are those in Lassus's four-voice setting, Cardoso's setting for six voices, and Kerle's: in the first two of these pieces 'quia pius es' is sung twice, Lassus using quasi-chordal texture both times, and Cardoso three-voice quasi-chordal texture the first time. Kerle begins his extended treatment of 'quia pius es' with imitation based upon the relevant chant motive, but ends the section with two further statements both involving homorhythmic declamation in three of the four voices. Lobo also employs a double statement of 'quia pius es' in both of his Requiems (using contrapuntal and imitative textures): in each case the first phrase is for a reduced number of voices and the second for all voices. Clemens likewise repeats 'quia pius es', and his final four-voice statement of it is homorhythmic. In the unattributed Requiem in Montserrat, Abadía, 1085, 'quia pius es' is repeated in the lower three parts in free homorhythm to conclude the setting.

The 'Phrygian' cadence which ends the first statement (b. 21–2) involves *B fa* in the Bassus coinciding with the peak of the phrase, *d″* in Cantus I, and the peak note (*a′*) of the chant phrase here, itself emphasised at the relevant point by being treated as a suspension.[94] In contrast, during the second statement (b. 22–5) Cantus I ascends via *b′ mi*, and the two Tenor parts decorate the peak of this Cantus ascent (the *c″* at 'pius') with shorter-note figures involving *b mi*.[95] In the third and final statement (b. 25–7) a *b′ mi* in Cantus I is strikingly contradicted by a final *b fa* in Tenor II, the latter being a closing surprise which colours the cadence onto G. The *mi* / *fa* oppositions in the setting of 'quia pius es' apply not only to B but also to F. In the first statement of 'quia pius es' Victoria inflects the second note of the chant phrase E – F – G – A so that its second note is *f♯′* (Cantus II, b. 19),[96] but this ascent through a tetrachord is accompanied by an ascent in the Altus which takes it from *c♯′* to *f♮′*, and in the second statement of 'quia pius es' the same contrast between *f′ mi* in Cantus II and *f′ fa* in the Altus is used again. If *Versa est in luctum* were sung next (as it appears in the print), this would highlight the shared emphasis on *mi* / *fa* conflicts in the 'quia pius es' passage (with which the Communion ends) and the motet. In each case the *mi* / *fa* instability involves both B and F. The latter instability is built into one of the two concurrent motives of the motet's opening, but also occurs between Altus and Cantus II in b. 4–5. As far as B *mi* and *fa* are concerned, I have noted above how the motet generally inhabits *cantus durus* in these terms but makes telling use of B *fa* to mark the conclusion of the opening section (b. 12) and of course at 'vocem flentium'.

The opening of Victoria's Communion setting is likewise coloured by contrasts between natural/sharp versions of a note, although a mistake (or misguided intervention) in Pedrell's edition dilutes the effect. The imitative figure sung first by Tenor II (b. 1–2) includes both *c♮′* and *c♯′*, with just one note intervening. Of course, this distinction between the two positions of

---

[94] The Bassus *B♭* is not so signed in the print, but is obligatory given the *f* in the Altus.

[95] Some modern editors suggest a flat for one or both of the relevant occurrences of *b* in the Tenor parts: Bruno Turner indicates a flat for both (presumably so that the relevant gestures incorporate a perfect rather than augmented fourth), and Samuel Rubio just for the first.

[96] Victoria used the stepwise version of the Communion verse chant in both of his Requiems; it occurs in (for example) the *Proprium missarum* printed by the Royal Press in Madrid in 1597. Another version, reflected in many polyphonic settings and found in (for example) the *Graduale Romanum* (Venice: Angelo Gardano, 1591), leaps from the F to the A. Although Victoria's inflexion of the chant here (with F ♯) is exceptional within the Requiem repertory, Victoria uses it likewise in his four-voice Requiem, and it is also found in Contino's and Heredia's settings and the unattributed Requiem in Tuy Cathedral, L 5. In Aichinger's Requiem the Tenor presents this chant phrase with *f♮*, and then repeats it with *f♯*.

C makes sense here in terms of melodic direction, with the $c\natural'$ falling and the $c\sharp'$ ascending to d' (although that does not negate the fact that Victoria *chose* such a shape), but the effect of instability is heightened by the fact that the chant-bearing voice sings a sustained $c\natural''$ (the second note of the chant) just a semibreve later (b. 3), supported by the same pitch class in the Bassus and indeed then in Tenor II. (Since this c' in Tenor II again rises to d', the singers would surely have expected to treat is as $c\sharp'$ once again when looking at their line alone, but the other parts prevent them from doing so.) Pedrell omitted the Tenor II sharp in b. 2. If not simply an error, this omission was perhaps motivated by the fact that the Bassus – singing the same imitative motive a breve after Tenor II does so – has no equivalent sharp, but if so Pedrell chose to ignore the Tenor I entry (b. 5–6), which matches Tenor II's in terms of intervals but a fifth lower, and thus has both $f\natural$ and then $f\sharp$. Whatever his reasons, Pedrell's version renders the passage more bland than it is in the 1605 edition, and this is one of the points in the *Officium defunctorum* where it is unfortunate that several modern editors looked to the edition by Pedrell rather than to the 1605 volume itself: the omission of the Tenor II $c\sharp'$ is reproduced in the editions by David Wulstan (who regarded the sharp as 'probably an error'), Bruno Turner, and Jon Dixon, and this watered-down effect is now the familiar one in concerts and recordings: approximately twice as many recordings have the $c\natural'$ as those that reproduce the gesture intended here.

The $c\sharp' - d'$ in Tenor II here reinforces the D tonality which Victoria employed at the start of the Communion, and this choice of tonality contributes to the focus on a particular pair of tonalities – *Ut* on F and *Re* on D – in Victoria's music for the second day of the exequies. This choice for the opening of the Communion was common but not inevitable: the chant here (which, as noted, is in mode 8) has an opening gesture for 'luceat eis' of $a' - c'' - b' - c'' - a'$, and several composers chose in consequence to construct the opening of their Communion settings using harmonies on A with minor third, and/or imitative entries on A and E:[97] settings of the Communion in Requiems of this period typically employ paraphrase technique in the opening section, constructing *fuga* from the chant motive. Other composers, however, treated the first chant note, a', as the upper note of a $d' - a'$ first-species pentachord (*re – la*, belonging to the protus modes) and used imitative entries on

---

[97] For example: Asola's four-voice setting published in *Messa pro defunctis a quatro voci pari* (Venice: Angelo Gardano, 1576, A2529), Belli's four-voice setting, and Cardoso's four-voice setting.

D and A.[98] The use of *Re* tonality on D for this polyphonic opening makes sense given that the chant incipit includes an *f♮'*. In Victoria's setting, the Altus entry supplies the lower note of the pentachord below the *a'* in Cantus II, and then sings the *f♮'* (i.e. *fa*) in between. This tonal emphasis is strengthened by the fact that the next two entries (in Tenor II and Bassus) of the opening passage are likewise on D. A similar tonal treatment of the Communion's first paragraph is found in Victoria's four-voice Requiem, but a comparison of the two settings here highlights a frequent difference between these Requiems, namely the more highly coloured language of the later work: the four-voice Communion uses neither the C sharps of the opening section in the six-voice setting nor the B flats of its 'cum sanctis tuis' section.

Overall, one finds a similar approach to crafting a Requiem in terms of tonalities in Victoria's four- and six-voice Requiems. It is true that in one important respect – his handling of the Gradual – Victoria went less far in the earlier work in producing a focus on D- and F-final tonalities than he did in 1603, but even so one sees an effort to bring the music within the same tonal sphere as other movements. As in the six-voice Mass, the Gradual of the four-voice Requiem is notated with the chant at the normal pitch for mode 2, with both of its principal sections ending on A. However, whereas the Gradual of the later Requiem has *chiavette* cleffing, indicating downwards transposition of a fifth, the clef combination of the four-voice Gradual is the same as that used for the Introit and Kyrie (c_1 c_2 c_3 f_3) and does not therefore denote such transposition (and indeed in the Introit and Kyrie here the relevant chants are presented at the normal pitches for those chants). Thus, while in the six-voice Requiem the Gradual as performed has section-ending cadences on D, matching the Offertory, in the four-voice work these cadences are on A. However, in this earlier setting Victoria steers the music some distance towards the tonal territory of the Introit and Kyrie by writing much of the movement in the sixth *tuono* (to use church-key terminology) of those earlier movements, with the beginnings of phrases and sections in F-tonality.

In one case within the six-voice Requiem – the Introit verse – Victoria's periodic steering of a section with F-mode chant towards D *Re* tonality was quite conventional (among Requiems),[99] and is apparent also (albeit to

---

[98] Works that do so include Esquivel's four-voice setting and Cardoso's six-voice setting. The latter may indeed have been influenced by Victoria's six-voice work since Cardoso employs the same imitative motive as does Victoria.

[99] Two earlier examples are the five-voice Requiems of Morales and Lassus, and a later instance is in the six-voice Requiem by Cardoso.

a lesser extent) in his four-voice Mass, but is here made dramatic. Although, as noted, this verse is based on a chant using the sixth psalm tone, and which duly cadences onto F at its end, composers tended to orient their harmonisation of much of the verse around a D tonality with minor third (perhaps encouraged to do so by the similarity between the first and sixth psalm tones, already mentioned), and Victoria did so from the fourth breve (b. 36) onwards. At 'Hierusalem' he cadences onto A (b. 41–2), the note with which this chant phrase ends, but inserts a suspended dissonance into this cadence, driving it onwards to a cadence on D one breve later, and thus linking this part of the verse with the next.[100] Shortly afterwards (b. 48–50), the quicker declamation at 'orationem' uses (as mentioned above) a D – C♯ – D figure in imitation which reinforces the D tonality, and leads to a climactic D cadence at 'meam' (b. 51–2) emphasised by the dotted rising gesture in the Bassus. Only after this, for the final phrase of the verse ('ad te omnis caro veniet') does the music move back to F tonality, reflecting the termination of the psalm tone and allowing a tonally smooth junction with the repetition of the antiphon.

While the tonal character of Victoria's setting is in this case not unusual, his treatment of the Sanctus, Agnus Dei, and Communion is suggestive of the broader scheme (as I have posited it above) for his Requiem as a whole, in terms of the focus upon and balance between *Ut* F and *Re* D tonalities. The Communion has already been discussed in this regard. It will be remembered that the Sanctus chant (except for its final phrase) is close to the sixth psalm tone, and Victoria might well have chosen to clothe it with polyphony using essentially F tonality (or in the sixth church key), but instead he made D tonality at least as prominent as F. The opening melodic gesture of the movement, in the Altus, establishes D tonality, and the second and third of the three polyphonic sections, after the 'pleni sunt' and 'Benedictus' chant intonations, both begin with a D-minor harmony and a D cadence, while the cadence before the first 'Hosanna' (b. 25–6) is likewise on D. But Victoria has not simply eschewed F tonality in favour of D in the relevant sections: they rub shoulders as they do in the Introit. Moreover, the striking 'circle-of-fifths' sequential passage which opens the Sanctus – discussed above regarding its reliance on the

---

[100] In most Iberian settings, including that in Victoria's four-voice Requiem, there is a break between these two parts of the verse, although harmonically Victoria's four-voice setting is here similar to his six-voice one, with the first sonority after the rest completing a cadence onto D; those settings which avoid such a break, besides Victoria's six-voice treatment, are the two by Esquivel, Guerrero's, Garro's, Morales's four-voice setting, and the setting in the Requiem by Dávila y Páez.

syncopated cadential figure and therefore its links with *Versa est* – serves to link the D and F tonalities through a dynamic process, since its succession of cadences is D – G – C – F.

Turning to the Agnus Dei, the chant phrase to which 'qui tollis peccata mundi' (the first part of each polyphonic section) is sung outlines A – G – A – F – G – A, and is therefore amenable to similar treatment to the bulk of the Sanctus, and Victoria certainly adopts a similar tonal practice: both polyphonic sections begin with D harmony; the first then cadences on F (b. 5) before returning to D for the cadence ending the section (b. 8, before 'dona eis requiem'); the second Agnus Dei reverses this procedure, cadencing on D in b. 19 and emphatically on F in b. 23–4 (the cadence before 'dona eis requiem').

Polyphony and Chant

In planning and fashioning his six-voice Requiem, Victoria faced various other basic decisions, for some of which conventional practice – whether in the Peninsula or beyond it – would have exerted significant influence: which liturgical items to set, which element of these texts to treat polyphonically, how much and in what ways to make use of the relevant chants in the polyphony, and (beyond this) what manners of polyphonic writing to adopt.

In the selection of items set Victoria's six-voice Requiem typifies Iberian practice, and thereby also corresponds with customs north of the Alps, but differs from Italian usage. Victoria's music for the Mass itself comprises the following seven items:

Introit
Kyrie
Gradual
Offertory
Sanctus
Agnus Dei
Communion

Of the Requiems by Spanish composers or by composers working in Spain up to the mid seventeenth century, more than twice as many set the Gradual (or part of it) as omit it, and all the Portuguese settings from this period have a Gradual.[101] In Italy, however, it was rare to set this

---

[101] The Requiems by Spanish composers which omit the Gradual typically include the Tract; among them are both Requiems by Esquivel and that by Vivanco. Among the very few

item.[102] Conversely, almost all polyphonic Requiem Masses by Italian composers in the period up to 1650 incorporate the Sequence, but the Spanish and Portuguese (and also the French and other northerners) very rarely did so, despite the inclusion of this Sequence in the reformed Roman Missal and the fact that it was sung polyphonically during at least some royal exequies in Spain:[103] as noted in Chapter 2, the surviving draft order of service for Philip II's court *honras* indicates that a polyphonic setting of the Sequence be used, while at the exequies for Philip III organised by the city of Murcia the Sequence was sung *alternatim* at both of the Requiem Masses.[104]

In terms of *how much* of a given text is provided with polyphony in the *Officium defunctorum*, while we again find conformity with typical Iberian practice in some respects, other facets are unusual. Below I again use **bold** to show which segments of text are set in polyphony; chanted sections not provided in the 1605 edition are shown in brackets, and an arrow indicates where there is no break in the music between sections of text.

INTROIT

Antiphon: Requiem æternam **dona eis Domine, et lux perpetua luceat eis.**

Requiems (internationally) which provide settings of both Gradual and Tract are those by Garro, Guerrero, and Vázquez. The draft order of service for Philip II's court exequies specifies that both Gradual and Tract were to be sung in polyphony, using Guerrero's settings; see Robledo, 'Questions of Performance Practice', 209.

[102] I am aware of only ten Italian Requiems of the period (out of a field of approximately one hundred) which include the Gradual; a similar number include the Tract.

[103] Victoria did not set the Sequence as part of his four-voice Requiem, despite that work's Roman origins. Most Iberian settings of the Sequence are in any case atypical of Italian practice, according to which sufficient music is provided to allow either an *alternatim* performance of the text or a fully polyphonic one. For example, Esquivel in his four-voice Requiem sets only the last two verses, from 'Lachrimosa' onwards. The four-voice setting of the Sequence which forms part of Duarte Lobo's six-voice Requiem appears at first sight closer to the Italian model, since he sets the first three odd-numbered verses. However, he then – oddly – breaks the *alternatim* scheme, setting verses 8 and 14, and finally includes the text from 'Lachrimosa' to the end of the Sequence; the Sequence published as part of Dávila y Páez's Requiem is likewise brief, including just verses 1, 8, and 13, together with the concluding 'Pie Jesu'. A similarly selective treatment of the *Dies iræ* is found in one Italian Requiem, that by Tamburini, who sets verses 2, 7, 9, 14, 18, and the 'Pie Jesu'. Morales's five-voice Requiem includes a setting of just the 'Pie Jesu'; since the same occurs in the Requiem by Charles d'Argentil, who was a colleague of Morales in the Cappella Pontificia, one wonders whether this was a practice of that chapel, or whether one of these two settings influenced the other. On the use of a version of the 'Pie Jesu' text as an Elevation motet in seventeenth-century France, see Montagnier, *The Polyphonic Mass in France*, 241–2.

[104] See Enriquez, *Las honras*, 62–3. The decrees resulting from a visitation of the Royal Chapel in March 1594 include the instruction that the Sequence be included in Requiem Masses (although there is no stipulation that polyphony be used), indicating that this had not previously been the chapel's practice; see Robledo, 'La música en la casa del rey', 163 and 349.

Verse: Te decet hymnus Deus in Sion: **et tibi reddetur votum in Hierusalem. Exaudi orationem meam: ad te omnis caro veniet.**

KYRIE[105]

Kyrie eleison
Christe eleison
Kyrie eleison

GRADUAL

Requiem æternam **dona eis Domine, et lux perpetua luceat eis.**
Verse: In memoria æterna **erit iustus: ab auditione mala non timebit.**

OFFERTORY

Domine Iesu Christe rex gloriæ, **libera animas ... in lucem sanctam.** →
Repetendum: **quam olim Abrahæ ... et semini eius.**
[*Verse*: Hostias et preces ... de morte transire ad vitam.]
[*Repetendum*: quam olim Abrahæ ... et semini eius.]

SANCTUS

Sanctus, **sanctus, sanctus Dominus Deus Sabaoth.**
Pleni sunt **cæli et terra gloria tua. Hosanna in excelsis.**
Benedictus **qui venit in nomine Domini. Hosanna in excelsis.**

AGNUS DEI

Agnus Dei **qui tollis peccata mundi, dona eis requiem.**
[Agnus Dei qui tollis peccata mundi, dona eis requiem.]
Agnus Dei **qui tollis peccata mundi, dona eis requiem sempiternam.**

COMMUNION

Lux æterna **luceat eis Domine:** →
Repetendum: **cum sanctis tuis in æternum, quia pius es.**
Verse: Requiem æternam dona eis Domine: **et lux perpetua luceat eis.** →
Repetendum: **cum sanctis tuis in æternum, quia pius es.**

Regarding the inclusion or omission of entire sections of text, the fact that Victoria did not set the Offertory verse 'Hostias et preces' aligns with typical Spanish and Portuguese practice, whereas polyphony for this verse was usually included in Requiems by Franco-Flemish composers and more often than not by Italians.[106] One issue facing modern performers at this point in Victoria's Requiem is how to perform the repetendum

---

[105] Possible *alternatim* performance of the Kyrie is discussed below.
[106] Franco-Flemish custom was to leave the first part of the verse to be chanted, beginning the polyphony at 'tu suscipe', and this practice was also quite common in Italy.

section of the antiphon text, 'quam olim Abrahæ promisisti et semini eius', which is to be sung again after the verse. In his four-voice Requiem Victoria had provided a break in the polyphony before the beginning of the repetendum, and in both the 1583 and 1592 editions of the work this repetendum section is placed on a new opening, with the chant for the verse given below it, thus facilitating performance with the necessary repetition, which is indeed indicated by an 'ut supra' instruction in both editions. Similar breaks in the polyphony before 'Quam olim' occur in a small number of other Iberian Requiems – those by Brito, Cardoso (both Masses), Cererols (the four-voice Requiem), Guerrero, and Magalhães – and are not uncommon in Italian settings (for example, all four Requiems by Giovanni Matteo Asola) and northern works (such as those by Aichinger, Ammon, Clemens non Papa, Clereau, Févin, Moulinié, and Sermisy).[107] In contrast, in Victoria's six-voice setting and in most Requiems attributed to Iberian composers there is no break in the polyphony at 'quam olim'. Whoever undertook the casting off of this movement when the *Officium defunctorum* was printed may, however, have had polyphonic repetition of the repetendum in mind: he laid out the Offertory in such a way that the final cadence note in each part immediately preceding 'quam olim' falls on a new opening of the choirbook. Although the voices' entries at 'quam olim' are not simultaneous, the singers would have had relatively little difficulty beginning from this point.[108] However, such a restart would have been highly unconventional and somewhat unsatisfactory: the first entries of 'quam olim' (b. 62) begin not on the *thesis* but on the *arsis*, whereas in the polyphonic style of this period pieces (and independent sections of pieces) always begin on the *thesis*; also, the Altus holds a *d'* on the last syllable of the previous text-phrase ('-tam') during

[107] It is common in Franco-Flemish settings for the repetition of 'Quam olim . . . ' to follow the end of the verse without a musical break; this occurs in the Requiems by Bonnefont, Bournonville, Clemens, Du Caurroy, Lauverjat (where new music is provided for the repetition of 'quam olim . . . '), Monte, Prioris, and Richafort. The same procedure is also found in the four- and five-voice Requiems by Lassus, and in a number of Italian Requiems, such as Belli's five-voice Mass, those by Biondi and Zucchini, both of the four-voice Requiems by Pontio, and Viadana's three-voice Mass.

[108] We can presume that a similar treatment of the Offertory, with both occurrences of the repetendum in polyphony and the verse in chant, was envisaged by Brito and Guerrero, who (like Victoria) do not set the verse but who do leave the relevant gap in the polyphony to facilitate repetition. In two Iberian Requiems which provide polyphony for the verse but where no gap is inserted before 'Quam olim' – Morales's five-voice setting and Lobo's six-voice setting – an altered repetition of the original music for the repetendum is written out. Such an altered repetition is also found in the Offertory of Palestrina's Requiem, where the verse is set in polyphony.

these entries, completing the harmony as the Cantus parts and the Bassus begin 'olim', and the absence of that Altus note if starting a repeat from the 'quam olim' entries produces a brief but uncomfortable gap in the harmony and sonority. Such problems are reflected in the variety of solutions chosen by those modern editors and performers who adopt a polyphonic repetition of the repetendum: on a number of recordings the Altus part is re-written here so that it is present from the beginning of the repetition but underlaid with the repetendum text (with the necessary dividing-up of its first note to accommodate 'quam olim'),[109] and in others the first notes of the initial entries on 'quam' are extended backwards so that they begin on the *thesis*.[110] Given the need for such revision in order to make the passage work, it seems most likely – since Victoria provided no break in the music – that he did not intend that the repetendum be sung in polyphony after the verse, but rather that it be chanted. As noted above, the 1605 edition specifies a similar approach in the case of the 'quando cœli' section of *Libera me Domine*, which is initially sung polyphonically and then chanted (in this case the chant being provided in the edition). A polyphonic repetition of the Offertory repetendum is nevertheless the most common approach on those recordings which include the Offertory verse.

More unusual than his treatment of the Offertory was Victoria's provision of polyphony for just two of the three sections of the Agnus Dei. The Agnus Dei text for Requiems consists of a threefold petition, the first two petitions being textually identical and the third extended by the addition of the word 'sempiternam' at the end. Victoria provided one setting of the text of the first (or second) petition, and then a setting of the final petition. In this case he is out of line with typical international practice: both in the Peninsula and beyond it composers of Requiems normally set all three sections, as indeed Victoria himself had done in his four-voice Requiem.[111] The reduction in number of Agnus Dei sections between Victoria's two Requiems is mirrored in his other Masses, where there is a striking division between the works originally published during his period in Rome (as, of course, was the four-voice Requiem) and those published for the first time after his return to Spain: all but one of the former include two polyphonic sections in the Agnus Dei, whereas all but one of the latter have settings of only the first

---

[109] See for example the edition by David Wulstan.

[110] See for example the edition by Jon Dixon.

[111] Two Peninsular works pre-dating Victoria's which have only two Agnus Dei invocations in polyphony are the Requiems by Escobar and Vázquez.

invocation.[112] While this might represent an independent decision by Victoria, more probably it reflects a difference in performance custom between Rome and Madrid. Three means of performing Victoria's setting in the *Officium defunctorum* suggest themselves:

1. The setting was sung as it stands, as a twofold invocation.
2. The polyphony of Agnus I was sung twice.
3. The second Agnus was chanted.

Regarding option 1, an indication that such twofold polyphonic performance of the Agnus in a Requiem Mass was considered acceptable, at least in some contexts, is that the Agnus of the four-voice Requiem by Cererols has the same amount of text as does Victoria's, but in a through-composed form and hence not allowing for repetition of the polyphony. However, the Agnus of Cererols's seven-voice Requiem (which is likewise through-composed) includes all three petitions, suggesting inconsistent practice even within a single institution. Option 2 is rendered feasible by the fact that the chant for the first two petitions is identical, and indeed this is the performance method indicated in the Segorbe Cathedral copy of the *Officium defunctorum*, where 'dos veces' ('twice') was written in the margin at the beginning of each voice part.[113] The nineteenth-century editions by Haberl and Bordes left Victoria's twofold Agnus as printed, but the performing editions of a century later by Bruno Turner and Jon Dixon adopted the third option above, providing chant for a second Agnus. Turner's version was used for the well known recordings by Westminster Cathedral Choir and The Tallis Scholars, both from 1987, and attained the status of orthodoxy, appearing on almost all subsequent recordings, although a few groups have followed option 2, which is also the approach set out in David Wulstan's edition.

Conversely, modern editors and performers have usually left Victoria's printed threefold Kyrie alone, without attempting an *alternatim* treatment in order to make the Kyrie ninefold as it was when chanted.[114] As in the vast majority of polyphonic Requiems (and, of course, other types of

---

[112] The exception among the works published in Rome is the *Missa O quam gloriosum*, and the unusual case among the works published during his time in Spain is the *Missa pro victoria*: the Agnus Dei here consists of a single section of music, but this incorporates both 'miserere nobis' (the words which end the first and second invocations of the Agnus Dei text) and 'dona nobis pacem'.

[113] Such repetition of the first polyphonic section is marked also in the edition (Paris: Robert Ballard, 1656) of Charles d'Helfer's Requiem.

[114] The exception among modern editions is that of David Wulstan. Samuel Rubio indicated in his edition that Victoria's polyphonic sections should be repeated sufficient times to produce

polyphonic Mass), Victoria's Kyrie has just three polyphonic sections, setting 'Kyrie eleison', 'Christe eleison', and 'Kyrie eleison' respectively. It is common in polyphonic Requiems for the third of these sections to incorporate reference to the chant melody used to sing the final Kyrie in the ninefold structure, and in the case of Victoria's Mass this Kyrie IX chant – with its distinctive opening leap downwards from C to the modal final, F – is laid out as a cantus firmus in Cantus II. In an *alternatim* performance of the Kyrie as a nine-part structure, the third polyphonic segment would therefore have to be sung as Kyrie IX, resulting in the following scheme (where 'Kyrie IX' is used to distinguish the second of the two Kyrie settings which Victoria provided):

1. **Kyrie**
2. Kyrie
3. **Kyrie**
4. Christe
5. **Christe**
6. Christe
7. **Kyrie**
8. Kyrie
9. **Kyrie IX**

One Iberian Requiem, by Estêvão Lopes Morago, provides clear evidence of *alternatim* performance according to such a scheme, since Morago includes separate settings for the five sections shown in bold above. However, in order to fill out such a nine-part scheme using the Kyrie polyphony in Victoria's *Officium defunctorum*, his first polyphonic Kyrie would have to be sung three times in all (segments 1, 3, and 7 as shown above). Evidence of repetition of a polyphonic Kyrie section may indeed be found in the copy of the Requiem by Charles d'Argentil in Cappella Giulia XII.3, mentioned above, which includes the instruction that the first Kyrie be repeated. A number of Requiems from beyond the Pyrenees – by Antoine de Brumel, Claudin de Sermisy, Giovanni Contino, and Gregor Aichinger – have quadripartite Kyrie settings (Kyrie, Christe, Kyrie, Kyrie) which might also have been performed according the scheme above, with the first polyphonic segment sung twice (as segments 1 and 3 of the scheme).[115] However, an unattributed Requiem in a manuscript from the

---

a ninefold performance, rather than alternating chanted and polyphonic sections.

The recording by Capella de Ministrers follows the approach advocated by Rubio.

[115] In Aichinger's setting the Tenor sings the Kyrie IX melody as a cantus firmus in the last of the four polyphonic sections.

monastery of Santa Cruz in Coimbra (Coimbra, Biblioteca Geral da Universidade, MM 6) is copied with segments 1, 4, and 7 in chant and the other six segments in polyphony, while – to complicate the picture further – Antonio Gallego's Requiem preserved in Valladolid Cathedral, Archivo Musical 5 is shown with a six-part scheme:

Kyrie
Kyrie
Christe
Christe
Kyrie
Kyrie

The two Requiems by Manuel Cardoso are unusual in that they have four-section polyphonic Kyries but with separate polyphony for two Christe sections. (The final Kyrie in each case once again uses the Kyrie IX chant.) Since therefore they cannot have been sung with a strict scheme alternating chant and polyphony (no such scheme will fit), one wonders if a pattern similar to that found in the Coimbra manuscript just mentioned was intended (the two polyphonic Christe settings here being labelled 'Christe V' and 'Christe VI'):

1. Kyrie
2. **Kyrie**
3. **Kyrie**
4. Christe
5. **Christe V**
6. **Christe VI**
7. Kyrie
8. **Kyrie**
9. **Kyrie IX**

With the Coimbra and Antonio Gallego cases in mind, an alternative solution to the performance of Victoria's Kyrie might be to sing each polyphonic section only once, preceded by one or two chanted sections.[116] But it seems very possible also that Victoria's Kyrie (and other threefold polyphonic settings like it) could be performed – on some occasions at least – simply as they stand, without additional chanted sections. Evidence that entirely polyphonic performance of Requiem Kyries was employed both in the Spanish royal chapel and at the

---

[116] The latter is the approach taken on the recording by La Stagione Armonica (Symphonia, 2002).

Descalzas is found in the Requiems by Pierre de Manchicourt and Francisco Dávila y Páez, which both have a through-composed Kyrie movement setting the whole Kyrie text.[117] An Italian example is in the Requiem by Bernardo Strozzi published in 1626 in a collection of Masses described on the title page as 'composed with the greatest brevity, to suit the impatience of modern times'.[118] Partly with such a remark in mind, we might imagine that treatment of the Kyrie (in Requiems and other Masses) varied to suit the occasion, reflecting requirements for concision on the one hand or due ceremoniousness on the other: as observed in Chapter 2, in accounts of royal exequies the lengthiness of the ceremonies is frequently highlighted, as evidence of their due solemnity. Thus it is conceivable that at María's exequies Victoria's Kyrie polyphony was deployed in a ninefold structure, but that its performance on some other occasions at the Descalzas and elsewhere was simply threefold.

In terms of the lengths of chant intonations at the starts of movements and sections, Victoria's practice is in many respects typically Iberian. As mentioned regarding *Libera me Domine* above, the locations of the junctions between chant and polyphony in such cases reflected the points at which soloists' chant gave way to choral chant in a plainchant performance, and practices varied in these regards. It is normal in Iberian Requiems for the chanted intonations of the Introit, Gradual, and Offertory to be longer than those in Requiems from elsewhere:[119]

---

[117] Manchicourt was the Spanish royal chapelmaster, and his Requiem was certainly in the repertory of the royal chapel. Both Requiems by Joan Cererols likewise have through-composed Kyries, as does that attributed to Mateo Romero. A slightly different scheme is followed in Richafort's Requiem, which was one of the settings proposed for use at the court exequies of Philip II: there are two polyphonic sections, the first setting 'Kyrie eleison' and 'Christe eleison', and the second 'Kyrie eleison'. The same occurs in the Requiem by Francisco Garro (chapelmaster of the Portuguese royal chapel), the second section in this case concluding with a cantus-firmus statement of the Kyrie IX chant. Outside the Iberian world, another example of a through-composed Kyrie is found in the Requiem of Simon de Bonnefond.

[118] 'fatte con la maggiore brevita che si convenga alla poca pacienza del tempo d'hoggi'. Bernardo Strozzi, *Messe a Cinque Sei & Otto voci . . . opera settima* (Venice: Gardano/ Bartholomeo Magni, 1626, S6991).

[119] On these distinctions, see for example Robert Snow, 'An Unknown Missa pro defunctis by Palestrina', in Emilio Casares and Carlos Villanueva (eds), *De musica hispana et aliis: miscelánea en honor al Prof. Dr. José López-Calo, S.J., en su 65°Cumpleaños*, 2 vols (Santiago de Compostela: Universidad de Santiago de Compostela, 1990), I, 387–428, at 392, and Wagstaff, 'Music for the Dead', 206–7, 235–6, 279, 290, 292–3, and 431. The most widely used modern edition of Victoria's *Officium defunctorum*, that by Bruno Turner, gives an erroneous indication of the way that the chant intonations worked in the Introit, Gradual, and Offertory, i.e. in those cases where Victoria's (and typical Iberian) practice differs from the normal

INTROIT AND GRADUAL

Normal Iberian practice: Requiem æternam **dona eis Domine**

Normal practice elsewhere: Requiem **æternam dona eis Domine**

OFFERTORY

Normal Iberian practice: Domine Iesu Christe rex gloriæ, **libera animas**

Normal practice elsewhere: Domine Iesu Christe **rex gloriæ, libera animas**

However, exceptions to these broad geographical distinctions are sufficiently numerous to highlight the need for further investigation of local and regional chant traditions, and also of possible influences within the polyphonic repertory. In the case of the Introit, while the longer intonation is extremely rare among Northern works,[120] there are quite a few Italian examples, and one likewise finds instances of the longer Gradual intonation among the relatively scarce Italian Requiems which include this movement.[121] An intriguing case is the Requiem of Giovanni Contino (d. 1574), published in Milan in 1573, which has the longer intonation for Introit, Gradual, and Offertory; Contino also omits the Offertory verse (as noted above, this was common Iberian practice, but less common in Italy), and in the Gradual verse he uses reduced scoring until the final words, 'non timebit', where full scoring returns, a practice found in a number of Iberian

practice elsewhere and in modern liturgical books, and the resulting distorted approach has become common in performances and is heard on many recordings, particularly those by British ensembles. Turner's edition shows a change from 'solo' to 'tutti' chanting at the points where this transition occurs in modern Roman liturgical books, so that (for example) in the Introit a soloist sings the first word and then other singers join the chanting at 'æternam'. In fact, the same forces would have been used throughout each of these chant intonations. Independently of Turner's edition, the same problem is apparent in the recording by the Choir of the Church of the Advent, Boston (Afka, 1985), where the chant intonations are taken from the *Liber usualis*.

[120] They include the Requiems by Bonnefont and Moulinié; the latter has the longer intonation for the Gradual also. Maillard's setting is likewise in this category, using the longer intonation for both Introit and Gradual, but might be of Spanish provenance.

[121] Italian Requiems with the longer Introit intonation, besides that by Contino, include those by Giovanni Francesco Anerio (which also has the longer Offertory intonation), Heredia, Ruffo, Tamburini, Tristabocca (the four-voice Mass), and Orazio Vecchi. Also in this category are two unattributed settings (the provenance of which is therefore uncertain) in manuscript sources in Rome: Basilica di San Giovanni in Laterano, Archivio Musicale, Rari, st. mus. 69, and Biblioteca Casanatense, Fondo Baini II, 189; this latter piece also has the longer Offertory intonation. The longer Gradual intonation appears both in Contino's Requiem and in the four-voice Requiem by Pontio published in 1584. Conversely, among Iberian Requiems the shorter Introit intonation appears in those attributed to Basurto and Gallego, and the shorter Offertory intonation in that by Escobar.

Requiems from Morales's five-voice setting onwards. As we shall see, there are other parallels between Contino's approach to setting the Requiem and those found in significant numbers of Iberian works, and the circumstances leading to his adoption of such characteristics deserve exploration.[122]

The treatment of the Gradual verse represents one of the peculiarities in Victoria's handling of the chant–polyphony interface: Victoria leaves the opening three words ('In memoria æterna') as a chant intonation. I know of only two other Requiem Masses which adopt this approach, and one of these is Victoria's own four-voice Mass. The other is the four-voice Requiem by Morales, which circulated only in manuscript, and which – according to Juan Bermudo – was composed for Juan Téllez Girón, Count of Ureña. It seems likely that Victoria was influenced by Morales's setting here, and that the institution for which Morales wrote it had a distinctive practice of treating these three words as a solo intonation in chanted performance. Victoria's two Requiems likewise correspond with Morales's four-voice work in treating the words 'Pleni sunt' within the Sanctus as a chant intonation. The more usual Iberian practice here matched that beyond the Pyrenees, namely that these words were set in polyphony.[123] A final locus of distinction between Iberian custom and that elsewhere concerns the opening of the Benedictus: as in the great majority of Iberian Requiems which set the Benedictus, the opening word is left as a chant intonation in both of Victoria's Requiem Masses,[124] whereas most Italian settings treat this word as part of the polyphony.[125]

---

[122] Contino worked in Brescia and Mantua, and was a client of Bishop (later Cardinal) Cristoforo Madruzzo. Contino's Mass appeared in *Missæ cum quinque vocibus ... liber primus* (Milan: Paolo Gottardo Ponzio, 1573, C3543); modern edition by Ottavio Beretta in *Giovanni Contino, Missae cum quinque vocibus liber primus (1572)*, Monumenti musicali italiani 20 (Milan: Edizioni Suvini Zerboni, 1997), 200–58. The use of reduced texture for the bulk of the Gradual verse and a return to full texture for 'non timebit' is found in Guerrero's setting, both of those by Duarte Lobo, and one of the settings copied as part of the Requiem by Manuel Mendes.

[123] Iberian works which leave 'Pleni sunt' in chant, besides those by Victoria and Morales's four-voice work, include the Masses by Bernal, Brito, Esquivel (both Requiems), Gallego, Ribeiro, and Vivanco.

[124] The few Iberian exceptions include the Masses of Escobar, Vázquez, and Garro.

[125] Requiems from North of the Alps reveal no predominant practice in this regard. Several of those that do leave the opening of the Benedictus in chant have a longer chant intonation – 'Benedictus qui venit' – than one finds in Iberian and Italian works.

Chant Use and the 'Spanish Tradition'

Within the polyphony of the *Officium defunctorum* Victoria assigns the chant (where present) mainly to the Cantus II part,[126] although the Altus takes this role in the Offertory and *Libera me Domine*, and as we shall see the presentation and use of the chants varies considerably between and within items in the collection. The degree to which – and the ways in which – chant is incorporated into the polyphony of Requiem Masses has been identified by scholars as a key means of distinguishing Spanish or Iberian practice within the genre from that of other parts of Europe. It has been observed that Iberian settings more frequently incorporate the chant in relatively unadorned fashion, laid out as a cantus firmus, and most commonly in the topmost voice, and the adoption or otherwise of such procedures has been used to assess how 'Spanish' or 'foreign' is the approach to composition in a particular work. I explore below the degree to which this view may represent undue exceptionalism, and in painting a more complex picture I aim to contextualise Victoria's chant use in the music of 1603.

The view of Spanish practice just outlined is firmly expressed in Harold Luce's 1958 doctoral study of polyphonic Requiems up to 1600, where he concluded – when considering evidence for 'national schools' in the composition of Requiems – that 'the long-note treatment of the *cantus firmus* in the soprano, which prevails in Spanish Requiems, is likewise unique'.[127] Luce goes on to highlight, as have many others, a more general emphasis (beyond the cantus-firmus voice) on long note-values and sobriety of texture and style as distinguishing marks of the Spanish Requiem tradition. The concept that there existed a standard Spanish practice with regard to chant-treatment in such music was developed considerably by Grayson Wagstaff, who concludes that 'the Spanish developed a unique way of approaching these texts'.[128] When considering the Requiem by Pedro de Escobar, Wagstaff states:

---

[126] In this respect Victoria's Requiem resembles the five-voice setting by Esquivel and the six-voice Requiem by Cardoso, both of which have two Cantus parts one of which bears the chant for much of the work, but with the other Cantus part frequently singing higher than it. It is of course irrelevant in terms of the musical results that in the *Officium defunctorum* Cantus II bears the chant at the relevant points, whereas in Esquivel's and Cardoso's Masses Cantus I does so. In the manuscript copy of Victoria's Mass in Augsburg, Staats- und Stadtbibliothek, Tonkunst Schletterer 21 the two Cantus parts are, indeed, reversed.

[127] Luce, 'The Requiem Mass', I, 270.   [128] Wagstaff, 'Music for the Dead', 607.

Escobar's *Missa pro defunctis* embodies several important characteristics that were to be a part of the approach taken by Hispanic composers throughout much of the history of the genre. First, and perhaps most important, is the presentation of the chant melody in the cantus in an unadorned manner ... Although the chant may be prefigured by melodic fragments used imitatively in other voices, the preexistent melody is not integrated into the web of voices as it is in the Northern tradition ... Escobar's work presents the chant in such a way that it is not obscured by compositional artifice but, rather, it is supported by the other voices in ways that never obscure the clarity of the preexistent melody.[129]

Having thus established Escobar's approach – marked by 'respect for the chant'[130] – as an archetype for Spanish Requiems, Wagstaff then tests the Spanishness or otherwise of further works and sections of works through comparison with that archetype. Thus he characterises the Requiem music by Basurto (which he considers alongside Escobar's work in a chapter on 'Early Settings of the *Missa pro defunctis* in Spain') as follows:

[A] primary distinguishing factor between Basurto's work and more stereotypically Spanish settings of the Mass is the approach to incorporating the chant melody. As was discussed with Escobar's setting, composers in the Spanish tradition usually placed the chant in unadorned form in the cantus, where it was distinguished from the other voices by being presented in breves. Thus it was recognisable and not allowed to become enmeshed in the polyphonic web. In contrast, Basurto often incorporates the melody so that it becomes entwined in the polyphonic texture and indistinguishable from the other voices. Because this approach was much more typical of the Northern tradition, its use adds to the overall impression of the setting as more Franco-Flemish than Spanish ... Although later composers in Spain did occasionally ornament the preexistent melodies more than Escobar, the degree of modification found in the setting by Basurto is much more in line with the practice of Northern musicians.[131]

When considering the five-voice Requiem by Morales, Wagstaff high-lights the distinction between sections 'embodying Spanish attributes' (presenting the chant as a long-note cantus firmus in the topmost voice, and with little imitation of the chant in the other voices) and others more akin to Italian and Northern practice (with heavier use of imitation, including of motives from the chant).[132] He likens Morales's placement of the chant in an Altus part in the Gradual with those Requiems by Italians or published in Italy where the chant is in the tenor. Wagstaff proposes, indeed, that those movements of Morales's work – such as Introit and Kyrie – which reveal a 'Spanish approach' may have been composed in

---

[129] *Ibid.*, 197–8.   [130] *Ibid.*, 227.   [131] *Ibid.*, 237.   [132] *Ibid.*, 432–40.

Spain and the others in Rome.[133] He emphasises the supposed distinctiveness of the Spanish approach by observing that Morales's presentation of
the chant in such sections as the Introit 'contrasts with almost all of the
settings published in Italy in the fifty years after Morales's *Liber secundus*'
in which the five-part Requiem appeared.[134]

The type of chant treatment highlighted by Wagstaff undoubtedly
became common in Spanish Requiems in the later sixteenth century and
the seventeenth century, among the works exemplifying such an approach
being Victoria's four-voice Requiem first published in 1583, both
Requiems by Esquivel, both settings by Cardoso, and the Requiem of
Mendes. However, Iberian composers' practice was very far from
uniform,[135] and furthermore such variety is also apparent among the
early examples of Requiem Mass polyphony by Spaniards which
Wagstaff analyzes in detail: the Requiem movements by Basurto, Juan
Vázquez's Mass, and the two Masses by Morales. Wagstaff himself observes
that all of these depart in significant ways, in some sections, from the
supposedly archetypal practice which he sees in Escobar's Mass.
The cases of Basurto's setting and Morales's five-voice Mass have already
been mentioned, and one should note that in Morales's work not only is the
chant given to Altus II (rather than the Cantus) in the Gradual but also it is
assigned to the (only) Altus part in the Offertory, the most substantial
section of the Requiem. In Morales's four-voice Mass, as Wagstaff remarks,
the chant is taken by the Tenor rather than the Cantus in the Gradual, and
the Communion turns away from cantus-firmus treatment, while in
Vázquez's Mass (again as Wagstaff observes) the cantus firmus frequently
migrates between voices.[136] Indeed, even in Escobar's Mass there is considerable variation in the behaviour of the Cantus line, which not infrequently has free or faster-moving passages, so that it does not consistently
stand apart from the other voices; there is also some migration of the chant
(for example, to the Tenor in the final Agnus Dei). There are, moreover,
other examples of relatively early Spanish Requiems, beyond those considered by Wagstaff, which do not conform to the model of cantus-firmus
treatment which he views as typically Spanish: in the Requiem by Pujol –
bearing the date 1546 in the source – and the Requiem movements by
Cubells, both in the apparently lost manuscript of which photographs are
preserved in Barcelona, we find no movements in which one of the voices is

---

[133] *Ibid.*, 441.   [134] *Ibid.*

[135] To mention just one example, in the Requiem by Antonio Pallares clear use of the chant is
absent, as observed by Wagstaff, *ibid.*, 602–3.

[136] *Ibid.*, 484.

distinguished as a cantus-firmus part.[137] In the light of all this, we might do well to treat with caution the notion of a normative Spanish approach to chant-treatment in the Requiem, established in Escobar's setting, against which the 'Spanishness' of other Requiems may be judged.

Furthermore, when considering more widely the Iberian repertory of Requiems composed before about 1650, it is important to note that the disposition of the chant as a long-note cantus firmus in the topmost voice is more often found in settings of some of the constituent texts than others. It is most common in the Introit, Sanctus, and Agnus, whereas in the Communion (for example) paraphrase technique is frequent, in other words elements of the chant are distributed among the various voices (the practice that is supposedly Northern or Italian rather than Iberian). Even in those Communion settings where the chant is more clearly present in the Cantus than in other voices, it is less often presented as a long-note cantus firmus than is the case in settings of the Introit, Sanctus, and Agnus. Paraphrase technique is common in Kyrie settings also, as is migration of the chant between voices.[138] In the Gradual and Offertory the chant is frequently located in the Altus or Tenor part rather than the Cantus, even in Masses in which it is otherwise taken by the Cantus. The cases of the two Masses by Morales have already been mentioned in this regard, and Victoria used the Altus to carry the chant in the Offertory of his six-voice Requiem. Other examples within such Masses are as follows (with the chant-bearing voice shown in parentheses):

1. Brito: Gradual verse (A), Offertory (A)
2. Cardoso (four-voice Mass): Gradual respond (T)[139]
3. Cardoso (six-voice Mass): Gradual respond (A I), Gradual verse (A II)
4. Juan Pau Pujol: Gradual (A), Offertory respond (A), Offertory verse (T)[140]
5. Ribeiro: Offertory (A)
6. Vivanco: Offertory (T)

Two Portuguese settings – the Requiem by Bernal and the six-voice work by Lobo – further exemplify the contrast that sometimes exists between the

---

[137] This Pujol is to be distinguished from the later Juan Pau Pujol by whom a four-voice Requiem survives.

[138] Examples of chant migration in Kyrie settings occur in the Requiems by Bernal, Cererols (the four-part Mass), Esquivel (the five-part work), Guerrero, Lobo, Morago, and Juan Pau Pujol, and in both of Victoria's Masses.

[139] In this Mass, the chant likewise moves to the Tenor for part of the Communion.

[140] In the unattributed four-voice Requiem in Tuy Cathedral L 5, the chant is in the Cantus in the Introit and Gradual verse, but is given to the Altus in the Offertory.

treatment of chant in particular sections. In the Requiem by Bernal the chant is placed in the highest voice as a cantus firmus in all sections except the Kyrie, where it migrates, and the Offertory, which not only lacks a cantus firmus but is almost entirely free of references to the chant.[141] In his six-voice Requiem Lobo assigns the chant to the Cantus in the Introit and the Mass Ordinary items (Kyrie, Sanctus, and Agnus), sometimes with a nearly monorhythmic presentation, whereas in the Gradual, Offertory, and Communion the chant – where it is present – is distributed amongst various voices: in the Gradual it passes between the two Altus parts, while in the Offertory and Communion paraphrase technique is employed, with chant motives appearing in all voices.

One finds within Victoria's six-voice Requiem elements of these distinctions between movements that treat the chant as a long-note cantus firmus and those in which it is more integrated into the texture and makes greater use of shorter values. Victoria followed convention in favouring the former approach in his Kyrie, Sanctus, and Agnus, and the latter approach in his Gradual and Offertory, but the discrimination between these two types of chant-treatment is not always clearly maintained. In the Sanctus and Agnus, breve movement predominates in the chant-bearing voice except where the line is decorated in the later parts of phrases, while in the Gradual Victoria's approach is more diversified in terms of fidelity to and treatment of the chant: he begins with the chant in breves (b. 1–6) but then abandons it for the conclusion of its first phrase, turns to minim declamation of the chant at 'et lux perpetua' (b. 9–10), and reverts to breves for 'luceat' (b. 14–18), but then severely truncates the last part of the respond's chant. In the Gradual verse, he refers to the chant at 'erit iustus' (b. 23–8), but transposes this motive, then uses minim declamation once again for the chant's monotone recitation of 'ab auditione' (b. 31–2),[142] while at the end of the verse ('non timebit', b. 37 onwards) he again makes reference to the chant at first but then abandons it.

In the Introit antiphon Victoria lays out the chant very largely in breves and semibreves, as was common practice in setting this section of text, while (as is once again typical) his treatment of the verse includes some use of shorter values during the recitational elements of the psalm tone,

[141]   The chant also migrates from Cantus to Altus in one verse of the setting of *Libera me Domine* preserved in the same manuscript source as the Requiem.

[142]   In the treatment of 'ab auditione mala' here he drew (whether consciously or unconsciously) on his own setting of this same phrase of text in the psalm *Beatus vir* (the setting of the even-numbered verses) preserved in Rome, Biblioteca Nazionale Centrale Vittorio Emanuele II, Ms Musicali 130.

employing minims in the chant line at 'reddetur' (b. 36–7) and 'ad te omnis' (b. 52–3). A similar practice is found in (for example) Victoria's four-voice setting and in Morales's four-voice Mass. The chant deployment in the Communion of the *Officium defunctorum* has an analogous profile to that in the Introit: the antiphon likewise features extensive long-note cantus-firmus treatment, although here the chant is distributed between Cantus II and Altus, and the final repetition of the concluding 'quia pius es' is free of chant-reference. In the verse the psalm-tone recitation again uses some shorter note-values, although we shall see below that Victoria's handling of the chant is in other respects unusual here, as indeed is his use of a long-note cantus firmus in the antiphon, paraphrase technique being more common here (as noted). A mixture of chant treatment is likewise apparent in the Kyries of Victoria's Requiem: the first Kyrie presents the chant almost entirely in breves, while in the Christe and final Kyrie a mixture of breves and semibreves is employed, as in the Introit and Communion antiphons. As noted, chant migration is quite common in Kyrie settings, and here it occurs in the Christe: the Cantus II sings the first part of the chant phrase in breves, but the Tenor imitates this an octave lower and two breves later, and it is the Tenor that goes on to sing the entire Christe chant melody.[143]

The use of the Altus rather than Cantus as the chant-bearing part in the Offertory settings of a number of Requiems, including Victoria's six-voice work, has a simple explanation: the range of the chant concerned. This mode-2 chant reaches up only to G (with one occurrence of A in the verse), and descends several times to the A below. It is thus unsuitable for Cantus parts notated in c_1 clef. We consequently find four solutions in Iberian Requiems where the Offertory makes significant reference to the chant:

1. The chant is assigned to an Altus part, notated in c_2 or c_3 clef, well suited to the ambitus of the chant.[144]
2. It is given to a Cantus part in a low range, again using a c_2 clef.
3. It is transposed upwards by a fourth, so that its final becomes G rather than D, and a B♭ *cantus mollis* signature used.
4. It is transposed upwards by a fifth, so that its final becomes A.

---

[143] One likewise finds a migration of the chant to the Tenor in the Christe of Guerrero's Requiem.

[144] However, in the unattributed Requiem in Coimbra, Biblioteca Geral da Universidade, MM 6 the chant is presented an octave lower than in those Masses using the Altus to bear this chant; here it is in the (low) Tenor part (as throughout this Mass), written out using chant notation and with f_3 and f_4 clefs.

These last two solutions allowed the chant to be placed in a Cantus part of 'normal' range, notated with c_1 clef, or a Tenor part notated in c_3 or c_4 clef.[145] Victoria adopted the first of these four approaches in his six-voice Requiem, placing the chant with D final in the Altus; in his four-voice Requiem he took the second approach, giving the chant to his low Cantus part, using c_2 clef. Other Requiems by Iberian composers exemplifying the first approach include those by Brito, Garro, Morales (the five-voice Mass), Juan Pau Pujol,[146] and Ribeiro, while the second approach is found in the Requiems by Escobar, Esquivel (the four-voice Mass), and Morales (the four-voice setting).[147] The third solution, with the transposed chant given to a 'normal-range' Cantus part, was employed by Cardoso (in both of his Requiems), Magalhães, and Mendes, and the fourth solution occurs in the Offertories by Gallego and Vivanco, the former dividing the chant between Cantus and Tenor, and the latter assigning it to the Tenor.

As noted above, in the case of the Gradual also we find a number of Iberian Requiems which assign the chant to an Altus part. Another similarity with the treatment of the Offertory is that composers presented the chant at different pitches, in this case with A final and D final, and this variety is indeed found in contemporary chant sources. When notated with D final, the chant has almost the same ambitus as that of the Offertory, and in a few cases (such as Escobar's, Guerrero's, and Magalhães's settings, and the second Gradual setting copied with Mendes's Requiem) composers accordingly assigned the chant at this pitch to a low-range Cantus part (using c_2 clef in Guerrero's case), as we saw in several Offertory settings. However, the approach of other composers was to notate the chant with A final (perhaps to reflect its notation thus in the relevant chant sources, which include the *Graduale Romanum*), and several of these – including of course Victoria in the six-voice work – employ 'high clefs' for this section (only) of their Requiem, thus indicating downwards transposition by a fifth (the normal transposition when pieces used high clefs but no flat in the

---

[145] In the Requiem by Cesare Tudino, the Tenor cantus firmus in the Offertory – presented in the transposition with G final and a flat signature – is notated in f_3 clef, while in the six-voice work by Michele Varotto the Sextus part (using c_4 clef) carries the chant, using this same transposition. The great majority of Italian Requiems consulted use G final and a signature of one flat for the Offertory, whether or not they make reference to the chant.

[146] As mentioned, Pujol transfers the chant to the Tenor in the Offertory verse,

[147] Vázquez's setting of the Offertory distributes the chant between the Cantus (notated in c_2 clef), Altus (with c_3 clef), and Bassus (with f_4 clef). In the four-voice Requiem by Cererols, the chant is in the Cantus part, but is notated with c_1 clef rather than c_2.

signature).[148] In almost all of these settings the chant is present in the Cantus, although Vázquez places it in the Tenor (the middle part of the three-voice scoring here). The clef combination used by Guerrero in his Gradual setting – c_2 c_4 f_3 f_4 – positions each clef a fifth below those in the common high-clefs combination of g_2 c_2 c_3 c_4, and Andrew Johnstone has proposed that works notated using this c_2 c_4 f_3 f_4 combination in printed editions by such as Scotto may indeed represent high-clef works notated at 'performing pitch'.[149] Still other Requiems, however, notated the Gradual chant at the A-final level but without using high clefs and thus with no implication of transposition downwards: this approach is found in, for example, Morales's five-voice Mass (with the chant in Altus II), Cardoso's four-voice setting (where the chant is in the Tenor during the respond), the same composer's six-voice setting (with Altus I taking the chant in the respond and Altus II in the verse), and the Requiem by Juan Pau Pujol (with the chant in the Altus in the respond and Altus II in the verse). Brito's setting of the Gradual – which likewise does not use high clefs – actually incorporates both pitches of the chant: in the respond he assigns the chant at its D-final pitch to the Cantus, but in the verse he moves the chant to the Altus and to the A-final pitch.[150] Victoria's four-voice setting employs cleffing of c_1 c_2 c_3 f_3 (as had Morales in the equivalent section of his four-voice Requiem), and here the situation regarding implied transposition is

---

[148] See Andrew Johnstone, '"High" Clefs in Composition and Performance', *Early Music* 34 (2006), 29–54, at 31 and 44–5. The recordings of the *Officium defunctorum* by the Gabrieli Consort and La Stagione Armonica duly transpose the Gradual downwards by a fifth.
The modern edition of the work by Jon Dixon transposes the Gradual downwards by a major third and all other movements upwards by a minor third, so that the appropriate pitch-alignment of the Gradual with other sections is achieved. However, the much-used edition by Bruno Turner transposes the Gradual downwards by a minor third and the other sections of the *Officium defunctorum* upwards by a tone, so that the relevant pitch-alignment is absent, and most recordings (for example, those by Westminster Cathedral Choir, The Tallis Scholars, The Sixteen, Collegium Vocale Gent, Tenebræ, Magnificat, and KammerChor Saarbrucken) adopt these pitches, as does that by the Choir of St John's College Cambridge (which pre-dates Turner's edition). On other recordings – those by the Cor de la Generalitat Valenciana, Musica Ficta, and Choeur In illo tempore – the Gradual is transposed downwards by a tone and the other sections sung at written pitch, and the equivalent relationship between the pitches of these movements is found on the recording by the Escolania & Capella de Música Montserrat, where the general transposition is up a semitone and the Gradual is performed a semitone below written pitch. The editions by Haberl, Walter, and Wulstan transpose the Gradual downwards by a tone and the other movements upwards by a minor third, so that the relevant alignment of pitches is again absent.

[149] *Ibid.*, 39–40.

[150] Contino likewise employs both pitches of the Gradual chant, but in this case the Cantus switches from the lower pitch to the higher during the Gradual verse, the transposition occurring at 'æterna'.

less clear-cut than in his six-voice work, since this cleffing is used in the Introit and Kyrie also, where the relevant chants are presented 'at pitch' and so no transposition is implied according to the conventions of high clefs.

Besides the Offertory, the other item in the *Officium defunctorum* in which Victoria generally places the chant not in the second Cantus part but in the Altus is the *Libera me Domine*.[151] Both of the relevant chants have *protus* modality, with D final, and with a strong emphasis on the final for much of the time.[152] It is therefore not surprising to discover that Iberian settings of *Libera me* which make significant use of the chant adopt the same approaches which we find in Iberian settings of the Offertory: the chant is typically sung either by a low-lying Cantus part notated with c_2 clef or by the Altus, but may also be transposed by a fourth so that it has a G final (with a signature of one flat).[153] This latter approach is adopted by Estêvão de Brito, while the former approach (with the chant in a low-range Cantus) can be seen in the settings by Juan de Anchieta, Manuel Cardoso, Aires Fernandez, Hernando Franco, and Juan Pau Pujol, and in Victoria's setting appended to his four-voice Requiem. In Guerrero's setting (published with his Requiem in the edition of 1582), the chant is likewise in the Cantus (with c_2 clef) except in the third verse ('Requiem æternam'), in which it moves to the Tenor. Manuel Mendes divides the chant between his Cantus (in c_2 clef) and Altus, and Alonso Lobo similarly uses the Altus and the second Cantus part to carry the chant in various parts of his five-voice setting. The chant is again assigned to the Altus in the setting by Vázquez, except that it moves to the Tenor in the Kyrie section. In Victoria's six-voice setting of *Libera me Domine* we likewise find some migration of the chant. The three-voice setting of the first verse, 'Tremens factus sum', was borrowed from the composer's four-voice Requiem (as discussed above), and that setting's chant-bearing Cantus part (originally notated in c_2 clef) became a low Cantus part (notated in c_1 clef) in the new context. Besides

---

[151] In addition, the chant migrates to the Altus for one passage during the Communion: at 'cum sanctis tuis in æternum' the chant phrase is begun by the second Cantus, but then passes to the Altus, which sings the phrase from its beginning and in cantus-firmus style (in breves and semibreves), but transposed downwards by a fifth.

[152] In part of the last section of the respond of *Libera me Domine*, at 'dum veneris iudicare', the chant uses a higher range, ascending to c'' in the pitch-level used here in the *Officium defunctorum*. This section of the respond is left in chant in the *Officium defunctorum*, and thus the need to use ledger lines (given that the Altus part is notated in c_3 clef) is avoided.

[153] Some Iberian settings make scant (or no) reference to the chant, including those by Cererols (both the four-voice and the seven-voice setting) and Cubells, and the second setting which follows Morago's Requiem in the manuscript copy in Viseu, Arquivo Distrital, Cod. 3.

this, the chants of the concluding two 'Kyrie' settings – which occupy a higher range than is typical of the preceding chant of the responsory – are given to Cantus II.

In scrutinising Italian *Libera me Domine* settings, Antonio Chemotti has noted similarities of chant handling between Victoria's four-voice setting composed in Rome and various other settings which were likewise written there and/or formed part of Roman institutions' repertories. As mentioned above, Victoria's setting conforms to Roman practice in that he sets the text of the respond up to the end of the first repetendum as one polyphonic unit. Like Victoria's, the setting by Festa and two of those attributed to Palestrina place the chant in the topmost voice during the respond, and such features as the level of decoration of the chant are similar between Victoria's setting and these others.[154] To be sure, however, Roman settings of the *Libera me Domine* respond are not consistent in their chant use: for example, in the setting by Charles d'Argentil the chant appears initially in the cantus but with a greater proportion of free material, and migrates to the Bassus during the first repetendum.

More generally, while we should indeed recognise the especial frequency with which Spanish and Portuguese composers of Requiems opted to place the chant in the highest voice and relatively unadorned (particularly in the Introit, Sanctus, and Agnus Dei), we should be aware that there was no neat separation between Iberian and Italian practice (in other words, that Spanish practice was not 'unique', as suggested by Luce and Wagstaff), since among the Requiems by Italian composers dating from the mid to late sixteenth century one finds works in which the chant is assigned to the highest voice some or much of the time, including as a long-note cantus firmus, and among these works – as in Iberian ones – the Introit, Sanctus, and Agnus are the most common sites for this approach. Perhaps the earliest of the relevant Italian works is the Requiem by Bernardino Lupacchino (also known as Carnefresca), who was attached to San Giovanni in Laterano in Rome from 1546 to 1550 and possibly in 1552–3, and whose four-voice Requiem – consisting of Introit, Kyrie, Sequence, Sanctus, and Agnus – is preserved in a book of the composer's Masses belonging to that basilica.[155] Lupacchino located the chant mainly

---

[154] See Chemotti, 'Polyphonic Music', 207–12.

[155] For information about the composer's life, see Luigi di Tullio (ed.), *Bernardino Carnefresca detto il Lupacchino dal Vasto, opera omnia*, 2 vols, Monumenti Musicali Abuzzesi 1 (Milan: Edizioni Suvini Zerboni, 2000), I, xix–xxi. The manuscript source of the Requiem is Rome, Basilica di San Giovanni in Laterano, Archivio musicale, Rari, Ms 25, at 173v-188 (in the modern pencil foliation). There is no modern edition.

in the Cantus: for example, it appears as an unadorned cantus firmus laid out in breves in much of the Sanctus and in the Agnus Dei, and using mainly breves and semibreves in the Introit.[156] Thus in an Italian Requiem forming part of the repertory of one of Rome's great churches and which may be approximately contemporary with Morales's five-voice setting published in Rome, one finds chant presentation similar to that which has been characterised as distinctively Spanish in Morales's work and other Iberian Requiems.

The Requiem by Giovanni Contino likewise resembles the common Iberian practices in its chant use, but there are reasons to treat this as a special case. As mentioned above, this piece also features the longer chant intonations for the Introit, Gradual, and Offertory which were normal in Iberian Requiems, and (as will be shown later) it likewise resembles many Iberian works in its mensural practice. One wonders therefore whether there were particular reasons for the similarities between Contino's approach and those of Peninsular composers. Contino laid out the chant in the Cantus part in the whole of the Introit antiphon and the first part of the verse (moving it to the Altus for the rest of the verse), and treated it mainly in undecorated fashion, using breves and semibreves.[157] He likewise placed the chant in the Cantus in the Sanctus, Benedictus, Agnus Dei, and Communion (frequently in undecorated form), as well as for one section of the Kyrie and for much of the Gradual verse.[158] Contino's assigning of the chant to the Altus rather than the Cantus in the Offertory of his Mass once again has Iberian parallels, as discussed above.

In some other Italian Requiems the chant is placed in the Cantus, albeit either in fewer sections than in the cases just mentioned, or with less use of cantus-firmus technique than in those cases. Several of these works are among the Requiems that – like Contino's – use the longer 'Spanish' chant intonation for one or more movements: the Requiems by Vincenzo Ruffo, Giovanni Francesco Anerio, and Pedro Heredia, together with the setting

---

[156] The Cantus also takes the chant in the first Kyrie (using breves and semibreves) and parts of the Sequence: the Sequence alternates verses for two Cantus parts and verses for four lower voices, and in the former Cantus I usually makes the clearest reference to the chant, although in the (identical) music used for verses 7 and 13 the two Cantus parts both use the chant extensively. The Tenor takes the cantus firmus in the Christe and the second Hosanna.

[157] At 'et lux perpetua' in the Introit antiphon the Tenor also sings the chant as a cantus firmus. See the modern edition by Beretta, *Giovanni Contino: Missae cum quinque vocibus, Liber primus*, 202.

[158] The migration of the chant in the Kyrie seen in the Requiems of Lupacchino and Contino, and also in the three-voice Requiem by Viadana, is found also (as noted above) in a number of Iberian works. Viadana lays out the chant undecorated and in semibreves in the Bassus in the first Kyrie, the Altus in the Christe, and the Tenor in the final Kyrie.

by Charles d'Argentil that was presumably composed in Rome and was copied for the Cappella Giulia. The conjunction of chant-treatment and intonation practice in these pieces once again raises intriguing questions regarding local practices and/or about influence.[159] In Ruffo's Requiem the chant is assigned to the highest voice during most of the Agnus Dei and parts of the Sanctus, and is laid out in longs, breves, and semibreves at the opening of the Sanctus. Anerio gave the chant to the Cantus in the Introit verse, the Sanctus, and the first Agnus Dei. Like Victoria, Anerio was connected with Philip Neri's Congregazione dell'Oratorio, and he might well have come to know Victoria's *Officium defunctorum* through the (surviving) copy send to the Oratorians (see Chapter 3). Heredia's Requiem refers heavily to chant, again assigning it to the Cantus in the Introit verse, and also in the Offertory verse and the first two petitions of the Agnus Dei, for example.[160] Charles d'Argentil gives the chant to the Cantus in the Introit, Sanctus, first Agnus Dei (mainly undecorated and in long note-values), and Communion antiphon. Among other Italian Requiems with the longer Introit intonation, Tamburini's uses cantus-firmus technique in the Introit (where Tenor I carries the chant), and periodically in other movements (most often in Tenor I, but also in the Cantus). But one also finds extensive chant use in the Cantus in some Italian Requiems that have the shorter chant intonations. For example, in the four-voice Requiem by Giulio Belli the top voice sings the chant in part of the Introit, the Benedictus, and (with some alterations) the Communion antiphon, while Palestrina's five-voice Requiem assigns the chant most frequently to the topmost voice and the two Tenor parts, and makes sporadic use of cantus-firmus treatment of the chant.

Cantus-firmus technique appears in a number of other Italian Requiems of this period, but with the Tenor rather than the Cantus as the favoured voice to carry the chant. An extreme case is Cesare Tudino's Requiem, in which the Tenor behaves strictly as a cantus-firmus part throughout, presenting the chant unaltered, in semibreves, and using chant notation. Costanzo Porta's Requiem uses a Tenor cantus firmus in all movements except the Offertory and parts of the Kyrie, laying out the undecorated

---

[159] One wonders, for example, whether Ruffo's periods of service in Spanish-governed Milan might be relevant to the characteristics of his Requiem discussed here.

[160] When considering the characteristics of this work, including its use of the longer Introit intonation, it might be worth nothing that although Heredia spent his entire life in Italy, he was of Spanish ancestry. Alternatively, it might be relevant that he (like Anerio) worked mainly in Rome, where Spanish influence was strong.

chant mainly in breves in the Introit antiphon, while of the four Requiems by Giovanni Matteo Asola the four-voice work published first in 1574 employs a (very largely unadorned) Tenor cantus firmus in the Sanctus and Agnus Dei, and his setting included in the *Officium defunctorum* (published initially in 1586) does likewise in these same movements and in the Introit verse.[161] In Michele Varotto's six-voice Mass, the Tenor bears the chant in the Introit and Sanctus, and parts of other movements, and the Sextus (a tenor-range part) in the Offertory.[162]

The sixteenth-century repertory of Requiems by Northern composers gives further grounds for caution in treating as a peculiarly Spanish trait assignment of the chant to the Cantus, particularly in the Introit,[163] Sanctus, and Agnus Dei, and its treatment as a long-note cantus firmus. Works which exemplify such traits in one or more movements include the following:

1. Pierre Certon: the Cantus presents the chant in all movements, albeit with quite frequent decoration or alteration.
2. Pierre Clereau: the Cantus presents the chant as a cantus firmus in the Introit and the first two petitions of the Agnus Dei.
3. Antoine de Févin:[164] the Cantus carries the chant in the Introit antiphon and (as a long-note cantus firmus) in the Sanctus.
4. Jacobus de Kerle: the Cantus bears the chant in the Introit (although frequently decorated), much of the Sequence, and the Agnus (undecorated), as well as in the final verse of the associated setting of *Libera me Domine*.
5. Johannes Mangon: the Cantus is the main chant-bearing voice, with cantus-firmus treatment appearing frequently.
6. Johannes Prioris: the chant is assigned almost throughout to the Cantus, its presentation varying between unadorned (long-note) and decorated forms.

---

[161] Only the Tenor part of Pietro Pontio's *Missa mortuorum* – as published in his *Missarum cum quatuor vocibus liber primus* (Venice: heir of Scotto, 1584, P5079) – is known to survive. This Tenor part presents the chant unadorned as a cantus firmus in the Introit and Kyrie.

[162] In addition to the examples cited here, the unattributed four-voice Requiem copied for San Giovanni in Laterano in the seventeenth century (in Archivio Musicale, Rari, st. mus. 69) assigns the chant variously to the Cantus and Tenor, but rather more often to the latter than to the former.

[163] Jean-Paul Montagnier has observed that in France the tendency to make prominent use of the chant in the Introit antiphon continued in the late seventeenth and eighteenth centuries: *The Polyphonic Mass in France*, 257–8.

[164] Attributed in one source to Divitis.

With regard to the Requiem by Pierre de Manchicourt, while it is conceivable that he wrote it during his five years of service in the royal chapel of Philip II (1559–64), and while it is preserved in a manuscript from that chapel,[165] it is more likely that the piece dates from his extended career in France: indeed, Manchicourt's setting conforms to normal French practice in many respects.[166] Manchicourt assigns the chant to the Cantus in most sections, presenting it as a cantus firmus in the Introit, the Sanctus, and the first and third sections of the Agnus Dei. In Lassus's five-voice Requiem the Tenor has the chant in many sections but the Cantus for much of the Agnus Dei. One also finds extensive use of Tenor cantus-firmus technique in the Requiem by Claudin de Sermisy and in those by the rather later German composers Gregor Aichinger and Christian Erbach, while Philippe de Monte's Requiem has the first Tenor sing the chant in the Introit and Sanctus, and Charles d'Helfer constructs his setting of the Introit antiphon around a monorhythmic presentation of the chant in the Tenor, given in chant notation by the publisher Ballard.[167]

Sobriety of Style, 'Spanishness', and the *proportio dupla* Manner

Beyond the issues of chant presentation (but in some degree related to them), a recurrent observation in writing about polyphonic Requiems in this period, and about the Spanish repertory in particular, is that Spanish works are characterised by a distinctive sobriety of style, a simplicity which

[165] Montserrat, Abadía, 772. One motet in this manuscript bears the inscription 'P. de Manchicourt faciebat 1560', and the title-page of the book includes 'A Petro de manchicourt regie cappelle magistro conscriptus et compositus'. The manuscript appears in an inventory of music books of the royal chapel dated 1603.

[166] The Offertory provides several examples: he sets the Parisian-rite version of the text, with 'de manu inferni' instead of 'de pœnis inferni' and 'memoriam agimus' rather than 'memoriam facimus', and including 'tenebrarum loca' after 'obscurum' and 'sanctam' after 'ad vitam'; the polyphony of the verse commences at 'Tu suscipe', which is standard practice in Northern Requiems; as in many French settings, the repetendum ('Quam olim . . . ') is written out after the verse, and there is no break between the end of the verse and the repetendum (as in at least nine other settings by French and other Northern composers). Likewise, the text of the final Agnus Dei ends with 'et locum indulgentiæ', conforming to the Parisian rite. On such textual differences between the Requiem texts in the Roman and Parisian rites, as reflected in polyphonic settings by French composers, see James Eby, 'A Requiem Mass for Louis VI: Charles d'Helfer, François Giroust and the *Missa pro defunctis* of 1775', *Early Music* 29 (2001), 218–32, at 225–6.

[167] In addition to the attributed works mentioned here, in the unattributed Requiem in Munich, Bayerische Staatsbibliothek, Mus. BS 65 the chant is presented as a cantus firmus in the Bassus in most sections, and mostly unadorned.

was particularly appropriate to the liturgical occasions concerned and which – again – is seen as setting this repertory apart from Requiems composed elsewhere. Such attitudes represent part of the broader tendency – within Peninsular musicology but also well beyond it – to emphasise distinctive qualities in the Spanish golden-age repertory, a tendency apparent in much writing from the nineteenth century to the present day. These qualities have often been associated with a peculiarly intensive religiosity and, particularly since the publication of Collet's *Le mysticisme musical espagnol* in 1913, with mysticism. Writings in this vein have tended to associate some of all of the following: simplicity, expressivity, Spanishness, and spirituality. Such *topoi* have been notably prominent in discussions of Victoria's music and life.

The view that the Spanish cultivated a particularly spartan style for Requiems was expressed thus by Samuel Rubio:

Two routes or styles can be seen in the manner of conceiving music for exequies: the common, universal style, to which non-Spanish European composers comply, and which serves equally well for a motet or a Mass as for a Requiem Mass, and another style, typical of our country: austere, sober, stripped down, and especially fitted to that liturgy.[168]

He continues by characterising the style of the Requiem Masses by Morales, Vázquez, Guerrero and Victoria as 'exclusively Spanish',[169] and by observing that this distinctive style – firmly separated from the approach of foreigners who applied the international 'Palestrinian' style to Requiems – was followed by Iberian composers as late as Manuel Cardoso and afterwards. Thus for Rubio the Spanish Requiem repertory provided a particularly pure example supporting the belief (as Manuel Sancho García has aptly summarised it) that Spanish music of the 'golden age' constituted 'an autochthonous school, fundamentally different from foreign schools, and definable by the specific qualities of simplicity, mysticism, purity and expressive profundity'.[170] The status of such works, and

---

[168] 'Se aprecia una doble vía o estilo en la manera de concebir la música exequial: el estilo común, universal, al que se atienen los compositores europeos no españoles, que lo mismo sirve para un motete, o misa de Gloria, que para uno de difuntos, y otro típico de nuestro país: austero, sobrio, esquelético, especialmente aplicado a dicha liturgia.' Samuel Rubio, *Juan Vázquez: Agenda defunctorum (Sevilla, 1556): Estudio tecnico-estlistico y transcripcion* (Madrid: Real Musical, 1975), xv.

[169] 'exclusivamente español': *ibid.*, xvi.

[170] 'una escuela autóctona y radicalmente diferente de la extranjera, definible por las cualidades específicas de sencillez, misticismo, pureza y profundidad expresiva': Manuel Sancho García, 'De Teixidor a Pedrell: Tomás Luis de Victoria en la historiografiá musical español del siglo XIX', *Revista de Musicología* 35/1 (2012), 443–57, at 445–6.

the appropriateness of their austerity, is associated with and heightened by their function: not only sacred, and not only liturgical, and not only for Mass, but for a particularly solemn type of Mass. (We have, indeed, seen in Chapter 2 that in *relaciones* of Spanish Habsburg exequies the music is not infrequently characterised as 'contemplative' and that a slow and solemn manner of performance was employed, but this leaves open the question of whether the polyphony itself was different from *pro defunctis* polyphony employed outside the Iberian world.) Such a belief that one can identify a 'Spanish style' of Requiem, characterised by sobriety of melodic and rhythmic approach, was held also by Luce,[171] while José Sierra linked the austere style to the prominent use of the chant by Spaniards, producing (he believed) works 'of markedly Spanish hue'.[172]

Even August Wilhelm Ambros, who did not subscribe to the idea of an independent Spanish 'school' of polyphony (while nevertheless acknowledging the relevance of the 'mystical' for the Spanish approach), suggested in his description (1868) of Morales's five-voice Requiem that its sombre austerity was in some way related to Morales's nationality.[173] The passage was quoted in translation in Robert Stevenson's seminal *Spanish Cathedral Music in the Golden Age* of 1961:

The *Missa pro defunctis*, though magnificent, inspires terror. One shivers in the presence of this somber, nocturnal masterpiece. One feels as if he were wandering in dark hollows beneath leaden vaults supported by heavy pillars. In it, all adornment has been stripped away, and everything is as plain as could be. Before the face of death all colors fade, and all gaiety ceases. Morales, the Spaniard, conceives death in all its terrible seriousness. . . . Coming from his Requiem immediately upon that of Palestrina, one is struck by the strange feeling that into the blackness of the graves has shot a ray of heavenly light, and that the stern messenger from an unknown land whom Morales presented to us has given way to an angel, serious but benign.[174]

---

[171] 'The Requiem Mass'; see, for example, 255.

[172] 'de tinte marcadamente español'. He observes that 'the seriousness and austerity proper to this style is compositionally related to the greater presence of the chant . . . which suggests sobriety more than the play of art or contrapuntal artifice, more limited, but without thereby losing expressivity' ('la seriedad y austeridad propias de este estilo está relacionada composicionalmente con la mayor presencia del canto llano . . . que hace pensar más en la sobriedad que en el juego del arte o artificio contrapuntístico, más limitado, pero sin que por ello pierda expresividad'); *Pedro de Escobar: Missa pro defunctis* (Zaragoza: Institución Fernando el Católico, 2009), 10–11.

[173] Ambros, *Geschichte der Musik*, 5 vols (Breslau and Leipzig: F. E. C. Leuchart, 1862–82), III, 573–4.

[174] *Spanish Cathedral Music in the Golden Age*, 60.

The 'sober' style described here and by later writers on Spanish Requiems is indeed not difficult to find among the relevant works by Spanish and Portuguese composers, but one should signal the fact that it is quite frequently associated with the use of *proportio dupla* mensuration (that is, with a breve rather than semibreve tactus) in particular sections (only) of these works. The 'sobriety' is thus partly a notational phenomenon (at least in some works), rather than necessarily one of marked sobriety in the actual sounding music, since under a *proportio dupla* signature each note value occupies less time than it does under an *integer valor* signature. This leads to consideration of a different way in which the Iberian polyphonic Requiem tradition may indeed have been distinct from those elsewhere in Europe: the distinctiveness consists not simply in the more widespread employment of genuinely *proportio dupla* writing in Iberian settings, but more specifically in the exploitation by a significant number of Iberian composers of contrast – within a Requiem – between sections using *proportio dupla* and *integer valor*. Furthermore, one can detect certain conventions about which parts of the Requiem were most likely to be written in each of these two 'manners', and also a linkage between the two 'manners' and the use of long-note cantus firmus technique on the one hand and paraphrase treatment of chant on the other.

The sections of the relevant Iberian Requiems which employ *proportio dupla* mensuration move predominantly in the longer note values, breves and semibreves. Minims – where present – are frequently used to provide inessential-note movement, and semiminims (i.e. crotchets) are rare or absent. Such sections are usually given the relevant mensuration signature, with a vertical stroke indicating *tempus imperfectum diminutum*. Those sections employing *integer valor* mensuration employ a different rhythmic spectrum, typically making more frequent use of semiminims (and perhaps including decorative pairs of fusæ (i.e. quavers)) and regularly employing minims as the unit of declamation and harmonic change. Another distinction between the two ways of writing is that under *proportio dupla* the dissonance in a suspension will (ignoring decorative elements) typically last for a semibreve, while under *integer valor* it will more frequently last for a minim. A survey of Iberian Requiems of the sixteenth century and the first half of the seventeenth reveals a tendency – in those pieces which distinguish between *proportio dupla* and *integer valor* writing – for the Sanctus and Agnus Dei to employ the former manner, and the Gradual, Offertory, and Communion the latter.[175] The Introit is frequently in *proportio dupla* also,[176] but one quite often finds variation of style and rhythmic profile within Introit settings: a shift from the *proportio dupla* 'manner' to that belonging to *integer valor* can be observed in several works from 'et lux perpetua' onwards in the antiphon (with minim declamation for 'et lux perpetua'), and the verse likewise may use this latter manner, with the chant sung in relatively shorter values than in the antiphon. Such 'speeding up' occurs at 'et lux perpetua' in Victoria's six-voice setting of the Introit (from b. 15), as well as in Morales's two Masses, Esquivel's four-voice Mass, Cardoso's six-voice Mass, Mendes's, Vivanco's, and both of those by Duarte Lobo.

The distinctions between *proportio dupla* and *integer valor* just described are already apparent in Morales's five-voice Mass, with the *proportio dupla* rhythmic spectrum used in the Introit, Kyrie, Sanctus, and Agnus Dei (as well as for the setting of the conclusion of the Sequence), and the *integer valor* spectrum in the Gradual, Offertory, and Communion.[177] Other Iberian Requiems displaying such distinctions include those by:[178]

1. Bernal
2. Cardoso, four voices
3. Cardoso, six voices
4. Esquivel, four voices
5. Esquivel, five voices
6. Gallego
7. Lobo, six voices
8. Lobo, eight voices

---

[175] In some cases, the distinction is made even within a movement of a Requiem. In the Sanctus of the unattributed Requiem in Coimbra, Biblioteca Geral da Universidade, MM 6, the two polyphonic 'Sanctus' acclamations use *proportio dupla* and the remainder of the setting (from 'Dominus Deus' onwards) *integer valor*, and the relevant change of mensuration signature is present in the source. In both of Cardoso's Requiems, the respond of the Gradual employs *proportio dupla*, and the Gradual verse *integer valor*, while in the Gradual and Gradual verse of the unattributed Requiem in Braga, Arquivo Distrital 965 these mensurations appear the other way round.

[176] However, in Bernal's and Morago's settings the Introit has an *integer valor* signature, and behaves accordingly, leaving only the Kyrie, Sanctus, and Agnus in *proportio dupla*.

[177] The distinction is blurred somewhat by the use of minim declamation at the opening of the final Agnus Dei, as well as at 'et lux perpetua' in the Introit, as already mentioned. The presence of two different mensurations in this Mass was ignored in, for example, Moderne's edition, where the composer used a *proportio dupla* signature throughout the work.

[178] Another work in an Iberian source which falls into this category is the unattributed Requiem in Braga, Arquivo Distrital 965. In Garro's Requiem the behaviour of the music is predominantly that of *integer valor*, but the Sanctus clearly behaves as if in *proportio dupla*.

9. Mendes
10. Morago
11. Ribeiro[179]
12. Vivanco

Those (many) Iberian Requiems which do not exploit clear distinction between *proportio dupla* and *integer valor* writing encompass a significant number that avoid *proportio dupla* style – and hence the (at least notationally) 'sober' style – throughout. Works in this category include the following:[180]

1. Brito[181]
2. Cubells
3. Guerrero
4. Pujol
5. Juan Pau Pujol
6. Victoria (the four-voice Requiem)

Much of the writing in these works is not significantly less 'decorated' or elaborate than was typical in sacred polyphony of the period. At the other extreme is the Requiem by Filipe de Magalhães, which is entirely in *proportio dupla*, using only notes of minim value or greater with the exception of two pairs of semiminims in the Gradual verse. But one should emphasise that this work – which seems perfectly to represent the supposed general sobriety of Spanish Requiems – is exceptional within the Iberian repertory: its long-note rhythmic profile and associated contrapuntal practices (with, for example, all suspensions operating at the *proportio dupla* level) is much more consistent than in – for instance – the Requiem by Escobar (a piece which has, as noted, been viewed as in many respects of seminal importance for the genre in the Peninsula), which in some passages likewise relies almost entirely on the longer note-values but in others is much more rhythmically active.

---

[179] The copyist of this work in the manuscript Braga, Arquivo Distrital 965 did not reflect – in his choice of mensuration signatures – the use of two mensurations: as is commonplace, the Introit, Kyrie, Sanctus, and Agnus operate in *proportio dupla*, and the Graduals (there are two settings), Offertory, and Communion in *integer valor*.

[180] The unattributed Requiem in Tuy Cathedral L 5 is another written throughout in *integer valor* style, and notated with *integer valor* signatures.

[181] Brito's Requiem is notated (in Málaga, Catedral, Archivo Capitular 4) with *integer valor* signatures except in the Sanctus and Agnus, but the *proportio dupla* signatures applied to those two sections do not reflect the behaviour of the music: for example, the Agnus Dei includes semiminim declamation.

To summarise: there did not exist a general 'Spanish' approach to composing Requiem Masses characterised by austerity, plainness, and absence of ornament. That being said, a significant number of Iberian composers distinguished two groups of items within the Requiem: on the one hand, the Kyrie, Sanctus, and Agnus Dei (together with, in many cases, the Introit), and on the other the Gradual, Offertory, and Communion, applying to them different types of writing in terms of mensuration and associated rhythmic profile. The movements in the first group are also those most likely to feature long-note (often breve-based) and relatively undecorated presentation of the chant as a cantus firmus, whereas in the second group it is more frequent to find rhythmically freer and decorated chant, or chant material which is incorporated into the texture through paraphrase rather than cantus-firmus technique. The correlations just mentioned are far from exact, and exceptions are easy to find. Nevertheless, it is clear that certain conventions about how one might set different parts of the Requiem had quite widespread and certainly long-lasting influence within the Peninsula, even though such conventions are observable in a minority of Iberian Requiems.

The practice of making such distinctions seems to have been both much more widespread and much longer-lived in the Iberian Peninsula than elsewhere in Europe, to the extent that we may justifiably regard it as a distinctive element of Iberian traditions. A survey of nearly fifty Italian and Northern Requiems of the period from approximately the middle of the sixteenth century to the middle of the seventeenth reveals no work which makes the distinction as clearly as do many Iberian settings of the same period: rather, although these pieces almost all bear *proportio dupla* signatures in their sources,[182] the overwhelming majority are composed in the *integer valor* manner throughout.[183] An exception, however, is the

---

[182] Although this signature supposedly indicated *proportio dupla* (or *tempus imperfectum diminutum*), in most sources of the period it had in general ceased to have any such particular mensural significance, but was used as the ubiquitous signature for *tempus imperfectum*. However, that the distinction between *tempus imperfectum* (the Spanish *compasillo*) and *tempus imperfectum diminutum* (or *compás mayor*) continued to have significance for some Iberian composers, at least in certain contexts, is revealed both by the Requiems discussed here (in the sources of which the meaningful distinction between the relevant mensuration signatures continued more often to operate) and also by (for example) the Magnificat settings of Vivanco, as observed by Bruno Turner in 'Spanish Liturgical Hymns: A Matter of Time', *Early Music* 23 (1995), 473–82, at 481.

[183] The Requiem by Pierre Certon, first published in 1558, has passages in both *proportio dupla* and *integer valor* 'manners' in most movements; for example, the Sanctus displays *proportio dupla* characteristics, and the Benedictus *integer valor* ones. The Agnus Dei is more clearly in *proportio dupla*. Among the Requiems by Northern composers from a somewhat earlier period

Requiem by Giovanni Contino, which has already been mentioned both for its extensive use of cantus-firmus technique and for the fact that it includes the longer chant intonations commonly found in Iberian settings.[184] The distinctions in mensural behaviour in this Mass are distributed similarly to those in the relevant Iberian Requiems: the Introit, Kyrie, Sanctus, and Agnus behave mainly as if in *proportio dupla*, while the Gradual, Offertory, and Communion suggest *integer valor*.[185] The adoption of one 'manner' or the other here is not entirely consistent within movements, and is less marked than in some Iberian works. Nevertheless, the *proportio dupla* behaviour of (for example) the Kyrie – connected in some degree to its extensive employment of a cantus firmus in breves – is clear.

It should be noted, as an aside at this point, that although *integer valor* behaviour was apparently the norm in Italian and Northern Requiems of the period, this does not exclude the appearance of very 'austere' writing in these works, which is quite common in settings of the Agnus Dei, for example.[186] The 'sober' style here – these are concise, largely syllabic, and often homophonic settings of the text, using few semiminims – is comparable to that of many Iberian settings, and fits as well as do they with Rubio's and others' characterisation of the 'Spanish' approach to Requiem composition, further weakening the claims that such sobriety was a peculiarly Peninsular trait in *pro defunctis* polyphony.

Traces of the conventions regarding different mensural 'manners' (and associated chant-treatment) applied to particular movements in the Requiem may be found in Victoria's six-voice work, although the distinctions are not so consistently apparent there as they are in many other Iberian Requiems. These traces are observable if one compares Victoria's approach to the Kyrie and the Offertory. The first Kyrie incorporates the chant, with little adornment, laid out in breves in the Cantus II part. The other parts move largely in breves and semibreves (the Bassus entirely so); minims are rare and semiminims very rare, the appearances of these shorter values being mainly concentrated in a brief passage in the two Tenor parts (b. 9–11, discussed below) shortly before the final cadence. All

---

one finds a wide variety of mensural profiles, including within movements as well as between movements and between pieces.

[184] It is also one of the few Italian Requiems to include a setting of the Gradual, a practice more common (as noted) in Spain.

[185] The printed edition of 1573, as was common practice at the time, uses a *proportio dupla* signature indiscriminately for all the imperfect-time music in the Mass.

[186] Instances include the Agnus Dei settings in all three Requiems by Giulio Belli, Lassus's four-voice Mass, and those by Certon and Clemens.

suspensions in this first Kyrie and the final Kyrie operate at the *proportio dupla* level, and the rate of harmonic change is once per breve, reflecting the progress of the chant in breves, except (once again) at the approach to the final cadence of the first Kyrie.[187] In the Offertory, in contrast, almost all the suspensions – except for the string of suspensions at 'de pœnis' (b. 14–18) – are of the shorter-note type common under an *integer valor* signature,[188] declamation in minims is ubiquitous, and indeed semiminim declamation appears at 'repræsentet' (b. 52–5) and various other points. The rate of harmonic change is very varied, but is frequently at the level of the semibreve or minim. The pace of the chant-bearing line is correspondingly less consistent than in the Kyrie, and this line has a higher proportion of shorter note-values,[189] so that it is frequently integrated with the other voices in its rhythmic profile.

Convention and Invention: The F – G – A Chant Motive

Victoria's crafting of polyphony from and around the Requiem chants runs the gamut from the strongly conventional to the extraordinary. This range of approaches is well illustrated by the varied ways in which he treats the chant motive F – G – A which features repeatedly in the first two sections of the Requiem: at 'dona' (the opening of the Introit antiphon polyphony); as intonation formula in the Introit verse (at 'et tibi' and 'exaudi'); and as the opening gesture of the first Kyrie and the Christe. The first four of these five occurrences will be considered in turn. Among them, the first represents the most conventional polyphonic handling of this motive, the second epitomises a particular habit of Victoria's (both in this Requiem and in his works for more than four voices throughout his career), while the third and fourth are unconventional and striking gestures. The contrapuntal and harmonic module used at the beginning of Victoria's Introit is a commonplace one

---

[187] Other sections of Victoria's Mass which come close to the approach described here include the second part of the Sanctus ('Pleni sunt cæli . . . Osanna in excelsis'), where the chant again proceeds almost entirely in breves.

[188] The signature here in the 1605 publication is nevertheless *proportio dupla*, as throughout the *Officium defunctorum* except for *Tædet animam meam*, which has an *integer valor* signature. There is a printer's error in the Cantus I part on f. 24v, where the final verse of *Libera me Domine* is given an *integer valor* signature, whereas all other voice-parts here have a *proportio dupla* signature.

[189] However, there are also passages of breve- or semibreve-based cantus-firmus treatment in the Offertory, as at 'de pœnis' (where all voices employ the longer note-values, and where – as noted – a succession of longer-value suspensions appears), 'libera eas', 'in lucem sanctam', and 'et semini eius'.

Example 4.8 Conventional module for openings involving an F – G – A progression

in pieces whose openings involve this F – G – A progression, whether chant-derived or not, and is shown in its essential form in Example 4.8: the opening three-note ascent of the chant interlocks with a preceding entry of the same rising motive beginning on C, to form a simple two-voice *fuga* cell, while the Bassus underpins this with the progression *f – d – c*. This module appears at the start of the Introit in Victoria's six-voice Requiem, the five-voice Requiem by Morales, the Requiems by Guerrero and Mendes, two of the four-voice Requiems by Asola,[190] and the Requiem by Blasius Ammon.[191] It is also found at the openings of other sections of Requiems in which the chants begin with the same F – G – A ascent: instances are the Introit verse of Prioris's Mass, Isnardi's four-voice Mass, and Helfer's Mass, the Kyrie of Morales's four-voice Mass, and the 'Pleni' section of the Sanctus in Mendes's Requiem. Victoria had used the same module when setting another chant with tritus modality which begins with the F – G – A ascent, namely *Tantum ergo* (a verse of the hymn *Pange lingua*): see Example 4.9. The resemblances between this passage and the opening of the Introit in the *Officium defunctorum* extend beyond their use of the basic module described above: in both cases, the chant is assigned to the second of two Cantus parts, and the first Cantus part sings an ascending line *a' – b♮' – c'* while the chant-line has its initial *f'* and *g'*. In addition, the Tenor part in *Tantum ergo* corresponds (in terms of its first three pitches) with the Tenor I part in the Requiem Introit. The line ascending A – B – C is used also by other composers when deploying this module; for example, Morales places this line in the Altus II part of his five-voice Introit setting, and Asola (in the setting in his *Officium defunctorum*) likewise in the Altus.

---

[190]   The work initially published as *Messa pro defunctis* in 1576, and the setting within the *Officium defunctorum* first issued in 1586.

[191]   The F – G – A element of the module constitutes a pre-imitation of the chant's opening figure in the cases of Morales's and Guerrero's settings, but is the entry of the chant itself in the cases of Mendes's and Victoria's. Asola's polyphony begins at 'æternam' rather than 'dona', but the chant for 'æternam' commences with the same F – G – A motive as occurs at 'dona'.

Example 4.9 Thome Luis de Victoria, *Pange lingua*, opening of 'Tantum ergo' verse

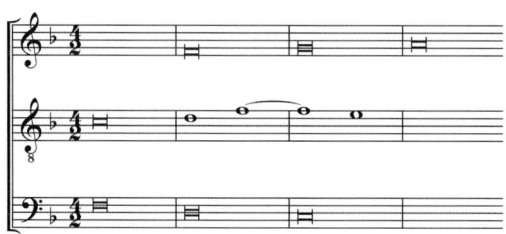

Example 4.10 Alternative conventional module for openings involving an F – G – A progression

Another form of this basic module exists in which, instead of the simple C – D – E line, the relevant voice leaps from its D to an F which then becomes a suspended dissonance (Example 4.10). This version of the module is found in, for example, the settings of the Introit by Lupacchino and Vázquez, and at the opening of the Kyrie in the Requiem items by Basurto. (Victoria had used such a module in his early motet *O decus apostolicum*.) A related passage by Victoria is the opening of the first Kyrie setting in *Libera me Domine* from the *Officium defunctorum*, where once again one finds a chant line rising F – G – A (b. 77–9). In this case the suspended *f'* (in the Altus) does not form part of the C – D – F figure just described, but echoes the suspended *c''* in Cantus I formed against the Bassus progression from *f* to *d*. The countersubject C – D – F with suspension of the F appears also at the opening of the Introit in the Requiems of Richafort and Magalhães, although the Bassus lines here are different from that in the module discussed above. Yet another instance of the module is at the opening of Morales's setting of *Circumdederunt me dolores mortis*, antiphon to the invitatory psalm at Matins of the Dead, the chant of which likewise begins F – G – A.[192]

The second and third occurrences of the F – G – A chant motive in Victoria's Introit are, as mentioned, at the beginning of the verse (setting 'et tibi', b. 33–5) and later in that verse (at 'exaudi', b. 43–5), where they constitute an intonation formula of the sixth-tone chant of the verse. Victoria handles these two moments in conspicuously different ways. For the first he uses an harmonic sequence (D – G – C – F) constituting a four-step segment of the circle of fifths. He was not alone in such a choice: two Portuguese Requiems employ the same harmonic device at this point in the text.[193] Use of this type of sequence (and other sequential patterns) is, in fact, rather common in the *Officium defunctorum*: instances involving four or more harmonic steps occur in every item except the Kyrie (which, however, includes a prominent three-stage progression (b. 4–6) culminating in an E♭ harmony, to be discussed below) and Gradual (which nevertheless includes another type of sequence). Such extensive use of sequence was not a peculiarity of the *Officium defunctorum* within Victoria's output, but was a common part of his compositional technique when writing in more than four parts.[194] Besides the Introit verse, two other sections of the Requiem – Offertory and Sanctus – open with a circle-of-fifths sequence as a means of harmonising the chant, and in the Offertory another prominent example occurs in the passage leading to the final cadence (b. 70–74).[195] The beginning (b. 1–6) of the Sanctus has the same harmonic sequence as in the Introit verse (but beginning one stage earlier in the pattern: A – D – G – C – F), here used as a means of harmonising the opening descent

---

[192] The lowest-sounding voice in this case again differs from the Bassus progression in the module shown in Ex. 4.10. The sharing of this module between Morales's piece and the Requiem Introit openings of Richafort and Magalhães was highlighted by Bernadette Nelson in her paper '*Missas de Requiem* in Early 17th-Century Lisbon: Traditions, Compositional Processes, Influences', Medieval and Renaissance Music Conference, University of Sheffield, 8 July 2016.

[193] Cardoso's four-voice Requiem and Lobo's eight-voice Requiem.

[194] For example, in the *Motecta* of 1572 circle-of-fifths sequences of significant length (i.e. incorporating four or more steps) are rare in the four-voice works (most of these motets containing no such sequences), but occur in all but two of the five-voice works and in all of the six- and eight-voice works. The four-voice Requiem includes no significant circle-of-fifths sequences and almost no other significant sequential devices, in marked contrast to the music of the *Officium defunctorum*. Only in his Mass collection of 1592 does one find such sequential writing more often in four-voice works.

[195] Furthermore, in *Versa est in luctum* the phrase 'parce mihi Domine' is set using two imitative motives concurrently, one of which outlines a sequence of fifths and produces the corresponding harmonic sequence.

A – G – F in the chant. The sequential construction is particularly empha-sised by making each progression into a cadence, signalled principally by the use (at every stage) of the syncopated minim-semibreve-minim figure which provides the pre-cadential suspension using a consonant fourth. At the beginning of the Offertory (b. 1–4), the Altus (carrying the chant), Tenor I, and Bassus enter at a breve's distance on *e'*, *a*, and *d* respectively, and the Bassus then falls a fifth to *G*, the resultant passage again outlining a harmonic sequence. The second note of the chant's opening gesture here, E – C – D, is raised to *c♯'*, so that the harmony at that point is major, strengthening the sequential effect, as also does the use of *f♯'* in Cantus II at the next stage of this sequence.[196]

Victoria's handling of the F – G – A chant motive at the opening of the Introit verse – with sequential Bassus movement leaping by fifths and introducing the *b' mi* of *cantus durus* – contrasts markedly with his treatment of 'exaudi' later in that verse (b. 43–5), where the same intona-tion formula occurs. Here he accompanies the F – G – A ascent with a motive moving by semitones, *d – e♭ – d*, in the Bassus; the *g'* of the chant motive is thus here accompanied by *e fa*, whereas at 'et tibi' the equivalent chant *g'* had been accompanied by *b' mi*. The Bassus's semitonal motive is also sung by Cantus I, as *a' – b♭' – a'*, in stretto at the fifth with the Bassus, and is then repeated by Tenor II using these same pitch classes (b. 46–8); this last statement of the motive is highlighted by the behaviour of the Cantus I part, which rises to *a'* against the *b fa* of the Tenor, thus creating the unusual 'consonant seventh' mentioned above, found nowhere else in the *Officium defunctorum*. The semitonal move to E♭ at 'exaudi' is employed by no other composer at the equivalent point in the Introit verse, so far as I am aware, although in his eight-voice Requiem Pérez Roldán (who did not use the chant at this point) likewise employed E♭ harmony. More generally, Victoria's treatment of the 'exaudi orationem meam' passage departs considerably from the traditions of setting the Introit verse of the Requiem in declamatory homorhythm, as a relatively simple harmonisation of the psalm tone, a tradition which was not restricted to the Iberian Peninsula (as discussed below). Victoria, using more complex textures, dramatises and intensifies his setting through the imitative repeti-tion and striking harmonisation of the semitonal 'exaudi' motive, and by means of the subsequent quickening of declamatory and harmonic pace at

---

[196] Other composers had the same idea, presumably independently: similar sequential progressions occur at the beginning of the Offertory settings in the Requiems by Contino and Morago.

'orationem',[197] but also by his handling of 'Hierusalem' (leading into the 'exaudi' setting), where he goes beyond other settings in his dissonant treatment. Almost all Iberian composers of Requiems employed a suspension of the A as the chant mediation formula falls from B♭ to A to G at 'Hierusalem':[198] either a seventh, as in Victoria's setting (b. 42), or a ninth, as in both settings by Esquivel and Lobo's six-voice Mass, for example.[199] However, Victoria highlights this segment by also using a suspended ninth two breves earlier (b. 39) at the previous descent from A to G in the chant. No other attributed Iberian Requiem of the period adopts this approach, so far as I am aware.[200]

The final notable example of Victoria's treatment of the F – G – A chant motive in the opening two movements of the Requiem is that at the beginning of the Kyrie. Here, as at 'exaudi' in the Introit verse, the results are unusually powerful. The Requiem Kyrie chant used by Victoria ascends beyond F – G – A to B♭.[201] He here employed a simple imitative interlock similar to the type discussed above with regard to the opening of the Introit antiphon, but in this case the chant-bearing voice (Cantus II, as usual) precedes rather than follows the imitation in another voice (Cantus I), and that imitation is at the fourth above rather than the fourth below. The result is striking: the Cantus I part thereby reaches *e″* as the peak note of this

---

[197] In Lupacchino's Requiem one similarly finds imitative writing in the free voices at 'orationem', with entries at the unison and octave beginning on D, and minim declamation as in Victoria's treatment.

[198] The Iberian repertory of Requiem settings reflects variants in the manner of intoning the Introit verse. Some settings follow the Roman tone for this verse, while in other cases the more elaborate Iberian forms are found. At 'orationem meam' (b. 48–52) Victoria uses the Roman formula, remaining on the reciting note A rather than using the mediation formula found in Iberian sources here, but at 'Hierusalem' in the first part of his verse Victoria follows Iberian practice in using a mediation formula more elaborate than the Roman one, and which includes the descent from A to G discussed here (b. 41), whereas the Roman formula omits this A. For a summary of the differences between the Roman and Iberian formulæ for the Introit verse, see João Pedro d'Alvarenga, 'Two Polyphonic Settings of the Mass for the Dead from Late Sixteenth-Century Portugal: Bridging Pre- and Post-Tridentine Traditions', *Acta Musicologica* 88 (2016), 5–33, at 14–15; however, the observation there that Victoria uses the Roman tone is not entirely correct, as just noted.

[199] Among non-Iberian works this is rarer, but a ninth suspension occurs here in the Requiems by Blasius Ammon and Claudin de Sermisy.

[200] Lobo's eight-voice Requiem likewise has a suspended ninth at the first descent in the chant, but avoids the second descent and therefore the opportunity for a second suspension.

[201] This was the chant employed for the Kyrie of the Requiem Mass in the *Graduale Romanum* of the relevant period. It also appears, for example, in Morales's five-voice Requiem, Cererols's four-voice work, both of the Requiems by Duarte Lobo, and those by Contino, Magalhães, Morago, and Juan Pau Pujol, while many other Iberian Requiems employ different chants. Iberian chant melodies for the Kyrie, and their use in certain polyphonic settings, are considered in Alvarenga, 'Two Polyphonic Settings', 15–17.

gesture, a note not used in the Introit and which makes only rare appearances within the music of the *Officium defunctorum*,[202] these occasional uses including climactic moments such as the ending of the second 'Hosanna', the setting of 'sempiternam' at the conclusion of the Agnus Dei, and the extraordinary treatment of 'nihil enim sunt dies mei' in *Versa est in luctum* which – as noted above – constitutes the expressive zenith of that item and indeed of the *Officium defunctorum* as a whole. However, the occurrence of *e″* in the Kyrie is separated from all of the others in that it must be sung as *e♭″* – although no flat is indicated in the printed edition – since the Bassus reaches *e♭* at this moment (and so that the Cantus I phrase outlines a rising perfect fourth rather than an augmented fourth). Victoria's engineering of a powerfully shaped gesture by his handling of a chant motive in *fuga* again exemplifies the manner in which his six-voice Requiem not infrequently stands out among contemporary works in the genre.

Unconventional Elaboration: Introit Verse and Communion Verse

For two of those parts of the Requiem Mass texts which were commonly set (at least partly) in polyphony – the verses of the Introit and the Communion – a recitational formula, similar to a psalm tone, was employed in chanted performances. The first parts of these verses were left in chant, and the remainder set in polyphony (from 'et tibi' in Introit verses, and from 'et lux perpetua' in Communion verses). Many composers throughout Catholic Europe (whether or not they incorporated the chant in their polyphony here) dealt with the relevant polyphonic sections in a manner which reflected the recitational character of the chant, using homorhythmic or quasi-homorhythmic textures and declamatory treatment of the text (without textual repetition), reminiscent to some degree of *fabordón / falsobordone*, the technique commonly used for polyphonic singing of psalms and canticles. However, Victoria's settings in the *Officium defunctorum* stand somewhat apart from this convention: they are generally more elaborate in textural terms, and as a result lie towards one end of the spectrum of approaches to these parts of the Requiem. Grayson Wagstaff regarded Victoria's rather elaborate writing in the

---

[202] For these purposes appearances of *e″* in the Gradual are ignored, since this item was subject to transposition downwards by a fifth.

Introit verse – and the consequent lack of stylistic or textural contrast between the verse and the Introit antiphon – as one symptom of the separation that he sees between the composer's six-voice Requiem and Spanish traditions,[203] but in fact Victoria's procedure in this instance is not specifically 'un-Spanish' so much as internationally atypical, and more complex styles appear sufficiently frequently in the Introit verses of Iberian Requiems – at least for parts of the verse – to encourage further caution about labelling this aspect of Victoria's writing as specifically 'non-Iberian'.[204] Admittedly, the proportion of Iberian works featuring more complex settings of the Introit verse does seem to be somewhat smaller than the equivalent proportion of Northern settings, but the difference is not great, and the picture in Italy appears rather similar to that in the Iberian world in these terms. Victoria's setting of the Introit verse is not just more elaborate texturally than was typical, but is also unusually long.[205] It occupies 26 breves, which is more than almost all of the approximately forty-five non-Iberian settings which I have examined for this purpose.[206] Of the twenty-six Italian settings in this sample, all but five

---

[203] Wagstaff, 'Music for the Dead', 591.

[204] The relevant settings include Cardoso's six-voice version, Guerrero's, Lobo's eight-voice setting, and the settings by Pujol, Juan Pau Pujol, Ribeiro, Rimonte, and Vázquez. Chordal or quasi-chordal writing predominates in the Introit verse settings by the following Iberian composers: Cererols (in the four-voice Requiem), Escobar, Esquivel (in both Requiems), Garro, Lobo (the six-voice setting), Magalhães, Mendes, Morales (in both Requiems), Romero, and Vivanco. Wagstaff regards Rimonte's Requiem as standing outside the 'Spanish' norms he has identified, in terms of chant presentation and (for example) treatment of the Introit verse. He argues that 'the most obvious characteristic of most previously discussed [Spanish] settings, the obvious presentation of the chant in longer notational values, is completely absent from Ruimonte's work. When they are present, the chant melodies are so ornamented and stated in shorter notes so that they become almost completely indistinguishable from the newly composed music surrounding them.' ('Music for the Dead', 595) However, Rimonte does indeed use cantus-firmus technique in several parts of the Mass: in the second section of the Sanctus ('Pleni sunt . . . Hosanna in excelsis') the chant is presented without decoration as a monorhythmic breve cantus firmus in Cantus II; the same occurs throughout the Benedictus, with the chant in Cantus I; and all three sections of the Agnus Dei use an unadorned cantus firmus, the chant being assigned to the Tenor, Cantus II, and Altus I respectively. Besides this, the chant is given to Cantus I for most of the Introit verse and to Cantus II in the Communion verse.

[205] In making comparisons of the lengths of Introit verse settings, one has to take into account the use of *proportio dupla* style for many Iberian settings and a very few non-Iberian ones. In these *proportio dupla* settings, the density of musical events is significantly lower than in settings – such as Victoria's – which adopt *integer valor* style, and their effective length in comparison to the latter settings is reduced given the faster pace of performance under a *proportio dupla* signature.

[206] In similar fashion, of the twelve Iberian settings examined which do not use *proportio dupla* style and which set the same amount of the verse text as does Victoria's, only one (that by Vázquez) is longer than Victoria's six-voice setting.

are less than 20 breves in length,[207] and Victoria's verse is longer than any of the twenty-three Northern settings in the sample except Bonnefond's and three in *proportio dupla* style. With regard to Communion verse settings, Robert Snow likewise suggested that there was a distinction between Spanish and Italian practice, but in this case (contrasting with Wagstaff's view regarding the Introit verse) he believed that the Italians almost always used a quasi-chordal style while the Spaniards often adopted a more complex style akin to that employed for the Communion antiphon.[208] My survey again suggests, however, that no such national or geographical distinction existed: chordal or quasi-chordal declamation in the Communion verse is common internationally, and the Spanish repertory does not stand apart in these terms from either Italian settings or those from North of the Alps. More specifically, one frequently finds – in all parts of the international repertory – that the first words of the polyphonic section of the verse, 'et lux perpetua', are set in chordal or quasi-chordal fashion, but that after this – at 'luceat eis', where the chant moves away from its reciting note – the writing typically becomes more contrapuntal and elaborate.[209] (It was likewise an international convention that the antiphon and repetendum sections of the Communion were set using imitative textures paraphrasing the chant, so that the declamatory opening of the verse polyphony contrasts with the rest of the setting.) This approach to the verse was adopted by Victoria himself in his four-voice work, and also by the composers listed here, for example:[210]

Iberian composers
Bernal
Cardoso (six-voice Requiem)
Guerrero (both settings of the Communion published in 1582)
Lobo (eight-voice Requiem)
Morales (five-voice Requiem)
Juan Pau Pujol
Ribeiro

[207] For example, those by Bernardi and Biondi occupy 12 breves, Viadana's four-voice setting from the *Officium defunctorum* 13 breves, those by Giovanni Francesco Anerio, Canale, Ghizzolo (from his five-voice Requiem), and Heredia 14 breves, the three settings by Belli between 13 and 16 breves, and the four settings by Asola between 15 and 18 breves. The shortest setting discovered is that by Petrucci, which takes just 9 breves.

[208] Robert Snow, 'An Unknown *Missa pro defunctis* by Palestrina', 415.

[209] This change in texture is common even in settings which make little or no reference to the chant.

[210] It also occurs in the unattributed Requiems in Montserrat, Abadía 1085 and Braga, Archivo Distrital 965.

Italian composers[211]

Anerio

Asola (the four-voice Requiems first published in *Il segondo libro delle messe*, AA2540a, and *Officium defunctorum*, A2565)

Bacilieri

Belli (eight-voice Requiem)

Biondi

Contino

Ghizzolo (five-voice Requiem)

Isnardi

Porta

Viadana (the three-voice setting, and the four-voice work published in the *Officium defunctorum*, 1600)

Zucchini

Northern composers

Bournonville

Certon

Clemens

Clereau

Helfer

Kerle

Lassus (five-voice Requiem)

Lauverjat

Prioris

Sermisy

With these facts in view, we can see that Victoria's contrapuntal and imitative setting of the Communion verse lies significantly outside international norms. Rather than beginning in chordal or quasi-chordal manner, Victoria employs a more elaborate texture, laying out the psalm-tone formula in canon at the octave between Cantus II and Tenor, and giving both of these entries a countersubject which is then treated further in imitation in Altus, Tenor I, and Bassus. As well as the contrapuntal texture itself, his extension of this section through repetition of 'et lux perpetua' is highly unusual. Other Iberian settings using contrapuntal textures for

---

[211] Of the works listed here, those by Belli, Ghizzolo, and Zucchini use unmeasured chanting in the manner of *falsobordone* for 'et lux perpetua', returning to mensural writing at 'luceat eis'. A similar technique is employed in several other parts of Zucchini's Requiem, including both the antiphon and the verse of the Introit.

'et lux perpetua' in the verse are (*pace* Snow) in a very small minority: they include the four-voice Mass by Esquivel, the four-voice Requiem by Morales, and Vivanco's setting, in the last two of which one finds repetition of 'et lux perpetua'. Among the – likewise very rare – non-Iberian works where the Communion verse opens contrapuntally are those by Bonnefond, Contino, Heredia, Monte, and Tamburini. Of these, Heredia uses imitative textures built around two statements (in the Tenor and then the Bassus) of the chant for 'et lux perpetua luceat eis', while Tamburini likewise has two statements of the chant, in Cantus and then Tenor I, with freely contrapuntal textures around them. However, the closest of all to Victoria's is Rimonte's setting (which one might justifiably treat as either a Spanish or a Northern work): the chant recitation is again assigned to two voices (here Cantus II and Altus I) in loose canon, each being accompanied by essentially the same contrapuntal module, which here involves two voices besides the part carrying the chant.

Animating Chant-based Polyphony

While the Introit verse and Communion verse of the *Officium defunctorum* represent unusually elaborate treatments of their chants (in terms of the generic conventions of how to set these sections), elsewhere in the chant-based parts of the work Victoria quite frequently employs fundamentally very simple textures animated by straightforward means, the kind of textures which seem well characterised by Noel O'Regan's term 'pseudo-polyphony', discussed above. A good example is the second section of the Sanctus (b. 17–31, setting 'cæli et terra gloria tua. Osanna in excelsis'). Victoria here laid out the chant (in Cantus II, as usual) in breves, decorating and/or departing from it just twice, at 'tua' (b. 24) and 'excelsis' (b. 30), and thus marking the division of the text into two sections, a structure highlighted by his use of exactly the same syncopated and decorative figure in Cantus II at both of these points.[212] It would be an easy task to strip Victoria's setting of this section – in which breve and semibreve movement predominates in the free voices also – down to a simple homorhythmic harmonisation of the chant notes, with one harmony per breve. In fact, there is only one brief deviation from this harmonic rhythm in the whole section (at b. 29). Except during the two passages where the chant is

---

[212] However, the first is harmonised with a 'Phrygian' cadence whereas the second cadences on A and therefore introduces *g♯'* at the cadence approach.

decorated, the role of adding contrapuntal and rhythmic interest to this plain framework is usually assigned to just one voice at a time: thus at the opening (b. 17) the Cantus I entry is delayed by a semibreve, its first note is then suspended, and the resolution is decorated with a semiminim figure, this standard figure then reappearing at all but one of the other suspensions in the section, including the two decorations of the chant line.[213] Victoria then passes the task of propelling the music from Cantus I to Tenor I for an extended passage (b. 19–22), using octave leaps, semiminims, and syncopation, the striking contrasts of high and low pitch also serving pictorial purposes ('cæli' / 'terra').

Another instance of extremely simple writing warranting the label 'pseudo-polyphony' is the first of the two Kyrie settings concluding *Libera me Domine* (b. 76–81). This is once again essentially a series of breve-length chords, with a few rhythmic displacements creating one suspension in Cantus I and two in the Altus. The part writing is otherwise notably plain: after its opening suspension, Cantus I sings only breves on c' for the remainder of the Kyrie, while Tenor II likewise has only two pitches, and uses nothing except breves. The first of the Altus suspensions belongs (as noted above) to a common formula for treating the chant figure F – G – A, as here. This is, of course, the same chant figure as at the start of the Introit, and both the Bassus and one of the Tenor lines are identical for the first four notes of this Kyrie and the equivalent passage in the Introit (Tenor II in the Introit matching Tenor I in the responsory). Once Victoria had generated the first four breves of his Kyrie setting by such simple and formulaic means, all that remained was to add two breves of cadential material.

If one were searching for symptoms of the brief period of time within which Victoria may have had to compose his music for María's exequies (and especially *Libera me Domine*, if it was sung at her burial), such a passage – and others using simple 'pseudo-polyphony' – might be cited (alongside his re-use of the 'Tremens' verse in *Libera me*). Of course, the fact that Victoria sets other sections of the Requiem with unusual elaboration suggests that we should be cautious in applying this interpretation: the pressure of time was not apparently so great as to encourage consistently simple writing. However, a very surprising technical solecism in the Benedictus may indeed be an indicator of haste: in b. 34–5 Cantus II and

---

[213] Morales relies heavily on this particular figure (usually – as here in Victoria's setting – constituting a decorative way of resolving a suspension) to provide animation and momentum in those movements of his five-voice Requiem which behave in the *proportio dupla* manner: it occurs, for example, no fewer than twenty times in the Introit, and sixteen in the Agnus Dei.

Tenor I proceed in consecutive (parallel) octaves. This error is all the more surprising because Cantus II here has the chant, and one might have expected Victoria to be particularly aware of how the chant-bearing part moved when conceiving counterpoint around it, especially given that this counterpoint is so simple and unadorned. The lapse is highlighted because Victoria harmonises the *a'* to *g'* movement in the chant here so as to produce a cadence onto G, by sharpening the *f'* in Cantus I: both Cantus II and Tenor I thus take the same role (that of the *clausula tenorizans*) in this directed progression, falling by step to the cadence note. One wonders why Victoria did not amend this passage when, as he states in the dedicatory epistle of the *Officium defunctorum*, he inspected the music for accuracy before publication.[214] Admittedly, the avoidance of consecutive fifths and octaves becomes more difficult the larger the number of parts in play, but the consecutive octaves here could easily have been avoided or expunged.[215] The fact that Victoria's other output of music for six or more voices reveals only one other set of forbidden consecutives[216] whereas the *Officium defunctorum* has two[217] increases the possibility that they resulted from hurried composition. The use of 'pseudo-polyphony' in the Benedictus may itself point in the same direction: as in the other passages described above, the music is based upon a simple chordal framework harmonising the chant, which again proceeds in breves, and the animation of the passage is achieved by the familiar means, such as the decorated suspension figure (Altus, b. 33) which had provided the 'motor' for the preceding section of the Sanctus.

Elsewhere in the *Officium defunctorum* Victoria kills two birds with one stone, introducing shorter-note movement both to animate his 'pseudo-polyphony' and to avoid forbidden consecutive intervals. Several examples involving the Tenor parts occur in the final section of the Kyrie: the minim movement in Tenor II at the ends of b. 29 and b. 30 removes what would otherwise be consecutive fifths with the Bassus, the similar motive in Tenor I at b. 35–6 avoids parallel octaves with the chant line in Cantus II, and the

[214] The relevant word in Victoria's epistle is 'recognoscerem'. I am grateful to Angus Bowie for his advice about its meaning.

[215] However, the 'amendment' of the Tenor I part in Wulstan's edition of the Benedictus (p. 21), by which the Tenor I note at the start of the fourth bar is moved down by a fifth, causes two sets of parallel fifths in succession between Tenor I and Bassus.

[216] In the Agnus Dei of the eight-voice *Missa Ave regina cælorum* there are parallel octaves between the Tenor of choir II and the Cantus of choir I at the change-over of choirs as choir I begins 'qui tollis peccata mundi'.

[217] There are parallel fifths between Cantus I and Altus in b. 38–9 of the Kyrie, as noted by two editors of the work, Walter and Wulstan.

new entry of Tenor II in b. 34–5 obviates consecutive octaves with the Bassus by means of its second note and with the Altus by means of its fifth note. Imitation of the opening (falling-fifth) chant motive of Kyrie IX, again in the two Tenor parts and again narrowly avoiding forbidden parallel movement with the Bassus, provides a further burst of animation to highlight the final section of this Kyrie (b. 39–40).

However, the animating counterpoint woven around the cantus firmus part moving in breves is sometimes considerably more motivically consistent and imitatively developed than this. For example, to set 'dona eis' in the first Agnus Dei, he developed material from the rising third figure G – A – B in the chant: Altus and Cantus I sing this motive as a *fuga* cell (b. 8–9), each voice accompanied by a countersubject which falls a fifth and rises a fourth. This pair of countersubject statements (in Tenor II and Bassus) is extended sequentially to harmonise the stepwise ascent from *g'* to *a'* in the chant-bearing Cantus II, and is then treated as an independent *fuga* cell, repeated a fourth higher in the same two voices from b. 11, and with Tenor I (from b. 12) joining in to interlock with the sequential extension to the cell.

As we have seen, the means by which Victoria animates (often simple) textures constructed on the basis of the chant line are employed to shape passages through acceleration of – and increased density of – activity, and this is particularly prominent in the opening paragraphs of sections of the work. Such techniques should be viewed within the larger topic of Victoria's meticulous manipulation of pace in the *Officium defunctorum*, whether or not a cantus firmus is present. Such control of pace was highlighted in the discussion of bipartite climactic structures in the *Libera me* and elsewhere, but the opening of the Introit provides another fine example. The first two breves-worth of music have no minim movement, the first minim occurring in the Altus in b. 3, gently marking the first cadence of the piece (and the end of the conventional module which begins the Introit) but without any propulsive dissonant suspension; in b. 5 the harmonic rhythm doubles, to one harmony per semibreve, and at that same point Tenor I has a new entry on the *arsis* rather than the *thesis* of the tactus (if one treats this passage as operating in *integer valor*): up to this point, the music has seemed to be in *proportio dupla*, but the events of this bar begin to muddy that perception; b. 6 sees the first suspension (indeed the first dissonance of any kind), while at the end of that bar Tenor I has a syncopated rhythm; in b. 7 the first semiminim movement occurs, the Altus echoes the first Tenor's syncopated rhythm from the previous bar, and both Cantus I and Tenor II syncopate their entries. The appearance of the consonant fourth figure in b. 9 marks the next stage in this gradual enlivening of the music. (This figure is commonly used in the *Officium defunctorum* to achieve momentum when the parts are otherwise moving largely in breves and semibreves, including where the cantus firmus proceeds in breves, and where the harmonic rhythm may accordingly be breve-based: the start of the Sanctus provides a good example.) Furthermore, the *f♯'* which begins that figure causes a melodic and harmonic surprise, diverting the music from the expected *f'* resolution of the cadential figure in the preceding bar; the suspension and resolution involved in the consonant fourth figure operate at the typical *integer valor* level, whereas the only two previous suspensions in the Introit were at the more leisurely *proportio dupla* level.

The music which Victoria published in 1605 unites coherence and eclecticism. With its recurrent and distinctive harmonic gestures (serving in part as Marian emblems), its linking of movements but employment of *chiaroscuro* effects within them, its dramatic manipulations of pace, its use of chant on the one hand and of a famous Marenzio madrigal on the other, and its occasional shattering of expectations (as at the climax of the motet), the *harmoniam* – as Victoria described it – composed for María's exequies represents a remarkable response to the demands, challenges, and opportunities of this form of cultural production. Its combination of unity and variety, and of convention and novelty, echoes that apparent in the ephemeral art and spoken and written texts which surrounded the work at its first performances, and more generally the ideals of Spanish preaching of the period. Those attending the exequies were presented with countless reproductions of a single symbol – María's coat of arms, placed on the catafalque, altar, pulpit, candles, and pillars – but they also experienced a profusion of images (and indeed of languages: Spanish, Latin, Greek, and Hebrew) in the sermons, orations, poetry, and hieroglyphs. Like an effective preacher, Victoria cast new light on familiar themes – using richly varied and sometimes dramatic means to do so – while reinforcing the listener's focus upon the principal overarching subject.

5 | 'The Crowning Work of a Great Genius'

The seeds from which the modern knowledge and status of Victoria's Requiem grew seem most likely to have been the copies of the *Officium defunctorum* which he sent to Rome, considered in Chapter 3. The current chapter traces various stages in that widening knowledge and evolving perception of the work from the early eighteenth century to the late twentieth, proceeding essentially in a chronological fashion, but with particular geographical foci at various points: it begins with Roman church musicians of the early to mid eighteenth century, and moves thence to the English writers of general music histories of the later eighteenth century, before turning to the nineteenth-century Cecilian movement in Germany and the editing (by Franz Xaver Haberl) and liturgical performance of the work in that context. I then focus on Paris at the end of that century, and the performing edition by Charles Bordes, before considering the awareness and use of the work in Catholic contexts in England and Ireland, partly thanks to Haberl's and Bordes's editions. Two manifestations of Spanish reappropriation of the work are then examined. The first of these is the edition by Felip Pedrell published in 1909 as part of his *opera omnia* of Victoria, a (flawed) edition which has left its mark to an extraordinary degree on modern performing editions and hence on performances and recordings. The second manifestation of Spanish reappropriation is the choice of Victoria's Requiem for the funeral of Manuel de Falla in 1947, exemplifying the incorporation of Victoria and of this piece within the sphere of Spanish (musical) nationalism.

Rome and Bologna

I turn first to two Roman church musicians active between the late seventeenth century and the mid eighteenth, Giuseppe Ottavio Pitoni (1657–1743) and his pupil (and biographer) Girolamo Chiti (1679–1759). Both exploited the holdings of Roman archives in pursuing their interests in the music of earlier periods: Pitoni compiled an extensive biographical dictionary of composers, the *Notitia de contrapuntisti e de compositori di musica*, and Chiti was a vigorous collector of musical sources, and was generous in sharing both information and music with the famous Bolognese writer, collector, and scholar Giovanni Battista ('Padre') Martini (1706–1784), with whom Chiti maintained a voluminous correspondence over an extended period.

Pitoni's awareness of the *Officium defunctorum* emerges in his entry on Victoria in the *Notitia de contrapuntisti*. The last of the three paragraphs of that entry begins thus: 'Nell'anno 1605, quando morì l'Imperatrice, per le sui essequie, trovandosi cappellano della Sacra Cesarea Maestà, compose l'offizio de' morti a 6 voci, che poi stampò in Madrid il medemo anno.' ('In the year 1605, when the Empress died, [Victoria], finding himself chaplain of her Holy Imperial Majesty, composed the *Officium defunctorum* for six voices, which was then printed in Madrid in the same year.')[1] It seems likely that, as was the case elsewhere in the *Notitia*, Pitoni derived this information directly from a copy of the *Officium defunctorum*. His error in believing that María died in 1605 reflects the fact that the death-date is not mentioned in Victoria's book. Pitoni was director of music for the Collegium Germanicum, a post which Victoria had himself held, as Pitoni highlights in the entry in the *Notitia*. As we saw in Chapter 3, Victoria sent a copy of the 1605 publication to the Germanicum, reflecting his connections with the College,[2] and it may have been this copy that Pitoni inspected, but Pitoni also became *maestro di cappella* at two institutions whose collections include copies of the *Officium defunctorum*: San Giovanni in Laterano and the Cappella Giulia. Before we move on from Pitoni's entry on Victoria, it is worth noting a biographical error there, one which seems to have proved influential (as we shall see): he states that for the final years of his life Victoria returned to Rome and became a musician within the Cappella Pontificia.

Martini may initially have learned of the existence of the *Officium defunctorum* through Pitoni, but whether or not this was the case he certainly then obtained information about the book from Chiti, who consulted the copy at the Lateran. Pitoni had provided Martini with biographical and bibliographical information regarding various musicians,[3] and a letter from Martini to

[1] For the full text of Pitoni's entry on Victoria, see Cesarino Ruini (ed.), *Giuseppe Ottavio Pitoni: Notitia de' contrapuntisti e compositori di musica* (Florence: Leo S. Olschki, 1988), 172.

[2] Pitoni lived at the College from 1686 until his death.

[3] For example, the entry on Carissimi in Martini's manuscript *Notizie storiche degli scrittori di Musica, e loro opere* incorporates a page of information provided by Pitoni, as is indicated by Martini's annotation at the top of the page concerned. See Elisabetta Pasquini, *Giambattisa Martini* (Palermo: Epos, 2007), 97–8 and Plate 13.

Chiti of 18 September 1745 indicates that Victoria was one of these: Martini there asks Chiti for details of printed works by specified composers including Victoria, Morales, Alonso Lobo, and Manuel Cardoso, and states that he already has some information on these and their works through Pitoni's kindness.[4] Martini sought from Chiti details of any editions which Martini did not yet have, and in a letter of 24 March 1746 Chiti provided bibliographical descriptions of a number of printed collections of the relevant composers' music which he had perused in the cupboard containing the Lateran music archive, among which is: 'Thome Ludovici de Vittoria Abulen[sis] Messa e Salmo Defunctorum – stampato in Madrid a 6 voci facto in obitu sacre Imperatricis, con l' Arme Imperiale d'Austria in mezzo ex Typographia Regia Anno *1605* a d. Margherita figlia di Maria, e Massimiliano Imperatore in foglio'.[5] Thus he erroneously described the contents as a Mass and a psalm of the dead: he had apparently not looked through the entire book, and perhaps guessed wrongly that 'officium' in the title indicated the inclusion of at least one psalm from the Office of the Dead. It seems clear, then, that the complete contents of the *Officium defunctorum* were not familiar to Chiti through performance at the Lateran (of which he had been *maestro di cappella* for twenty years) or elsewhere in Rome. In his response of 2 April, Martini indicated that he had no copy of the *Officium defunctorum*.[6]

London

The granting of special status to the Requiem within Victoria's output emerges in the renowned general histories of music by John Hawkins and Charles Burney in the 1770s and 1780s. The relevant section of Burney's

---

[4] 'dalla gentilezza del Sig. Pittoni fui favorito di varie notizie di Autori, e delle loro Opere'. The correspondence between Chiti and Martini is available online on the 'Carteggi' section of the database http://www.bibliotecamusica.it, hosted by the Museo internazionale e Biblioteca della Musica, Bologna. Transcriptions of many letters are in Federico Parisini, *Carteggio inedito del P. Giambattista Martini coi più celebri musicisti del suo tempo* (Bologna: Zanichelli, 1888); for the passage quoted here see I, 124. See also Anna Schnoebelen, *Padre Martini's Collection of Letters in the Civico Museo Bibliografico Musicale in Bologna: An Annotated Index* (New York: Pendragon, 1979), 137, where the letter concerned is no. 1213.

[5] The letter, no. 1236 in Schnoebelen, *Padre Martini's Collection*, may be viewed at www.bibliotecamusica.it. An (inaccurate and incomplete) transcription is in Parisini, *Carteggio*, I, 168–72, where the description of the *Officium defunctorum* is at 171.

[6] 'Tengo solamente tre libri in foglio stampati in Roma et uno in 4° in Milano di Tom. Ludovico de Victoria.' This letter is no. 1239 in Schnoebelen, *Padre Martini's Collection*, may be viewed at www.bibliotecamusica.it, and is transcribed in Parisini, *Carteggio*, 175–9, where the relevant passage is at 176.

account of Victoria – including his treatment of the Requiem – derives from Hawkins's, while Hawkins's information about the piece was clearly Italian in origin, although we cannot currently trace the route by which it reached him. In Hawkins's brief account of Victoria within his *A General History of the Science and Practice of Music* of 1776, he comments that 'one of the best' of the composer's published works 'is that called La Messa de' Morti'.[7] This wording – treating 'La Messa de' Morti' as if it were the title of the work, rather than a generic description of it – suggests that he may not have had direct experience of the piece, but was reliant on a previous writer's comment, and the language in which he gives this 'title' indicates that the information derived (at least ultimately) from Italy. Indeed, while it is entirely possible that Hawkins had seen Victoria's four-voice Requiem, since it was copied by Henry Needler (a fellow musical antiquarian, who like Hawkins was a member of the Academy of Ancient Music),[8] I know of no evidence that the six-voice Requiem reached England between its publication and Hawkins's time. Hawkins's comment that this 'Messa de' Morti' was 'one of the best' works of Victoria would certainly have encouraged other English musical antiquarians and collectors – men who formed close-knit networks in Hawkins's London – to seek copies if they did not already know the piece, and to make further copies if any were found; the fact therefore that no eighteenth- or early-nineteenth-century copy survives from these circles, or is mentioned in the sales catalogues of their collections, again makes one believe that Hawkins never held a copy in his hands.[9] Although we do not know whence or from whom Hawkins obtained this information about the piece (among the numerous sources on which he drew during the many years' preparation of his *History*), it may be significant that he reproduces the erroneous information that

---

[7] John Hawkins, *A General History of the Science and Practice of Music*, 5 vols (London: Payne & Son, 1776), III, 196. It seems likely that Hawkins was here referring to the six-voice Requiem rather than the four-voice setting, since he mentions the 1583 book of Masses (containing the four-voice Requiem) as a distinct entity earlier in the same sentence. A wide-ranging study of the reception and circulation of Victoria's works in England between the sixteenth century and the early twentieth century is Tess Knighton, 'Victoria and the English Choral Tradition', in Suárez-Pajares and Sol (eds), *Estudios*, 455–75. A survey of the representation of Spanish music in histories and reference works during the eighteenth and nineteenth centuries may be found in Judith Etzion, 'Spanish Music as Perceived in Western Music Historiography: A Case of the Black Legend?', *International Review of the Aesthetics and Sociology of Music* 29 (1998), 93–120.

[8] Needler's copy of the entire contents of Victoria's Mass collection of 1583 is British Library, Add. Ms 5047.

[9] On these networks, see for example the present author's 'Adventures of Portuguese "Ancient Music" in Oxford, London, and Paris: Duarte Lobo's *Liber missarum* and Musical Antiquarianism, 1650–1850', *Music & Letters* 86 (2005), 42–73.

Victoria was a singer in the pontifical chapel, a mistake which (as noted) occurs in Pitoni's account of Victoria. Indeed, the only other information about the composer's professional posts which Hawkins mentions – that he was *maestro di cappella* at Sant' Apollinare – is highlighted in Pitoni's account, and one can easily believe that Hawkins's information derives indirectly from Pitoni's *Notitia*. The fact that Pitoni gives more detail about the *Officium defunctorum* than any other of Victoria's printed works, so that the 1605 publication stands out from his list of printed collections, may have caused the work to become spotlighted in an account or accounts derived from Pitoni which may have been the ancestors of Hawkins's description, and at some point in that process (and perhaps thanks to Hawkins himself), that spotlighting spawned a qualitative elevation of the piece to 'one of the best'. As noted, Pitoni provided Martini with information about Victoria, and it is possible that Martini was the means of the information reaching London's antiquarian musical circles. For example, among Martini's correspondents was Johann Christoph Pepusch, a key figure in such circles and a founder-member of the Academy of Ancient Music, from whom Hawkins acquired many of the books used in compiling his *History*.

Charles Burney, unlike Hawkins, had direct contact with Martini (whom he visited), but he relied upon Hawkins for substantial parts of his own account of Victoria.[10] The most telling sign of this reliance is his repetition of an egregious error made by Hawkins: Hawkins referred, for the final part of his entry on Victoria, to Henry Peacham's *The Compleat Gentleman*,[11] but misread the relevant passage. Having mentioned Victoria very briefly as his second favourite composer of sacred music (after Byrd), Peacham proceeds within the same paragraph to consider Lassus (whom he ranks third), noting that he worked at the Bavarian court and citing specifically his settings of the seven Penitential Psalms and of *Susanne un jour*. Hawkins mistakenly transfers these comments about Lassus – including the employment at the Bavarian court, and the authorship of the works just mentioned – to Victoria. This error was repeated by Burney and in subsequent musical reference works.[12] It seems very likely that Burney likewise

[10] *A General History of Music: From the Earliest Ages to the Present Period*, 4 vols (London: for the author, 1776–89), III, 298.

[11] London: Francis Constable, 1634; Hawkins's reference is to the edition of 1661.

[12] See Ernst Ludwig Gerber, *Neues historisch-biographisches Lexikon der Tonkünstler*, 4 vols (Leipzig: Kühnel, 1812–14), IV, col. 444. The resulting misattribution of the penitential psalms also occurs in John Sainsbury's *A Dictionary of Musicians, from the Earliest Ages to the Present Time*, 2 vols (London: Sainsbury and Co., 1824), II, 513, and Thomas Busby's *A General History*

had Hawkins's account in mind when he remarked that Victoria's 'burial service, or *Messa de' Morte*, was much celebrated'.[13] In 1814 Ernst Ludwig Gerber – drawing in turn upon Burney – echoed this, giving *Messe de' Morti* as its title and describing the piece as 'besonders berühmt', and thus matching Burney's expression 'much celebrated'.[14] Similarly, five years later Thomas Busby included the *Messa de' Morte* in his brief list (drawing upon those of Hawkins and Burney) of those works by Victoria which were 'much applauded in their time'.[15]

The Cecilian Movement

Moving beyond this early thread of comments in music histories and reference works, the development of the modern reception of Victoria's *Officium defunctorum* needs to be understood within the context of the overlapping nineteenth-century movements for the reform of church music and the revival of Renaissance sacred polyphony, and first and foremost the Cecilian movement in Germany. Within such contexts Victoria's Requiem was re-introduced in liturgical performances, while published editions of the work originating in these contexts allowed it to become known and performed more widely. It is easy to see how Victoria's setting could have been regarded as epitomising the qualities – dignity, sublimity, grandeur, serenity, purity, restraint, and relationship to chant – which were so highly prized within such circles. In 1835 Carl Proske, who became the father-figure of the Regensburg Cecilian movement,[16]

---

of Music, from the Earliest Times to the Present, 2 vols (London: Whittaker and Simpkin and Marshall, 1819), II, 136.

[13] John Sainsbury reproduced Burney's remark on the Requiem verbatim in *A Dictionary of Musicians*, II, 513. In his article on Victoria ('Vittoria') in Abraham Rees's *The Cyclopædia; or, Universal Dictionary of Arts, Sciences, and Literature*, 45 vols (London: Longman, Hurst, Rees, Orme, and Brown, 1802–20), XXXVII, Burney does not mention the *Messa de' Morte*, but restricts his comments to another printed collection of Victoria's works to which he had referred in *A General History*, namely the *Motecta festorum totius anni* (Rome: Basa, 1585, V1433), and which – as he notes – he had actually seen, in the copy in the library of Christ Church, Oxford: he mentions this copy in *A General History*, III, 298.

[14] Gerber, *Neues historisch-biographisches Lexikon*, IV, col. 444. The entry on 'Vittoria' in Gerber's earlier *Historisch-biographisches Lexikon der Tonkünstler*, 2 vols (Leipzig: Breitkopf, 1790–1792), II, col. 734, makes no mention of the six-voice Requiem.

[15] Busby, *A General History*, II, 136.

[16] An insightful introduction to – and contextualisation of – this movement is provided in James Garratt, 'Performing Renaissance Church Music in Nineteenth-Century Germany: Issues and Challenges in the Study of Performative Reception', *Music and Letters* 83 (2002), 187–236. On Proske's attitudes and approach, see Annie Cœurdevey, 'Édition et interprétation:

transcribed Victoria's *Officium defunctorum* into score, using a copy in the archive of S. Giacomo degli Spagnoli in Rome, during a stay of nearly two years in Rome during which he wrote out and acquired great quantities of sacred music.[17] Proske did not include the work in the original series of volumes of the liturgically oriented series *Musica divina* (dedicated to four-voice music, including two Requiems) issued between 1853 and 1863, nor in the *Selectus novus missarum* series issued between 1855 and 1861 (which contained Orazio Vecchi's eight-voice Requiem), but after his death in 1861 his manuscript copy was used as the basis for an edition of *Tædet animam meam* by Joseph Schrems and an edition of the Mass by Franz Xaver Haberl, included in separate volumes of the second series of *Musica divina*, published in 1869 and 1874 respectively.[18] These editions seem to have constituted the first publication of the music of the *Officium defunctorum* since the original volume of 1605, and they reflected liturgical performance of the works in Regensburg at the General Assemblies of the Allgemeinen Cäcilien-Vereins. Schrems notes, in the volume which includes *Tædet animam meam*, that the motets in that volume were sung at the relevant performances in August 1869 (the year of publication), and

les choix scientifiques et esthétiques du chanoine Proske', in Philippe Vendrix (ed.), *La Renaissance et sa musique au XIXe siècle*, Épitome musical (Paris: Klincksieck, 2000), 133–54. On Proske's editorial work and his contribution to the movement for the reform of church music, see also Bernhard Janz, 'Das editorische Werk Carl Proskes und die Anfänge der Kirchenmusikalischen Reformbewegung', in Winfried Kirsch (ed.), *Palestrina und die Idee der klassischen Vokalpolyphonie im 19. Jahrhundert: Zur Geschichte eines Kirchenmusikalischen Stilideals* (Regensburg: Gustav Bosse, 1989), 149–69.

[17] Proske's manuscript score of the *Officium defunctorum*, dated 22 April 1835, is Regensburg, Bischöfliche Zentralbibliothek, Sammlung Proske, Ms M Victoria II. See Gertraut Haberkamp and Jochen Reutter (eds), *Bischöfliche Zentralbibliothek Regensburg: Thematischer Katalog der Musikhandschriften III: Sammlung Proske Mappenbibliothek* (Munich: G. Henle, 1990), 397. Proske revealed his use of this particular printed copy in the biographical note on Victoria included in the prefatory matter of *Musica divina: sive thesaurus concentuum selectissimorum omni cultui divino totius anni juxta ritum sanctæ ecclesiæ catholicæ inservientium*, Annus Primus, I (Regensburg: Pustet, 1853), liii. Franz Xaver Haberl subsequently noted, regarding Proske's transcription of the work in Rome, that the archive of S. Giacomo degli Spagnoli had been transferred to Santa Maria di Monserrato: 'Tomas Luis de Victoria: eine bio-bibliographische Studie', *Kirchenmusikalisches Jahrbuch* 11 (1896), 72–84, at 81, n. 1.

[18] *Tædet animam meam* was issued together with motets by other composers in the first fascicle of vol. II of the series, edited by Schrems: *Tædet* is item 6, at pp. 29–32. Victoria's Mass is item 5 in vol. I of the series, edited by Haberl; each Mass in this 'volume' was issued as a separate fascicle with its own title page. *Versa est in luctum* was omitted from this edition. Regarding the second series of *Musica divina*, see Raymond Dittrich, 'Dokumentation zum zweiten Jahrgang und zur zweiten Auflage des Messenbandes aus dem ersten Jahrgang der *Musica Divina*', *Musik in Bayern* 56 (1998), 55–78, and Johannes Hoyer, *Der Priestermusiker und Kirchenmusikreformer Franz Xaver Haberl (1840–1910) und sein Weg zur Musikwissenschaft* (Regensburg: Verlag des Vereins für Regensburger Bistumsgeschichte, 2005), 283.

specifically that *Tædet animam meam* was used at a Requiem Mass at the Dominican Church of St Blasius on 4 August. Similarly, Victoria's Requiem Mass was performed in the General Assembly on 5 August 1874, the year of Haberl's edition. In the introduction to that edition, dated 21 June, Haberl notes that this was the first occasion on which a Requiem on this scale had been sung at the General Assembly, although there had already been three successful previous performances of the piece.[19] He highlights the contrast between Victoria's writing and those modern styles of Requiems in which grand instrumentation and tone-painting transgress 'ecclesiastical styles': Victoria's chant-based polyphony is, he argues, much better suited than were those modern styles to the solemnity of such a liturgical context and to the 'devout grief' ('andächtigen Trauer') proper to the celebration of a Requiem Mass. Likewise Friedrich Könen, writing about the appearance of Haberl's edition and the singing of the work by the choir of Regensburg Cathedral – of which Haberl was the director, as Schrems had been – highlighted the work's qualities of 'gravity' and 'dignity' ('Ernst' and 'Erhabenheit').[20] Such attributes were, as noted, central to the ideals of the Cecilian movement, as was the 'noble simplicity' ('edle Einfachheit') for which Schrems praised *Tædet animam meam*.[21] Schrems's and Haberl's editions reflect in other ways their concerns with liturgical performance. For example, Schrems altered the text of *Tædet animam meam*, inserting the word 'me' after 'calumnieris', in accordance with the then current Breviary,[22] while Haberl replaced the chant intonations of the 1605 edition with the official Regensburg versions, as edited by himself and published by Pustet.[23] He also transposed the Mass and *Libera me*,[24] and added breathing and accentuation markings. The former indicate a highly articulated manner of performance at odds with the typical modern

[19] Vorwort, p. [i].
[20] Könen's comment is quoted by Haberl in 'Tomas Luis de Victoria', 81, n. 2.
[21] This comment is on p. 36 of the relevant volume of *Musica divina*.
[22] Schrems also took the opportunity here to correct Victoria's faulty accentuation of the word 'calumnieris' by altering the musical rhythm. He replaced the minim with which Victoria sets the first word of 'si calumnieris' with two semiminims, and moved the syllables forward accordingly, such that the accent falls (correctly) on the penultimate syllable of 'calumnieris' rather than (as in Victoria's version) on the antepenultimate syllable.
[23] Hoyer, *Der Priestermusiker*, 307.
[24] All movements are transposed upwards by a minor third, except the Gradual, which is transposed downwards by a tone. William Smith Rockstro described Haberl's decision as 'the altogether needless transposition with which the work is disfigured, from beginning to end'; his comment appears in the 'Requiem' article of the first edition of George Grove's *A Dictionary of Music and Musicians*, 4 vols (London: Macmillan, 1879–1890), III, 109.

emphasis on sustained continuity of line; the latter are intended to highlight textual accentuation or syncopations.[25]

Proske had provided a biographical note about Victoria in the first volume (1853) of *Musica divina*, in which he said of the *Officium defunctorum*: 'Es ist diess die Krone aller Werke unsers Meisters und gehört zu dem Erhabensten, was jemals für die Kirche geschaffen wurde.' ('This is the crown of all the works of our master, and is one of the most sublime ever created for the church.')[26] His appraisal of the work as 'die Krone aller Werke unsers Meisters', representing an inflation of the work's status above that observed in the Hawkins/Burney/Gerber family of descriptions, has had an enduring presence in the subsequent literature: it was quoted by Haberl in both the introduction to his edition of 1874 and in his study of Victoria published in 1896,[27] and then by the hugely influential Catalan musicologist Felip Pedrell in his 1918 monograph on Victoria.[28] J. R. Milne – in the article on Victoria published in 1890 within the first edition of Grove's *Dictionary* – observed (without specific reference to Proske) that 'this work is universally described as the crown of all the works of the master'.[29] While the fourth volume of August Wilhelm Ambros's *Geschichte der Musik*, published posthumously in 1878, does not use Proske's phrase, its reference to the *Officium defunctorum* as 'Victoria's Hauptwerk' ('masterpiece') and as 'diese erhabene Trauermusik' ('this sublime funeral music', c.f. Proske's 'Erhabensten') may well reflect Proske's influence.[30] Proske's phrase was subsequently paraphrased as 'la corona de las obras del gran maestro' by Ferreol Hernández Hernández in his *Tomás Luis de Victoria 'el Abulense'*, written for the celebrations of the 400th anniversary of Victoria's birth in 1940 [sic],[31] and also by Robert Stevenson in 1961 (who translated it somewhat loosely as 'the crowning work of a great genius')[32] and by David Wulstan in the preface to his edition of 1978; it was further echoed in Paul H. Lang's description of the piece (in 1941) as 'the crowning glory of his

---

[25] Haberl's edition contains few significant errors, two of which involve pitch.

[26] *Musica divina*, Annus Primus, I, liii.   [27] 'Tomas Luis de Victoria', 81, n. 1.

[28] *Tomás Luis de Victoria Abulense*, 140: 'Recuerda que Proske llamó a esta *Requiem* "la corona de las obras del gran maestro".'

[29] J. R. Milne, 'Vittoria, Tommaso Ludovico da', in Grove (ed.), *A Dictionary of Music and Musicians*, IV, 316.

[30] August Wilhelm Ambros, *Geschichte der Musik*, IV, ed. Gustav Nottebohm (Leipzig: F. E. C. Leuchart, 1878), 72. Ambros's comments on the work were also cited by J. R. Milne in his article for Grove's *Dictionary*.

[31] Published posthumously: Ávila: Diputacion Provincial de Ávila, 1960. The relevant passage is at 170.

[32] Stevenson, *Spanish Cathedral Music*, 413.

art',[33] while Samuel Rubio subjected Proske's assessment to critical scrutiny in an essay on the *Officium defunctorum* originally written to accompany a recording of 1981.[34] Allan Atlas in 1998 likewise declared the *Officium defunctorum* to be Victoria's greatest work, and said of *Versa est in luctum* that 'it is as heartbreaking a piece of music as the sixteenth or any other century has ever produced'.[35]

Charles Bordes

Some two decades after the appearance of Haberl's *Musica divina* edition, Charles Bordes included Victoria's six-voice Requiem in the first collection (1893) of his *Anthologie des maîtres religieux primitifs des quinzième, seizième et dix-septième siècles*.[36] Bordes was a key French proponent of Renaissance music both within the liturgy and in concert, as director of the Chanteurs de Saint-Gervais in Paris and co-founder of the Schola Cantorum,[37] and he added the six-voice Requiem to the repertory of the Chanteurs in 1892 (the series title of the *Anthologie* is 'Répertoire des Chanteurs de Saint-Gervais'), performing it in Saint-Gervais for Mass on All Souls' Day that year and the next.[38] The work, with its heavy reliance on chant, would have had particular appeal for Bordes given his belief that the rhythmic and melodic qualities of plainchant were also those which the

---

[33] *Music in Western Civilization* (New York: Norton, 1941), 267.

[34] 'El *Officium defunctorum* de Tomás Luis de Victoria', 22–3. Rubio suggests that Proske was referring not to the intrinsic worth of the piece but simply to the fact that it was the last to be published by the composer.

[35] *Renaissance Music: Music in Western Europe, 1400–1600* (New York & London: Norton, 1998), 615.

[36] Paris: Au siège de l'Association des Chanteurs de Saint-Gervais, 1893. The edition of Victoria's Mass is at pp. 119–51 in the 'Livre des Messes' volume of the *première année* of the series, dedicated to Pope Leo XIII. The Mass was also available separately, as were the Offertory and the *Libera me*.

[37] On Bordes's role in the cultivation of Renaissance sacred music in France, see Catrena Flint, 'The Schola Cantorum, Early Music and French Political Culture, from 1894 to 1914', unpublished PhD thesis, McGill University (2006), and Katharine Ellis, *Interpreting the Musical Past: Early Music in Nineteenth-Century France* (Oxford University Press, 2005), 105–11.

[38] See Flint, 'The Schola Cantorum', I, 123, II, 7, II, 12. The relevant notice in *Le Ménestrel* of 30 October 1892 specifies that the work concerned was the six-voice Requiem; although the equivalent notice in *Le Ménestrel* of 29 October 1893 does not state the number of voices, Flint is surely correct to presume that this was the same work, even though Bordes went on to publish Victoria's four-voice Requiem in the 'Livre des Messes' of the *Troisième année* (1895) of the *Anthologie*. I am grateful to Katharine Ellis for furnishing me with information about the 1892 performance.

finest sacred polyphony exemplified,[39] and he highlights the chant line in his edition by labelling the relevant voice-part at the beginning of each movement and by using a bold typeface for the underlay in that voice.

Bordes clearly used Haberl's edition as the basis of his own (although without acknowledgement), as is revealed by his reproduction of the three errors of pitch in Haberl's version.[40] He retained Haberl's transpositions, and omitted both *Tædet animam meam* (which, as noted, had been published in a separate volume of *Musica divina*) and *Versa est in luctum* (which is not in Haberl's edition). Bordes sought to produce 'popular' editions for the use of both choir schools and amateurs, and accordingly (and in contrast to Haberl) used modern clefs, halved the note values, and included a keyboard reduction.[41] But what separates Bordes's edition from Haberl's most strikingly is the former's provision of a great abundance of 'nuances et indications d'exécution' (as the title-page puts it), including indications of changes of speed within sections, which presumably reflect his interpretation of the piece in the liturgical performances under his direction at Saint-Gervais. Some of the texts within the Requiem – and Victoria's treatment of them – caused him to apply an even greater density and range of such markings than was his wont (although he usually left the chant-bearing voice relatively free of such nuance), endowing each voice-part with an almost continuous stream – and great variety – of articulation signs, including tenuto, marcato, and accent marks, and *sostenuto* and *legato* instructions. The later parts of the Offertory, where the text is particularly vivid and dramatic, provide the most striking example: 'tartarus' is marked *Più vivo*, and the sudden *piano* at 'in obscurum' is immediately followed by *fff* and *Allegro* for 'sed signifer Sanctus Michael', before the momentum is gradually arrested during the setting of 'repræsentet eas' through markings of *Meno vivo*, *Rall.* and *Più rall.*, leading to *Lento*, *pp*, and *Mezza voce* for the opening of the repetendum at 'quam olim'; the repetendum section then attracts markings of *Expressivo*, *Dolce*, and *Più dolce*, and ends *ppp*. It is worth noting that Bordes's edition of Lassus's five-voice Requiem, published in a later volume of the *Anthologie*, is more sparing in its addition of 'indications

---

[39] On Bordes's views in this regard, see Flint, 'The Schola Cantorum', I, 276–85.

[40] Bordes introduces one further significant (rhythmic) error, in the Tenor II part during the seventh bar of verse 3 of *Libera me Domine*.

[41] The title-page of the edition of the Requiem includes: 'édition populaire à l'usage des maitrises et des amateurs en notation moderne avec clefs usuelles, nuances et indications d'exécution et réduction des voix au clavier'. For discussion of Bordes's editorial and performative approach, see Katharine Ellis, 'Palestrina et la musique dite "palestrinienne" en France au XIXᵉ siècle: questions d'exécution et de réception', in Vendrix (ed.), *La Renaissance et sa musique*, 155–90.

d'exécution' in the equivalent part of the Offertory, and the dynamic range is more limited (from *ff* to *p*).

England and Ireland

Haberl's and Bordes's editions were certainly available to some of those working in Catholic institutions in England and Ireland and who were significant figures within the movement to restore Renaissance polyphonic repertoire to liturgical use.[42] Among the subscribers to Bordes's *Anthologie* was Edwin Bonney, choirmaster between 1899 and 1917 of the Catholic Ushaw College, near Durham,[43] and it was apparently Bordes's edition which was used for one or more performances of Victoria's Requiem between 1898 and 1901 by the Palestrina Choir in Dublin directed by Vincent O'Brien, a prominent force in the Cecilian movement in Ireland.[44] Haberl's edition of the Requiem was included in the *List of Church Music Approved for use in the diocese* published by the diocese of Salford in 1904,[45] and liturgical use of the work in England also received encouragement from Richard Terry (a member of the team that drew up the Salford *List*), famous for his creation of the choral tradition at the new Westminster Cathedral, of which he was Master of Music from 1901.[46] Terry's sympathies regarding sacred music are well summed up in the following: 'I think we may say that modern individualistic music, with its realism and emotionalism, may stir human feeling, but it can never create that atmosphere of serene spiritual ecstasy that the old music generates.

---

[42] On this movement, see Chapter 6 of Thomas Muir, *Roman Catholic Church Music in England, 1791–1914: A Handmaid of the Liturgy?* (Aldershot: Ashgate, 2009).

[43] See Knighton, 'Victoria and the English Choral Tradition', 465.

[44] The fact that the Palestrina Choir included the Victoria Requiem in its repertoire, and that it made use principally of Bordes's editions when first building up its library, is reported in Edward Martyn's article about the foundation and early activities of the choir, 'La Società Palestriniana di Dublino', *Cosmos catholicus* 4/2 (January, 1902), 54–5. Martyn does not state unequivocally that the work performed was the six-voice Requiem, rather than the four-voice work, but his description of it as 'la grande "Messa dei Morti", di Vittoria' implies that it was the former. A number of copies of Bordes's edition survive in the library of the Palestrina Choir; I am grateful to the librarian of the Choir, Jimmy Reynolds, for supplying this information.

[45] Salford: Diocese of Salford, 1904. On the compilation of this and other diocesan lists of approved music at this time, see Thomas Muir, '"Full in the Panting Heart of Rome": Roman Catholic Music in England: 1850–1962', unpublished PhD thesis, University of Durham (2004), 256–7.

[46] An introduction to this aspect of Terry's work is Timothy Day, 'Sir Richard Terry and 16th-Century Polyphony', *Early Music* 22 (1994), 296–307.

It is a case of mysticism *versus* hysteria.'[47] Terry had contributed, alongside Bordes, to the lecture-debates which formed part of an early-music festival organised by the Paris Schola Cantorum in Bruges in 1902, and at which the Chanteurs de Saint-Gervais were the principal performers.[48] Appendix A of Terry's *Catholic Church Music* of 1907 is 'A List of Music suggested for General Use in Choirs', and includes a selection of six Requiem Masses, the last of which is Victoria's six-voice setting.[49] Surprisingly, however, the piece does not feature in the extensive lists of repertoire (collections of scores, and lists of music performed) in English Catholic contexts compiled by Muir and covering the period up to 1962, lists within which Victoria's music is generally well represented.[50] Perhaps the demands of its six-voice scoring discouraged performance in many institutions: it is the only six-voice work in Terry's list. At Westminster Cathedral, where Victoria's Holy-Week responsories (introduced under Terry) maintained an enduring place in the repertoire for decades, Victoria's Requiem was not sung liturgically in the period surveyed in detail by Muir, 1949–1962; rather, the four-voice Requiem by Giovanni Felice Anerio (which was likewise on Terry's lists) was the setting regularly employed for All Souls' Day during these years.[51]

However, in 1950 the Victoria Requiem was among the works chosen for a series of four broadcasts of the composer's works on the BBC Third Programme (then in only its fourth year).[52] The performance was by Schola Polyphonica, directed by Henry Washington, who was Director of Music at the Brompton Oratory, and familiar to many as an editor of repertory published by J. & W. Chester in the series *Latin Church Music of*

---

[47] Terry, *Catholic Church Music* (London: Greening, 1907), 47.

[48] The event is described by Charles Maclean in 'Bruges and the "Schola Cantorum": A Note from Tour', *The Musical Times and Singing Class Circular* 43, no. 715 (1 September 1902), 595–8.

[49] *Catholic Church Music*, 203. Terry assigned to each work in the appendix a level of difficulty to assist choirmasters in choosing repertory, and the Victoria Requiem is labelled 'difficult', as is Lassus's five-voice setting. Terry here gives the publisher of the Victoria Requiem as Breitkopf; since Breitkopf & Härtel were the distributors both of Bordes's *Anthologie* editions and of Pustet's volumes from Regensburg, it is not clear from Terry's reference whether he had Haberl's or Bordes's edition in mind. Terry likewise included Victoria's Requiem in the list of 'Music Suggested for Choir Use', Appendix A of his *The Music of the Roman Rite* (London: Burns Oates & Washbourne, 1931), 238. Here he gives the publisher as Chester, and this firm certainly distributed the Bordes edition of the Requiem.

[50] See Muir, '"Full in the Panting Heart of Rome"'. The numerous institutions – including cathedrals, other churches, abbeys, colleges, schools, and a seminary – from which surviving materials were scrutinised are listed on pp. 411–24 of the thesis. The databases recording the relevant information are available at Durham E-Theses Online: http://etheses.dur.ac.uk/2918/.

[51] The Choir went on to record this work for a CD released by Hyperion in 1990.

[52] The broadcast of the Requiem was on 21 February 1950.

the Polyphonic Schools (although the Victoria Requiem never appeared in that series). Schola Polyphonica was a mixed choir founded as an extension of the Oratory's choir, created in 1947 at the suggestion of Basil Lam, the BBC producer responsible for many early-music broadcasts. In Washington's account of musical traditions at the Oratory published in 1984 he suggests that the work was a staple in the liturgical repertory there, although he does not specify when it was introduced (he became Director of Music in 1935, and left the post in 1971): 'Weddings and requiems ... came in abundance. These were graded musically and ceremonially according to taste and expense. Requiems were either plainsong; small choir (Casciolini); or full choir (Victoria).'[53] The Victoria Requiem was sung at the Memorial Mass for Washington at the Brompton Oratory in 1988.[54]

The influence of Bordes's interpretative view of the Requiem, as represented by the 'nuances et indications d'exécution' provided in his edition (available from J. & W. Chester until at least the 1930s), can still be heard, remarkably, in the first commercial recording of the piece by an English choir: that by the Choir of St John's College, Cambridge, directed by George Guest, issued in 1968.[55] Guest retained not only some of Bordes's idiosyncratic decisions concerning dynamics but also tempo indications such as the puzzling direction to sing *Più lento* not at the start of the repetendum of the Communion but at the third bar of this section. It was through this recording that a significant number of listeners in the UK, America, and Australia will have come to know the work, since (besides sales of the recording) it was played repeatedly by the BBC and other networks in the 1970s.

Felip Pedrell

However, most modern editions of the *Officium defunctorum* trace their ancestry not to Bordes's performing edition, nor to Haberl's, but to the publication of the collected edition of Victoria's works. Such a project took a very long time to come to fruition: as early as 1841 Proske wrote to two

---

[53] Henry Washington, 'The Oratory Musical Tradition', in Michael Napier and Alistair Laing (eds), *The London Oratory Centenary 1884–1984* (London: Trefoil, 1984), 152–71, at 160.

[54] A notice of this service appeared in *The Times* of 10 September. The service was on 16 September.

[55] *Victoria Requiem Mass sex vocibus*, Argo ZRG 570. In 1967 there appeared another recording of the work directed by Guest, performed by the Berkshire Boy Choir from the United States.

publishers (Schott, and Breitkopf & Härtel) regarding a plan to publish the composer's complete output,[56] and Haberl likewise intended to issue such an edition, a project about which he corresponded in 1895 with the Catalan musicologist Felip Pedrell.[57] But it was Pedrell – generally regarded as the most influential founding figure of modern Spanish musicology – rather than Haberl who undertook this task, the fruits of which were published by Breitkopf & Härtel in eight volumes between 1902 and 1913.[58] Both Victoria's four-voice Requiem and the music of the *Officium defunctorum* were included in volume 6, which appeared in 1909. Pedrell's expressed intent was to 'reestablish the true original text' of the work:[59] the edition presents itself as an authoritative diplomatic transcription, and in correspondence he stated that his transcription was made from the 1605 edition.[60] Despite this, it contains many significant errors of pitch or rhythm, as is indeed true of other parts of the *opera omnia*,[61] and some (but not all) of these errors reflect the fact that Pedrell did not in fact work from a copy of the 1605 book, but from a (surviving) transcription made from the Segorbe Cathedral copy by the *maestro de capilla* of the Cathedral, José Perpiñán Artíguez, which he sent to Pedrell.[62]

Quite a few of the mistakes in Pedrell's edition – including some very obvious errors of pitch – can be heard on early recordings of the piece,

---

[56] See Janz, 'Das editorische Werk', 152.   [57] Hoyer, *Der Priestermusiker*, 382, n. 10.

[58] *Thomae Ludovici Victoria Abulensis Opera omnia ex antiquissimis, iisdemque rarissimis, hactenus cognitis editionibus in unum collecta, atque adnotationibus, tum bibliographicis, tum interpretatoriis* (Leipzig: Breitkopf & Härtel, 1902–1913).

[59] 'restablecer el verdadero texto original'. The relevant passage from a letter of 1902 is quoted in Arroyas Serrano and Martínez Molés, 'La primera transcripción moderna', 483.

[60] Arroyas Serrano and Martínez Molés, 'La primera transcripción moderna', 482.

[61] A partial list of the errors in Pedrell's edition of the *Officium defunctorum* is given in the critical commentary to the edition of the Mass and *Libera me* from the *Officium defunctorum* by Walter. The errors include wrong pitches in the Introit (in one passage the Altus is shown a sixth too low), Kyrie, Gradual, Offertory, and Communion, and in *Tædet animam meam*, and erroneous rhythms in the Offertory, Sanctus, and *Libera me*.

[62] See Arroyas Serrano and Martínez Molés, 'La primera transcripción moderna'. In his *Tomás Luis de Victoria*, 137, Pedrell notes that Perpiñán also provided him with photocopies of the *Officium defunctorum*; it is not entirely clear from Pedrell's wording whether these photocopies were of only the liminary matter (as Arroyas Serrano and Martínez Molés argue, 483) or of the entire book. Pedrell also provided bibliographical details of the *Officium defunctorum* (*Tomás Luis de Victoria*, 135–6) which suggest either that Perpiñán furnished him with a precise description of the book or that Pedrell did consult the original at some point between the preparation of his edition and 1918. The underlay in Pedrell's edition is at odds with that in the 1605 edition in several instances, and some of his underlay decisions involve the breaking of ligatures in the original, for example in the (chant-bearing) Cantus II part in the Introit antiphon. Perpiñán's transcription does in fact indicate ligatures (by means of slurs), but perhaps Pedrell did not realise that Perpiñán had used slurs with this meaning. The altered underlay in Cantus II of the Introit antiphon is found also in the 1978 edition by Wulstan.

dating from the 1950s, by the Accademia Corale di Lecco and the
Netherlands Chamber Choir.[63] More significant, however, has been the
perpetuation of several of Pedrell's departures from the 1605 print in most
later editions of the *Officium defunctorum*.[64] These flawed readings have
thence been transmitted in numerous recorded performances by groups
using one of these performing editions. To be sure, a few of the divergences
between the 1909 edition and that of 1605 may represent editorial decisions
on Pedrell's part, rather than errors of transcription or mistakes in the
type-setting of his edition, and in one of these cases Pedrell's emendation
was almost certainly correct,[65] but in another case his judgement was
flawed, and caused a significant problem in terms of musical grammar.
At b. 48 of the Introit, the initial note of the Bassus entry on 'orationem' is
a semibreve in the 1605 edition, but Pedrell shortened this note to a minim
and moved the entry one minim later, presumably so that the rhythm of the

---

[63] Vox, 1954; Columbia, 1959.

[64] Including those by Wulstan (1978), Turner (1988), Dixon (1994), and Rubio (completed 1981;
published 2000). The correct readings are, by way of contrast, given in editions based on one of
the Roman copies of the *Officium defunctorum*: those by Walter (1962) and Michael Noone
(*Missa pro defunctis a4, 1583; Requiem responsories, 1592; Officium defunctorum a 6, 1605*,
Boethius Editions 10 (Aberystwyth: Boethius Press, 1990)). In the commentary to his edition (p.
[45]) Wulstan notes that he had compared Pedrell's edition with the original of 1605, but that
only 'a limited examination' of the latter was possible, while Dixon states in the Preface to his
edition (p. 3) that 'the present edition has been based on the 1605 edition'. Wulstan did indeed
correct most of Pedrell's errors, but retained the following four mistakes: in the Offertory, at
b. 22 in the Bassus, the last two notes should be a dotted crotchet and a quaver; in the same
movement, at b. 48, the Altus should have a semibreve rather than a minim and a minim rest; in
the Communion, the sharp to the *c'* in Tenor II in b. 2 is missing; and in *Tædet animam meam*
the Cantus is lacking its sharp in b. 22. The first three of these four errors are present also in
Turner's and Dixon's editions. In Rubio's edition these errors do not appear, but he does derive
from Pedrell one other error: in b. 5 of the 'Quando cæli' section of *Libera me Domine*, the
Bassus is given a breve rather than a semibreve followed by a semibreve rest. Aspects of Dixon's
edition reveal that his was based on Pedrell's, but that he also consulted a copy of the 1605
edition and made use of Turner's edition, since he reproduces from there an error in *Tædet
animam meam* (showing an accidental actually present in the source as an editorial accidental,
in the Cantus at b. 6) which is not in Pedrell's. It is regrettable, in light of this situation, that
publication of the new complete edition of Victoria's works – *Tomás Luis de Victoria: Opera
omnia, nueva edición* – by Higini Anglès was cut short by Anglès's death in 1969 before the
appearance of the *Officium defunctorum* in that series. This edition was explicitly advertised as
a revised replacement for Pedrell's.

[65] In the Gradual (b. 5–6), the second occurrence of the imitative figure for 'dona eis' in Tenor
I falls on a page-break in the 1605 edition, and the third note of this figure, which should surely
be a dotted minim as in other occurrences, is divided into a minim on the first page and
a semiminim on the second. Pedrell gave this note as a dotted minim (as had Haberl also), and
all subsequent editors have followed suit, albeit generally without noting that they are
correcting an apparent error in the original edition. By what seems to be an extraordinary
coincidence, there is a page-break at the relevant point in Bordes's edition, and a misprint
whereby the continuation of the Tenor part's tie is not shown on the new page.

entry matched those of Tenor I in b. 47 and Cantus I in b. 49. However, this 'emendation' cannot be correct, since it produces a basic technical solecism: where the Bassus has its new minim rest (on the third minim beat of b. 47) there results a fourth between the lowest sounding note (the *a* in Tenor II) and the *d'* in Tenor I (this *d'* not being treated as a suspended dissonance). This unfortunate decision by Pedrell has likewise been reproduced in most later editions,[66] and the resulting faulty musical effect is thus to be heard in almost all recordings of the work: nineteen out of twenty-two recordings sampled (and dating from the 1960s onwards) adopt this reading. Besides this solecism, and the mistakes in transcription or printing, Pedrell's edition perpetuated an error in the Segorbe Cathedral copy of the 1605 edition: as mentioned in Chapter 3, that copy is in poor condition, and contains repairs to several pages involving manuscript replacements for missing notes and *custodes*, but one of the replacement notes is at the wrong pitch.[67] This error has again been reproduced in several later modern editions (including those by Dixon, Rubio, Turner, and Wulstan) and hence is to be heard in many recordings.[68]

A bizarre consequence of Pedrell's use of Perpiñán's transcription rather than the 1605 edition itself is that Pedrell presented *Tædet animam meam* in note-values twice as long as those used by Victoria for this item. This error occurred because Perpiñán's transcription employed halved note-values for all other items of the *Officium defunctorum* but (unbeknown to Pedrell) kept the original note-values for *Tædet animam meam*, reflecting the fact that *Tædet animam meam* – alone of the items in the *Officium defunctorum* – has an *integer valor* signature and employs a style involving declamation mainly in minims and semiminims. Pedrell, as was his policy throughout the *Opera omnia*, wished to restore the original note-values, and accordingly but incorrectly doubled the note-values for *Tædet animam meam* that he saw in Perpiñán's transcription.[69]

---

[66] The user of these editions is given no reason to suspect that the reading presented is an editorial intervention, since the reading is not marked as a departure from that in the 1605 source.

[67] Offertory, Tenor II, b. 57: the first note in the bar should be *b* (as in my edition in the Online Appendix) not *c'* (as in the Segorbe copy, and hence Pedrell's edition and several other modern editions). The error is understandable in that the *c'* makes this imitative entry resemble those in other voices.

[68] Of twenty-one recordings sampled, seventeen have this erroneous reading, and four the correct reading.

[69] Pedrell's approach has again had much later echoes. Wulstan's and Rubio's editions use halved note-values throughout except in *Tædet animam meam*, obscuring the metrical and stylistic distinction between this item and the others. In Wulstan's edition there is no prefatory staff here to tell the user about what is effectively a change in editorial approach, nor is it mentioned in the editorial note. Pedrell's distortion of the mensural/rhythmic nature of *Tædet animam*

'The Only Canopy Worthy to Shelter the Tomb of the Greatest Spanish Musician of our Times'

Pedrell's *opera omnia* edition provided ready means for the Spanish composer Manuel de Falla, who was a pupil of Pedrell, to acquaint himself with Victoria's works, and Falla made so-called 'expressive versions' (with added dynamic and other markings) of a number of those works. The writings of Falla's friend and pupil Henri Collet (who was likewise a pupil of Pedrell) further influenced his attitudes to Victoria. Collet developed and popularised the idea of Spanish musical 'mysticism' in his *Le mysticisme musical espagnol au XVIe siècle* (Collet's doctoral thesis from the University of Paris), which appeared in the year (1913) in which the publication of Pedrell's *opera omnia* was completed, while his *Victoria* came out the following year. As it happens, these were Falla's final two years in Paris. Carol Hess observes:

Falla ... took comfort in the concentrated intensity of Golden Age polyphony ... he immersed himself in the music of Cristóbal de Morales and Tomás Luis de Victoria, especially the latter, who represented the spirit of the Counter-Reformation to many Spanish Catholics. ... From Falla's annotations in his signed copy it is clear that Collet's descriptions of Victoria's 'austere Catholicism' and 'ardent mysticism' deeply impressed him.[70]

Upon Falla's death it was Victoria's six-voice Requiem that was selected for use at the funeral in Cádiz Cathedral on 9 January 1947.[71] The music was performed by the Capella Clàssica of Mallorca, directed by Falla's friend Juan María Thomas, who gave the following emotive account:

We entered the quire [where] our souls were able to unleash, with love, trembling, and reverence, all their emotion that had been restrained until then, casting it into the ardent and harmonious storm of divinely composed polyphonies that form the Requiem of the great man from Ávila, the only canopy – as Joaquin Rodrigo

---

meam misled other modern editors: of the editions available online via the *Choral Public Domain Library* at the time of writing, one (by Sabine Cassola) preserves Pedrell's note-values, and another (by Rafael Ornes) restores the original values but presents these as having been halved. In terms of recordings, Pedrell's mistake led Felix de Nobel to adopt a strikingly slow pace for *Tædet animam meam* in his 1959 recording with the Netherlands Chamber Choir, whereas the other sections of the *Officium defunctorum* are performed briskly.

[70] Carol A. Hess, *Sacred Passions: The Life and Music of Manuel de Falla* (Oxford University Press, 2005), 201.

[71] I am most grateful to the following for providing information regarding this event and the use of the six-voice Requiem: Nancy Lee Harper, Dácil González Mesa of the Archivo Manuel de Falla, and Elena García de Paredes (Falla's great niece).

correctly wrote – worthy to shelter the tomb of the greatest Spanish musician of our time.[72]

Others writing about the occasion took the opportunity to draw parallels between the two composers, Antonio Fernández-Cid remarking that they were 'so far separated in time, but so similar in aesthetic ideals',[73] while Luis Calvo explicitly emphasised the aspect of Spanish mysticism, portraying Victoria as the 'ancestor of Falla in religious piety and artistic meditation, compatriot and contemporary of Saint Teresa and one of the figures whom Falla venerated most highly in Spanish art'.[74] Eva Moreda-Rodríguez has situated such comments within a tendency – in the contemporary Francoist musical press – to emphasise Falla's alleged mysticism and religiosity, chiming with the nationalist ideals of Franco's regime. She argues that Falla's funeral, attended by the Minister of Justice representing the government in Franco's place, 'was also seized by the regime … to exploit the composer's mystic associations, in the context of the theatricality which characterised the large-scale displays of patriotism and religiousness typical of the Franco regime'.[75]

Victoria's Requiem was thus reinvested, for this moment in 1947, with something akin to the dual dynastic and personal-commemorative functions which it had served in 1605. In the epilogue to this book, I turn back to the wider reception of the work which has been traced above, but focusing on more recent decades, and particularly the 1980s onwards, which have witnessed the explosion in its popularity as a work consumed in secular contexts in the concert hall and through recordings.

---

[72] 'Entramos en el coro y en aquella magnífica sillería que había sido de la Abadía sevillana de Santa María de las Cuevas, nuestras almas pudieron desatar, con amor, temblor y reverencia, toda su emoción hasta entonces refrenada, lanzándola en la ardiente y armoniosa tempestad de polifonías divinamente concertadas que forman el Requiem del gran abulense, único dosel – como acertadamente escribió Joaquín Rodrigo – digno de cobijar el túmulo del mayor de los músicos españoles de nuestro tiempo.' Juan María Thomas, Manuel de Falla en la Isla (Palma de Mallorca: Ediciones Capella Classica, 1947), 316–17.

[73] 'Qué lejos en el tiempo! Qué próximos en el ideal estético!' Antonio Fernández-Cid, 'Los restos de Falla recibieron sepultura en la catedral de Cádiz', Arriba, 9 January 1947, 1, quoted in Eva Moreda-Rodríguez, 'A Catholic, a Patriot, a Good Modernist: Manuel de Falla and the Francoist Musical Press', Hispanic Research Journal 14 (2013), 212–26, at 219.

[74] 'Predecesor de Falla en piedad religiosa y recogimiento artístico, coterráneo y contemporáneo de Santa Teresa y una de las figuras más veneradas por Falla en el arte español.' Luis Calvo, 'Ayer recibieron sepultura en Cádiz, en medio de una imponente manifestación de duelo popular, los restos del insigne músico d. Manuel de Falla', ABC, 10 January 1947, 7–9, at 7, quoted in Moreda-Rodríguez, 'A Catholic', 219.

[75] Ibid.

Epilogue: Requiem for Our Age?

Since the start of the new millennium, recordings of the Victoria Requiem have appeared at the rate of approximately one a year, reflecting the extraordinary status which the work has attained. There is of course nothing unusual about the fact that most of those who hear the piece now do so in non-religious contexts – through the media of recordings and concert performances – rather than within the liturgy. But the meaning and impact of this work in such contexts seems nevertheless to draw particularly heavily on evocations of its profoundly and solemnly sacred nature, an emphasis which matches the ubiquitous preoccupation in modern writings on Victoria with his being a priest and his (and Spanish) mysticism, but intensified because the object concerned is a Requiem. In descriptions of the work associated with such recorded and concert performances – and sometimes in the manner in which the work is presented in such contexts – one witnesses strenuous efforts to evoke, recreate, or preserve the 'aura' pertaining to it even as the work moves (as it is transmitted through such media) beyond the ritual contexts from which that 'aura' in part derived.[1]

A striking case is that of the highly influential paired recording by Westminster Cathedral Choir and performing edition by Bruno Turner, which appeared in 1987 and 1988 respectively. Turner's edition rapidly became and remains much the most frequently used for recordings and performance of the work, and has played a major role in widening knowledge of the work. It was employed (before publication) for the Westminster Cathedral LP, and that recording project was put together under Turner's guidance, which included the decision to include chanted

---

[1] Deployment of the term 'aura' when considering an historical work of art naturally evokes Walter Benjamin's famous but elusive uses of the concept. An oft-quoted passage from his best known essay (originally of 1935) may be of relevance here: 'The earliest artworks originated in the service of rituals – first magical then religious. And it is highly significant that the artwork's auratic mode of existence is never entirely severed from its ritual function. In other words: the unique value of the "authentic" work of art always has its basis in ritual.' Benjamin, 'The Work of Art in the Age of its Technological Reproducibility', in Michael W. Jennings, Brigid Doherty, and Thomas Y. Levin (eds), *The Work of Art in the Age of Its Technological Reproducibility, and Other Writings on Media* (Cambridge, MA: Belknap Press of Harvard University Press, 2008), 24.

items from Matins and Lauds of the Dead 'in order to place this music in context, and to give some impression of what should lead up to the Mass itself'.[2] Turner played a central role in the growth of interest in Spanish polyphony in the English-speaking world and well beyond it, through his talks on the Third Programme, his performances and recordings as director of Pro Cantione Antiqua from 1968, and his launching in the 1970s of the Mapa Mundi imprint of Renaissance performing scores, within which the *Officium defunctorum* edition appeared.[3] The sleeve design of the Westminster Cathedral LP (by Terry Shannon) and the design of Turner's edition strongly evoke the original book of 1605, suggesting to the listener and performer a proximity to Victoria's work and its material form: the record cover is dominated by the coat of arms which is the main element of Victoria's title page, and the back cover shows the first opening of the Introit from the original. But these reproductions and the title wording are set against an entirely black backdrop, used also for the cover of the Mapa Mundi edition, which renders them *more* instantly evocative of *pro defunctis* liturgical books (and vestments and drapery) than was the original 1605 book itself, and indeed sets this edition and work apart from those of other Iberian Requiems published by Mapa Mundi. The 'aura' of grave and solemn liturgy engendered by the Westminster Cathedral recording is intensified through the use of Latin titles – which are not used by Victoria in the 1605 volume. Thus the services represented on the recording (Matins, Lauds, the Mass, and the Absolution) are labelled 'Officium defunctorum ad Matutinum', 'In Laudibus', 'Absolutio', etc., and items within them are likewise exoticised with Latin labels, so that *Versa est in luctum* is headed 'motectum'. This all echoes the terminology of Latin liturgical books, and transports the listener into a world of largely lost ritual. It is striking, in this context, that Turner appended the following 'Editor's Personal Note' to the Introduction of his edition: 'This great masterpiece can only be presented with respect and humility. The purpose of this edition is to encourage performance in the same spirit, with dignity and simplicity.'

The use of the medium of recording to provide the listener to Victoria's Requiem with an aurally immersive simulacrum of liturgical performance

---

[2] Liner notes to *Victoria Requiem, Officium defunctorum 1605* (Hyperion, 1977).

[3] On Turner's role in these respects, see Tess Knighton, 'Introduction: A Heart of Pure Gold', and Luis Gago, 'Pure Passion: A Conversation with Bruno Turner', in Knighton and Nelson (eds), *Pure Gold*, xv–xxvii and 385–407 respectively. A concert performance of the work by Pro Musica Sacra under Turner's direction in October 1982 was broadcast by the BBC; the recording is in the British Sound Archive.

was taken further still in a recording by the Gabrieli Consort directed by Paul McCreesh, issued in 1995. Although (unlike in the Westminster Cathedral recording) the liturgy of Matins is not represented (*Tædet animam meam* being sung as an isolated item for that service), the chanted parts of the Mass – Collect, Epistle, Tract, Sequence, Gospel, etc. – are added at the relevant points between Victoria's polyphonic items. A vast resonant acoustic and 'distant' recording appear designed to heighten the sense that the listener is witnessing the piece unfold in its proper space: in fact, there would have been very little resonance in the Descalzas chapel at the first performances, given that the space (which is in any case not particularly large) was lined with drapery.

Turner's edition was also used by The Tallis Scholars, directed by Peter Phillips, for their recording which likewise appeared in 1987, and the burst of exposure which the work received at that time included broadcast performances by that group at the Utrecht Early Music Festival in 1987 and the Proms in 1988, as well as a performance at the Three Choirs Festival in 1987, and another in the Early Music Centre Festival at Westminster Cathedral in the same year. A measure of the work's popularity as a concert item is the fact that The Tallis Scholars performed it no fewer than eighty-six times between 1986 and 2015.[4] Phillips has written (in a manner contrasting with the approaches of Turner and McCreesh) of the advantages he sees in presenting sacred polyphonic works divested of their 'aura' of liturgical ritual and removed from the ecclesiastical spaces for which they were written into the concert hall, so that they can be appreciated for their pure musical worth alongside the masterworks of the instrumental repertoire.[5] But he acknowledges that the special popularity of Requiems with the modern concert audiences for polyphony does nevertheless draw upon elements of that 'aura' which in large measure reside in the texts set:

Settings of the Requiem Mass are among the most frequent requests for concert music. This may seem unlikely, given the subject matter, but in fact it is just that subject matter which makes them so compelling. There is a drama inherent in the text which never fails to move audiences, having, in the first place, brought out the best in the composer. It is not a modern kind of drama such as we are used to seeing in the cinema or on television, but rather of the opposite: of the light which is shining on the deceased (whose body would have been present in the original

---

[4] Information kindly supplied by Peter Phillips.
[5] See Peter Phillips, *What We Really Do: The Tallis Scholars* (London: The Musical Times, 2003), 45–6.

performances), of the immediacy of heaven, of the peace which death will bring. Put in words this may sound a bit far-fetched, but from the split second that the opening 'Requiem aeternam' chant is heard, every listener is inevitably transported.[6]

Phillips proceeds to exemplify further how, in his view, the dramatic intensity and emotional range inherent in a polyphonic Requiem makes it particularly arresting to the modern listener. This is immersive and transporting escapism of a kind deeply attractive to modern sensibilities, and it may be also that the particular combination of variety and coherence which – as argued in Chapter 4 – characterises the Requiem of 1603 makes it all the more successful as a concert work. Victoria's 'excellent *Officium*', which apparently achieved limited fame in the seventeenth century, is enjoying an extraordinary afterlife.

---

[6] Peter Phillips, booklet notes to *Requiem* (Gimell Records, 2005).

Appendix 1: *Officium defunctorum*: Texts and Translations of the Paratextual Material

Translations by Leofranc Holford-Strevens

Dedicatory Epistle

Serenissimæ principi, ac dominæ D. Margaritæ, imperatorum Maximiliani, & Mariæ Filiæ Madriti in Regio Monasterio Matris Dei in Consolatione Christo iuxta institutum Primæ Regulæ D. Claræ, militanti: Thomas Ludovicus á Victoria Abulensis, humilis eius Capellanus, Salutem & incolumitatem precatur.

Mos fuit antiquis gentibus (Serenissima Princeps) divis suis eiusmodi sacrificia & munera offerre, qualia ab iisdem acceperant; sic Pani oves, Cereri fruges, Baccho racemos, Pomonæ fructus, Apollini arcus & sagittas, gratæ mentis indicia dare assueverunt, ita enim & divorum potentiam, & benignitatem, pariterque beneficiorum modum, & qualitatem omnium conspectui proposuerunt. Mihi vero cogitanti, quomodo tua in me beneficia, aliqua ex parte compensare gestiam: nulla se commodior via ostendit, quam ut eiusmodi dona tibi offeram qualia mihi tua, & familiæ vestræ Austriacæ, benignitate contigerunt, Musica nimirum, & Harmonica. Et quum vestro propitio in me favore hæc mihi otia facta fuerint, fructus eorundem vobis solum debitos, hilari & læta fronte, tanquam mustum Baccho, aut uniones Amphitritæ, tibi donare. Rude nimirum, & levidense munus, nec tanta Heroina, aut tanta prosapia dignum. Quid enim sunt hæc quæ offerantur

For the Most Serene Princess and Lady, doña Margarita, daughter of the emperors Maximilian and María, a soldier for Christ at Madrid in the Royal Monastery of the Mother of God of Consolation according to the ordinance of the First Rule of St Clare, Thome Luis de Victoria of Ávila, her humble chaplain,[1] prays for health and security.

It was the custom with ancient peoples (Most Serene Princess) to offer such sacrifices and gifts to their gods as they had received from them; thus as token of their gratitude they were wont to give Pan sheep, Ceres crops, Bacchus grapes, Pomona fruit, Apollo bows and arrows; for thus they displayed both the gods' power and kindness, and equally the degree and quality of their favours for all to see. Now, as I pondered how I may strive in some measure to recompense your favours to me, no more suitable way reveals itself to me than that I should offer you such gifts as have befallen me through your and your Austrian family's kindness, musical, naturally, and harmonic. And since it is by your[2] propitious support for me that I obtained this leisure, I give you its fruits, owed to you alone, with happy and cheerful countenance, like grape-juice to Bacchus or pearls to Amphitrite. Of course it is an unprepossessing and trivial gift, nor worthy of so

---

[1] An alternative, but less likely, reading is 'its humble chaplain', i.e. chaplain of the Monastery; after María's death, Victoria was assigned one of the new chaplaincies attached to the Descalzas which were founded through her estate. If the reading 'her humble chaplain' is correct, then this is intriguing, being the only known reference to Victoria serving Margarita in such a capacity, or indeed of her having one or more personal chaplains whilst a nun.

[2] 'Your' is here plural, i.e. including the House of Austria.

familiæ Austriacæ? perpetua gloria per tot sæcula iam fulgenti, à Regibus, Imperatoribus, & Principibus totius orbis celeberrimis, prosapiam suam ducenti, & ad tale fastigium fortunæ, & Imperii evectæ, quale nulla unquam humana vidit ætas, ita ut eam non modo clientes omnes fideliter colant, hostes tremunt & adorent, sed & ipsa invidia eam velit nolit, omnibus orbis terræ familiis præponit? Hæc est illa quæ Scipionum instar non milites sed Imperatores producit, tales nimirum qui servilis iugi impatientes parere nesciunt, nec tamen cum inferioribus certare; instar Aquilarum, aut Leonum, qui passeres, aut lepores venari dedignantur: aut instar Alexandri Magni, qui in ludis Olimpicis non nisi cum Regibus currere voluit: tales sunt Austriaci, non milites ensiferi, sed Heroes ensibus pariter & Sceptris adornati: nec tamen Ottomannorum instar Imperio inhiantes parricidiis intenduunt, aut mutuis se vulneribus conficiunt, sed concorditer viventes horam Imperii placide expectant, & tunc revera se quales sint ostendunt. Quid multa? Hoc solum addam, hæc familia quibus artibus ad Imperium orbis terræ potentissimum aspiravit (hoc est pietate & modis legitimis) iisdem illud & retinet, & gubernat. Heroes illos innumeros belli & pacis artibus insignes, qui in hac familia floruerint, quid opus est recensere? Ut alios taceamus invictum illum orbis terrorem Carolum V. Qui instar novi Solis in Occasu fulgere cœpit contra Solem Orientis, Herculis etiam columnas, audacia plusquam Alexandri superare ausus, Plus ultra, pro Non ultra, inscripsit. Magnanimum demum Philippum, qui avitum Imperium, Nec spe, nec mœtu, Sed armis, & consilio rexit & auxit? Philippum denique III. Paternæ, & avitæ virtutis, & fortunæ spem summam præ se ferentem? Quid insignes illas Heroinas dicam? & inter alias Serenissimam Mariam, Imperatricem matrem tuam, cuius illustris & nulli secunda nobilitas, quamvis eam ornet, quod Cæsareo sanguine, longa & vetusta serie orta, Imperatorum etiam filia, neptis, nurus, coniux, soror & mater, Regum

great a heroine or so great a lineage. For what gifts are there that could be offered to the House of Austria, already shining for so many generations with unbroken glory, which traces its lineage from the most famous kings, emperors, and princes of the whole world, and raised to such a peak of fortune and empire as no human age has ever seen, so that not only do all its subjects faithfully honour it, its enemies tremble and do it reverence, but Envy herself willy-nilly sets it before all the houses of the world? This is the house that like the Scipios produces not soldiers but commanders, such as cannot bear the yoke of slavery and know not how to obey, nor yet to contend with inferiors, in the manner of eagles and lions, which scorn to hunt sparrows or hares, or Alexander the Great who at the Olympic Games was willing to run only against kings: such are the Austrians, not sword-bearing soldiers but heroes equally adorned by swords and sceptres, yet they do not, like the Ottomans, panting for power, make their way to murdering their kin, or kill each other with mutual wounds, but living in concord peaceably await their hour of rule, and then truly show what manner of men they are. Why need I say more? I will add only this, that the arts by which this House aspired to the most powerful empire in the world (that is, by piety and lawful means) are those same arts by which it both keeps and governs it. What need is there to list those countless heroes, eminent in the arts of war and peace, who have flourished in that house? To say nothing of the others, that invincible terror of the world, Charles V, who like a new sun began to blaze in the West against the sun of the East, who with a boldness greater than Alexander's durst pass the Pillars of Hercules, and changed the inscription from *Non ultra*[3] to *Plus ultra*[4]; then the great-hearted Philip II, who governed and expanded his ancestral dominion 'neither by hope nor by fear' but by arms and counsel; lastly Philip III, who manifests the highest hope of his father's and grandfather's virtue? What shall I say of those eminent heroines? And among them of the Most Serene María, the empress, your

---

[3] 'No further'.

[4] 'Beyond'.

potentissimorum soror & socrus esset, summo tamen pietatis & religionis studio (quod Gentilitium vestrum fuit semper decus) generis sui gloriam, superavit & auxit? Celebris est hæc ubique non generis modo, sed progeniei nomine, quod quattuor filios, hodie superstites, orbis terræ lumina produxerit, è quibus unus Imperator, alii authoritate Regibus æquales, filias potentissimis Regibus nuptas, & è filia nepotem Regem maximum viderit. Magna quidem hæc sunt, multo vero maior laus ei fuit, te in lucem protulisse: te inquam quæ generis tui claritatem & divitias excellens, etiam formæ donum præ Christo contemnens, Principum maximorum nuptias recusans, delitias & luxum aulicum fastidiens, maluisti Christi coniugio vinciri, vitam Monasticam eligendo (ut de tuis excellentibus virtutibus nihil dicam, neque enim Sol indiget tædarum lumine ut magis splendeat, nec mare influentibus rivis ut maius appareat, nec tuæ virtutes ullis encomiis ut magis clarescant, quum illæ sint omni laude & præconiis maiores.) Huic tuo sancto proposito quum ego gratulari diu in animo habuerim, nihil mihi magis idoneum visum est, quam ut Harmoniam illam, quam in exequias Serenissimæ tuæ Matris composui, recognoscerem, & tanquam Cygneam cantionem, sub tui nominis patrocinio in lucem æderem. Accipe ergo (Serenissima Princeps) ieiunos hosce, sed tamen tui agri, proventus. Accipe inquam eodem animo quo Artaxerxes Persa, oblatam à rustico aquam accepit. Rusticus videns Regem terrarum orbem iam possidentem, & victorias terrestres adeptum, nil potuit illi optare præter Imperium aquarum, & tanquam earundem arrham, aquas hasce ei obtulit. Ego cum magnam terræ marisque partem pedibus Austriacorum subiectam video, quid optare possum, nisi ut coronis Diademata perpetuo cumulantes, ultimam tandem in cælo adipiscantur coronam, cuius ego arrham hanc, Musicam nimirum sacram, & Harmonicam[5] cælestem do. Tu vero non munus, sed animum dantis, &

mother, whose illustrious nobility, second to none, for all the ornament of her being born of imperial blood in a long and ancient line and also being the daughter, niece, daughter-in-law, wife, sister,[6] and mother of emperors, and the sister and mother-in-law of the mightiest kings, surpassed and enhanced the glory of her line in her supreme zeal for piety and religion (which was always your family's honour)? She is renowned everywhere on account not only of her lineage, but of her offspring, in that she bore four sons now living, the lights of the world, of whom one is emperor, the others are equal in authority to kings, and saw her daughters married to the most powerful kings, and her grandson by one of those daughters the greatest king. These are indeed great things, but a far greater theme for praise was her bearing you; you, I say, who excelling the lustre and wealth of your line, spurning even the gift of beauty for Christ, refusing marriage to the greatest princes, scorning the delights and luxury of court, preferred to be bound in marriage to Christ, choosing the monastic life (to say nothing of your outstanding virtues, for neither does the sun require the light of torches to shine the more, nor the sea the inflow of streams to appear larger, nor your virtues any encomia to gleam with more lustre, for they are greater than all praise and preachings). Having long had in mind to congratulate you on this holy purpose, nothing seemed to me more suitable than to revise the music that I wrote for the exequies of your Most Serene mother, and publish it as a swan-song under the protection of your name. Receive, therefore, Most Serene Princess, this produce, jejune but from your field. Receive it, I say, in the same spirit as Artaxerxes the Persian received the water offered him by a peasant. The peasant, seeing a king who already possessed the world, and had obtained earthly victories, could wish him nothing else but dominion over the waters, and as an earnest of them offered him this water. What can I, seeing a great part of the earth and sea lying under the feet of the Austrians, wish for but that, ever piling diadems on crowns,

---

[5] 'Harmonicam' should read 'Harmoniam'.

[6] This is erroneous: María's brother Philip II was not Emperor.

humillimum in Serenissimam Matrem tuam defunctam, in te, tuosque omnes obsequium respiciens, his incœptis fave, maiora, si Deus mihi dies longiores dederit, olim expectans. Salve & vale Serenissima Princeps. Madriti idibus Iunii, Anno reparatæ salutis 1605.

they should at last obtain the final crown in heaven, of which I give you this earnest, namely sacred music and celestial harmony. But may you – regarding not the gift but the spirit of the giver, and his most humble devotion to your late Most Serene mother, to you, and to all yours – show favour to this enterprise, expecting that one day, if God grant me longer life, they will be greater. Hail and farewell, Most Serene Princess. Madrid, 13 June, in the year of recovered salvation 1605.

Eulogistic *carmen* by Martin Pesserio

Martini Pessenii Hasdale, in laudem Auctoris Collegæ sui Carmen.

Martin Pessenio Hasdale in praise of his colleague the author's composition.

Nominis omen habes (Victoria) victor amenos,
Therpsichores colles, iucundaque prata Timoli
Lustrasti Clarios victor fœliciter hortos:
Hinc tibi partus honos meritæque encomia laudis,
Hinc tibi Phæbea cinguntur tempora lauro.
Ipse Chelyn Phæbus tibimet donasse videtur
Orpheus ipse Lyram, Cytharam vocalis Arion,
Amphion dedit ipse suæ modulamina vocis,
Pierus & natas in te superesse triumphat
Pierides, quas tu vocali carmine vincis.
Te fera, te volucres, silices & saxa sequuntur,
Arboribusque suis nudantur Thessala Tempe,
Cyrrha virens, Pindus, Parnassus & Herculis Oeta
Dum tua sublimi modularis carmina plectro.
Te Phæbus, Musæ Charites audire canentem
Gaudent, quærentes redivivus num foret Orpheus,
Precipuè celebras mœsto dum carmine celsam,
Sanguine Cæsareo, necnon Diademate Claram
Induperatricem MARIAM, cui gloria soli
Contigit ut Cæsar natus, pater atque maritus
Cæsar & ipse Socer, Regum soror ipsa socrusque
Esset, Nobilitas insignis! At altior illi
Gloria contigerat CHRISTUM, quod pectore tote
Fovit, & illius totam se addixit amori
Talibus exequiis, cantu (Victoria) tali
Comunis nostræ Dominæ pia funera defles,
Quales Euridices in funere Thracius Orpheus,
Aut quales cygnus moriens, vel Daulias ales,
Ingeminat tristes lugubri voce querelas.
Vive diu fœlix coniunge trophæa trophæis,
Musica, Timotheus sis alter in arte canendi
Summa petens alis Phæbeis Sydera cygnus,
Nominis augurium rerum successibus implens.

Your name is an omen, Victoria; as a victor you patrolled the pleasant hills of Terpsichore, and delightful fields of Tmolus, as a victor in good fortune the gardens of Claros; hence you acquired honour and encomia of deserved praise, hence your temples are girt with Phoebus' bay. Phoebus himself seems to have given *you* his tortoiseshell,[7] Orpheus himself his lyre, singing Arion his cithara, Amphion himself gave you the melodies of his voice, and Pierus is triumphant that in you his daughters survive, the Pierides, whom you defeat in vocal contest. You wild beasts, you birds, stones[8] and rocks follow, and denuded of their trees are the Thessalian Tempe, green Cyrrha, Pindus, Parnassus, and Hercules' Oeta, when you play your songs with sublime plectrum. You Phoebus, the Muses, and the Graces rejoice to hear singing, wondering whether Orpheus had come back to life, especially when you honour with sad song the elevated, Caesar-blooded, and diadem-lustrous Empress María, to whom alone fell the glory that a Caesar should be her son, her father, and her husband, a Caesar himself her father-in-law, and that she herself should be the sister and mother-in-law of kings, a marked nobility! But a higher honour had befallen her, that she nurtured Christ with her whole bosom, and gave herself entirely to his love. With such exequies, with such a song, Victoria, do you bewail the pious funeral of our common mistress as Thracian Orpheus (lamented) at the death of Eurydice, or such sad plaints as the dying swan or the Daulian bird[9] redoubles with mournful voice. Live long and happy, join musical trophies to trophies, be another Timotheus in the art of singing, a swan seeking the lofty stars on Apolline wings, fulfilling the prophecy of your name with achievements in facts.

---

[7] I.e. his lyre.   [8] Literally 'flints'.
[9] The nightingale.

Appendix 2: Requiem Masses by Italian Composers Printed between 1560 and 1650

Note: Publication details refer to the first publication, where the work concerned was published more than once.

Composer	Voices	RISM	Publication date	Place of publication	Publisher
Anerio, Giovanni Francesco	4	A1110	1614	Rome	Giovanni Battista Robletti
Asola, Giovanni Matteo	4	AA2540a	1574	Venice	Sons of Antonio Gardano
Asola, Giovanni Matteo	4	A2529	1576	Venice	Angelo Gardano
Asola, Giovanni Matteo	4	A2565	1586	Venice	Giacomo Vincenti & Ricciardo Amadino
Asola, Giovanni Matteo	3	A2609	1600?	Venice?	
Bacilieri, Giovanni	5	B566	1619	Venice	Bartolomeo Magni (sub signo Gardani)
Balbi, Lodovico	5	B739	1595	Venice	Angelo Gardano
Bartei, Girolamo	8	B1061	1608	Rome	Bartolomeo Zannetti
Bartolini, Orindio	8	B1144	1633	Venice	Bartholomeo Magni
Bellazzi, Francesco	8	B1724	1628	Venice	Gardano/Bartholomeo Magni
Belli, Giulio	5	B1745	1586	Venice	Angelo Gardano
Belli, Giulio	8	B1749	1595	Venice	Ricciardo Amadino
Belli, Giulio	4	B1758	1599	Venice	Angelo Gardano
Belloni, Gioseppe	5	B1790	1603	Milan	Heirs of Simone Tini, & Filippo Lomazzo
Bernardi, Stefano	4	B2051	1615	Venice	Giacomo Vincenti
Bidelli, Matteo	8	B2619	1616	Antwerp	Pellegrino Bidelli
Biondi, Giovanni Battista	3	B2714	1609	Venice	Giacomo Vincenti
Borsaro, Arcangelo	8	B3780	1608	Venice	Ricciardo Amadino

(*cont.*)

Composer	Voices	RISM	Publication date	Place of publication	Publisher
Brunelli, Antonio	4	B4650	1619	Venice	Giacomo Vincenti
Brunelli, Antonio	4	B4650	1619	Venice	Giacomo Vincenti
Brunelli, Antonio	7	B4650	1619	Venice	Giacomo Vincenti
Canale, Floriano	4	C770	1588	Brescia	Tomaso Bozzola
Capuana, Mario	8	C950	1645	Venice	Alessandro Vincenti
Capuana, Mario	4	C953	1650	Venice	Alessandro Vincenti
Cavaccio, Giovanni[1]	5	C1546	1580	Venice	Alessandro Gardano
Cavaccio, Giovanni	4	C1551	1593	Venice	Ricciardo Amadino
Cavaccio, Giovanni	5	C1551	1593	Venice	Ricciardo Amadino
Cavaccio, Giovanni	4	C1554	1611	Milan	Heirs of Simone Tini, & Filippo Lomazzo
Cavaccio, Giovanni	5	C1554	1611	Milan	Heirs of Simone Tini, & Filippo Lomazzo
Contino, Giovanni	5	C3543	1573	Milan	Paolo Gottardo Ponzio
Donati, Ignazio	4/5	D3400	1633	Venice	Alessandro Vincenti
Gallerano, Leandro	5	G152	1615	Venice	Ricciardo Amadino
Gastoldi, Giovanni Giacomo	4	G504	1607	Venice	Ricciardo Amadino
Ghizzolo, Giovanni	4	G1785	1612	Milan	Heirs of Simone Tini, & Filippo Lomazzo
Ghizzolo, Giovanni	8	G1786	1613	Milan	Filippo Lomazzo
Ghizzolo, Giovanni	5	G1800	1625	Venice	Bartolomeo Magni (stampa del Gardano)
Girelli, Santino	8	G2515	1627	Venice	Bartolomeo Magni (stampa del Gardano)
Grancini, Michel'Angelo[2]	4	G3398	1624	Milan	Filippo Lomazzo
Graziani, Tomaso	5	G3704	1599	Venice	Ricciardo Amadino
Gualtieri, Alessandro	8	G4790	1620	Venice	Alessandro Vincenti
Heredia, Pedro (de)	4	1646/1	1646	Rome	Lodovico Grignani
Isnardi, Paolo	5	I108	1568	Venice	Antonio Gardano

[1] The Requiem Mass in C1546 may be the same work as one of those in published in C1551 and C1554.
[2] Three movements added to the Requiem by Rognoni Taeggio.

Composer	Voices	RISM	Publication date	Place of publication	Publisher
Isnardi, Paolo	4	I116	1573	Venice	Sons of Antonio Gardano
Lappi, Pietro	4	L695	1625	Venice	Bartolomeo Magni (stampa del Gardano)
Marini, Giuseppe	8	M675	1621	Venice	Bartolomeo Magni (stampa del Gardano)
Micheli, Domenico	5	M2681	1584	Venice	Angelo Gardano
Moro, Giacomo	8	M3731	1599	Venice	Ricciardo Amadino
Mortaro, Antonio	8	M3737	1595	Venice	Ricciardo Amadino
Pacelli, Asprilio	8	P29	1629	Venice	Alessandro Vincenti
Palestrina, Giovanni Pierluigi da	5	P658	1591	Rome	Alessandro Gardano
Pasino, Giovanni Battista	4	PP964 II,1	1630	Brescia	Paolo Bizardo
Pasino, Stefano	4	P966	1635	Venice	Bartolomeo Magni
Pellegrini, Vincenzo	5	P1177	1603–4	Venice	Monastery of Santo Spirito
Petrucci, Sante	4	P1657	1621	Venice	Alessandro Vincenti
Pietragrua, Gasparo	4	P2345	1629	Milan	Giorgio Rolla
Pontio, Pietro	4	P5079	1584	Venice	Heir of Girolamo Scotto
Pontio, Pietro	5	P5081	1585	Venice	Heir of Girolamo Scotto
Pontio, Pietro	4	P5084	1592	Venice	Ricciardo Amadino
Porta, Costanzo	5	P5180	1578	Venice	Angelo Gardano
Radesca (di Foggia), Enrico Antonio	4	R9	1604	Milan	Heirs of Simone Tini, & Filippo Lomazzo
Rambelli, Giovanni	5	not in RISM	1613	Milan	Filippo Lomazzo
Rognoni Taeggio, Giovanni Domenico	4	G3398, 1624/6	1624	Milan	Filippo Lomazzo
Rossi, Giovanni Battista	4	R2739	1618	Venice	Bartolomeo Magni (sub signo Gardani)
Ruffo, Vincenzo	6	R3055	1574	Venice	Heir of Girolamo Scotto
Sabino, Ippolito	4	S40	1575	Venice	Angelo Gardano
Serra, Michelangelo	4	S2830	1615	Venice	Giacomo Vincenti
Strozzi, Bernardo	5	S6991	1626	Venice	Bartolomeo Magni (stampa del Gardano)

(*cont.*)

Composer	Voices	RISM	Publication date	Place of publication	Publisher
Titi, Placido	5	T845	1626	Venice	Alessando Vincenti
Tristabocca, Pasquale	5	T1247	1590	Venice	Giacomo Vincenti
Tristabocca, Pasquale	4	T1248	1591	Venice	Heirs of Girolamo Scotto
Tudino, Cesare	5	T1336	1589	Venice	Giacomo Vincenti
Varotto, Michele	6	V987	1563	Venice	Girolamo Scotto
Varotto, Michele	8	V994	1595	Milan	Heirs of Francesco & Simone Tini
Vecchi, Lorenzo	8	V1002	1605	Venice	Angelo Gardano
Vecchi, Orazio	8	V1008, 1607/1	1607	Venice	Angelo Gardano & brothers
Vecchi, Orfeo	5	V1065	1598	Milan	Heirs of Simone Tini, & Giovanni Francesco Besozzi
Viadana, Lodovico	3[3]	not in RISM	1592	Venice	Ricciardo Amadino
Viadana, Lodovico	4	V1357	1600	Venice	Giacomo Vincenti
Viadana, Lodovico	5	V1374	1604	Venice	Giacomo Vincenti
Vitali, Filippo	4	V2125	1646	Florence	Luca Franceschini & Alessandro Logi
Zucchini, Gregorio	4	Z364	1616	Venice	Giacomo Vincenti

[3] And basso continuo.

Select Bibliography

Works Published Before 1700

Ángeles, Juan de los, *Sermon que en las honras de la catolica ceserea magestad de la emperatriz nuestra señora predicó el padre fray Iuan de los Angeles . . . en 17 de março de 1603* (Madrid: Juan de la Cuesta, 1604)

Carrillo, Juan, *Relación histórica de la real fundación del monasterio de las descalzas de santa Clara de la villa de Madrid* (Madrid: Luis Sánchez, 1616)

Cervantes de Salazar, Francisco, *Túmulo imperial dela gran ciudad de Mexico* (Mexico City: Antonio de Espinosa, 1560)

Céspedes, Baltasar de, *Relacion de las honras que hizo la universidad de Salamanca a la magestad de la reyna doña Margarita de Austria* (Salamanca: Francisco de Cea Tesa, 1611)

de la Vera, Martín, *Ordinario y ceremonial según las costumbres y rito de la orden de nuestro padre san Geronymo* (Madrid: Imprenta Real, 1636)

Enriquez, Alonso, *Las honras que celebró en la muerte del muy alto, y religioso monarca rey don Felipe tercero la muy noble ciudad de Murcia* (n.p., 1622)

Fernandez de Cordova, Geronimo, *Relacion de las funerales exequias que la nacion española hizo en Roma a la majestad del rey n(uestro) s(eñor) d(on) Philippo III de Austria, el piadoso* (Rome: Giacomo Mascardo, 1622)

Gómez de Mora, Juan, *Relación de las honras funerales que se hizieron por la reyna doña Margarita de Austria nuestra señora, en esta villa de Madrid por su magestad del rey don Felipe nuestro señor* (Madrid, n.d.)

Guzmán, Diego de, *Reina catolica: vida y muerte de d(oña) Margarita de Austria* (Madrid: Luis Sánchez, 1617)

Iñiguez de Lequerica, Juan, *Sermones funerales, en las honras del rey nuestro señor don Felipe II* (Madrid: heirs of Juan Iñiguez de Lequerica, 1601)

León, Martín de, *Relacion de las exequias q(ue) el ex(celentisi)mo s(eño)r d(on) Iuan de Mendoça y Luna Marques de Montesclaros, Virrey del Piru hizo en la muerte de la reina nuestra s(eñora) doña Margarita* (Lima: Pedro de Marchán y Calderón, 1612)

Libro de las honras que hizo el colegio de la compañia de Iesus de Madrid, à la m(agestad) c(æsarea) de la emperatriz doña Maria de Austria, fundadora del dicho colegio, que se celebraron a 21. de abril de 1603 (Madrid: Luis Sánchez, 1603)

López de Hoyos, Juan, *Hystoria y relación verdadera de la enfermedad felicíssimo tránsito, y sumptuosas exequias funebres de la serenissima reyna de España doña Isabel de Valoys nuestra señora* (Madrid: Pierres Cosin, 1569)

López de Hoyos, Juan, *Relacion de la muerte y honras funebres del s(ereni)s(simo) principe D. Carlos, hijo de la mag(estad) del catholico rey d(on) Philippe el segundo nuestro señor* (Madrid: Pierres Cosin, 1568)

Manrique, Ángel, *Exequias, túmulo y pompa funeral que la universidad de Salamanca hizo en las honras del rey . . . Felipe III* (Salamanca: Antonio Vásquez, 1621)

Méndez Silva, Rodrigo, *Admirable vida, y heroycas virtudes de aquel glorioso blasón de España . . . la esclarecida emperatriz María* (Madrid: Diego Díaz de la Carrera, 1655)

Palma, Juan de, *Vida de la serenissima infanta sor Margarita de la cruz, religiosa descalça de s(anta) Clara* (Madrid: Imprenta Real, 1636)

Pompa funeral honras y exequias en la muerte de la muy alta y católica señora doña Isabel de Borbon (Madrid: Diego Díaz de la Carrera, 1645)

Primeira parte do index da livraria de musica do muyto alto e poderoso rey dom Ioão o IV nosso senhor (Lisbon: Paulo Craesbeeck, 1649)

Relacion de las honras que se hizieron en la ciudad de Cordova, à la muerte de la serenissima reyna señora, doña Margarita de Austria (Córdoba: widow of Andres Barrera, 1612)

Relatione del solenne mortorio fatto nell morte del cattolico Filippo II re di Spagna (Rome: Bartholomeo Bonfadino, 1598)

Ribera Florez, Dionisio de, *Relacion historiada de las exequias funerales de la magestad del rey d(on) Philippo II nuestro senor* (Mexico City: Pedro Balli, 1600)

Roales, Francisco, *Exequias del serenissimo principe Emanuel Filiberto* (Madrid: Juan Gonzales, 1626)

Rodríguez de Monforte, Pedro, *Descripcion de la honras que se hicieron a la catholica mag(esta)d de d(on) Phelippe quarto rey delas Españas y del nuevo mundo* (Madrid: Francisco Nieto, 1666)

Sariñana, Isidro, *Llanto del occidente en el ocaso del mas claro sol de las Españas, funebres demonstraciones, que hizo, pyra real, que erigio en las exequias del rey n(uestro) señor d(on) Felipe IIII* (Mexico City: widow of Bernardo Calderon, 1666)

Valcaçar, Ivan de, *Relacion de las exequias que se celebraron en Napoles, en la muerte de la serenissima reyna Margarita señora nuestra* (Naples: Tarquinio Longo, 1612)

Victoria, Thome Luis de, *Thomæ Ludovici de Victoria abulensis, sacræ cæsareæ maiestatis capellani, officium defunctorum, sex vocibus, in obitu et obsequiis sacræ imperatricis* (Madrid: Juan Flamenco, 1605)

Works Published After 1700

Abreu y Bertodano, Joseph Antonio de, *Coleccion de tratados de paz, alianza, neutralidad, garantia, proteccion* (Madrid: Diego Peralta, Antonio Marin, Juan de Zuñiga, 1740–1752)

Agee, Richard, *The Gardano Music Printing Firms, 1569–1611* (University of Rochester Press, 1998)

Allo Manero, María Adelaida, 'Exequias de la Casa de Austria en España, Italia e Hispanoamérica', unpublished PhD thesis, University of Zaragoza (1993)

Alvarenga, João Pedro d', 'Two Polyphonic Settings of the Mass for the Dead from Late Sixteenth-Century Portugal: Bridging Pre- and Post-Tridentine Traditions', *Acta Musicologica* 88 (2016), 5–33

Anglès, Higini, 'Latin Church Music on the Continent – 3: Spain and Portugal', in Gerald Abraham (ed.), *The New Oxford History of Music*, 10 vols (Oxford University Press, 1954–1990), IV, 372–418, at 400

Arbury, Andrew, 'Spanish Catafalques of the Sixteenth and Seventeenth Centuries', unpublished PhD thesis, Rutgers University (1992)

Arroyas Serrano, Magín, and Vicente Martínez Molés, 'La primera transcripción moderna del *Oficio de difuntos* de Victoria: el manuscrito del maestro José Perpiñán', *Revista de Musicología* 35/1 (2012), 473–89

Baade, Colleen Ruth, 'Music and Music-Making in Female Monasteries in Seventeenth-Century Castile', unpublished PhD thesis, Duke University (2001)

Barnett, Gregory, 'Tonal Organization in Seventeenth-Century Music Theory', in Thomas Christensen (ed.), *The Cambridge History of Western Music Theory* (Cambridge University Press, 2008), 407–55

Bernstein, Jane, 'Made to Order: Choirbook Publications in Cinquecento Rome', in M. Jennifer Bloxam, Gioia Filocamo, and Leofranc Holford-Strevens (eds), *Uno gentile et subtile ingenio: Studies in Renaissance Music in Honour of Bonnie J. Blackburn* (Turnhout: Brepols, 2009), 669–76

Bernstein, Jane, *Music Printing in Renaissance Venice: The Scotto Press (1539–1572)* (Oxford University Press, 1998)

Bianconi, Lorenzo, *Music in the Seventeenth Century*, translated by David Bryant (Cambridge University Press, 1982)

Burney, Charles, *A General History of Music: From the Earliest Ages to the Present Period*, 4 vols (London: for the author, 1776–89)

Butt, John, 'The Seventeenth-Century Musical "Work"', in Tim Carter and John Butt (eds), *The Cambridge History of Seventeenth-Century Music* (Cambridge University Press, 2005), 27–54

Cabrera de Córdoba, Luis, *Relaciones de las cosas sucedidas el la corte de España, desde 1599 hasta 1614* (Valladolid: Junta de Castilla y León, Consejería de Educación y Cultura, 1997)

Checa Cremades, Fernando, 'Monasterio de las Descalzas Reales: origenes de su colección artística', *Reales Sitios* 102/4 (1989), 21–30

Chemotti, Antonio, 'Motets and Liturgy for the Dead in Italy: Text Typologies and Contexts of Performance', in Esperanza Rodríguez-Garcia and Daniele V. Filippi (eds), *Mapping the Motet in the post-Tridentine Era* (London: Routledge, 2018), 57–84

Chemotti, Antonio, 'Polyphonic Music pro mortuis in Italy (1550–1650): Context and Intertext', unpublished PhD thesis, Ludwig-Maximilians-Universität, Munich (2017)

Cœurdevey, Annie, 'Édition et interprétation: les choix scientifiques et esthétiques du chanoine Proske', in Philippe Vendrix (ed.), *La Renaissance et sa musique au XIXe siècle*, Épitome musical (Paris: Klincksieck, 2000), 133–54

Collet, Henri, *Le mysticisme musical espagnol au XVIe siècle* (Paris: Félix Alcan, 1913)

Collet, Henri, *Victoria* (Paris: Félix Alcan, 1914)

Cramer, Eugene Casjen, *Studies in the Music of Tomás Luis de Victoria* (Aldershot: Ashgate, 2001)

Cusick, Suzanne, *Valerio Dorico: Music Printer in Sixteenth-Century Rome* (Ann Arbor, MI: UMI Research Press, 1981)

Dadson, Trevor, 'Music Books and Instruments in Spanish Golden-Age Inventories: The Case of Don Juan de Borja (1607)', in Iain Fenlon and Tess Knighton (eds), *Early Music Printing and Publishing in the Iberian World* (Kassell: Edition Reichenberger, 2007), 95–116

Diario de Hans Khevenhüller, embajador imperial en la corte de Felipe II, ed. Félix Labrador Arroyo, with introduction by Sara Veronelli (Madrid: Sociedad estatal para la conmemoración de los centenarios de Felipe II y Carlos V, 2001)

Dittrich, Raymond, 'Dokumentation zum zweiten Jahrgang und zur zweiten auflage des Messenbandes aus dem ersten Jahrgang der *Musica Divina*', *Musik in Bayern* 56 (1998), 55–78

Eire, Carlos M. N., *From Madrid to Purgatory: The Art and Craft of Dying in Sixteenth-Century Spain* (Cambridge University Press, 1995)

Ellis, Katharine, *Interpreting the Musical Past: Early Music in Nineteenth-Century France* (Oxford University Press, 2005)

Ellis, Katharine, 'Palestrina et la musique dite "palestrinienne" en France au XIXe siècle: questions d'exécution et de réception', in Philippe Vendrix (ed.), *La Renaissance et sa musique au XIXe siècle*, Épitome musical (Paris: Klincksieck, 2000), 155–190

Escrivà Llorca, Ferran, 'Eruditio, pietas et honor: Joan de Borja i la música del seu temps (1533–1606)', unpublished PhD thesis, Universitat Politècnica de València (2015)

Escrivà Llorca, Ferran, 'La vida en las Descalzas Reales a través de los epistolarios de Juan de Borja (1584–1604)', in Javier Suáres-Pajares and Manuel del Sol (eds), *Estudios. Tomás Luis de Victoria. Studies*, Colección Música hispana, textos, estudios 18 (Madrid: Instituto Complutense de Ciencias Musicales, 2013), 437–52

Filippi, Daniele V., 'Carlo Borromeo and Tomás Luis de Victoria: A Gift, Two Letters and a Recruiting Campaign', *Early Music* 43 (2015), 37–51

Filippi, Daniele V., *Tomás Luis de Victoria* (Palermo: L'Epos, 2008)

Fischer, Klaus, 'Unbekannte Kompositionen Victorias in der Biblioteca Nazionale in Rom', *Archiv für Musikwissenschaft* 32/2 (1975), 124–38

Flint, Catrena, 'The Schola Cantorum, Early Music and French Political Culture, from 1894 to 1914', unpublished PhD thesis, McGill University (2006)

Fuhrmann, Wolfgang, 'Pierre de la Rues Trauermotetten und die *Quis dabit*-Tradition', in Stefan Gasch and Birgit Lodes (eds), *Tod in Musik und Kultur. Zum 500. Todestag Philipps des Schönen*, Wiener Forum fur ältere Musikgeschichte 2 (Tutzing; Hans Schneider Verlag, 2007), 189–244

García López, Consuelo, *Archivo del Monasterio de las Descalzas Reales de Madrid*, 2 vols (Madrid: Patrimonio Nacional, 2003)

Gómez, Maria Carmen, 'Precisiones en torno a la vida y obra de Matheo Felcha el joven', *Revista de Musicología* 9 (1986), 41–56

Guillo, Laurent, *Pierre I Ballard et Robert III Ballard: Imprimeurs du roy pour la musique (1599–1673)*, 2 vols (Sprimont: Mardaga, 2003)

Haberl, Franz Xaver, 'Tomas Luis de Victoria: eine bio-bibliographische Studie', *Kirchenmusikalisches Jahrbuch* 11 (1896), 72–84

Haggh-Huglo, Barbara, 'Singing for the Most Noble Souls: Funerals and Memorials for the Burgundian and Habsburg Dynasties in Dijon and Brussels as Models for the Funeral of Philip the Fair in 1507', in Stefan Gasch and Birgit Lodes (eds), *Tod in Musik und Kultur. Zum 500. Todestag Philipps des Schönen*, Wiener Forum fur ältere Musikgeschichte 2 (Tutzing: Hans Schneider Verlag, 2007), 57–85

Hathaway, Janet, 'Spirituality and Devotional Music in the Royal Convent of the Descalzas, Madrid', *Journal of Musicological Research* 30 (2011), 202–26

Hawkins, John, *A General History of the Science and Practice of Music*, 5 vols (London: Payne & Son, 1776)

Hernández Castelló, Esteban, 'Il manoscritto musicale 130 della Biblioteca Nazionale Vittorio Emanuele II di Roma', *Revista de Musicología* 29/1 (2006), 326–31

Hernández Ying, Orlando Amado, 'Angels in the Americas: Paintings of Apocryphal Angels in Spain and its American Viceroyalties', unpublished PhD thesis, The City University of New York (2009)

Hoyer, Johannes, *Der Priestermusiker und Kirchenmusikreformer Franz Xaver Haberl (1840–1910) und sein Weg zur Musikwissenschaft* (Regensburg: Verlag des Vereins für Regensburger Bistumsgeschichte, 2005)

Huff, Kelly, 'Demystifying the Life and Madrid Works of Tomás Luis de Victoria', unpublished PhD thesis, University of Kansas (2015)

Janz, Bernhard, 'Das editorische Werk Carl Proskes und die Anfänge der Kirchenmusikalischen Reformbewegung', in Winfried Kirsch (ed.), *Palestrina und die Idee der klassischen Vokalpolyphonie im 19. Jahrhundert: Zur Geschichte eines Kirchenmusikalischen Stilideals* (Regensburg: Gustav Bosse, 1989), 149–69

Johnstone, Andrew, '"High" Clefs in Composition and Performance', *Early Music* 34 (2006), 29–54

Jordan, Annemarie, 'Las dos águilas del Emperador Carlos V. Las colleciones y el mecenazgo de Juana y María de Austria en la corte de Felipe II', in Luis A. Ribot García (ed.), *La monarquía de Felipe II a debate* (Madrid: Sociedad estatal para la conmemoración de los centenarios de Felipe II y Carlos V, 2000), 429–72

Judd, Cristle Collins, 'Modal Types and *Ut, Re, Mi* Tonalities: Tonal Coherence in Sacred Vocal Polyphony from around 1500', *Journal of the American Musicological Society* 45 (1994), 428–67

Khevenhüller, Hans, *Geheimes Tagebuch, 1548–1605*, ed. Georg Khevenhüller-Metsch (Graz: Akademische Druck- und Verlagsanstalt, 1971)

Kirk, Douglas, 'A Tale of Two Queens, Their Music Books, and the Village of Lerma', in Tess Knighton and Bernadette Nelson (eds), *Pure Gold: Golden Age Sacred Music in the Iberian World. A Homage to Bruno Turner*, DeMusica 15 (Kassel: Edition Reichenberger, 2011), 79–92

Kirk, Douglas, 'Churching the Shawms in Renaissance Spain: Lerma, Archivo de San Pedro Ms Mus. 1', unpublished PhD thesis, McGill University (1993)

Kirkman, Andrew, *The Cultural Life of the Early Polyphonic Mass: Medieval Context to Modern Revival* (Cambridge University Press, 2010)

Knighton, Tess, 'Music for the Dead: An Early Sixteenth-Century Anonymous Requiem Mass', in Tess Knighton and Bernadette Nelson (eds), *Pure Gold: Golden Age Sacred Music in the Iberian World. A Homage to Bruno Turner*, DeMusica 15 (Kassel: Edition Reichenberger, 2011), 262–88

Knighton, Tess, 'Preliminary Thoughts on the Dynamics of Music Printing in the Iberian Peninsula during the Sixteenth Century', *Bulletin of Spanish Studies* 89 (2012), 521–56

Knighton, Tess, '"Through a Glass Darkly": Music and Mysticism in Golden Age Spain', in Hilaire Kallendorf (ed.), *A New Companion to Hispanic Mysticism* (Leiden and Boston: Brill, 2010), 411–36

León Pinelo, Antonio de, *Anales de Madrid desde el año 447 al de 1658*, ed. Pedro Fernández Martín (Madrid: Instituto de Estudios Madrileños, 1971)

Lewis, Mary, *Antonio Gardano, Venetian Music Printer, 1538–1569: A Descriptive Bibliography and Historical Study*, 2 vols (New York and London: Garland, 1988, 1997)

Llorens, José M., *Le opere musicali della Cappella Giulia* (Vatican City: Biblioteca Apostolica Vaticana, 1971)

López-Calo, José, 'La música en la Orden y en el Rito Jeronimianos', *Studia Hieronymiana* 1 (1973), 123–38

López-Vidriero, María Luisa, 'Por la imprenta hacia Dios', in Pedro M. Cátedra and María Luisa López-Vidriero (eds), *De libros, librerías, imprentas y lectores* (Salamanca: Ediciones Universidad de Salamanca, Seminario de Estudios, 2002), 193–218

Luce, Harold, 'The Requiem Mass from its Plainsong Beginnings to 1600', unpublished PhD thesis, The Florida State University (1958)

Marín López, Javier, 'Music Books for an *iglesia principal y calificada*: The 1657 Inventory of Jaén Cathedral in Context', in Tess Knighton and Emilio Ros-Fábregas (eds), *New Perspectives on Early Music in Spain*, Iberian Early Music Studies 1 (Kassel: Reichenberger, 2015), 108–62

Marín López, Javier, 'Tomás Luis de Victoria en las Indias: de la circulación a las reinvención', in Alfonso de Vicente and Pilar Tomás (eds), *Tomás Luis de Victoria y la cultura musical en la España de Felipe III* (Madrid: Centro de Estudios Europa Hispánica and Machado Libros, 2012), 403–60

Martínez Gil, Fernando, *Muerte y sociedad en la España de los Austrias* (Cuenca: Ediciones de la Universidad de Castilla-La Mancha, 2000)

Millán Martínez, José, 'La emperatriz María y las pugnas cortesanas en tiempos de Felipe II', in Ernest Belenguer Cebrià (ed.), *Felipe II y el Mediterráneo*, 4 vols (Madrid: Sociedad Estatal para la Conmemoración de los Centenarios de Felipe II y Carlos V, 1999), III, 143–60

Moll, Jaime, *De la imprenta al lector: estudios sobre el libro español de los siglos XVI al XVIII* (Madrid: Arco/Libros, 1994)

Moll, Jaime, 'Problemas bibliográficos del libro del Siglo de Oro', *Boletín de la Real Academia Española* 59 (1979), 49–107

Montagnier, Jean-Paul C., *The Polyphonic Mass in France, 1600–1780: The Evidence of the Printed Choirbooks* (Cambridge University Press, 2017)

Moreda-Rodríguez, Eva, 'A Catholic, a Patriot, a Good Modernist: Manuel de Falla and the Francoist Musical Press', *Hispanic Research Journal* 14 (2013), 212–26

Mota Murillo, Rafael, *Sebastián López de Velasco (1584–1659), Libro de missas, motetes, salmos, magnificas y otras cosas tocantes al culto divino*, 4 vols (Madrid: Sociedad Española de Musicología, 1980–1993)

Muir, Thomas, '"Full in the Panting Heart of Rome": Roman Catholic Music in England: 1850–1962', unpublished PhD thesis, University of Durham (2004)

Muir, Thomas, *Roman Catholic Church Music in England, 1791–1914: A Handmaid of the Liturgy?* (Aldershot: Ashgate, 2009)

Nelson, Bernadette, 'Ritual and Ceremony in the Spanish Royal Chapel, *c.* 1559–*c.* 1561', *Early Music History* 19 (2000), 105–200

Noone, Michael, *Music and Musicians in the Escorial Liturgy under the Habsburgs, 1563–1700* (Rochester, NY, and Woodbridge: University of Rochester Press, 1998)

Noone, Michael, 'Processions to the "City of the Dead": The Spanish Royal Chapel and an Anonymous Requiem from El Escorial', in Juan José Carreras and

Bernardo García García (eds), *The Royal Chapel in the Time of the Habsburgs: Music and Court Ceremony in Early Modern Europe*, Studies in Medieval and Renaissance Music 3 (Woodbridge: Boydell, 2005), 144–61

Olmos Sáez, Ángel Manuel, 'Aportaciones a la temprana historia musical de la Capilla de las Descalzas Reales de Madrid (1576–1618)', *Revista de Musicología* 26/2 (2003), 339–489

O'Regan, Noel, 'Historia de dos ciudades: Victoria como mediador musical entre Roma y Madrid', in Alfonso de Vicente and Pilar Tomás (eds), *Tomás Luis de Victoria y la cultura musical en la España de Felipe III* (Madrid: Centro de Estudios Europa Hispánica and Machado Libros, 2012), 279–300

O'Regan, Noel, 'Victoria in Rome', *Leading Notes* 15 (Spring 1998), 26–30

Orso, Steven N., *Art and Death at the Spanish Habsburg Court: The Royal Exequies for Philip IV* (Columbia, Missouri: University of Missouri Press, 1989)

Parisini, Federico, *Carteggio inedito del P. Giambattista Martini coi più celebri musicisti del suo tempo* (Bologna: Zanichelli, 1888)

Pedrell, Felip, 'Estudio biográfico-bibliográfico sobre el Maestro abulense Tomás Luis de Victoria y la presente edición completa de sus obras', in Pedrell (ed.), *Thomae Ludovici Victoria abulensis opera omnia* VIII (Leipzig: Breitkopf and Härtel, 1913)

Pedrell, Felip, *Tomás Luis de Victoria Abulense* (Valencia: Manuel Villar, 1918)

Pérez Pastor, Cristóbal, *Bibliografía Madrileña: ó, descripción de las obras impresas en Madrid*, 3 vols (Madrid: Tipografía de los huérfanos, Tipografía de la Revista de Archivos, Bibliotecas y Museos, 1891–1907)

Pettas, William, *A History and Bibliography of the Giunti (Junta) Printing Family in Spain, 1526–1628* (New Castle, DE: Oak Knoll Press, 2005)

Phillips, Peter, *What We Really Do: The Tallis Scholars* (London: The Musical Times, 2003)

Pogue, Samuel, *Jacques Moderne, Lyons Music Printer of the Sixteenth Century* (Geneva: Librairie Droz, 1969)

Proske, Carl (ed.), *Musica divina: sive thesaurus concentuum selectissimorum omni cultui divino totius anni juxta ritum sanctæ ecclesiæ catholicæ inservientium*, Annus Primus, I (Regensburg: Pustet, 1853)

Ramos López, Maria Pilar, 'The Construction of the Myth of Spanish Renaissance Music as a Golden Age', in Karol Berger, Lubomir Chalupka, and Albert Dunning (eds), *Early Music – Context and Ideas (International Conference in Musicology, Kraków 18–21 September 2003)* (Krakow: Jagiellonian University, 2003), 77–82

Ramos López, Maria Pilar, 'Mysticism as a Key Concept of Spanish Early Music Historiography', in *Early Music: Context and Ideas II (International Conference in Musicology, Kraków)* (Krakow: Jagiellonian University, 2008), 69–82

Rees, Owen, 'Motets *pro defunctis* in the Iberian World: Texts and Performance Contexts', in Esperanza Rodríguez-Garcia and Daniele V. Filippi (eds), *Mapping the Motet in the post-Tridentine Era* (London: Routledge, 2018), 85–101

Reynaud, François, *La polyphonie tolédane et son milieu, des premiers témoignages aux environs de 1600* (Turnhout: Brepols, 1996)

Robledo Estaire, Luis, Tess Knighton, Cristina Bordas Ibáñez, and Juan José Carreras (eds), *Aspectos de la cultura musical en la corte de Felipe II* (Madrid: Fundación Caja Madrid / Editorial Alpuerto, 2000)

Robledo, Luis, 'Questions of Performance Practice in Philip III's Chapel', *Early Music* 22 (1994), 198–218

Rose, Stephen, 'Music, Print & Authority in Leipzig during the Thirty Years' War', unpublished PhD thesis, University of Cambridge (2002)

Rose, Stephen, 'Publication and the Anxiety of Judgement in German Musical Life of the Seventeenth Century', *Music and Letters* 85 (2004), 22–40

Rose, Stephen, 'Schein's Occasional Music and the Social Order in 1620s Leipzig', *Early Music History* 23 (2004), 253–84

Ros-Fábregas, Emilio, 'Cristóbal de Morales: A Problem of Musical Mysticism and National Identity in the Historiography of the Renaissance', in Owen Rees and Bernadette Nelson (eds), *Cristóbal de Morales: Sources, Influences, Reception* (Woodbridge: Boydell, 2007), 215–34

Rostirolla, Giancarlo, *L'Archivio musicale della Basilica di San Giovanni in Laterano: Catalogo dei manoscritti e delle edizioni (secc. XVI–XX)*, 2 vols (Rome: Ministero per i beni e le attività culturali, Direzione generale per gli archivi, 2002)

Rubio, Samuel (ed.), *Juan Vázquez: Agenda defunctorum (Sevilla, 1556): Estudio tecnico-estilistico y transcripcion* (Madrid: Real Musical, 1975)

Rubio, Samuel, 'El *Officium defunctorum* de Tomás Luis de Victoria', *Tomás Luis de Victoria: Officium Defunctorum a seis voces* (Ávila: Caja d'Ahorros d'Ávila, 2000), 13–23

Ruini, Cesarino (ed.), *Giuseppe Ottavio Pitoni: Notitia de' contrapuntisti e compositori di musica* (Florence: Leo S. Olschki, 1988)

Ruiz Jiménez, Juan, *La librería de canto de órgano: creación y pervivencia del repertorio del Renacimiento en la actividad musical de la catedral de Sevilla* (Granada: Junta de Andalucía, 2007)

Ruiz Jiménez, Juan, 'Recepción y pervivencia de la obra de Victoria en las instituciones eclesiásticas de la Corona de Castilla', in Alfonso de Vicente and Pilar Tomás (eds), *Tomás Luis de Victoria y la cultura musical en la España de Felipe III* (Madrid: Centro de Estudios Europa Hispánica and Machado Libros, 2012), 301–51

Sánchez, Magdalena S., 'Empress María and the Making of Political Policy in the Early Years of Philip III's Reign', in Alain Saint-Saêns (ed.), *Religion, Body and Gender in Early Modern Spain* (San Francisco: Mellen Research University Press, 1991), 139–47

Sánchez, Magdalena S., *The Empress, the Queen, and the Nun: Women and Power at the Court of Philip III of Spain* (Baltimore and London: The Johns Hopkins University Press, 1998)

Sánchez Hernández, Maria Leticia, 'La vida cotidiana de la primera comunidad de las Descalzas Reales de Madrid', in Ana García Sanz (ed.), *Las Descalzas Reales:*

orígines de una comunidad religiosa en el siglo XVI (Madrid: Patrimonio Nacional / Fundación Caja Madrid, 2010), 107–47

Sánchez Hernández, Maria Leticia, *Patronato regio y órdenes religiosas femeninas en el Madrid delos Austrias: Descalzas Reales, Encarnación, y Santa Isabel* (Madrid: Fundación Universitaria Española, 1997)

Sancho García, Manuel, 'De Teixidor a Pedrell: Tomás Luis de Victoria en la historiografía musical español del siglo XIX', *Revista de Musicología* 35/1 (2012), 443–57

Schnoebelen, Anna, *Padre Martini's Collection of Letters in the Civico Museo Bibliografico Musicale in Bologna: An Annotated Index* (New York: Pendragon, 1979)

Schwartz, Roberta, '*En busca de liberalidad*: Music and Musicians in the Courts of the Spanish Nobility, 1470–1640', unpublished PhD thesis, University of Illinois at Urbana-Champaign (2001)

Sebastián Lozano, Jorge, 'Emblemas para una emperatriz muerta. Las honras madrileñas de la Compañía por María de Austria', in Rafael García Mahíques and Vicent Francesc Zuriaga Senent (eds), *Imagen y cultura: La interpretación de las imágenes como Historia cultural*, 2 vols (Valencia: Biblioteca Valenciana, 2008), II, 1453–62

Simón Díaz, José (ed.), *El libro español antiguo: análisis de su estructura*, 2nd edition (Madrid: Ollero & Ramos, 2000)

Simón Díaz, José (ed.), *Historia del Colegio Imperial de Madrid*, 2 vols (Madrid: Consejo Superior de Investigaciones Científicas, 1952)

Simón Díaz, José (ed.), *Relaciones breves de actos públicos celebrados en Madrid de 1541 a 1650*, El Madrid de los Austrias, Serie Documentación 1 (Madrid: Instituto de Estudios Madrileños, 1982)

Stevenson, Robert Murrell, *Spanish Cathedral Music in the Golden Age* (Berkeley and Los Angeles: University of California Press, 1961)

Terry, Richard Runciman, *Catholic Church Music* (London: Greening, 1907)

Thomas, Juan María, *Manuel de Falla en la Isla* (Palma de Mallorca: Ediciones Capella Classica, 1947)

Turner, Bruno, 'Glimpses of P-Rex: Aspects of the Gentle Art of Music in the Reign of Philip II', *Leading Notes* 8/1 (Spring 1998), 2–8

van Orden, Kate, *Music, Authorship, and the Book in the First Century of Print* (Berkeley, Los Angeles, and London: University of California Press, 2014)

Varela, Javier, *La muerte del rey: el ceremonial funerario de la monarquía española, 1500–1885* (Madrid: Turner, 1990)

Vicente, Alfonso de, 'El entorno femenino de la dinastía: el complejo conventual de las Descalzas Reales (1574–1633)', in Alfonso de Vicente and Pilar Tomás (eds), *Tomás Luis de Victoria y la cultura musical en la España de Felipe III* (Madrid: Centro de Estudios Europa Hispánica & Machado Libros, 2012), 197–246

Vicente, Alfonso de (ed.), *El mayordomo de Tomás Luis y otros documentos de Victoria* (Ávila: Miján, 2015)

Vicente, Alfonso de, *Libros y obras de Tomás Luis de Victoria (y otros) en Aragón*, Cuadernos Tomás Luis de Victoria 4 (Ávila: Miján, 2016)

Vicente, Alfonso de, *Tomás Luis de Victoria: Cartas (1582–1606)* (Madrid: Fundación Caja Madrid, 2008)

Vieira, Ernesto, *Diccionario biographico de musicos portugueses*, 2 vols (Lisbon: Mattos Moreira de Pinheiro, 1900)

Villanueva, Joaquin Lorenzo, *De la obligacion de decir la Misa con circunspeccion y pausa* (Madrid: Imprenta Real, 1788)

Vindel, Francisco, *Manual gráfico-desriptivo del bibliófilo hispano-americano (1475–1850)*, 10 vols (1930–1931)

Vistarini, Antonio Bernat, John T. Cull, and Tamás Sajó (eds), *Book of Honors for Empress Maria of Austria Composed by the College of the Society of Jesus of Madrid on the Occasion of her Death, 1603*, Early Modern Catholicism and the Visual Arts Series 5 (Philadelphia, Saint Joseph's University Press, 2011)

Voet, Leon, *The Golden Compasses: A History and Evaluation of the Printing and Publishing Activities of the Officiana Plantiniana at Antwerp*, 2 vols (Amsterdam: Vangendt / New York: Abner Schram, 1969–1972)

Voet, Leon, *The Plantin Press (1555–1589): A Bibliography of the Works Printed and Published by Christopher Plantin at Antwerp and Leiden*, 6 vols (Amsterdam: Van Hoeve, 1980–1983)

Wagstaff, Grayson, 'Cristóbal de Morales's *Circumdederunt me*: An Alternate Invitatory for Matins for the Dead and Music for Charles V', in David Crawford (ed.), *Encomium musicæ: Essays in Honor of Robert J. Snow* (Hillsdale, NY: Pendragon, 2002), 27–45

Wagstaff, Grayson, 'Morales's Officium, Chant Traditions, and Performing 16th-Century Music', *Early Music* 32 (2004), 225–43

Wagstaff, Grayson, 'Music for the Dead and the Control of Ritual Behavior in Spain, 1450–1550', *The Musical Quarterly* 82 (1998), 551–63

Wagstaff, Grayson, 'Music for the Dead: Polyphonic Settings of the *Officium* and *Missa Pro Defunctis* by Spanish and Latin American Composers before 1630', unpublished PhD thesis, The University of Texas at Austin (1995)

Washington, Henry, 'The Oratory Musical Tradition', in Michael Napier and Alistair Laing (eds), *The London Oratory Centenary 1884–1984* (London: Trefoil, 1984), 152–71

Wiering, Franz, *The Language of the Modes: Studies in the History of Polyphonic Modality* (New York & London: Routledge, 2001)

Modern Editions of the *Officium defunctorum*

Bordes, Charles, 'Messe pro defunctis (à 6 voix)', Anthologie des maîtres religieux primitifs des quinzième, seizième et dix-septième siècles, Première année, Livre des Messes (Paris: Au siège de l'Association des Chanteurs de Saint-Gervais, 1893), 119–51; reissued, New York: Da Capo Press, 1981

Dixon, Jon, *Tomás Luis de Victoria (1548–1611): Requiem Mass for Six Voices and Settings for the Office of the Dead* (JOED: Carshalton Beeches, 1994)

Haberl, Franz Xaver (ed.), *Missa pro defunctis sex vocum auctore Thoma Ludovico a Victoria*, Musica divina: sive thesaurus concentuum selectissimorum omni cultui divino totius anni juxta ritum sanctæ ecclesiæ catholicæ inservientium, Annus II, I (Regensburg, New York, & Cincinnati: Pustet, 1874)

Noone, Michael, *Missa pro defunctis a4, 1583; Requiem responsories, 1592; Officium defunctorum a 6, 1605*, Boethius Editions 10 (Aberystwyth: Boethius Press, 1990)

Pedrell, Felip, *Thomae Ludovici Victoria Abulensis Opera omnia ex antiquissimis, iisdemque rarissimis, hactenus cognitis editionibus in unum collecta, atque adnotationibus, tum bibliographicis, tum interpretatoriis*, 8 vols (Leipzig: Breitkopf & Härtel, 1902–1913), VI (1909), 124–51

Rubio, Samuel, *Tomás Luis de Victoria: Officium Defunctorum a seis voces* (Ávila: Caja de Ahorros de Ávila, 2000)

Turner, Bruno, *Tomás Luis de Victoria (1548–1611): Officium defunctorum, Requiem, 1605*, Mapa Mundi Renaissance Performing Scores, Series A, No. 75 (London: Vanderbeek & Imrie, 1988)

Walter, Rudolf, *Tomás Luis de Victoria: Missa pro defunctis cum responsorio Libera me domine, 1605, 6 gemischte Stimmen a cappella*, Musica divina 15 (Regensburg: Friedrich Pustet, 1962)

Wulstan, David, *Tomás Luis de Victoria: Requiem à 6 (1605)*, revised edition (Oxford: Oxenford Imprint, 1984)

Discography

Recordings of Victoria's *Officium defunctorum*

Accademia Corale di Lecco, dir. Guido Camillucci, *Victoria: Missa pro defunctis* (Vox, 1954)

Agrupación Coral de Cámara de Pamplona, dir. Luis Morondo, *Victoria: Officium defunctorum. El renacimiento español* (Ducretet-Thomson, n.d.)

Armonico Consort, dir. Christopher Monks, *Tomás Luis de Victoria: Requiem* (Deux-Elles, 2005)

The Berkshire Boy Choir, dir. George Guest (BBC, 1967)

Capella de Ministrers, dir. Carles Magraner, *Tomás Luis de Victoria: Requiem* (Licanus, 2006)

The Chapel Choir of Lincoln College, Oxford, dir. Joseph Mason, *For the Fallen* (Regent, 2013)

Chœur In illo tempore, dir. Alexandre Traube, *Tomás Luis de Victoria: Requiem 1603* (Gallo, 2004)

The Choir of the Church of the Advent, Boston, dir. Edith Ho, *Tomás Luis de Victoria: Missa Pro defunctis cum sex vocibus (1605)* (Afka, 1985)

Choir of Clare College, Cambridge, dir. Graham Ross, *Requiem: Music for All Saints & All Souls* (Harmonia Mundi, 2015)

Choir of St. John's College, Cambridge, dir. George Guest, *Victoria: Requiem Mass sex vocibus* (Argo, 1968)

Christ Church St Laurence Choir and Gregorian Schola, dir. Neil McEwan, *Requiem: Victoria Requiem a6, Tallis Motets* (St Laurence Music Inc, 2002)

Collegium Vocale Gent, dir. Philippe Herreweghe, *Tomás Luis de Victoria: Officium defunctorum* (Phi, 2012)

Coral San Ignacio, dir. Jesús María Unanue, *Tomás Luis de Victoria: Officium defunctorum. Reconstrucción litúrgico musical* (ausArtrecords / Quincena Musical Donostia, 1996)

Coro de Radiotelevisión Española, dir. Alberto Blancafort, *Victoria: Officium defunctorum*, Colección de Música Antigua Española 21 (Hispavox, 1973)

Cuarteto Vocal 'Tomás Luis de Victoria', dir. Samuel Rubio, *Tomás Luis de Victoria: Officium Hebdomadae Sanctae. Roma 1585. Officium Defunctorum, Madrid 1605* (Columbia, 1981)

Dessoff Choirs, dir. Paul Boepple, *Spanish Church Music of the 16th Century* (Fantasy / Vista, 1960)

Escolania and Capella de Música Montserrat, dir. Ireneu Segarra, *Tomás Luis de Victoria: Missa pro defunctis 6 vocum* (Deutsche Harmonia Mundi, 1977)

Gabrieli Consort, dir. Paul McCreesh, *Victoria: Requiem, Officium defunctorum, 1605* (Archiv Produktion, 1995)

KammerChor Saarbrücken, dir. Georg Grün, *Tomás Luis de Victoria: Requiem, Officium defunctorum* (Rondeau, 2012)

Magnificat, dir. Philip Cave, *Tomás Luis de Victoria: Officium defunctorum* (Linn, 1996)

Musica Ficta, dir. Raúl Mallavibarrena, *Tomás Luis de Victoria: Officium defunctorum* (Enchiriadis, 2003)

Netherlands Chamber Choir, dir. Felix de Nobel, *Tomás Luis de Victoria (1548–1611): Officium defunctorum and other sacred works* (Columbia / Angel, 1959)

Prazstí madrigalisté, dir. Miroslav Venhoda, *Victoria: Officium defunctorum* (Valois / Das Alte Werk, 1965)

The Sixteen, dir. Harry Christophers, *Tomás Luis de Victoria: Requiem 1605, Officium defunctorum* (Coro, 2005)

La Stagione Armonica, dir. Sergio Balestracci, *Tomás Luis de Victoria: Requiem for Empress Maria of Austria (Madrid, 1603)* (Symphonia, 2002)

Sydney University Chamber Choir, dir. Neil McEwan, *In Celebration of the 1986 Papal Visit: The Victoria Requiem* (Australian Broadcasting Corporation, 1986)

The Tallis Scholars, dir. Peter Phillips, *Victoria Requiem* (Gimell, 1987)

Tenebrae, dir. Nigel Short, *Tomás Luis de Victoria: Requiem Mass, 1605* (Signum Classics, 2011)

Westminster Cathedral Choir, dir. David Hill, *Tomás Luis de Victoria: Requiem Mass, Officium defunctorum (1605)* (Hyperion, 1987)

Index

-god's composer-